FRESH from the WORD

the Bible for a change

Foreword by Pam Rhodes
Edited by Nathan Eddy

MONARCH
BOOKS

Published by
Lion Hudson Limited
Wilkinson House, Jordan Hill Business Park,
Banbury Road, Oxford OX2 8DR, England
www.lionhudson.com
and by the **International Bible Reading Association**
5–6 Imperial Court, 12 Sovereign Road, Birmingham, B30 3FH
Tel: 0121 458 3313; Fax: 0121 285 1816
www.ibraglobal.org
Charity number 1086990

ISBN 978 1 80030 001 9
eISBN 978 1 80030 002 6
ISSN 2050-6791

First edition 2020

A catalogue record for this book is available from the British Library

Printed and bound in the UK, June 2020, LH26

Fresh From The Word aims to build understanding and respect for different Christian perspectives through the provision of a range of biblical interpretations. Views expressed by contributors should not, therefore, be taken to reflect the views or policies of the Editor or the International Bible Reading Association.

The International Bible Reading Association's scheme of readings is shown daily on the IBRA website at www.ibraglobal.org and the full scheme for 2021 may be downloaded in English, Spanish and French.

Contents

Foreword

I first remember hearing stories from the Bible when I was a toddler at Sunday school. I may have forgotten the names of the children I shared those times with, but locked in my memory are the fascinating biblical characters and the places where their stories unfolded. So, a few years back, I was thrilled to have the chance to go on a pilgrimage to the Holy Land, when I'd be with about 40 others who also wanted to visit those places with names we'd known since childhood.

It was on that coach trip, as we rushed from one iconic location to another, that I found a friend in an elderly lady called Phyllis. Many passengers were grumbling about her being slow and holding everybody up, because she was wearing completely the wrong shoes for the terrain – flat leather soles with a band across the toes that looked far too big for her. She was an accident waiting to happen!

And it did. When we were in Bethlehem Square, Phyllis took a tumble – so, after that, we walked around slowly together. She told me it was her lifelong dream to visit the Holy Land, so she'd booked the tickets a year in advance. Most of all, she was thrilled when her son said he wanted to go too, so that he could share the experience with his mum. But in the months leading up to the trip, her son contracted a serious form of cancer and became too ill to travel – so the shoes that Phyllis was wearing were his shoes. She wanted him to have the chance to walk in the footsteps of Christ.

I felt so humbled by Phyllis's faith, and her love not just for her son, but for God's Son too. For Phyllis, the truth and the miracle of Christ's time on earth, and God's constant presence in her life were as powerful today as they'd ever been. I came away thinking that, in spite of being a Christian all my life, I still have so much to learn of this God I love and long to know better – and that the best place to learn more about the nature and mystery of God is where Phyllis learned it, in the pages of the Bible.

This is a longing I now share with thousands of Christians around the world who read passages from the Bible every day through this book, *Fresh From The Word*. In our own languages, reading the same stories and insights, we join together in prayerful study and worship as the family of Christ across the globe. One prayer, one body, one God.

Pam Rhodes

How to use *Fresh From The Word*

How do you approach the idea of regular Bible reading? It may help to see daily Bible reading as spiritual exploration. Here is a suggestion of a pattern to follow that may help you develop the discipline but free up your mind and heart to respond.

- Before you read, take a few moments – the time it takes to say the Lord's Prayer – to imagine God looking at you with love. Feel yourself enfolded in that gaze. Come to scripture with your feet firmly planted.

- Read the passage slowly before you turn to the notes. Be curious. The Bible was written over a period of nearly 1,000 years, over 2,000 years ago. There is always something to learn. Read and reread.

- If you have access to a study Bible, pay attention to any echoes of the passage you are reading in other parts of the biblical book. A word might be used in different ways by different biblical authors. Where in the story of the book are you reading? What will happen next?

- 'Read' yourself as you read the story. Be attentive to your reactions – even trivial ones. What is drawing you into the story? What is repelling you? Observe yourself 'sidelong' as you read as if you were watching a wild animal in the forest; be still, observant and expectant.

- What in the scripture or in the notes is drawing you forward in hope? What is closing you down? Notice where the Spirit of Life is present, and where negative spirits are, too. Follow where life is leading. God always leads into life, even if the way feels risky.

- Lift up the world and aspects of your life to God. What would you like to share with God? What is God seeking to share with you?

- Thank God for being present and offer your energy in the day ahead, or in the day coming after a night's rest.

- Finally, the † symbol is an invitation to pray a prayer that has been written for the day's reading. You are invited to say these words aloud or in silence with thousands of other readers around the world who will be reading these notes on the same day in dozens of languages.

Introduction from the Editor

One phrase jumped out at me in this year's *Fresh From The Word*: 'At the time of writing'. Whether it was a global pandemic, climate change, or political change, writers this year are more aware than ever of the churn of change happening all around us. 'Into the Unknown' is the title of our theme for Lent this year, and it could apply quite aptly to our world as a whole. From parliamentary debates in Westminster, UK, to the recent election in the USA, very little is predictable these days. We mean the theme in a slightly narrower sense, however; following the trend of recent church discussions in the UK at a national level, we consider *discipleship* as a journey 'into the unknown'. What does it mean to follow Jesus? What does it mean to grow with God and with one another? While discipleship is a journey into the solid promise of God in Jesus Christ, Jesus is also clear that it is a journey 'into the unknown'. This year we invite you on this shared journey.

The weekly headings for our Lenten theme could serve as a mission statement for IBRA as a whole: first steps, rooted and growing, walking as one. Each year we commit to reading the Bible daily, and doing so together; we read the same scripture each day of the year. Will you take the 'first steps' of this challenge with us in 2021 – to read the Bible daily, and to let God shape you into the person only you can be?

As is our hallmark, *FFTW* 2021 features creative and faithful writers from around the world. This year we feature writers with roots in South Africa, India, Argentina, Brazil, Nigeria, Jamaica, the USA and elsewhere, as well as a spread of regions within the UK. We have one writer reflecting on island life in Shetland, and another on island life in Samoa. Themes include the Bible through the seasons, surprising women in the Bible, family tensions in Genesis and more – as well as continuous readings from Mark, Job, Galatians and the Minor Prophets.

It is my hope that the reflections in this book will spur you on in your journey 'into the unknown'. This year also marks my last as editor and the continuing of my journey beyond *Fresh From The Word*. I leave with tremendous gratitude for the writers, the publishing team and the group that brainstorms our themes, but especially for you, the readers. Our journey together will continue, in the Spirit that makes us one.

Yours in Christ,

Nathan

Acknowledgements and abbreviations

The use of the letters a or b in a text reference, such as Luke 9:37–43a, indicates that the day's text starts or finishes midway through a verse, usually at a break such as the end of a sentence. Not all Bible versions will indicate such divisions.

We are grateful to the copyright holders for permission to use scriptural quotations from the following Bible versions:

The enlightening word – 1 A light to my path

Notes by **Ian Fosten**

Ian Fosten is the director of a community theatre and a poet. He retired two years ago from leading the ministry team in the Norwich, UK, group of United Reformed churches. He lives on the Suffolk coast with his wife and young children. He helped set up the St Cuthbert's Centre mission project on Holy Island (Lindisfarne). He has a particular interest in connections between theology and landscape. His poetry is found at www. fosten.com. Ian has used the NRSVA for these notes.

Friday 1 January
Savouring the familiar and seeing beyond

Read Psalm 19

The decrees of the Lord are sure, making wise the simple …
The commandment of the Lord is clear, enlightening the eyes.

(Psalm 19:7–8)

The midwinter evening was almost done. Washing up at the kitchen sink I gazed idly through the window at the street outside. Streetlights silhouetted the outline of summer shrubs now stripped back to their winter nakedness. The year was following its set path: spring promise, summer flowering, then autumn fruitfulness, then fall. Evenings had lengthened and the temperature had fallen in anticipation of this dormant time of year. But even as I took in this scene of predictable order and stillness, I caught a hint of movement at the periphery of my gaze. Not everything, it seemed, was static and set – a small, slender body followed by a long tail made its way up the dead stalks of a mallow. A mouse was busy taking seeds from papery husks then scurrying back to feed a brood or gather a store against the bleakness of winter.

That winter mouse sets a pattern for approaching our readings at the start of this year. Alongside our savouring of scripture as it has been given, recorded and valued down the centuries, we shall also be attentive to glimpses of how ancient texts can nevertheless speak freshly as God's living word for today.

† May these words of my mouth and this meditation of my heart be pleasing in your sight, Lord, my Rock and my Redeemer. Amen

1

Saturday 2 January
Seeing, sufficiently, in the dark

Read Psalm 119:105–112
Your word is a lamp to my feet and a light to my path.

(verse 105)

In some parts of the world that are subject to intense urban development and consequent, constant light pollution, there is a growing enthusiasm to create oases of deep darkness. City dwellers rarely see the stars, much less have opportunities to appreciate them in all their manifold glory. Many of us have little experience of living other than in the constant glare of artificial illumination.

If that sounds like you (and it's certainly true for me), then pause for a moment to gather the importance of the image used by the psalmist. In a night-time environment of pitch darkness, a fragile wick makes, at best, modest sense of what surrounds us. A small circle of brightness discloses how safely to make the next couple of steps and not much more. The darkness, both spiritual and physical, is dominant, but a lamp creates possibilities and hope – enough for the followers of the lamp to make tentative, faithful steps in a good and useful direction.

Maybe some Christians are indeed blessed with such extraordinary faith that the whole of life is bathed in God's self-evident glorious purpose ... for the rest of us, most of us I expect, life can be rather baffling and littered with obstacles. Our reading steers us sufficiently for today, and maybe even tomorrow ... beyond that, we'll have to trust the giver of the lamp to light our pathway sufficiently. And remember, the bearer of the lamp, the giver of the word, is Lord of all things – even the darkness!

† God of light and life, I want to know and see and anticipate everything that might be coming my way. Help me to know that you show me enough to be sufficient for my needs.

For further thought
Seek out a night-time location without light pollution. Enjoy the real darkness; enjoy the stars if they are visible; recalibrate your need for light.

The enlightening word – 2 Arise, shine!

Notes by **Ian Fosten**

For Ian's biography, see p. 1.

Sunday 3 January

Finding the 'sweet spot'

Read Proverbs 4:10–19

But the path of the righteous is like the light of dawn, which shines brighter and brighter until full day.

(verse 18)

Here's an experiment: what is your immediate response when you hear or read the word 'righteous'? My guess is that most people's reactions would range from, at best, cautious, qualified approval, through to unease that the word carries undertones of self-satisfaction, smugness or undeserved superiority. For many, this latter response is influenced by how Jesus criticised the Pharisees for their proud and meticulous keeping of the letter of the Law whilst missing out on the life-fulfilling spirit of the Law.

Today's reading encourages us to release the idea of righteousness from its customary bad-press position and instead to present it as a key positive indicator of the quality of our life. Maybe it helps if we alter the spelling slightly – for 'righteousness' read 'right-ness', and in doing so, think less about keeping to the rules and rather more about settings in which the idea of 'right-ness' can make a marvellous difference. Think of how with a single stroke of a pencil or brush an artist can bring an image alive, or how a timely, thoughtful word can reassure, encourage or give a real sense of being heard and understood. Sports players testify to the unique sweetness of hitting a ball in just the right place on a club, racquet or bat.

As Proverbs tells it, we can pick up some idea about right-ness – righteousness from study and learning, but as the artist, wise counsellor and sportsperson knows, we grow best in this quality by trying it out in the company of one who already knows where and how it is to be found.

† Loving God, as I accept your outstretched hand and travel companionably with you, may my life display right qualities of grace, peace and love. Amen

Monday 4 January
Just two faces of the same coin

Read Psalm 36

O continue your steadfast love to those who know you, and your salvation to the upright of heart! Do not let the foot of the arrogant tread on me, or the hand of the wicked drive me away.

(verses 10–11)

There is within humanity, it seems, a deep desire to account for the people around us in binary terms – good or bad, friend or foe, pro or anti, people like us and those who are not. On a first reading, writers of the psalms display a particular enthusiasm for this way of seeing and defining – almost invariably the good and godly (like the psalmist, of course) are up against the wicked and the sinful.

But, listening afresh to this psalm, I wonder if the good and godly are always exclusively thus? Are the wicked really so consistently evil? The more I have listened for a living Word within this ancient poem, the more I fancy that I've glimpsed another strand of truth. What if, instead of dividing humanity (naively?) into either good or bad, the real wisdom of the psalmist is to recognise that godliness and wickedness are to be experienced in all of us? The psalm then becomes not so much a description of 'them and us', but an acknowledgement of the daily, corrosive conflict that grumbles away within me – and, maybe, within you too!

Heard in this way, the psalm is about honesty, choice and gift. Through the psalmist's words we say, 'Loving God, I don't always live as you and I want me to – I get so easily derailed – so once again I'm taking your hand for guidance and strength in the certain knowledge that your love, your grace and your presence will never let me fall.'

† Loving God, preserve me from blaming others for my failings; help me recognise a kinship with others' imperfections. Save me from myself that I may live well within your purpose and your will. Amen

For further thought
Check out how readily you divide other people into 'us' and 'them'. Try thinking of others as 'conflicted people like me', instead.

Tuesday 5 January
What makes our beliefs authentic?

Read Psalm 112
Praise the Lord!
Happy are those who fear the Lord, who greatly delight in his commandments … They have distributed freely, they have given to the poor; their righteousness endures for ever …

(verses 1 and 9)

Roald Dahl in *Boy*, the first part of his autobiography, recounts being viciously caned by his school headmaster for having committed a minor misdemeanour. He remembered how uneasy he had felt at the apparent sadistic delight this adult took in hurting a child. Then he adds, almost in passing, how equally disturbed he was when much later in life he was reacquainted with this child beater – though now no longer a school headmaster, but as the Archbishop of Canterbury! For the rest of Dahl's life, the discrepancy between the man's profession of Christian belief and his brutal delight in harming a child remained unbridgeable.

For the psalmist, knowing the Lord's commands is foundational to faith, but those commands are only rendered valid by the truly and consistently upright, compassionate, generous, gracious actions of the believer. The faith we proclaim is only ever credible and effective for the good of others when our daily living provides an authentic expression of those beliefs.

In the 1980s a Cambridge academic, also an Anglican priest, became notorious among many believers for contributing to a collection of essays which questioned fundamental, and for many essential, elements of Christian belief. 'How can this man say such things, and still call himself a Christian?' many asked. For me, the answer came from someone who at that time was involved in running a night shelter for the homeless in that city. 'Night after night,' he told me, 'who do you think was there quietly ministering to the needs of the rough sleepers?' None other than the 'holy heretic'!

† In my speaking and my doing; in my believing and my faith, make me always consistent and real. Amen

For further thought
Thank God for 'maverick' Christians who have modelled true faith for you.

Wednesday 6 January (Epiphany)
Holy, intrusive light in dark places

Read Isaiah 60:1–6
Arise, shine; for your light has come, and the glory of the Lord has risen upon you. For darkness shall cover the earth, and thick darkness the peoples; but the Lord will arise upon you, and his glory will appear over you.

(verses 1–2)

Following a heart attack, I recently spent some time in hospital. At first it was simply a relief to be somewhere safe and contained, but as the days passed and a decision about how best to deal with me seemed elusive, I began to feel trapped in a steadily tightening spiral of waiting, uncertainty and anxiety. The nights seemed endless and I looked forward to each new dawn. One morning, as daylight crept reluctantly into an overcast sky, I realised that it was high time to address the deepening gloom within and without. So, I opened my prayer journal and started writing as I felt led. Here is what emerged:

By day, by hour, by moment the world contracts
into a small circumference – waiting for a test, a next step,
a word of clarification …
As time hangs heavy and grey
I might succumb to its leaden thrall:
alternatively, I might take a ride on eagles' wings;
shout the glory of love renewed;
and recline, as might a pool-side sunbather,
in the palm of Your hand!

Admittedly, these words didn't prompt a miraculous parting of the cloudy sky, but they were nevertheless a true Epiphany gift. They reassuringly reminded me that Isaiah's promises of a future hope are something I already know as a constant, present reality.

† Subversive God of light and life, seep into our sadness, our greyness, our abandonment of hope, and ignite us with your glory! Amen

For further thought
When Quakers remember people in prayer, they speak of 'holding them in the light'. Try this in your own prayers for others.

Thursday 7 January
In the beginning ... and unfailingly ever since

Read John 1:1–9

In the beginning was the Word, and the Word was with God, and the Word was God. ... All things came into being through him ... In him was life, and the life was the light of all people. The light shines in the darkness, and the darkness did not overcome it.

(verses 1, 3a, 4 and 5)

The opening of John's Gospel is like a classic riddle: when is a word the origin of all things ... but also God ... but also a life ... and also a light ... and also a great deal more besides? Though unlike a riddle – a brainteaser which begs for a solution to be found – these familiar words carry an invitation to hold them without immediately trying to understand, explain or unravel them. Word, origin, God, Life, unquenchable light – are not a puzzle waiting to be solved. Rather, by holding them all simultaneously within our gaze we stand a chance of glimpsing something which is deeper, truer and more powerful than any single one of them.

One Sunday, early on in the New Year, the morning service concluded by John's words being used as a closing affirmation: "The light shines in the darkness, and the darkness has not overcome it."

Afterwards, when there was an opportunity to talk, someone from the congregation shared just how potent those words had sounded for her. She spoke of a distressing series of disintegrations which were currently consuming her entire family. In that context, the assurance of inextinguishable light, no matter how dark the world became, was vital, tangible and, it seemed, the one thing that would sustain her through the coming difficult months. Following the family over the intervening years, I know the dark times have never been completely eliminated, but I also know that they have never triumphed.

† Thank you for your Word, alive, strong and utterly dependable at all times and in all places. Amen

For further thought

Being unable to understand something is not always a problem; sometimes it is the gateway to knowing truth for living which is too powerful to be confined by mere explanation.

Friday 8 January
Let it shine ... in whichever way you shine best

Read Matthew 5:14–20

'You are the light of the world ... let your light shine before others, so that they may see your good works and give glory to your Father in heaven.

(parts of verses 14 and 16)

I once had a colleague who is a 'promiscuous conversationalist'. This unflattering description came to me when he told me how, when travelling on buses or the underground trains in London, he really enjoyed the enforced close proximity with fellow travellers. 'What I really love doing', he told me, 'is striking up gospel conversations with people who can't escape from me!' I pictured myself, wedged in close confinement with him and his unsolicited, unavoidable conversation, and cringed at the thought! I also admire his boldness – and contrast it with my own reluctance to engage evangelistically with strangers.

Today's reading is a proper challenge to diffident 'lights to the world' like me – and maybe like you, too. In accepting the challenge I'm encouraged to realise that my colleague's strategy is not the only way to go in for 'light shining'. Jesus gave greater value to deeds than words, recognising that whatever we claim to believe or be, our actions provide the necessary authentication for those claims. In that respect, lepers, outcasts, women, Gentiles and others were frequently applauded in preference to the religious leaders of his day.

In his poem 'The Elixir', George Herbert points to the many ways in which we can shine as authentic lights of the kingdom. Even sweeping out a room with care and diligence can be a good witness. I think of that every time I cut the grass around our chapel. I pray, 'Whatever my conversational shortcomings, dear God, please use this tidy lawn and the labyrinth mowed into it as both sign and invitation to share in your kingdom.'

† In purposeful conversation, in quiet acts of generous love, in giving enthusiastically and in receiving with heartfelt gratitude, may I live out the life of your kingdom. Amen

For further thought

Room sweeping, grass cutting, conversations on a bus ... what otherwise mundane, everyday actions might nevertheless be useful signs of God's kingdom?

Saturday 9 January
The all-sufficient light of God in Jesus

Read Revelation 21:22–27
And the city has no need of sun or moon to shine on it, for the glory of God is its light, and its lamp is the Lamb.

(verse 23)

I first came across these words from Revelation, not as a Bible reading but as the lyrics of an anthem we sang in the junior choir of my Congregational church in suburban London. The song was, 'The Holy City', a late Victorian ballad and, with hindsight, the contrast between its majestic, triumphant celebration of the New Jerusalem of Revelation, and the just-starting-to-swing 1960s could not have been more extreme. On the one hand we had the culmination of humanity under the glorious, undisputed Lordship of God made known in Jesus, whereas on the other we had the beginning of the modern era characterised by individualism and freedom to make of the world whatever we may choose.

As I look back over half a century of the mixed experience which is life, I am surprised but heartened to realise that our childish anthem held within it the possibility of a deeper, richer freedom than any of the wild experimentation taking place in wider society at the time. Some of the consequences of that experimentation are found in our current urban landscapes, flooded with surveillance lighting and CCTV cameras in order to deter destructive behaviour. By contrast, the New Jerusalem, in which nothing needs to be hidden away, is bright with the easiness of right relationships, a just society from which no one is excluded, and humanity living as the Maker intends.

† Free me, dear God, from dark corners of unforgiveness, nursed grievances and clung-to disappointments; in their place allow your light, grace, truth, peace and welcome to flourish. Amen

For further thought
The light of God's presence is never withheld: sometimes, though, we choose to obscure its brilliance. Maybe today is the day we throw back the shutters and let the light shine.

The Bible through the seasons: winter

Notes by **John Proctor**

John is a retired minister of the United Reformed Church. He has served as a parish minister in Glasgow, a teacher of New Testament studies in Cambridge, and as the URC's General Secretary in London. John has written commentaries on Matthew (BRF, 2001) and the Corinthian letters (WJK, 2015) and several Grove booklets on New Testament books and themes. He is married to Elaine, and they live near Cambridge. John has used the NRSVA for these notes.

Sunday 10 January
Lights in the darkness

Read Genesis 1:14–19

And God said, 'Let there be lights in the dome of the sky to separate the day from the night; and let them be for signs and for seasons and for days and years' ... – the greater light to rule the day and the lesser light to rule the night.

(parts of verses 14 and 16)

Sun, moon and stars. Gravity, orbits, tides and eclipses. Seasons, shadows and solstice. Darkening, directing, determining, defining. Lighting the day, shading the evening, nursing us to rest at night, awakening the dawn. Beckoning growth from the soil, balancing the rhythms of creation, driving the motion of the days, sustaining the cycle of the years.

They take the gift of creation's first day – light – and give it shape and order. They enable it to serve the Earth. They give pattern to time, and purpose to the planet. They make Earth a home, not just a rock.

This is God's work, says Genesis. The lights are creatures, as we are. We depend on them, but we need not worship them. They testify to a world out there, shaping the world we live in down here. They tell of a God who is much greater than we are, yet who loves the world constantly. They talk of a creative hand, generous and open, and an Earth rich with promise.

Winter is a facet of that gift, a stage in the year's journey, meshing with all the other phases to make a good and blessed whole. We thank God for it all.

† Darkness is not dark to you, our God. Cold does not shrink your goodness. For light, for the years, for creation, we give you praise.

Monday 11 January
For everything a season

Read Ecclesiastes 3:1–8

For everything there is a season, and a time for every matter under heaven: a time to be born, and a time to die; a time to plant, and a time to pluck up what is planted.

(verses 1–2)

Is this passage about the purpose of life or the futility of it? About the fact that things fit together, like a jigsaw, with a picture to show at the end of it all? Or about the fact that things simply follow on, a little randomly and raggedly, so that, although you must grasp life's opportunities, you can never really discern its destination?

There isn't an obvious answer. Was Ecclesiastes an optimist or a pessimist? Or was he just a pragmatist, getting on with living as best he could? Is this a book of faith or of doubt? Or is it something in between, commenting on life, observing it astutely and intelligently, but continually wondering where it is all leading? No one really knows what to make of Ecclesiastes. This writer has left us with as many questions as answers – which might have been his intention.

Nonetheless, this wide-ranging and resonant little passage in chapter 3 does have a message. Live sensibly. Don't take your days for granted. Be observant and alert. Learn from experience. Value time, watch for the demands and delights it brings, and think about how you're using it. If we do, Ecclesiastes might say, this will give us the best chance of finding purpose in life – a purpose for ourselves, and a glimpse of the purposes of God. Time well used can be a window into eternity. Take it seriously, even in the harsh and short days of winter. It's a gift, and it might just open us to the Giver.

† God of my days and years, may time be a lens to bring you into focus, in my living and believing. In Jesus' name. Amen

For further thought

Think about the balance of your life – conversation and silence, accumulating and managing with less, making new plans and living with decisions already made. Is it right as it is? How might you change it?

Tuesday 12 January
Stormy sea, steadfast love

Read Psalm 107:23–32

They saw the deeds of the Lord, his wondrous works in the deep.
For he commanded and raised the stormy wind, which lifted up the
waves of the sea.
They mounted up to heaven, they went down to the depths; their
courage melted away in their calamity.

(verses 24–26)

This psalm is a fourfold tapestry of rescue. Its main panels portray four very different scenes of fear and distress. Yet none is beyond the reach of the Lord. From desert, prison, disease and storm God hears his people, brings them out of trouble and gathers them safely together. The psalm could well rise out of the Jewish people's experience of exile in Old Testament times. As a hymn of trust and gratitude, it would tell of return, renewal and recovery. God reaches. God redeems. God rescues. God relocates his people, to hope and health and home.

This last main movement of the poem is also the longest and most elaborate. It tells of waves that rise and crash, ships bouncing like driftwood, sailors stumbling to and fro, and minds and hearts that, like the sea itself, have lost all trace of steadiness and order. The world rages. There is no prospect of peace or stillness, no time to take evasive action, nowhere to run or hide or lie low. All you can do is pray.

Then God hears. The calm that follows is God's doing, as surely as the storm. Both are images of power, wonder and majesty. Yet the calm is also a scene of love and care, of prayer answered and protection assured.

And we travel through winter, with stormy days, frozen ground, cloudy skies, knifing wind and biting cold. Yet in this, and beyond it, God meets us, carries us and has good designs for us. 'Thank the Lord', says the psalm, 'for his steadfast love' (verse 31).

† Pray for someone you know who is living through stormy days just now. Ask God to bring them to a place of peace and relief.

For further thought

Look back across your own years. Remember the difficulties you have left behind, give thanks for the help God has given you and take courage for the journey ahead.

Wednesday 13 January
Signposts on the sea

Read Luke 8:22–25

... (he) rebuked the wind and the raging waves; they ceased, and there was a calm. He said to them, 'Where is your faith?' They were afraid and amazed, and said to one another, 'Who then is this, that he commands even the winds and the water, and they obey him?'

(part of verses 24–25)

The storms we meet in the Gospels have a meaning. They concern much more than weather. They are signposts to realities beyond themselves. In Mark, for example, the turbulence of the Sea of Galilee seems to symbolise the tense relationship between the people of Israel and their Gentile neighbours; yet Jesus can move without fear from one side to the other. And now, as Luke takes us onto these rough waters, the issues are pointed and personal.

'Who is Jesus?' is the question at the end of the episode. He controls the wild sea, like God moving surely across the waters at the dawn of time. He settles the waves, as in the psalm that we read yesterday. He seems to be in charge of it all, as if it belonged to him. This man is more than a carpenter.

This links to the earlier question that Jesus puts to the disciples in the boat, and perhaps also to us, sitting securely outside the story. 'Where is your faith?' Do we fear that the storms in our living might be too much for Jesus to handle? Or that he might be off-duty today, asleep perhaps? Or that he doesn't care? This Gospel incident invites us to think again, to trust afresh, to turn around and discover him journeying with us. If the water beneath us rages, he can keep its anger in check and hold it back from destroying us. He can give us a calm place when all seemed stormy. These sea scenes in the Gospels are about you and me too.

† What are the fears that shake and disturb you? Talk with Jesus about them, honestly, trustingly and confidently.

For further thought

Has a difficult situation in your life ever highlighted spiritual questions, so that your faith and knowledge of Jesus actually grew? Does that experience affect the way you deal with difficulty now?

Thursday 14 January
Darkness and danger

Read Acts 27:9–26

When neither sun nor stars appeared for many days, and no small tempest raged, all hope of our being saved was at last abandoned ... Paul then stood up among them and said, '... keep up your courage, for there will be no loss of life among you, but only of the ship.'

(parts of verses 20–22)

Autumn was well advanced, and the Mediterranean in winter was not a safe place to sail. But this ship was carrying Egyptian corn to Rome, and the owner wanted to find a better harbour for the months ahead. Julius the centurion, in charge of the group of prisoners on board, went along with the decision to travel. Then the weather overtook them badly. For a fortnight they were blown savagely, all the way from Crete to Malta – about 600 miles (or almost 1,000 kilometres). The lights went out, the wind was up, the sea was high and spirits were desperately low.

This is one of three 'we' sections in Acts. The storytelling slides into the first-person, as if to say, 'I, Luke, the writer, was present during this episode.' Certainly this long and graphic account of the voyage would fit with an author who had been there. It would not be an experience to forget quickly.

Paul, however, rather than Luke, is the central character. Although a prisoner, Paul claims the stage. His confidence comes, he says, from God. He is assured and assuring, practical and persuasive, resilient and realistic. The cargo will be lost, and profit with it. But the people will survive. They will get to shore and to safety. The prisoner will live to state his case in Rome. Acts will end at the centre of the ancient world. For faith, Luke reminds us, gives you steadiness in the tempests of life, and helps you to steady other people too.

† God of peace and hope, help me to be a person of strength and support for those around me. Give me steadiness to share amid the storms of living. In Jesus' name. Amen

For further thought

Who and what has helped you to be steady in times of crisis or fear?

Friday 15 January
So much hot air?

Read Jeremiah 36:20–32

Now, after the king had burned the scroll with the words that Baruch wrote at Jeremiah's dictation, the word of the Lord came to Jeremiah: Take another scroll and write on it all the former words that were in the first scroll, which King Jehoiakim of Judah has burned.

(verses 27–28)

Jeremiah's prophecy should have chilled the king's heart. In the event it merely warmed his hands. A word designed to be humbling ended up as part of the heating. Instead of disturbing the nation's leaders, it dissolved before them, a few paragraphs at a time, into hot air and ash. The outflow of Jeremiah's heart and faith – and a demanding and heartfelt ministry it was – ended in the grate. Baruch's patient secretarial work, writing by hand on rough paper, giving his friend's words shape and permanence, flamed for a minute and then fell apart.

Yet despite the arrest warrant against their names, Jeremiah started again. Baruch sourced another scroll and picked up his pen. The prophet dictated his message. The whole content of the original scroll was spelt out for a second time, line by line, one column after another. And still more of the same. As if to say, God doesn't back down. You can't wipe God out of the picture. Despise God, if you will, but don't think you have the last word. God does, always.

Jeremiah and Baruch must have had guts and stamina. They had spoken truth to power, and power had preferred to ignore them. Yet truth has power and persistence of its own. It energises people. It stands, when its cultured despisers pass and perish. King Jehoiakim would end up in the dust. But Jeremiah's memory would survive, challenging and compelling, a pattern perhaps for another suffering prophet, who eventually died on a cross.

† God of our troubled and divided world, we pray for people who speak truth to power in difficult places. Guide their speaking; give them courage; guard their safety. For Jesus' sake. Amen

For further thought

What truths do you think are threatened today, and what can you do to keep them alive?

Saturday 16 January
Starting again

Read John 10:22–30

'I give [my sheep] eternal life, and they will never perish. No one will snatch them out of my hand. What my Father has given me is greater than all else, and no one can snatch it out of the Father's hand. The Father and I are one.'

(verses 28–30)

John's Gospel revolves around a series of festivals at the Jerusalem Temple – several Passovers, Tabernacles, and now Hanukkah (the Feast of Dedication). As if to say that the whole of Israel's ancient calendar of worship finds its home and fulfilment in Jesus. He is the one in whom heritage and hope come together. He gathers the meaning of the past into himself. Even the Temple directs the eye to him, as the great meeting point between heaven and humanity.

Hanukkah lasts for eight days, during December. It remembers the moment in 165 BCE when the Jerusalem Temple was reclaimed for Israel's worship. After three miserable years of foreign rule, when a pagan tyrant treated Israel's holy place with spite and contempt, freedom had dawned. Proper worship was possible again. Hanukkah was a celebration of leadership, liberty, praise and hope. It meant a new start.

Jesus too was offering Israel and the world a new start. As the Messiah, God's anointed leader in Israel, he was asking his people to begin again with God, securely, confidently and hopefully. As the good shepherd he would gather his flock. Then, in laying down his life, he would dedicate himself as a new meeting point between the life of earth and the mercy and goodness of God. 'The Father and I are in this together,' he said, 'We belong to each other. Follow me and you will find the Father, who will never turn you away.'

† Remember anyone you know who needs a new start. Pray for them to take confident steps forward. Ask too that they may find in Jesus a guide and companion for the way.

For further thought

What qualities of leadership do you notice in Jesus? What guidance and example might these offer amid the responsibilities that you carry?

The Gospel of Mark (1) – 1 The beginning of the good news

Notes by **Sue Richardson**

Sue is Christian Aid's Theological Education Adviser. In that role she works with those responsible for ministerial training and formation across a number of denominations. She is Roman Catholic and has been inspired by the popular reading of the Bible as practised in Brazil, a country she knows well, and by the readings of poor communities in other parts of the global South which resource a commitment to justice and peacebuilding. Sue has used the NRSVA for these notes.

Sunday 17 January
The one who comes before

Read Mark 1:1–15

The beginning of the good news of Jesus Christ, the Son of God. As it is written in the prophet Isaiah, 'See, I am sending my messenger ahead of you, who will prepare your way; the voice of one crying out in the wilderness: "Prepare the way of the Lord."'

(verses 1–3b)

The Good News starts in Mark with someone other than Jesus. Despite Mark's urgency to tell his story he begins with John the Baptist proclaiming that change is coming and all need to be ready. People respond; they come from city and countryside into the wilderness. They seem hungry for 'good news'.

John the Baptist is the warm-up act. He is not the 'good news' Mark is referring to, but he is present and makes me remember all the people I've met and heard who have helped me to look for Jesus and to be ready for his impact on my life. The Baptiser was in the wilderness, a place of hardship and little promise, yet God was there and would prove to be active in the world.

As I encounter people of faith making homes for refugees, running literacy classes for just-released prisoners, accompanying the vulnerable through the bureaucracy and hostility of the UK's welfare system, I see the forerunners for Jesus. People who can sow hope that Good News is coming in the hearts of people who might not ever believe it was meant for them if they had to rely on buildings and public worship to speak of it.

† Thank you, God, for inviting us to walk before Jesus as well as following him, that hearts and minds may be opened to receive him.

Monday 18 January
The man who heard the truth

Read Mark 1:16–28

Just then there was in their synagogue a man with an unclean spirit, and he cried out, 'What have you to do with us, Jesus of Nazareth? Have you come to destroy us? I know who you are, the Holy One of God.'

(verses 23–24)

I always thought that a synagogue would be a formal, hushed space, a little like a small parish church. But apparently 'synagogue' was the name given first to the local assembly of people and only afterwards to a place. It was used for worship and for teaching but was also a school, a courtroom and a community centre. Unlike the Temple in Jerusalem, where access was restricted, all Jews could enter the synagogue and we often hear of Jesus turning up and getting drawn into worship, and also playing a role in the social exchanges which must have gone on there in the face of the difficulties affecting those gathered together.

In this passage he's heckled, not something I've ever experienced in the pulpit; people are usually far too polite to take up what they find unacceptable in that public way. They wait for the church door! The passage tells us the heckler is possessed with an unclean spirit, he's a bit unbalanced. Modern writers often point to the mental health impact of living under occupation, of living with insecurity of livelihood, of knowing hunger and suffering without the possibility of redress being what is described in scripture as 'having a demon'. His unpredictability probably meant no one wanted a conversation with this man, but he begins one with Jesus. His illness makes him attack Jesus as a threat, but as Jesus responds we see a new way of life for him is imminent. Around him in the synagogue are people who cannot hear this message. Perhaps God's presence is more easily felt by the marginalised?

† God, let your words enter our hearts in the places of fear and anger. Give us grace to hear their challenge to our confusion and resistance, and to recognise the promise of wholeness they carry.

For further thought

What are we protecting when we find ourselves resistant to the gospel message of peace, forgiveness and inclusivity brought by others?

Tuesday 19 January
The importance of reflection

Read Mark 1:29–39

In the morning, while it was still very dark, he got up and went out to a deserted place, and there he prayed. And Simon and his companions hunted for him. When they found him, they said to him, 'Everyone is searching for you.'

(verses 35–37)

We often relate to Jesus through his doings and his teachings and miss the number of times in the Gospels when he purposefully draws back from engagement and seeks solitude for reflection. I am a fan of a process called the Pastoral Cycle which is a way of bringing our faith and life into a dynamic conversation, by means of a journey from what we identify as our experience (as we go about in our daily lives) to a decision to act on it.

Many of us, with an activist temperament, are inclined to move straight from one to the other and often take with us misunderstandings about our actual experience, and our own ego and agenda. The Pastoral Cycle invites us to pause a while to subject our experience and how we have understood it to some critical questions and then to purposefully spend some time in reflecting on where God can be seen in what we identify. Reading scripture is helpful here, as are personal prayer and the practice of doing both communally, so that we might come to discern what is the most fruitful and effective course of action to take, instead of merely what we prefer to do.

But we are busy people and are reluctant to spend time unprofitably, especially when we are about the Lord's work. Reflection is a discipline and needs discipline – time formally inserted in schedules – and a purposeful focus, and a heart free from the guilt of 'not doing'.

† Help us see, O God, how precious is the time we surrender: in stillness of body and openness of mind, we wait for you and your inspiration.

For further thought

Look at your schedule for the week. How busy are you? When can you seek out others for reflection on what that busyness is about?

19

Wednesday 20 January
Jesus makes a choice

Read Mark 1:40–45

A leper came to him begging him, and kneeling he said to him, 'If you choose, you can make me clean.' Moved with pity, Jesus stretched out his hand and touched him, and said to him, 'I do choose. Be made clean!'

(verses 40–41)

The historical time and place in which Jesus carried out his ministry was one of conflict, suffering and division. For most people life was a struggle: to eat, to keep healthy, to provide for those dependent on them; and then there was the cultural bureaucracy! Lepers were officially diagnosed by a priest and instructed to live separately from the rest of the community. This would mean a double loss: of their health and sense of bodily well-being as well as an estrangement from the human support and comfort that might have eased their situation.

There was no cure, only a slow progression of a disease that gradually maimed and disfigured. Resignation was advisable, but here is a man who believes there is the possibility of new life. He challenges Jesus: 'if you choose, you can make me clean' (verse 40).

This invites us to think again about Jesus' healings. We read he healed many, but we take it for granted that not all who suffered in his society could be relieved. But that Jesus had a choice about the action he took is perhaps not something we consider. We also have the choice to act in a cruel and unjust world or turn away. We have a choice about the form our action takes. Jesus' choice was made from his compassion, not from his power. When we feel that we can do nothing to help those who suffer because the challenge is too great, or too far away, or we lack influence, we might feel the compassion and choose to act anyway, trusting in the power of God.

† We look to you, God, to fill us with your love and mercy so that we might choose to find what power is there for us when we respond to the needs of others.

For further thought

All of the great life-giving movements of our history started with one person choosing to act in compassion and ended with powerful change.

Thursday 21 January
What are friends for?

Read Mark 2:1–12

Then some people came, bringing to him a paralysed man, carried by four of them. And when they could not bring him to Jesus because of the crowd, they removed the roof above him; and after having dug through it, they let down the mat on which the paralytic lay.

(verses 3–4)

Often when Jesus heals he tells the recipient of his action that their faith is the decisive element in the successful result. Here he praises the faith of the afflicted man's friends. Their determination is impressive and located in strength of feeling for their friend who was unable to press for his own healing.

When they decided to act, the friends had no assurance of a good outcome. They truly had to act in faith. It is not so difficult for us to intervene for the good of those who are close to us. A family friend is heroic in the physical and mental efforts she makes to ensure her two disabled children get the support they need to live full lives. But in working for Christian Aid I have been privileged to see the love and commitment offered by people as they have made a 'friend' of those whose struggle is outside their social experience. They give of their own resources and organise, so others can also give to relieve hunger, injustice and insecurity. They write to those in power and lobby in person so that poor nations might enter the global community as equal partners. They have undertaken these tasks without any guarantee that they will be successful.

They have prayed too, of course. But their faith is also the faith that Jesus recognises here; the faith to physically act, to remove obstacles and clamour for the sake of someone whose voice is never heard.

† O God, make our actions prayers in faith, and teach us the importance of the solidarity and not just the outcome.

For further thought

Who around you today do you see acting in solidarity with those in need in our community, our nation, our world? How can you help?

Friday 22 January
The wrong dinner companions

Eating out alone is a challenge for me. I feel so exposed to scrutiny. Too much food on my fork? A splash on the tablecloth? A struggle with the peas? I always try to have a book with me so that I can hide my fears that I might not do it right.

Whom we choose to share table with is also revealing, as Jesus found when he accepted dinner invitations from people not considered respectable enough to be eating companions.

The custom of his time would be to gather around a set of communal dishes which each would help themselves from, or dip their accompanying bread into to scoop up some of the contents. This makes eating together a very intimate experience and an obvious thing to avoid with people who fail the purity code: those who are soiling their hands with the taxes of the occupying power, or those whose bodies are soiled with the impact of sin.

But to eat alongside someone is to show them that you trust them enough to risk the embarrassment of a misplaced mouthful and to share food with them is to give them the gift of your fellowship in the common dish. Jesus was always looking for opportunities to get close to people in the minutiae of daily life. In the give and take of a shared meal is the honesty and welcome of the life in the kingdom of God; where the outsider can find a place at the table without embarrassment and find some bread to share.

† Generous God, enlarge our tables to include those who must otherwise eat alone. Show us how to include those who are never invited and fill our private dishes with enough for sharing.

For further thought

How does your community, your church see food? As something to be distributed or something to be eaten together?

Saturday 23 January
What is real sabbath?

Read Mark 2:23–3:6

They watched him to see whether he would cure him on the sabbath, so that they might accuse him. And he said to the man who had the withered hand, 'Come forward.' Then he said to them, 'Is it lawful to do good or to do harm on the sabbath, to save life or to kill?'

(verses 3:2–4a)

We live in a frenetic world where a key mark of success is being seen to work all hours. Whereas for some this is an economic necessity, others view it as the sign that they are indispensable. We are often encouraged to see taking a sabbath (a sabbatical) as a reward for long service or hard work. But scripture is insistent: all need sabbath.

The fundamental question, however, is what is sabbath for? Is it merely a recovery period, or a time to enjoy leisure? Is going to church what makes it a sabbath day? At its heart, sabbath is an invitation to make time for God. To do nothing in order to realise how all that we can do pales beside the gift of God to us of life in his creation. To give ourselves a sense of perspective, and to have the space to soothe our disordered thoughts and restore weary bodies that we might live rightly in that creation. So sabbath implies wholeness.

Those who watched Jesus in the synagogue had made a straitjacket of the sabbath. They served it with religious ritual, which had blinded them to its gift of rest, recuperation and renewal. Its connection with people's needs was not appreciated. The question Jesus asked resonates for us centuries later when we ask how church ritual and practice serve life. Are we so concerned about following our religious rules that we ignore the demand for sabbath renewal from those immediately in front of our eyes?

† Lord of the sabbath, come, reside in our hearts. Help us to transform sabbath from one more thing we can do 'right' into that privileged space where you can give life.

For further thought

We have sometimes fought to 'keep Sunday special'. How might that truly look like sabbath? Is it better to be righteous than life-giving?

The Gospel of Mark (1) – 2 Good news for all

Notes by **Mark Woods**

Mark served as a Baptist minister in two churches before becoming a religious affairs journalist and commentator. He has edited several Christian publications including The Baptist Times *and* Christian Today, *and is currently editor at Bible Society. He likes good food, country walking, poetry and arguments, and is the author of* Does the Bible Really Say That? *(Monarch), which takes a hard look at some long-standing Christian assumptions. He lives in Cheltenham. Mark has used the NIVUK for these notes.*

Sunday 24 January
Deliver us from evil: how Jesus makes us whole

Read Mark 3:7–12

For he had healed many, so that those with diseases were pushing forward to touch him. Whenever the impure spirits saw him, they fell down before him and cried out, 'You are the Son of God.' But he gave them strict orders not to tell others about him.

(verses 10–12)

The hallmark of these early chapters of Mark's Gospel is the authority of Jesus. He's the centre of attention. Everyone wants to be near him. In this passage he's teaching on the beach, and the only way he can clear a space for himself is to have his disciples push him off a little way from the shore in a boat. There's a sense here of a world with needs to be met and questions to be answered, and Jesus is the one who can do it.

But there's more to it than that. Mark makes a great deal of Jesus' conflict with evil or 'impure' spirits. In some sections of the Church today we can be rather uncomfortable with such language. But we shouldn't be so modern and sophisticated that we lose sight of what's happening: as part of Jesus' announcement of the kingdom of God, real spiritual evil is being confronted and defeated.

The gospel is good news for body, mind and spirit. Jesus healed the sick and changed lives. He enlightened dark minds, teaching them about the love of God. But he recognised the reality of evil, and broke its power wherever he found it.

† God, help us to recognise the weaknesses, ignorance and sin in our lives. Thank you that Jesus has power over every kind of evil. Amen

Monday 25 January
How to get our spiritual priorities right

Read Mark 3:13–19a

Jesus went up on a mountainside and called to him those he wanted, and they came to him. He appointed twelve that they might be with him and that he might send them out to preach and to have authority to drive out demons.

(verses 13–15)

There's a detail in the calling of the first disciples that it's easy to miss. Jesus chooses 12 and sends them out to preach and to have authority to drive out demons. For young men in a small town it must have been very exciting. They would have prestige and significance. Perhaps they'd travel and see the world.

But that's not the first thing he chooses them for. Verse 14 says he appointed 12 'that they might be with him'. In other words, the priority is not the high-profile activism that impresses people so much. It's just being with Jesus.

Most of us, if we're honest, like to be admired. We like it when we're able to shine in public and have people speak well of us. Many preachers are buttressed by the admiration of their congregations – and there's nothing wrong with that! But like the apostles, we are chosen first and foremost to be with Jesus.

Being with Jesus means firstly being humble. If we are with the Creator of the universe, we have a proper sense of our own place. Secondly, it means being quiet and listening. The disciples who were with Jesus didn't try to dominate the conversation or force their own ideas on people. Thirdly, it means being willing to learn. It's only after this that we're ready to face the public gaze.

Ministry, of whatever kind – and all of us have ministries of some sort – starts with being with Jesus. Without that, whatever we do for him won't be worth very much.

† God, help us to be like the first apostles, who were called to be with Jesus. Help us not to be so busy about the things of Christ that we stop spending time with him. Amen

For further thought

We know quite a bit about some of these first disciples, but nothing about others. Perhaps being with Jesus means we don't need the limelight.

Tuesday 26 January
The unforgiveable sin, and how to avoid it

Read Mark 3:19b–35

'Truly I tell you, people can be forgiven all their sins and every slander they utter, but whoever blasphemes against the Holy Spirit will never be forgiven; they are guilty of an eternal sin.' He said this because they were saying, 'He has an impure spirit.'

(verses 28–30)

There is more than one sad story of someone who's convinced themselves they have committed the sin against the Holy Spirit and can never be forgiven. These people – the poet and hymn writer William Cowper was one of them – are invariably suffering from a form of mental illness. In the form in which Jesus puts his solemn warning, this sin is practically impossible to commit. At this stage of his ministry he has been accused of being in league with the devil and doing his miracles by the power of Satan. He answers his critics by pointing out how absurd the charge is, but he also says that such a fundamental wrongness about him and his work has eternal consequences. Anyone who believes Jesus is evil – even members of his own family – is outside any kind of moral framework.

No one would really say this today; even the fiercest opponents of Christianity never have a bad word to say about Jesus. But this doesn't mean that what he says here is irrelevant.

When Jesus walked the earth, God was doing something new and good, but many people refused to accept it. Suspicious and hostile, they clung to what they knew and wouldn't see that God was offering them something wonderful.

We can't commit the unforgiveable sin. But we can still resist good things just because they're different and we haven't seen them before. When we do that, we put ourselves on the wrong side of God's intentions for us.

† God, thank you that your grace and mercy are new every morning. Help us to be open to the new things you are doing, even if they seem strange or disturbing. Amen

For further thought

Have there been times when I've failed to see God at work because I haven't liked or trusted someone when I should have done?

Wednesday 27 January
More than crossword puzzles:
how do parables work?

Read Mark 4:1–12

Again Jesus began to teach by the lake. The crowd that gathered round him was so large that he got into a boat and sat in it out on the lake, while all the people were along the shore at the water's edge. He taught them many things by parables ...

(verses 1–2a)

We're very used to this parable, and to the explanation of it that Jesus gave his disciples later. We know that the seed is the word of God, and that the different soils are the different conditions in which the word of God flourishes, or doesn't. But to Jesus' first hearers, this would not have been obvious. There are other parables, too, where his meaning isn't immediately clear. It is a 'secret', he tells his disciples, whose solution is given to some but not to others.

At one level, teaching in this way makes sense. We are far more likely to remember something if we've worked it out for ourselves. Schoolteachers who rely on the 'chalk and talk' method, where they stand in front of a class and explain everything to them, aren't usually as effective as those who involve the students in their own learning. Working out the meaning of a parable makes it come alive to us.

But there's something more here: Jesus seems to imply that he is deliberately speaking in ways some people won't be able to understand. And behind this is the idea that understanding is about more than head knowledge. These parables are meant to educate the heart as well as the mind. They change us, and we have to be willing to be changed. They ask hard questions of us: what sort of soil am I? How deeply rooted is the word of God in me? Parables are more than crossword puzzles.

† God, help me to read your word prayerfully, humbly and carefully. Let the words of Jesus speak to my heart, and keep me from thinking I understand them if they haven't changed me.

For further thought

When the Bible stops surprising us, it's probably not because we know it so well but because we don't know it well enough.

IBRA's rich and long history

The International Bible Reading Association (IBRA) was founded in 1882 by the National Sunday School Union (NSSU) committee under Charles Waters, a bank manager in King's Cross. A devout young man and Sunday school teacher, Waters had arrived in London in 1859 to further his career, and there encountered the inspirational teaching of Charles Spurgeon. He threw himself, heart and soul, into working with Spurgeon and the NSSU who wrote to all members in Britain and overseas inviting them to join the newly formed International Bible Reading Association, circulating lists of daily Bible readings supported by short hints and tips for understanding The Word for the day.

Over 1 million readers

The response was amazing. By 1910 the readership had exceeded a million people and was touching the lives of soldiers fighting wars, sailors on long voyages to Australia, colliers in the coal mines of Wales, schools in Canada, Jamaica and Belfast and prisoners in Chicago. People all over the world, alone and in groups, felt comforted and encouraged by the idea of joining other Christians throughout the world in reading the same Bible passages. *And they still do!*

Continuing the IBRA legacy

It is humbling to read endorsements from readers spanning the years – here are some from two of our partners in South Africa:

66 *During my 11 years as district Secretary for South Africa, many letters have [come] from members, who, through the daily readings have found light in darkness, solace in sorrow, direction in difficulty, strength in weakness, power in prayer and joy in our Saviour. Our members are scattered over many thousands of miles. Pray for us!* 99

MJ Russell, Wynberg, South Africa – 1907 – quote taken from the illustrated books created to celebrate IBRA's Silver Jubilee and presented to Charles Waters in 1907

66 *IBRA is a ministry with an amazing impact on the lives of believers and I have enjoyed the opportunity immensely... The* Fresh From The Word *notes are superb in challenging the reader – as no other notes can – to probe and pray for deeper insights in the reading of the Bible.* 99

Dan Vaughan – 2014 – distributor of IBRA in South Africa since 1993

God is the same yesterday, today and forever – therefore our original mission continues today and will do into the future!

Thursday 28 January
Shedding light on a surprisingly dark parable

Read Mark 4:13–25

He said to them, 'Do you bring in a lamp to put it under a bowl or a bed? Instead, don't you put it on its stand? For whatever is hidden is meant to be disclosed, and whatever is concealed is meant to be brought out into the open.'

(verses 21–22)

At first glance, this parable of Jesus is one to which we can nod along – we get it. It's a vivid portrayal of something all his hearers would have understood, and which anyone today who has a garden will understand too – you have to get the soil right for the plants to grow.

As we think about it further, though, it starts to look a bit bleak. The soil is what it is. Someone turns into a good church-going Christian because they happen to have been good soil for the word of God. Someone else doesn't, because they weren't. It hardly seems fair.

What we need to bring to this story, though, is something from the very beginning of the Bible, and the very end of the Gospels.

In Genesis 2:8, we're told that God planted a garden 'in the East, in Eden'.

In John 20:15 we're told that Mary mistook the risen Christ for a gardener.

It's an interesting coincidence, which points us to a solution to our problem. The soil in which the seed falls might be unpromising – shallow, or choked with thorns, or dry and hard. But God is a gardener. He breaks up the hard ground and clears the weeds. The most unlikely people have heard his word and responded to it. We should never write off anyone, because we don't know how God is working in their lives – and he calls Christians to be co-workers with him, labouring alongside him to prepare the ground for his word.

† God, thank you that you haven't finished with me yet. Break up the hard ground in me, deepen the shallow soil and clear out the weeds. Let your light shine in my life. Amen

For further thought

'Whoever has will be given more' (verse 25): good soil brings a good harvest. How can I cultivate my spirit to make it more Christlike?

Friday 29 January
Signs of life: discerning the kingdom of God

Read Mark 4:26–34

Again he said, 'What shall we say the kingdom of God is like …? It is like a mustard seed, which is the smallest of all seeds on earth. Yet when planted, it grows and becomes the largest of all garden plants, with such big branches that the birds can perch in its shade.'

(verses 30a, 31–32)

Equating the growth of the kingdom of God with the growth of the Church is a recurring temptation. It's true that a full church might very well be better than a half-empty one. God's desire is for human flourishing in body, mind and spirit, and where better for spiritual flourishing than a church?

There's a lot more to it than that, however. The rule of God extends beyond a church's walls. It involves justice, peace and reconciliation, not just inspirational sermons or sweet music. So, there's a paradox: a tiny church where God is worshipped faithfully, relationships are healthy and a few believers really try to change the world might be a better sign of the kingdom than the megachurch where you have to arrive early to get a seat.

This paradox is echoed by the theme of Jesus' parables here, which is mystery. His hearers had no idea what made crops grow. Today, we know exactly what happens. We can even manipulate them to make them grow better. But we can still be wonderstruck by the yearly miracle of the green shimmer on a field in spring.

So, we shouldn't imagine we can control the kingdom's growth, as though if we found the right formula, we could make churches grow, or make righteousness and harmony break out. It's not up to us, Jesus says here; it's up to God.

That doesn't mean we shouldn't expect to work hard at church. But it does mean we look to God to bring results, in his own good time.

† God, help me to believe in miracles. Help me to trust in your power, and not to feel I have to do everything myself. Keep me alert for signs of your kingdom.

For further thought

How should we balance our responsibility to work for God's kingdom with our knowledge that he alone brings a harvest?

Saturday 30 January
All at sea: faith when God is silent

Read Mark 4:35–41

A furious squall came up, and the waves broke over the boat, so that it was nearly swamped. Jesus was in the stern, sleeping on a cushion. The disciples woke him and said to him, 'Teacher, don't you care if we drown?'

(verses 37–38)

The picture of Jesus fast asleep during the storm is very poignant. He is sleeping like a child in his father's lap. But when he wakes, he demonstrates divine power over the wind and the waves, which stand for the forces of darkness and chaos God overcame with a word at creation.

There's a wonderful old hymn that's associated particularly with the Royal Navy: 'Eternal Father, Strong to Save.' Its refrain is, 'O hear us, when we cry to thee/ For those in peril on the sea.'

It isn't just a hymn for seafarers. Most of us at some point in our lives have the sense of being all at sea, lost, frightened and on the point of being overwhelmed. We are not waving but drowning, as the poet Stevie Smith put it.

So, the story Mark tells is a very familiar one. Panic sets in because we don't think anyone is in charge. God is absent; Jesus is asleep, and we're going under.

Christians should not expect faith to insulate us from hard times, or that Jesus will come to our rescue when we are quite capable of working things out for ourselves. But there are times when it's very reasonable to feel afraid. Worries and fears, about money, health, work, our loved ones, pile up and fill our whole horizon.

This story tells us that even when Jesus is silent, he is profoundly present. He is there for those in peril on the roughest sea.

† God, you know the hard times I have to go through. Help me to believe you're with me even when you are silent; help me to trust that the waters will not overwhelm me.

For further thought

'Even the wind and the waves obey him' (verse 41). What difference does trusting Jesus make in my day-to-day life?

The Psalms of David – 1 Chosen and chased

Notes by **Edna Hutchings**

Edna lives in a market town in the beautiful county of Dorset and is a retired accounts assistant. She is a member of a United Church (Methodist and United Reformed) and shares the leading and facilitating for one of the church home groups. She enjoys writing short stories and poetry. Other hobbies include reading, knitting, walking and messing about with paints. Edna has used the NIVUK for these notes.

Sunday 31 January
David's psalm

Read Psalm 18:1–19

I love you Lord, my strength …
He brought me out into a spacious place;
he rescued me because he delighted in me.

(verses 1 and 19)

Psalm 18 is a wonderful prayer full of drama. Who cannot be moved by it? It begins with a simple declaration of David's love for his Lord, then articulates in some detail all that God has done for him and ends with the statement that God delighted in him. Despite his faults, God was uppermost in his mind and decision making. He communicates with God at all levels and with great honesty. This could be a blueprint for how we should direct our own prayers to God.

In the week ahead we shall follow David's up-and-down relationship with Saul, beginning with his first appearance at Saul's court. We shall discover how he uses praise with singing. And how he waits on God's guidance and remembers how God has answered his prayers. Above all David respected God and he always tried to do his will. God, he says, 'delighted in me'. God will delight in us too if we try to do the same.

† Father God, help us to be guided by you in all things and thank you that you always hear our prayers.

Monday 1 February
David the sweet singer

Read 1 Samuel 16:14–23

'I have seen a son of Jesse of Bethlehem who knows how to play the lyre. He is a brave man and a warrior. He speaks well and is a fine-looking man. And the Lord is with him.'

(verse 18)

David seems to excel at everything. He is brave, good-looking and articulate. A young shepherd, a healthy out-of-doors young man, I think he may have expected his bravery, or his handsome features, to win him favour at the royal court. But, no, it was his gentler side, his lyre-playing and singing, which brought him to the attention of Saul. Saul suffered periodically from an 'evil spirit', what today we would probably translate as depression or anxiety. Music can lift the soul and soothe away worries.

I love our church choir. Although most of the singers are past their youth, like David they make sweet music. And I know the membership is enjoyed. One lady said to me recently, when I told her how much I appreciate their singing every week, that it was an enjoyable part of her life. So, music brings joy to the giver as well as the receiver.

For me, singing hymns is a form of prayer. When I am troubled, I sing to myself – from 'Dear Lord and Master of Mankind' which calms me, to 'How Great Thou Art' to lift my spirits. I've inherited this habit from my mother who used to go about her many chores with quiet renderings of hymns, psalms and canticles. Of course, some of our greatest prayers in the Book of Psalms are attributed to David, the sweet singer, who knew how to pray. And we will be exploring two more of these on Wednesday and Friday.

† Father God, thank you for the gift of music and poetry and may we be always ready to sing your praises.

For further thought

Pray for those who may not be able to enjoy music and that they may find consolation in poetry and other art forms.

Tuesday 2 February
David hides out with rebels

Today we move forward in David's story. Saul has now become jealous of David's popularity. David flees and hides from Saul who plans to kill him, gathering a band of outlaws to support him. So, will he be able to keep his faith in God alive in this situation of fear and fighting and less than honourable company? We see from this passage that indeed he can. Prayer has become a good habit and the fact that he is concerned for his parents' safety shows obedience to the Ten Commandments. And he waits for God's guidance.

We are not in the same situation as David in our lives today, but we may often find ourselves among people of no faith, or even perhaps of less than exemplary behaviour, in our work and daily lives. To maintain our Christian values together with our popularity may not be easy. Or we have mental anxieties that won't go away, making prayer difficult. At these times our Christian discipline comes into play.

Only this Sunday, my busy life was getting on top of me. Would it not be better to get some chores out of the way instead of going to church? There were apples to pick, a mountain of ironing, a letter to a sick friend to write. But I decided it was more important to stick to my Christian rituals. I went along to church as usual and came away with my mood lifted, increased energies and the realisation that the chores could easily be left until the next day.

† Father God, help us to hold onto our Christian rituals and beliefs even in situations where prayer is difficult.

For further thought

Is there any part of your Christian discipleship that you have let slide? Jesus said: 'But seek first his kingdom and his righteousness' (Matthew 6:33a).

Wednesday 3 February
Prayer and praise in the cave

Read Psalm 57

Have mercy on me, my God, have mercy on me, for in you I take refuge. I will take refuge in the shadow of your wings until the disaster has passed.

(verse 1)

As we saw yesterday, David is hiding from Saul, and today's psalm is considered to have been composed by David concerning this period. It's a wonderful example of how to pray. We are unlikely to be hiding in a cave under the threat of death, but we may be suffering from an illness or bereavement. Or having to cope with living alone, redundancy, exam failure. So many worries in our modern way of life.

David begins his prayer here with affirmation of his faith in God and with praise. Then earnestly articulates his fears. No doubt he would put on a brave face in front of his men, but with God he is honest. Throughout the psalm he sings God's praises.

David has faith that God will protect him as a bird will protect its young under its wings. As a small girl I delighted in visiting my grandparents' smallholding at the time when the baby chicks were hatched. Such delicate, fragile bundles of soft yellow fluff. They would venture out away from the broody hen, which was kept in a hutch, and start to peck and find food for themselves. But at the least sign of danger they were quick to return to their mother hen, who would protect them under her wings. We, too, are fragile and get comfort in knowing that we can return to the shelter of God. God gives us free will, but we can always return to his safety.

† Father God, may we never stop praising you and know that we can take refuge in the shadow of your wings.

For further thought
Praising God in prayer is as important as petitions. Alternating our worries with praise, as David does here, will reaffirm our dependence on God.

Thursday 4 February
Pursued by Saul to Ziph

Read 1 Samuel 23:14–29

And Saul's son Jonathan went to David at Horesh and helped him find strength in God. 'Don't be afraid,' he said. 'My father Saul will not lay a hand on you. You shall be king over Israel, and I will be second to you. Even my father Saul knows this.'

(verses 16–17)

David is in real danger as Saul gets ever closer and, without the encouragement of Jonathan, we can imagine that his faith in God's protection is tested. Jonathan reminds David of God's promise that David will become king (2 Samuel 7). But Saul, as well as having a much larger army, has spies in Ziph. David must have thought there was little hope. But God moves in mysterious ways. When it looks as if there is no possible chance of escape, Saul is diverted in his mission to kill David (verse 27).

I knew that my deafness was not curable, despite someone with a deeper faith than mine praying for a cure. At that time, I had not even heard about the modern technology and skill of surgeons that would some years later replace my useless cochlea with electrodes. Someone had prayed for me to be able to hear again and years later it happened. Not a 'miracle' in the biblical sense but a miracle of science. And a positive answer to the prayer of the faithful.

In less dramatic ways you may have come across coincidences as answers to prayers. Often in life, friends turn up out of the blue just when you needed cheering up or practical help. As we sing in that wonderful hymn by William Cowper (1731–1800), 'God moves in a mysterious way.' So, we keep praying and, like with David here, a friend to boost our faith can be very helpful.

† Father God, thank you that, even though your timing and answers may not be those we expect, you always hear our prayers.

For further thought

Read that wonderful poem/hymn by William Cowper. 'God Moves in a Mysterious Way' can be found in most hymn books, or Google that first line.

Betrayed by the Ziphites

Read Psalm 54

Hear my prayer, O God;
listen to the words of my mouth.
You have delivered me from all my troubles ...

(verses 2 and 7a)

This psalm has been attributed to David whilst being pursued by Saul who knew of his whereabouts from the Ziphites. Another of his articulate prayers full of anguish, and pleading, but also of praise and continuing faith in God's promise. David must have felt overwhelmed with the betrayal and the coming ever nearer of his enemy. How could God possibly help him in this situation? He thinks of previous times when God has protected him and heard his prayer.

I think it is so easy for us to forget how worried we may have been about something once the problem is resolved. I have kept a personal journal for many years and looking back at random I find entries of prayers answered in God's own time and according to his will. For example, I had written that I was worried about the work I was doing and intended to give up and resign, but I needed the work and knew how difficult it would be to get alternative employment at that time. 'Must pray about it,' I'd written. Reading on, it seems my employer encouraged me to carry on with the job. Later I find entries showing, once I had persevered, how much I enjoyed that work. We tend to forget how God has guided us through difficult times when all is well in the end.

† Father God, thank you for all the times you have answered our prayers, guided and protected us.

For further thought

If it is not painful, you might like to think back to difficult times when God has answered your prayers in his own time.

Saturday 6 February
David spares Saul's life

Read 1 Samuel 24:1–7

The men said, 'This is the day the Lord spoke of when he said to you, "I will give your enemy into your hands for you to deal with as you wish."' Then David crept up unnoticed and cut off a corner of Saul's robe.

(verse 4)

This must have bewildered David's band of outlaws. Saul was now within their grasp. The outlaws used God's words to say that Saul can now be killed but David has picked up on the 'to deal with as you wish' and decides that he cannot kill God's anointed king. Later in the chapter we see that it works well for him as by confronting each other peace, for now at least, reigns. David has prayerfully come to a decision.

How often we find ourselves in a dilemma. God gives us free will too. I was introduced to a lady, no longer with us, who had rather an abrupt manner. That first time I met her, a comment she made, and the way she said it, upset me and I decided to keep my distance from her. However, on reflection, I thought I may have been too sensitive and decided to ignore the comment. She eventually became a friend and confided in me. A rather sad childhood had made her into the independent, tough old lady she was.

When I had been faced with the situation where I had to accept her ways or walk away, at first, I decided that neither would be wrong. I had free will on this occasion, but with prayer I took the former decision which turned out to be beneficial to both of us. Often, we are left with dilemmas 'to deal with as we wish'. It is wise in these situations to avoid rushing in, but to consider the problem prayerfully and wait on God.

† Father God, thank you that you have given us free will. May we always use it wisely.

For further thought

Is there is a situation where you have reacted too hastily? Perhaps you could reconsider how God would like you to deal with the situation.

The Psalms of David – 2 Broken open

Notes by **Delroy Hall**

Delroy has been in active ministry for over 30 years and is an ordained Bishop within the Church of God of Prophecy. He sits on the International Committee for Doctrine and Polity for the Church of God of Prophecy in Cleveland, Tennessee. He works as a student counsellor and well-being advisor at Sheffield Hallam University, UK, and as a sports chaplain for Sheffield United Football Club. Delroy still keeps fit and loves listening to smooth jazz. He is married to Paulette and is the father of 24-year-old twins, Saffron and Jordan. Delroy has used the NIVUK for these notes.

Sunday 7 February
Out of the cave

Read Psalm 142

When my spirit grows faint within me,
it is you who watch over my way.

(verse 3a)

I do not know how you feel reading this psalm, but I can almost feel David's perplexed and troubled mind, worn out, gasping for life and breath. It is a dark poem of despair. It seems to go farther down a dark, dead-end road. As I read this song it reminds me of the many people whom I see suffering with various levels of depression. There seems to be no freedom from their dark prison. A prison they did not ask for, but here they are, imprisoned and trapped, with no way out, it seems.

David cries much in this psalm, but there is something which catches my eye. David recognises that it is important to experience our feelings, when we are going through difficult times. There is no point denying it. In fact, the psalmist gives us some pointers, perhaps especially as men. Feeling and talking about the pain lead us to the possibility of freedom. David understands that in God, there is hope, amidst the darkness. He wants to be set free that he may praise God. He needs release to praise God and sometimes, before the release takes place, just the thought of things being better fills us with hope.

† Father and friend, let me remember, in those times, when all seems lost, having you in my thoughts can help in looking beyond my immediate circumstances.

Monday 8 February
Lost leader

Read 2 Samuel 11:1–15

'Put Uriah out in front where the fighting is fiercest. Then withdraw from him so that he will be struck down and die.'

(verse 15)

We see this in movies, don't we? Someone thinks of a wicked plan and then gets someone else to carry it out. It makes me think. As humans, in spite of our advancement in science, technology and other entities which portray success, have we changed much since some of these Bible stories were written aeons ago? Here are two different men. One who was the leader of the nation and should have been with his troops, and the other, a general maybe, who was with his men fighting alongside them. David is revered for many reasons, but for a moment, let us consider Uriah, the unsung hero in the story. He is abiding in his duties and living out his responsibilities. His leader is not.

David, after his night of passion with Bathsheba, Uriah's wife, some time later hears she is pregnant with his baby. He uses his power, status and influence in a manipulative way to get her husband to sleep with his wife. Two times David attempts to get Uriah to sleep with his wife, but fails because Uriah is a principled man. How can he be having pleasure with his wife when his men are out on the battlefield?

With further trickery, David involves other people in his scheme to get rid of Uriah. His night of deceit, far from the battlefield, but occurring under the nose of God, ultimately leads to a conspiracy to murder.

† Dear Lord, you have given us freedom of choice but we cannot always determine the consequences of our actions. Help us to choose wisely.

For further thought

While we are alive we will always be tempted. We must learn ways to be vigilant and discerning when faced with temptation.

Tuesday 9 February
David repents

Read Psalm 51

The sacrifices of God are a broken spirit,
a broken and contrite heart ...

(part of verse 17)

David's hidden act with Bathsheba was exposed by someone who was not there at the time. Frightening!

David had the pleasure of spending the night with Bathsheba, and now he had the most unpleasant, but needful task of admitting his transgressions. That takes courage. He does not mince his words in owning up. From the moment he acted on his desire for Bathsheba to the murder of Uriah it was an indication of the condition of his heart, but he does not allow his sinful act or feelings of guilt to crush his spirit into hopelessness. He seeks to be purged and be forgiven by God, and he has learnt that difficult task of forgiving himself.

Too often, when we have committed sin we are good at believing that God has forgiven us, but we have, at times, a huge task in forgiving ourselves. As a counsellor that is a common problem I have to work with on a regular basis with believers and non-believers alike.

Repenting for the things we have done and wanting to bring about a change of life brings healing and relief. We are not designed to, or rather, we do not function at our optimum when we carry emotional, spiritual and psychological burdens due to our actions.

From verse 8 onwards, David's restoration is categorised by a sense of joy and once again being in fellowship with God. How many times have we been wracked with guilt and condemnation over our actions, only to then experience the joy of the Lord once we have confessed our sins and been forgiven? What blessed relief. Hallelujah!

† Saviour, we struggle daily in living, but what peace we deprive ourselves of when we fail to seek your divine forgiveness when we have done wrong. Help us.

For further thought

God is waiting to receive us when we have done wrong. Stop struggling with your guilt. He wants to forgive and release you.

Wednesday 10 February
Fleeing from kin

Read 2 Samuel 15:13–23

But Ittai replied to the king, 'As surely as the Lord lives, and as my lord the king lives, wherever my lord the king shall be, whether it means life or death, there will your servant be.'

(verse 21)

As usual, the scripture features rich descriptive scenes. One hardly knows which theme to pursue, but I want to focus on David receiving help from the most unlikely place: from a foreigner, an alien, a stranger in the camp. David is fleeing for his life. His son is after his blood. What a predicament! His own family member, but this is not so far from reality. I recall going to the funeral of one of my schoolfriends. My schoolfriend and his 21-year-old son got into an argument at a party and his son stabbed him to death. Our story today, though, has twists.

In today's heightened environment of racism and increasing nationalism, here is a stranger who has bonded himself to David and is loyal to him, his new king. Ittai the Gittite, not an Israelite, but a new arrival, possibly not even signed up to the Official Secrets Act, promises to serve the king, and David, highlighting his social class and societal standing, is astonished at this newcomer's loyalty. This person recognises David's kingship and follows him, but there is another twist to this story that has meaning for us today. God will send us help from the most unlikely places and through unlikely people.

If we learn one aspect of this story, is it that we are challenged in allowing a stranger, someone who does not look like us, someone of a different racial background or social class, to draw alongside us to help us?

† Father and friend, as I experience a myriad of life's difficulties, help me to be open to how, and through whom, you will use anyone to help me.

For further thought

Consider this. We all have biases, but God does not. As his people, are we open enough to whom God might send to deliver us?

Thursday 11 February
Words of trust

Read Psalm 3
I lie down and sleep;
I wake again, because the Lord sustains me.

(verse 5)

One of the most difficult things to experience in life is when we are unable to sleep at night, when we are in physical pain or going through a crisis. It is as though the fallout of a crisis does not leave us alone. It perches on our shoulders continually annoying us, speaking so no one else can hear in every crevice of our mind and body. We lie down to sleep and sleep abandons us.

In this story, David is fleeing his son, but we may not be fleeing a family member. It could be fleeing an illness, the thought of redundancy, a failed relationship, our children not doing well at school, our child or us being bullied; even being embroiled in debt can cause us to lose sleep.

What did David do so he could sleep? He trusted in the sovereign nature of God. His mind was settled in God. Regardless of what others had said about God, David knew who God was. Listen to these five words spoken with confidence, 'I lie down and sleep' (verse 5); why could he sleep so peacefully? His confidence was in the loyalty and faithfulness of God. Listen again. 'But You, O Lord, are a shield around me, my glory, the One who lifts my head high' (verse 3).

David's confidence in God was developed when things were not so difficult. He knew the faithfulness of God, so when he had to flee he ran with the essence of God's grace inside him. He knew no one could take that away from him. Never!

† Beloved Father and friend, help us to take the time to be grounded in you, especially when things are going well, so when tough times come we can survive.

For further thought
Having a strong faith is not just for long-gone Bible days. How might you develop a faith so that during troubled times, you can sleep?

Friday 12 February
A tight spot

Read 2 Samuel 15:24–30

'Take the ark of God back into the city. If I find favour in the Lord's eyes, he will bring me back and let me see it and his dwelling-place again.'

(verse 25b)

David is now in a tight spot. He is running for his life. His back is against the wall. There are two things that leap out of the scriptures in this instance. While recognising he is under severe pressure, his loyalty to God is symbolised by his attention to the ark of the covenant being returned.

It takes godly character to give attention to the matters of God when you are under pressure for your life. Our natural tendency is to look after our own matters first and then consider God.

David displays further godly character. Although he is a king and acquainted with prestige, honour, status and privilege, he is not beyond weeping and mourning. You can almost hear and feel him weeping. It is common to see people in positions of power and authority laud their power over others, but David shows us the experience of a parent whose own flesh and blood is after him, by also showing vulnerability. What parent would not be heartbroken, fearful and vulnerable with a death threat from their own child? We have no idea of David's thoughts, but using our senses we sense his pain. David expresses despair and anguish as any parent would, longing for the return of their wayward child.

† Saviour divine, hear us in moments of despair where our tears are the only means of communicating with you how much pain we are in.

For further thought

Are you in a position of power? Do your followers ever see you vulnerable and needing God? It might be good if they did, periodically.

Saturday 13 February
In the wilderness

Read Psalm 63

I think of you through the watches of the night.
Because you are my help,
I sing in the shadow of your wings.

(verses 6b–7)

As a young boy I rarely enjoyed poetry, but the psalms have kindled in me a love of vivid images and descriptive language. The psalmist uses these to portray his life experience, the life of Israel and the beauty of God.

Even if you are not a professional theologian, you cannot escape the beauty of the scriptures in how the psalmist, once broken, vulnerable and in despair, recognises God's providence and protection. Absorb this. 'On my bed I remember you,' 'because you are my help,' 'I sing in the shadow of your wings' (verses 6–7).

God has been there for David in his moments of crisis. He is there for us in our crises, but often when the crisis is over we forget God's protection; we fail to meditate on him significantly and miss the joy of being in the shadow of his wings. A place of protection, comfort and joy while remaining close to the breast and heartbeat of the Father.

What I find interesting in the New King James Version is that David uses 204 words to pen his experience of the loving and protective God, but only 32 words to talk about his enemies. He is teaching us, through the beauty of his words, that we must be real and acknowledge our difficulties, but we need to spend most of our time focusing on the God of all possibilities. It is not so much mind over matter; it is about filling our minds and spirit with the power of God's love and his word. Just a thought.

† Father, you continue teaching us that while acknowledging our difficulties we must not spend much time considering them. We will find security and assurance meditating on you, the God of all possibilities and deliverance. Amen

For further thought

Consider this. The amount of words the psalmist uses focusing on God instead of dwelling on problems precedes the self-help industry by centuries.

Into the unknown: the spirit of discipleship – 1 First steps

Notes by **Catherine Williams**

Catherine is an Anglican priest who works as a freelance spiritual director, retreat leader and writer. She is also involved with vocational discernment and ministerial development within the Church of England. Living in the English town of Tewkesbury, Catherine is married to Paul, also a priest, and they have two adult children. In her spare time Catherine enjoys reading, singing, theatre, cinema and poetry. She is also passionate about butterfly conservation. Catherine has used the NRSVA for these notes.

Sunday 14 February
Called

Read Luke 5:1–11

'Put out into the deep water.'

(part of verse 4)

This week we explore what it means to follow Jesus, and the confidence we can have going into the unknown. God is there and has been with us and for us from before we were even aware of God's existence.

In today's passage Jesus meets some workers as they go about their business of fishing. Jesus suggests they might try fishing in a new way – going out in the daytime and casting into the deeper water. Listening to Jesus and following his suggestions, Simon (Peter) and the other fishermen suddenly find their work transformed and with the help of colleagues they land a huge catch. Simon recognises that God is at work and he is both scared and fascinated. Jesus calls: the fishermen drop everything and follow him.

God calls us, commissions us to work for the kingdom, enhances our skills and abilities, makes suggestions about new ways of working and serving others and encourages us into a deeper relationship of love and trust – with God and with one another. It's not all plain sailing, as we'll see this week. The faithful disciple needs to grow in confidence, courage, honesty, humility and, above all, love.

† Lord Jesus, as I explore and deepen my discipleship this week, help me to trust you as you lead me in the ways of love.

Monday 15 February
Chosen

Read John 15:9–16

'You did not choose me but I chose you.'

(verse 16a)

Are you a sporty person? I'm not! I can remember those embarrassing times at school when classmates picked teams during PE lessons and I was among those left towards the end whom no one wanted on their side. I definitely wasn't an asset and on a bad day I could be a sporting liability! Thank goodness this is not the way God chooses. It's from God's immense love that we are chosen: not through any ability of our own. Whilst we may think that we are choosing to follow Christ, in reality our choice is a subconscious recognition of and response to God who has already chosen us, and promises to never let us go – even when we drift away or give up on faith.

In the Farewell Discourses in John's Gospel, Jesus shares with his disciples all he wants them to remember when he is no longer physically with them. As today's disciples we are reminded that Jesus has chosen and commissioned us as his friends to carry on God's work of building the kingdom. We are to do this through being at home in God's love and allowing that love to shape all our relationships, words and actions. We are to love one another in the same way that Jesus loves us. This is sacrificial love which, rooted in God, goes many extra miles for the well-being of others, and through which – Jesus assures us – we will discover complete joy. Today, remember you are chosen by God who loves you completely. Allow that great love to flow through you to others.

† Thank you, Lord, for choosing me as your friend. Help me remain in your love so that I may offer your friendship to all those I meet.

For further thought

Ponder some of the recent choices you have made. Has the driving force for those choices been shaped by God's love – or something else?

Tuesday 16 February
Known

Read Jeremiah 1:4–10

'Before I formed you in the womb, I knew you, and before you were born, I consecrated you.'

(verse 5a)

When did you first become aware of God? Have you always known God, or is it only recently that you've realised God is there? In this passage from Jeremiah we're reminded that God knew us before we were born. God the Creator of the cosmos, is our Creator too. God made each of us, unique and holy, and knows us intimately. God knows who we are and whom we will become. From the womb God set us apart to be holy people.

For Jeremiah this is too much to grasp and he feels unworthy and ill-equipped: too young to be of use to God. This great prophet lacks confidence and courage. He is anxious and reluctant. How reassuring for us, when we too feel inadequate and unsure. God regularly calls us to that which requires some growing into: not just in the early stages of our faith journey, but continually throughout our discipleship as we are called deeper into God and become increasingly Christlike. Our ability is immaterial. It is God working in us who enables us to speak appropriately of faith, and to take stock, challenge, dismantle and rebuild when necessary. 'Don't be afraid,' says God, 'I am with you to deliver you.' It's not through our own strength that we are faithful followers of Jesus Christ, but by the power of God working in us. Remembering that God has made us, loves us, calls us and equips us reorients our attention away from ourselves and directs it towards God. We are not the centre of our world: God is.

† Lord, give me courage and confidence to serve you in the world. Help me become more fully the follower of Christ you are calling me to be.

For further thought

Spend time today meditating on Psalm 139.

Wednesday 17 February (Ash Wednesday)
Restored

Read Ezekiel 37:1–14

'I will put my spirit within you, and you shall live.'

(verse 14a)

Today is Ash Wednesday, the beginning of the Lenten season. Lent prepares us for the great celebration of Easter by encouraging us to renew our faith, strengthen our spiritual discipline and come into right relationship with God. Ash Wednesday is set aside as a day of fasting and repentance. We have Ezekiel's vision of the valley of dry bones as a fitting backdrop.

Ezekiel encounters a place where all seems lost. Dry bones are everywhere. Imagine a desert full of carcasses picked clean by vultures and whitened by the fierce sun. Everything is dead. But God has a plan. Ezekiel is to bring the word of the Lord to the bones and as he does so the bodies of the House of Israel begin to be reconstructed: bones, sinews, flesh and skin. But that's not enough for life. God breathes on the bones and they live again. One more act is needed for them to flourish. God places his Spirit within them and they become spiritually alive: back from the dead. It's a vision that prefigures the central acts of our faith – the death and resurrection of Jesus, and the coming of the Holy Spirit. We're reminded that with God nothing is impossible. Hope is restored.

Sometimes our faith can dry up, God appears absent and following Jesus becomes very difficult. At such times it's good to remember that at our baptism we received the Holy Spirit who fills us with God's life. When all seems lost, resurrection and new life are only a breath away. God is longing to restore us to life again.

† Holy God, help me to turn away from sin and follow Christ. Breathe your new life into me and fill me afresh with your Spirit.

For further thought

What spiritual discipline will you take up this Lent in order to deepen your relationship with the God who gives you life?

Thursday 18 February
Parented

Read Hosea 11:1–11

*I led them with cords of human kindness,
with bands of love.*

(verse 4a)

Most of us don't remember learning to walk, but if we are parents, we probably remember those first tottering steps our children took, and the way we encouraged them to step out and stagger small distances clinging onto the furniture. It wasn't long before they were running in all directions and we were struggling to keep up with them and keep them safe. If we have children unable to walk, then we will have taken even more care and attention over their development.

Today's reading imagines God as an exemplary parent who feeds us, heals us and teaches us to walk accompanied by cuddles and kisses. The analogy continues as we, the children of God, become rebellious young adults and go our own way – far from home. Like the committed parent, God cannot stop loving us. God loves us unconditionally and longs for us to come home. With the tough, fierce love of a lion, God roars and we come flying back, like migrating birds. It's a beautiful image and shows both a human and feminine side to God, which many find helpful and reassuring. Whatever we do and wherever we go, God will come looking for us to bring us home. This is not just an analogy. In Jesus God became one of us, showing us how to live full and fruitful lives, and raising us to become all that we can be, mirroring God's image. In Jesus we learn that even death is not the end, for nothing can separate us from God's eternal and perfect parental love for each one of us.

† Thank you, Lord, that you love me unconditionally. Help me to remember that you care about the way I live my life and are concerned for me to remain safe with you.

For further thought
Who are the people who taught you to walk in the Christian faith? Give thanks for them today.

Friday 19 February
Guided

Read Psalm 25

Lead me in your truth, and teach me, for you are the God of my salvation; for you I wait all day long.

(verse 5)

In today's psalm David turns to the Lord for guidance and deliverance. His song implores God not to let his enemies succeed and triumph over him. David asks God to show him the right paths to take and teach him the ways of truth and integrity. Despite having committed some serious sins, David asks God to be merciful and gracious towards him, forgiving him for past misdemeanours and setting him back on the way of faithfulness. David's relationship with God is such that he can be honest and humble, confident that God's covenant of faithful love will restore him. David expresses an intense longing for God to lead him in the right ways and a strong desire, and commitment to waiting, for God to act.

Whom do we turn to when we require help in our lives? Are we confident to cry out to God for guidance when our human nature gets the better of us? Do we come before the Lord humbly – like David or the tax-collector in Luke 18:13 – acknowledging our sinfulness and need for God's restoring love and grace? In our Christian journey we should never reach the point when we are beyond being led by God. Even when we are mature in faith, we still need to look to God to lead us in the way of truth and show us the path to life. Lifting up our souls to God daily in prayer reminds us to rely not on our own efforts but on God's secure and steadfast guidance.

† Lord God – thank you for your guidance. Teach me your ways that I may humbly learn your truth, and remain honest before you – confident in your love.

For further thought

Which areas of your life are in most need of God's guidance? Humbly ask God to act. Wait patiently for the outcome.

February

Into the unknown: the spirit of discipleship – 1 First steps

Saturday 20 February
Delivered

Read Psalm 71:1–9

In your righteousness deliver me and rescue me.

(verse 2a)

Our final passage this week reminds us again that God has been with us from before our birth and is on our side throughout life, into old age and beyond the grave. The psalmist cries out to God for deliverance and rescue. He acknowledges that he has been able to lean on God throughout his life and that God has been a strong fortress – a safe place and a refuge – continually. In his anxiety and despair the psalmist turns to God for rescue.

When we experience difficulties in our lives which threaten our faith and discipleship it's helpful to remember that God is a God who rescues and saves. In this psalm God is our midwife – enabling our birth, encouraging our growth and not tiring of us as we grow old. We can put our trust and hope in God because we have assurance that God is there for us and with us. Whilst we can't always make sense of the things that happen around us, and we might from time to time wonder where God is and why God allows certain things to happen, we can have confidence that ultimately God works in all things for good, and that no situation is beyond God's transforming love. We know this because of Jesus, who through his death and resurrection has overturned evil and saved us for eternity. This means that even when all is in crisis and we can see no way forward, we can have hope that God's goodness and love will ultimately break through. Follow Jesus and grasp tightly the eternal perspective!

† Lord Jesus – when life gets tough, help me to remember that you have already won the victory and ultimately all will be well.

For further thought

If you are able, make a donation to a charity that rescues people and gives them a future.

Into the unknown: the spirit of discipleship – 2 Rooted and growing

Notes by **Aileen Quinn**

Aileen is a copywriter, playwright and lay member of the Church of England who lives in South Manchester with her son, Isaac. Her blog, 'The (mal)Contented Mother: Motherhood, Mental Health, Miscellany', takes an honest look at parenting culture and mental illness. Aileen has had several short plays performed in Manchester and continues to write as much as possible from her box-room/office. Aileen has used the NRSVA for these notes.

Sunday 21 February
Fruit in its season

Read Psalm 1

They are like trees planted by streams of water, which yield their fruit in its season, and their leaves do not wither. In all that they do, they prosper.

(verse 3)

As I sit down to reflect on today's reading I find there is a yearning in me to feel like the 'tree planted by streams of water' described by the psalmist here. This kind of imagery conjures a sense of serenity, patience, wholesome nourishment; and this can feel far away from our own faith journey. Likewise, the righteous/wicked binaries we are offered here often don't feel wide enough to hold the diverse, complex world we know.

I know I cannot always identify closely with the people of faith depicted in these passages; my own spirituality feels much more messy and flawed. I'd hope I'm not wicked, but I certainly don't feel 'righteous' most of the time either. Do I delight in the law of the Lord? Do I even know what that means?

However much we may long for a close relationship with God, and however much we try to live that out in our lives, the whole thing is far from simple. This week's readings explore what it means to be 'rooted and growing' in our discipleship this Lent; let's journey through them together.

† Jesus, the Living Water, be with us now as we seek you, nourish us with your love, challenge us by your wisdom. Amen

Monday 22 February
A new covenant

Read Jeremiah 31:31-37

But this is the covenant that I will make with the house of Israel after those days, says the Lord: I will put my law within them, and I will write it on their hearts; and I will be their God, and they shall be my people.

(verse 33)

The language of 'the law' can feel very heavy, can't it? Flick through the Old Testament and you'll see reams of instructional language that is difficult to navigate through. Yet the Bible has never been a rule book, and this passage hints at the law being something that whispers from within, if we will listen.

In Matthew 22, Jesus teaches that the love of God and love of your neighbour are the two commandments on which 'all the law' hangs. This distillation of the law as a love that translates into action is something that helps me connect in a deeper way with many of this week's readings, and today's especially. When we are still, when we allow ourselves to connect with God's love for us, we also connect to this law written on our hearts. Of course, 'tuning in' to this connection is, in itself, a challenge: how do we do it?

There is a clue, for me, in the words 'I will be their God, and they shall be my people' (verse 33). When trying to practise discipleship, it is all too easy to fall into a 'performance of holiness'. We try to behave in ways that we imagine a righteous person would, but that isn't what is required of us; we can let God be God – we just have to be his people. Just a person. That's all I am required to be; what I already am. When I come to God open to love and accepting of my humanity, that's when the connection I find is the deepest.

† God, when I despair at being better, help me just be me. Amen

For further thought

What does it mean to you to 'love your neighbour as yourself'? How could you act on this commandment today?

Tuesday 23 February
Patience in our growth

Into the unknown: the spirit of discipleship – 2 Rooted and growing

Read Psalm 92

The righteous flourish like the palm tree, and grow like a cedar in Lebanon. They are planted in the house of the Lord; they flourish in the courts of our God.

(verses 12–13)

In today's reading we encounter again the righteous/evil binary; one which doesn't always fit with our understanding of ourselves or the wider world. It helps me to take the imagery and bring it into that internal context. I want to regard 'evildoers' and 'righteous' as propensities within myself; ones that I have to navigate between.

There are always nourishing, wholesome aspects of myself that I can draw on, but there, too, are just plain stupid ones that like to pipe up now and again! This psalm's imagery gives clues as to how we might discern which is which. Whereas 'the wicked sprout like grass' (verse 7), the righteous 'grow like a cedar' (verse 12). Grass grows and spreads quickly, whereas trees take much longer to reach maturity.

I once heard an Ignatian teacher offer the phrase 'the good spirit draws and the bad spirit drives' when discussing how to tell the difference between healthy and unhealthy impulses/ideas. This reminds me of the grass/cedar metaphor we find in today's reading. Often calls to life in all its fullness are subtle and slow-burning – they might nag at you, but they won't rush you. Meanwhile, that which will lead you away from being your best self can often feel urgent, like something you want or need to launch into. When we observe these impulses and examine their nature, it can help us stay rooted in God and grow at our own steady pace.

† God, you call us to be planted and flourish in your house. Grant us the patience and insight to grow slowly into being abundantly fruitful.

For further thought

Is there somewhere I'm being drawn to that is drowned out by things that drive me? How can I redress this balance?

Wednesday 24 February
God's presence in our seeking

Read Psalm 119:9–16

With my whole heart I seek you; do not let me stray from your commandments.

(verse 10)

Today's excerpt is from Psalm 119 which, at 176 verses, is the longest psalm in the Bible. Although our snippet seems fairly self-assured, the rest of the psalm gives a different picture. The psalmist is obviously wrestling with a lot, feeling adrift from God and yearning for divine comfort. The whole thing is, in many ways, an appeal for a renewal of relationship, for an intimacy that one can only imagine used to be felt.

Knowing the above context helps me engage with our reading, which could otherwise sound boastful; the 'perfect' supplicant listing all the ways in which they have been 'holy' and 'steadfast'. But no, this is not that. In many ways it is a person listing all the things they are trying to do, and all the things they are promising they will do, before asking God to come closer and help. Sound familiar?

Personally, I find myself feeling for the psalmist and wishing they would get out of their own way, and God's for that matter. The idea that God has left us is not, in my understanding, something that can ever be deeply true. It can feel true, of course; most of us have experienced that emptiness to some degree. But the idea that there is a list of righteous behaviours we must engage in before God 'comes back' is largely a human invention. God is always waiting to meet us where we are. Can we welcome God with our whole heart?

† Thank you, God, for the miracle that when we feel your absence, even then you are present.

For further thought

Are there ways you engage in the theory of a relationship with God, rather than the holistic practice? Can you change your attitude/ practice to acknowledge God's continual presence in your life?

56

Thursday 25 February
Deep-rooted wisdom

Read Proverbs 3:13–26

Do not be afraid of sudden panic, or of the storm that strikes the wicked; for the Lord will be your confidence and will keep your foot from being caught.

(verses 25–26)

For all my adult life I have lived with recurrent anxiety disorder. I can be well for long periods and then it will flare up so fiercely that even getting out of bed becomes a struggle. There is nothing that makes me feel less rooted in wisdom and faith than the blurry thoughts and sharp physical sensations of panic.

In this passage, wisdom is spoken of almost as a talisman; a 'tree of life' that protects us from both inner and outer turbulence. Of course, I don't mean this in terms that could be simplistic or unhelpful; telling someone in the midst of a panic attack to 'have faith' or reading them a verse as if it is a magical incantation can belittle what that person is going through. What's more, both responses would be missing the point of a calling into deeper knowledge and understanding of oneself and one's foundation.

Wisdom, we read, was present at creation (verse 19); it is a 'tree of life' (verse 18), the 'life for your soul' (verse 22). This reminds me of our reflection on Monday about God's law being 'written on our hearts'. There is something deep within us that we can draw on in turbulent times; something we can remain rooted in even if we might not always feel it. In fact, we definitely won't! But knowing that there is a quiet, solid, deep-rooted wisdom available to us and attempting to cultivate its presence in our lives may mean that in those times of sudden panic there is a still, small voice of calm to soothe and guide us.

† Dear God, all of whose paths are peace, teach us to cultivate your wisdom when we feel strong so that it can bolster us in turbulent times.

For further thought
What emotional/physical state leads you to feel less rooted in God's wisdom? Is there a way you could invite God into this aspect of your inner world?

Into the unknown: the spirit of discipleship – 2 Rooted and growing

Friday 26 February
Space to ask questions

Read Luke 2:41–52

After three days they found him in the temple, sitting among the teachers, listening to them and asking them questions. And all who heard him were amazed at his understanding and his answers.

(verses 46–47)

I have read and heard this passage many times, but until now I had missed the description of what Jesus is doing. He sat for a total of four days in the temple with the teachers, 'listening to them and asking them questions'.

I imagine the 12-year-old Jesus rather joyously drinking in the opportunity to probe into the mysteries he has been pondering. I wonder how many of us could approach our faith with such curiosity in adulthood? I wonder if we feel safe to. In many church environments a status quo – whether theological or social – develops in which questioning or offering of new ideas is seen as a threat, or at least a problem to be solved. There are many understandable reasons why this closed-off culture might occur, of course. Yet it is one that excludes difference and guards against changes: two things that Jesus actively embraced.

Meanwhile, there are those with burning questions that they don't feel they can ask for fear of looking stupid. When we are children, questioning is encouraged, but as we grow older there is a real vulnerability in admitting we don't know it all or have everything figured out. I wonder how many of us spend our lives in church wondering about things we are too afraid to ask? I wonder how many of us wonder about the same things. Can we create spaces like the one Jesus was welcomed into? Spaces where questions are asked and answers are listened to? I hope so; I think it would deepen our relationship with God and each other.

† God who is beyond all answers, we bring to you today our questions, to be held and listened to and unravelled in your patient presence.

For further thought

How could you make your church culture a safe space for questions? Why not create a 'question box' for people to contribute to anonymously and then have an open discussion in a Facebook group or Bible study?

Saturday 27 February
Cultivating your fruit

Read John 15:1–8

'I am the vine, you are the branches. Those who abide in me and I in them bear much fruit, because apart from me you can do nothing.'

(verse 5)

Most of my reflections this week have been very much focused on our internal worlds. It is important that we examine these storms within us and that we find places to welcome God into. But, of course, the purpose of being rooted and growing is to bear fruit. Today's passage reminds us that this is an integral part of being a disciple of Jesus.

But what is this fruit that Jesus speaks of? What does it mean to bear fruit? Just like the many varieties of plants, we all have something different to offer, our own unique way to bless and nourish others. Bearing fruit, for me, is an opening out to the world, an offering of my gifts and of kindness to others.

When my internal world is more grounded, when I have confidence in who I am and feel rooted in self-love and the love of God; this is when I am fruitful. But when I try to give of myself at a low ebb, I burn out and begin to retreat from the world.

In the Gospels we are gifted all of these metaphors of Jesus being 'the bread of life', 'the living water': a source of nourishment to draw from in order to flourish. So, when we are connected to this, we can bear fruit more easily and nourish others in turn. So it is my prayer for you that you go through Lent feeding your internal spiritual life in the knowledge that it will help you serve your loved ones, your community and the world at large.

† Jesus, the true vine, nourish us so that we may share your gifts with others.

For further thought

What is the fruit you bear when you are rooted in God? What do you need to flourish? And how can you share these gifts in a sustainable way?

59

Into the unknown: the spirit of discipleship – 3 Walking as one

Notes by **Joshua Taylor**

Josh is the Vicar of St John's Anglican Church in Timaru, New Zealand. He's married to Jo with three daughters (Phoebe, Esther and Eve) and together they've been exploring what it means to be a family on mission. Josh recently completed his Master's thesis on consumerism and its impact on how we do church. In his spare time, he loves to spend his days off being mocked by fish whilst holding a fishing rod. Josh has used the NRSVA for these notes.

Sunday 28 February
On the way

Read Leviticus 26:3–13

And I will walk among you, and will be your God, and you shall be my people. I am the Lord your God who brought you out of the land of Egypt, to be their slaves no more.

(verses 12–13a)

If you've ever spent time with a baby at a dinner table you may have experienced the joy of them dropping something, then you pick it up, then they drop it again, then you pick it up, then they drop it again. Babies are amazing scientists; they are constantly doing little experiments. One of their favourites is testing the theory of gravity, and their parent's patience. What babies learn is that each action has a reaction. There are consequences to actions. As we get older, we continue to figure this out, but the actions and consequences get more complex.

In Leviticus we hear about the natural consequences that flow from obedience. The laws given aren't just arbitrary rules. Rather they help people live with the grain of the universe, with God's creational intentions for humanity. The natural consequences of following God's ways are that the people will flourish. They will live fruitful lives. The greatest promise of all is that the Lord who has rescued the people from slavery in Egypt will continue to walk with his people. Far from being arbitrary rules, the law functions for the people as a guide for life with God, the natural consequences of which are a fruitful and flourishing life.

† Lord Jesus, thank you that you walked on earth among us proclaiming the good news of your kingdom. By the power of the Holy Spirit, walk among us this day that we may flourish. Amen

Monday 1 March
Life together

Read Psalm 133

How very good and pleasant it is when kindred live together in unity!

(verse 1)

All families have problems. But go camping with your family and you will really discover what those problems are. There is nothing like trying to put up a complicated family tent in a high wind and hot sun to test the bonds of love. Psalm 133 is a Psalm of Ascent. The people may have sung these psalms on their ascent to Jerusalem for religious festivals. The context of these psalms is one of pilgrimage, a bit like a family camping trip. We might imagine the pilgrims as they neared Jerusalem after weeks of travel, weary, blistered and hungry. Disagreements over cooking and gathering of water, over religious viewpoints and all manner of topics have come up along the way.

Family and community are always full of tension. This is the reality of life together. However, this psalm speaks of the blessing of sticking together through it all. It says unity is like oil and dew – both signs of the abundance and goodness of God.

Unity doesn't mean that all these people agree or get along all the time. Rather, unity here is a commitment to one another. In our conflicted and divided world this message is essential. Whatever our culture, language, politics or religion, we all share a common humanity. However, even this can be tenuous at times. We need Jesus to have the kind of community that Psalm 133 talks about. Psalm 133 mentions the High Priest Aaron. It takes another High Priest to make this psalm a possibility, and his name is Jesus. Jesus is the person we gather around as a Church. We don't gather around abstract principles, we gather around Jesus.

† God, thank you for welcoming us into your family through your Son. Bless our families, churches and neighbourhoods that we may stick together. Amen

For further thought
What difference might it make in our church if we focus on gathering around Jesus? What are the non-essentials that we can disagree on?

Into the unknown: the spirit of discipleship – 3 Walking as one

Tuesday 2 March
Sharp edges and blind spots

Read Proverbs 27:17–22

Iron sharpens iron, and one person sharpens the wits of another.

(verse 17)

I live in Timaru, a small city in the South Island of New Zealand with a population of about 30,000 people. In Timaru there are over 25 churches from all kinds of denominations. This could be a cause for great quarrelling or competition. Yet the churches co-operate with one another. Our Christian Ministers' association meets regularly to pray, drink coffee and talk. We also run combined prayer gatherings and services of worship. I have found this so enriching and helpful.

Today's proverb says, 'iron sharpens iron' (verse 17). This has been my experience in getting to know other Christians from different places and worshipping together. As an Anglican I enjoy rubbing shoulders with my Pentecostal brothers and sisters who remind me of the joy of worship and the gifts of the Holy Spirit. I enjoy coffee with my reformed Baptist friends who remind me of the centrality of scripture and how God reveals himself to us through the Word. I enjoy the reverent and contemplative spirit of our local Coptic brothers and sisters. Together we all sharpen each other's understanding of the Christian faith.

The reality is that we all have our own blind spots. We all have our favourite books of the Bible, our 'go-to' prayers, our well-known songs. Church traditions shape us to see God a certain way. Without the help of other Christians, we might think this is the only way to see God. What we discover as we appreciate one another is that God is so much bigger than we think. In my view, this can only be a good thing.

† Heavenly Father, open our eyes to see that we are all your children. May we appreciate our brothers and sisters in Christ that we may see you more clearly. Amen

For further thought

Do you have a Christian friend from another denomination? Do you talk with them about your differences, and appreciate them?

Wednesday 3 March
Love and hate

Read John 13:31–35

'I give you a new commandment, that you love one another. Just as I have loved you, you also should love one another. By this everyone will know that you are my disciples, if you have love for one another.'

(verses 34–35)

On 15 March 2019, in my hometown of Christchurch, an atrocity took place. An armed gunman stormed into a mosque, opening fire and taking the lives of 51 people. It was described by our Prime Minister as 'New Zealand's darkest day'. It surprised so many of us living in what we thought was a tolerant society. It revealed a level of hate that was truly horrifying. In the wake of these events, a Muslim man who lost his wife in the attack publicly proclaimed that he forgave his attacker, saying 'I don't hate him, I love him.' This had a profound influence on many people in the city and illustrated the power of love versus hate. Many Christians in New Zealand, including myself, were rightly humbled by this moment. It was a powerful witness of the faith of this Muslim man, it pointed to the credibility of his convictions and it had me asking, would I be so forgiving? Would I be so loving?

Jesus in John 13 teaches his disciples that their love will be the best evidence that they are his disciples. Their love will make their message credible. So too will ours. Jesus has demonstrated this himself. Earlier, Jesus takes a towel and washes his own disciples' feet. How will the world know we belong to Jesus? The world will know if we too pick up a towel, seeking to love one another. Not only this, elsewhere Jesus reminds us that we are called to love not only one another, but also our enemies. By this, too, it will become clear that we belong to Jesus.

† Loving God, help me, like Jesus, pick up a towel to serve and love others that they might see your love shining through me.

For further thought

Who are the people you are called to love and serve today?

Thursday 4 March
At one

Read John 17:20–26

'I ask not only on behalf of these, but also on behalf of those who will believe in me through their word, that they may all be one.'

(verses 20–21a)

Let's face it, parts of or those involved in the Church can be disappointing. Throughout history, some involved with the Church have been responsible for some serious mishaps. Violence, greed, sexual abuse. There is plenty of ammunition for the atheist who wishes to discredit Christianity.

I've talked to many sceptics who point out these issues with the Church. And their logic is in line with the logic of Jesus. If the Church follows Jesus, then the Church should look like the one whom they worship. Rather than being threatened, I see it as a reminder of just how important it is that we walk the talk. Jesus prays that we the Church may be one so that we may be a witness to the truth of his message, and so people will believe in Him.

Throughout history we have had many factions, disagreements and splits. It can be argued that the Protestant Church has made a good job of splitting into factions, time and time again over various theological disagreements. Today in our individualistic culture it is even more tempting to split or even create personalised forms of faith that are disconnected from the Church. But all is not lost. I don't for a second believe that Jesus' prayer of unity will forever remain unanswered; after all, it is the will of Jesus that the Church may be one. We might honour this prayer today by aligning ourselves with this will and taking the call to unity seriously. When we do, we align ourselves with the one who not only prays that we may be one but made it possible through his life, death and resurrection.

† Lord Jesus, align our hearts with your will that we may strive for unity in all we do. May we look for ways to work together for the sake of your kingdom. Amen

For further thought

Have you found yourself disappointed by the Church? How are you contributing to the unity of the Church?

Friday 5 March
A living temple

Read 1 Corinthians 3:10–23

Do you not know that you are God's temple and that God's Spirit dwells in you? If anyone destroys God's temple, God will destroy that person. For God's temple is holy, and you are that temple.

(verses 16–17)

The church in Corinth was divided in many ways. One of the big problems was that people were quarrelling over church leadership. Some people liked Apollos and some liked Paul. There were factions and quibbling over who was right. Sound familiar?

A key to understanding Paul's letters is to read them as written to communities, not individuals. Paul is writing to the church. Paul's concern is for a mature church, not only mature individual Christians. Paul uses three images to paint a picture of the church. He uses the images of the church being God's field, God's building and God's temple. The focus of today's devotion is the image of the temple.

Throughout scripture the temple is the place where God dwells with the people; his presence is there. Paul points out that the Church is God's temple; his presence is there. God's presence is the key reality that marks the Church as the people of God. Christians are not recognisable just by displaying a different way of life; we are recognisable by the presence of God amongst us.

As well as affirming the Church as the place where God dwells, Paul addresses those who are causing factions and trouble, sternly giving a warning: 'If anyone destroys God's temple, God will destroy that person.' That should give all of us reason to seek unity and withhold from causing factions or disunity. God takes this very seriously indeed.

† Holy and loving God, thank you that you dwell amongst us. May we always seek to be unified so that we may be a sign of your love and presence in a broken and divided world.

For further thought

Is there anyone in your Christian community that you are quarrelling with? How might you seek the restoration of unity?

March

Into the unknown: the spirit of discipleship – 3 Walking as one

Saturday 6 March
Disciplined disciples

Read Hebrews 10:19–25

And let us consider how to provoke one another to love and good deeds, not neglecting to meet together, as is the habit of some, but encouraging one another, and all the more as you see the Day approaching.

(verses 24–25)

In Christian circles it has become trendy to talk about spiritual disciplines. Some writers have talked about the recovery of the ancient disciplines and how they can help Christians live well today in the twenty-first century and deepen our relationship with God. When we think of spiritual disciplines, what comes to mind? We might think of fasting, meditation, solitude, silence, prayer and so forth. This recovery is wonderful. Yet so often in the recovery of these disciplines we encourage spiritual individualism.

What about gathering on Sunday as the church to worship? Do we see that as a spiritual discipline? I once mentioned this to a crowd of my peers, and they looked at me as if to say, 'That's not a discipline.' Solitude, silence and reading the Church Fathers might make us feel like a spiritual guru, but going to church? What a drag.

Yet I think the Bible teaches us that corporate worship is an essential spiritual discipline. Without this discipline it is so much harder to be a faithful Christian. The writer of Hebrews knows that the discipline of gathering with one another as believers is important. It functions as a school of discipleship. As we hear the Bible read and preached, as we sing, as we share in communion and pray, we are schooled in the good news of Christianity and encouraged in our faith.

† Lord Jesus, thank you for gathering us all together as your people that we may follow you side by side, encouraging one another and sharing our lives. Help us not to neglect this gift but to commit afresh to meeting in your name. Amen

For further thought

What do you appreciate about gathering for corporate worship with other Christians?

Into the unknown:
the spirit of discipleship –
4 Peter the disciple

Notes by **Jan Sutch Pickard**

Jan, poet, preacher and storyteller, now lives on the Isle of Mull, having worked and raised a family in Nigeria, Notting Hill and New Mills. Working as an editor for Methodism, *which nurtured her, she also joined the ecumenical Iona Community. After six years on Iona, becoming Warden of the Abbey, she served with the Ecumenical Accompaniment Programme in Palestine and Israel, continuing to pray, give practical support and bear witness. Meanwhile, an island community offers challenges, celebrations, wildlife, worship, co-operation and ceilidhs. Jan has used the NRSVA for these notes.*

Sunday 7 March
Calling and naming

Read John 1:35–42

Andrew brought Simon to Jesus, who looked at him and said, 'You are Simon son of John. You are to be called Cephas' (which is translated Peter).

(verse 42)

This passage from John's Gospel bustles with activity: conversations between named people, religious leaders, strangers, family members; curiosity and questions, comings and goings; the call to come and see what's going on. There will be times in our own lives full of busyness when it's hard to know where to focus, because our attention is being demanded here and there.

This morning I heard an outboard motor and watched a neighbour's boat arrive at the jetty opposite my house. He'd been out early, fishing. As he lifted out the mackerel he had caught, another neighbour came to join him and they gazed across the bay, deep in conversation. For Galilean fishermen the focus of interest and questions was Jesus. And Jesus himself, when Simon came to meet him, focused on this strong, busy, working man, a leader in his local community, looked him in the eye, called him by his given name and then gave him a new name: Cephas/Peter, which means a rock. This was a different kind of calling.

Read on: as his story unfolds, does Simon Peter prove rock-steady? Take time out this week from busyness, to explore that question, what it might mean to us.

† Jesus, of the fishermen, show us where you are at work in the lives of others; help us hear you call us by name. Amen

Monday 8 March
Risking all, becoming ourselves

Read Luke 9:18–27

Then he said to them all, 'If any want to become my followers, let them deny themselves and take up their cross daily and follow me. For those who want to save their life will lose it, and those who lose their life for my sake will save it.'

(verses 23–24)

'Who do you think you are?' This is a question we're asked when we get above ourselves. But Jesus needed to ask who others thought he was, because all kinds of theories were circulating; people were wondering whether great leaders and prophets of old had returned from the dead. They remembered John, recently murdered by the state. But who on earth was Jesus? Peter declared with conviction, 'the Messiah'.

Then Jesus spelled out for his disciples what this meant: not worldly power, but rejection, suffering and death. Though the Jewish people had long yearned for God's chosen leader, who would save his people, the rulers of the known world then were afraid of being challenged (and still are today). The integrity of Jesus, as he witnessed to the justice and love of God, would inflame their anger. Peter needed to imagine what it meant to be a follower of Jesus, sharing the vulnerability that's part of God's love.

As a supporter of Amnesty International, I read the stories of men and women of different faiths, who act or speak according to their conscience, and suffer for it.

An example is Iranian human rights lawyer Nasrin Sotoudeh, a prisoner of conscience as this is being written. Courageous people like her lose their liberty, even their lives, but they are no less themselves: indeed, through their witness for justice they become more fully the people God created them to be.

† Compassionate God, we pray for those whose caring and conscience put them at risk. We give thanks for their courage, challenging injustice and speaking truth to power. May we also bear witness. Amen

For further thought

Look in the mirror. Who do you think you are? What does it mean to be a child of God? Whose example has inspired you? How can you bear witness?

Tuesday 9 March
Dazzled by glory

Read Luke 9:28–36

Peter said to Jesus, 'Master, it is good for us to be here; let us make three dwellings, one for you, one for Moses, and one for Elijah' – not knowing what he said. … Then from the cloud came a voice that said, 'This is my Son, my Chosen; listen to him!'

(part of verses 33–35)

Driving east across the island at dawn, I'm dazzled by the rising sun. It's hard to see down-to-earth details of which travellers need to be aware – sharp bends, other cars, wandering sheep. I pull in, pause to reflect. Dazzled and distracted, I'm blessed, too. Dawn colours in the sky and the level rays of sun fill me with wonder. I hold the moment, thanking God for such beauty. Without it, our lives would be uninspiring.

But life goes on: there's a ferry to catch, commitments to other people. I must set off again, keeping my eyes on the road!

Building a shrine doesn't occur to me. For Peter on the mountaintop that seemed the most obvious thing to do – to hold on to the moment, and sanctify the place where they'd glimpsed the glory of God shining in Jesus' face. He imagined that Jesus, with Moses and Elijah, would stay to be worshipped there. It's a very human instinct, to hold on to the past.

On my journey east that day I pass a roadside chapel – beautiful but often empty. The congregation has dwindled; no young families come there now. But folk can't bear to think of closing this church. Standing beside a pilgrimage route, it could offer a place of welcome, reflection, preparation for continuing the journey. Would piped water help – for tea-making and toilets? Could the pews be taken out? Resisting such changes, some hold on to a familiar idea of 'God's house'. But the One who can't be contained is out there on the road with the passing pilgrims.

† God of our life's journey, you bless us with places to rest and reflect, and with transfiguring moments. Encourage us to travel on, seeing you too in the light of common day. Amen

For further thought

Where are the mountaintops in your life and work at the moment? Where is the pilgrimage route?

Wednesday 10 March
Walking on water

Read Matthew 14:22–33

But when [Peter] noticed the strong wind, he became frightened, and beginning to sink, he cried out, 'Lord, save me!' Jesus immediately reached out his hand and caught him, saying to him, 'You of little faith, why did you doubt?'

(verses 30–31)

The sudden storm on the lake whipped up waves, through which, amid flying foam, the disciples saw Jesus walking towards the boat. They cried out in fear, but he replied, 'Take heart, it is I' (verse 27). When Peter heard Jesus say 'Come', he did not hesitate: he stepped out of the boat.

He was out of his element. What does it feel like to walk on water? It's not impossible. Some creatures make it seem effortless, like the basilisk, which is nicknamed 'the Jesus lizard' because it runs lightly across the meniscus – the 'skin' on the water. But maybe Peter looked more like ducks or seagulls trying to keep their balance on an icy pond: ridiculous, in an improbable situation. Water is a shape-shifter. Waves move in patterns; currents have hidden power; eddies and whirlpools break the surface and draw things and people down; ice stills everything. How could this water bear the weight of a man? Could faith alone do it?

Peter started his walk in faith, needing to believe that he could do like Jesus. Seeing a hand stretched out to him across the wild waves, he responded impulsively. Maybe he had too much self-confidence. But he lost it all: suddenly realising the risk he was taking, feeling the inhuman strength of the wind, losing his footing in the untrustworthy waters, imagining the depths beneath.

Jesus caught hold of him as he floundered, scolded him, scooped him into the safety of the boat. For everyone, the storm of their fear lost its force, their faith in Jesus deepened, and they came safe to land.

† God who stills our inner storms, show us how this story reflects our doubts and discoveries about ourselves. Help us believe that our deepest fears can be overcome by your hand stretched out in love. Amen

For further thought

Find out more about insects and other creatures that walk on water: wonders of God's creation. Do not attempt to copy them!

Thursday 11 March
Love's transforming touch

Read John 13:1–20

'Lord, are you going to wash my feet?' ... 'You do not know now what I am doing, but later you will understand.' ...'You will never wash my feet.' ...'Unless I wash you, you have no share with me.' ... 'Lord, not my feet only but also my hands and my head!'

(parts of verses 6b–9)

For a moment the upper room fell silent. The only sound was the pouring of water. What was Jesus doing? Then Peter started to protest, his words staccato as he refused to be part of this acted parable, where their leader became their servant. Jesus persisted, gently responding: 'Later you will understand.' The disciples round the table must have listened in bafflement to this exchange. Whereas Peter suddenly 'got it' – wholeheartedly accepted the ministry Jesus was offering. Again, silence, just the pouring and lapping of water.

What does it feel like to have your feet washed? Do you enjoy holidays when you can paddle in the sea? Relishing the textures of sand and shells underfoot, cool waves flowing and drawing back over the feet we often neglect, caressing them. It may be hard to remember being a very small child, with muddy feet needing to be washed and dried, and rhymes to count the toes. But maybe your much older feet know the sure touch of a podiatrist? Or have you ever had a foot-massage? Was it easy to accept someone seeing and touching your feet? Did you resist it, like Peter? How does it feel, to be open to another's ministry?

Foot-washing: actions instead of words, the sound of water being poured; refreshing coolness on tired feet; caress of water on skin. The healing touch of hands that care is hard to explain, but transformative: a sign of love. Just as bread and wine are sacramental – remembering the Last Supper – so, as part of that story, the washing of feet is also a sacrament.

† Wash over us, God, with your love: not just our feet, but all of us. Teach us about mutual ministry, caring for each other; surprise us with the touch of your transforming love. Amen

For further thought

In your congregation, church fellowship or Bible Study group, have you ever washed each other's feet? If that seems impracticable, then foot or hand massage – done with care – can be a very moving way of communicating to each other God's love.

Into the unknown: the spirit of discipleship – 4 Peter the disciple

March

71

Friday 12 March
Broken faith, friendship denied

Read Luke 22:54–62

*'Man, I do not know what you are talking about!' At that moment
… the cock crowed. The Lord turned and looked at Peter. Then Peter
remembered the word of the Lord … 'Before the cock crows today, you
will deny me three times.' And he went out and wept bitterly.*

(part of verses 60–62)

Visiting Jerusalem for the first time, I found my courage and my faith
were challenged. I stood in the church of 'St Peter in Gallicantu' and
wondered about the instability of that man whom Jesus called 'a
rock', and also what I was learning about discipleship. I wrote this:

A church built on a rock at the sign of the crowing cock,
beside a worn flight of steps: a place to stop and take stock.
Here, in the sanctuary, rock juts out – powerful,
an undeniable statement of faith, rugged, reliable –
but underneath, deep as doubt, hollow dungeons and pits.
Close to the steps that Jesus trod,
this hollow place is a hallowed place:
and still a hard place to face yourself – or to meet God.

When Jesus knelt to wash the disciples' feet, Peter protested,
struggling to understand what was happening. Now, only a few
hours later, he knew too well what had happened. His friend Jesus,
whose surprising ministry had touched him with God's love, had
been arrested. And Peter, challenged by the High Priest's servants,
protested again, denying three times any connection with the
prisoner. Jesus, who had warned that this could happen, was also
the one who had called him Peter, saying, 'On this rock I will build
my church' (Matthew 16:18).

Human beings don't always live up to their name or their calling.
How does the Church cope with such unstable foundations? Do we
meet God even in our weakest moments?

† Compassionate God, take our tears of shame, our doubts and petty betrayals.
Take, hold and heal them in your love. There may we find our true foundations.
Amen

For further thought

Find, if you can, a stone or small rock. Hold it, feel its weight and
texture, as you reflect on this story and pray this prayer.

Love is more than words

Read John 21:15–17

'Simon son of John, do you love me more than these?' ... 'Yes, Lord; you know that I love you.' ... 'Feed my lambs.' ... 'Simon son of John, do you love me?' ... 'Yes, Lord; you know that I love you.' ... 'Tend my sheep.' ... 'Simon son of John, do you love me?' ... 'Lord, you know everything; you know that I love you.' ... 'Feed my sheep.'

(parts of verses 15–17)

By the lake of Galilee, among fishing boats drawn up on the sand, would there be sheep wandering, seeking grazing, as happens on Hebridean shores today? Maybe the local shepherds led their flocks to better pastures. Maybe no sheep were present when his risen Lord challenged Peter as they walked on the shore. Yet the questions and responses were relevant and still are.

Three questions brought the same heartfelt answer three times: 'Yes Lord, you know that I love you.' A similar conversation happened in the upper room, as Jesus knelt to wash feet. But now, with waves lapping gently on the shore, we imagine Peter not only remembering the example Jesus set, but recalling words round a fire, after Jesus was arrested. Three questions from the bystanders, three vehement denials from Peter. How could he escape the guilt of friendship betrayed?

How do we deal with guilt? Do we close our minds to it, or let it keep gnawing away, destroying our capacity to become better people? Is there another way? What do you think?

Christians from different traditions have gathered to worship on the shore in Mull (yes, the sheep are there too!). We kindle a fire to keep warm; fish grilling in the embers will feed us later. But first we talk about how, in that encounter on the shore, three questions from the risen Christ enabled Peter – who had failed and fallen again and again and again – to get up and follow his calling. Three denials became three affirmations of faith: we share a story about transformation and resurrection hope.

† Giving and forgiving God, thank you for encounters with others which make all the difference, thank you for times when your word in our hearts is transforming. Amen

For further thought

What do you think 'Feed my lambs ... tend my sheep ... feed my sheep' means in your situation? This coming week, do something to put that into action.

Into the unknown: the spirit of discipleship – 4 Peter the disciple

March

Into the unknown:
the spirit of discipleship –
5 Peter the church leader

Notes by **Tim Yau**

Tim is a Pioneer Missioner working for the Anglican Diocese of Norwich. His role is to establish a mission community in Round House Park, a new housing development in Cringleford. He also is a Diocesan Mission Enabler encouraging missional practice across the region: 'not trying to get people to go to Church, but trying to get the Church to go to the people.' He's frequently found immersed in the latest sci-fi cinematic epic, and loves mini-adventures with his family. Tim has used the NIVUK for these notes.

Sunday 14 March
Peter and prayer

Read Acts 3:1–16

Taking him by the right hand, he helped him up, and instantly the man's feet and ankles became strong.

(verse 7)

This week we continue to follow Peter as he grows into the leadership bestowed on him when Christ declared, 'I tell you that you are Peter, and on this rock I will build my church' (Matthew 16:18).

We meet Peter and John in the aftermath of Pentecost and the outpouring of the Holy Spirit upon the disciples, turning them from a fearful and directionless group hiding in an upper room, into a supernaturally empowered engine for God's transformative kingdom.

With 3,000 already added to their number, the embryonic Church begins to catalyse around Peter's leadership. With the busyness of getting organised, whilst trying to theologically make sense of what had happened to them, Peter and John go to pray and are confronted with the plea for money from a lame beggar.

Peter and John stop, giving the unnamed man holy attention. They call on the name of Jesus and implore the beggar to do the one thing he cannot: walk. Taking him by the hand they help him up: an incredible act of faith between the beggar and the hopeful disciples trusting in the power of Jesus' name. Leadership is about engendering trust; do you trust Jesus to lead you?

† Lord Jesus, help us to follow your Spirit's lead in all things, willing to be interrupted on our journeys to enable trust in others. Amen

Monday 15 March
Perjury and punishment

Read Acts 5:1–16

Then Peter said, 'Ananias, how is it that Satan has so filled your heart that you have lied to the Holy Spirit and have kept for yourself some of the money you received for the land?'

(verse 3)

The music was blasting out, my friends were crammed into my small student nurse room and I was jumping up and down on my bed singing along at full volume. It was so raucous that I didn't hear the knock at my door and see the warden enter in declaring, 'So, you're not sick then!'

It's a horrible feeling getting caught in a lie. The consequences of pulling a sickie, instead of turning up for my shift on the ward, cost me a day's bursary payment, weeks of being in the ward sisters' bad books and a negative report at the end of my placement. However, that's nothing compared to what happened to Ananias and Sapphira.

At face value the couple had done a positive thing; they'd sold their property and given the money to the Church. This seemingly generous act must have elicited great honour from the Church but Peter sees through their superficially noble actions. We don't know if someone had whispered in his ear, or if the Holy Spirit had revealed this matter to him; all we know is that the actions of the Holy Spirit in the early Church were shifting the focus from the primacy of the Jerusalem temple as the place of God's holy justice in the world, and here Peter becomes the focal point of that judgement.

There are some scriptural examples of God's instantaneous judgement against sacrilegious offenders, though these are not commonplace. In life liars often seem to get away with their deceit, but God sees through human deceptions and divine justice will always be done.

† Lord God, you are awesome and powerful. Forgive us when we ignore your ways and treat you indifferently and irreverently. Help us to recognise your divine justice in the way we act towards others. Amen

For further thought

Are you caught in a lie? How will you own up to it? What will the consequences be if you don't? Will you trust God?

Tuesday 16 March
Purity and prejudice

Read Acts 11:1–18

'So if God gave them the same gift he gave us who believed in the Lord Jesus Christ, who was I to think that I could stand in God's way?'

(verse 17)

I stood on the steps of the nightclub flanked by two hefty black-clad doormen, whilst the heavy bass beats thumped behind me and escaped into the chill night air. A huddle of would-be evangelists held up their hands in prayer towards the dance music as a couple of clubbers stared out through the entrance pointing and laughing at the escalating confrontation. One of the bouncers rolled their eyes as the zealous street preacher shook their finger at me, declaring God's disdain for this 'house of sin'.

In spite of the noise and the commotion I tried to humbly explain to the criticiser that I too was a Christian and that a team of us were working in the disco as club chaplains: loving and serving the staff and clients, creating community and sharing words of hope and truth. He shook his head and judged, 'This is not a place for Christians!' Then he stormed off, followed by his bewildered band of believers.

In that encounter it would be easy to dismiss those outside the club as 'religious fanatics', but their arrogant attitude and sense of holy certainty had been exactly my demeanour before I met Tracey who led the chaplaincy ministry. She helped me to understand the culture and challenged me not to dismiss what I didn't understand.

In the same way Peter had had to learn not to just unquestioningly follow the religious assumptions he'd grown up with, but to attend to God's new revelation to him. Leadership is about listening well, making sense of new information and knowing when to change your direction.

† Lord God, forgive us when we put words into your mouth. Help us to listen to you attentively, so that we may be continually surprised by the new things you want to show us. Amen

For further thought

Whom are you prejudiced against? When have you unfairly dismissed a person or a place? Where is God trying to show you something new?

Wednesday 17 March
Polity and power

Read Acts 15:1–20

'No! We believe it is through the grace of our Lord Jesus that we are saved, just as they are.'

(verse 11)

I used to live and work in Cambridge. The place probably conjures up images in your mind: gowned university students cycling down narrow lanes; gentlemen in straw boater hats punting along the river Cam; majestic colleges with pristine lawns and mystifying traditions.

Obviously, these things are true, but there's another side to the city's life. The hurly-burly of the centre, with its mix of academia, retail and tourism, is matched by the mundane life of the residents who service the educational institutions that dominate the place. It is as if two worlds inhabit the same space: a dynamic locally referred to as the 'town and gown'.

After living outside the power, privilege and prestige of the university for four years, I was surprisingly accepted for ordination training and commenced my formational studies at Ridley Hall College, also in Cambridge. I moved worlds!

My 'town' persona did not fit the grandeur of the establishments I began to inhabit and I often felt that I didn't deserve to be there. Whereas some of my associates looked the part, I didn't. They would stride into colleges and faculties freely, whereas I'd be regularly detained by the bowler-hatted porters. Then one day as I handed over my university identity card for inspection, I had an epiphany.

I had been chosen to study in Cambridge, my photo was on the card, I didn't have to earn my place; whether I failed or flourished, excelled or expired, I was chosen. Similarly, God's grace was enough for Peter, the believing Gentiles and ultimately for all of us. You are chosen!

† Lord God, thank you that we are chosen by your grace, forgive us when we try to earn your love. No one is unacceptable to you, pardon us when we act like anyone is. Amen

For further thought

In 2 Corinthians 12:9 God says, 'My grace is sufficient for you, for my power is made perfect in weakness.' Why has God chosen you?

Thursday 18 March
Prison and prayer

Read Acts 12:1–19

So Peter was kept in prison, but the church was earnestly praying to God for him.

(verse 5)

Norwich's imposing Victorian prison stands on a hill overshadowing the vibrant heart of the city. The prison's dark brick edifice can be glimpsed between the neon-lit malls and crumbling medieval buildings of the shopping centre. Its presence is a stark warning to all that nobody is above the law.

The prison's austere frontage has surprisingly become a popular viewing point for local people, because of its impressive vistas of Norwich's skyline. With the amount of footfall passing the prison, the governor took the bold decision to open up part of their historic buildings to the public and turned it into a café. Not only that, but the business was operated by prisoners, from kitchen staff to waiting on tables.

The café's set-up led to some interesting conversations with my children about who are the 'bad men'. I have to admit being confronted with perfectly normal-looking employees serving me cake with a smile didn't fit with my mental image of a convict. When something is on the margins of our experience it's easy to dismiss it, or misunderstand it, and fall into lazy stereotypes.

Peter was a prisoner, but when we think of him, we don't immediately imagine him in prison overalls, manacled and incarcerated. However, we do remember his selfless acts, inspiring words and flawed character.

So, let us pray for the prisoners like Peter, victims of political populist persecution. But let us also remember the wrongly accused, the lost men and women who've been failed by the system, the misguided, manipulated and maladjusted. Prisoners are people who need our prayers.

† Lord God, you know the heart of every person. Forgive us when we judge others without knowing them. Help us love people who are locked away. Let us see them as you see them. Amen

For further thought

In Luke 4:18 Jesus quotes the prophet Isaiah declaring, 'He has sent me to proclaim freedom for the prisoners.' How can you help the imprisoned? We consider these themes more next week.

Friday 19 March
Peter and Paul

Read Galatians 2:1–14

For God, who was at work in Peter as an apostle to the circumcised, was also at work in me as an apostle to the Gentiles.

(verse 8)

'That sounds great, but we just don't do that.'

The vicar's words hung heavily in the air whilst the other ministers shuffled uneasily in their seats. I'd been trying to convince the town centre church leaders to back me in engaging with the thousands of people who frequented Ipswich shopping centre on Saturdays. I understood that their congregations were cautious about evangelism and wanted to distance themselves from the more zealous placard-waving street preachers. So, I'd carefully pitched to them the new project 'Presence: faith on the street', aiming to be a creative response to the spiritual needs of Ipswich town centre.

Clearly, the churches I wanted to help me in my missional endeavour had been a presence in that central location for years, but for whatever reason the ebb and flow of weekend shoppers were not crossing their thresholds. Undesirably for them, I didn't want to get the shoppers into church, I wanted to get the church to go to the shoppers.

Seeing that I looked crestfallen, the vicar broke the silence, explaining that it was not because they didn't believe in the project, or that they disagreed with my thinking, it was just that they were called to something different. Actually, they didn't want to see the shopping precinct left to the 'religious crazies', but they trusted me to do the job that they could not.

Peter knew his limitations and was clear about what God was calling him to. There are thousands of things that could be done, but like Peter let us recognise and bless the mission of others.

† Lord Jesus, help us to see what others see and be grateful for their learned insight. Forgive us when we marginalise others by disregarding their experience and making our ministry the most important thing. Amen

For further thought

What are the missional needs that you see that others don't? Who is missionally misunderstood? Whom can you talk to, to get some wisdom and insight?

March

Into the unknown: the spirit of discipleship – 5 Peter the church leader

Saturday 20 March
Prophecy and priorities

Read John 21:18–19

Jesus said this to indicate the kind of death by which Peter would glorify God. Then he said to him, 'Follow me!'

(verse 19)

Today's reading interprets Jesus' words as a prediction of the way Peter would die. According to Church tradition Peter was martyred in Rome somewhere between 64 and 68 AD. Therefore, for around 30 years Peter may have had an inkling about when and how his life would end. How would you cope with that knowledge?

When my eldest son graduated from school recently, on his last day there was an air of rebellion about his classmates. The usual uniform regulations were ignored as leavers signed each other's shirts and lessons were abandoned for a huge water fight. The end was in sight, so the usual rules didn't apply anymore. I wonder if that's what it was like for Peter? Did knowing he was going to be much older when life ended give him the courage and the licence to not hold back?

Similarly, the father of my friend was diagnosed with incurable cancer and was given only a few years to live. Instead of feeling sorry for himself he decided to organise lots of holidays and parties with friends and family. He wanted to make the most of his time left and treasure every moment.

Knowing that your time is running out does bring priorities into focus. What do we do with the time we've got? Peter continued living Jesus' great commission (Matthew 28:18–20) and had the courage to end well – to the extent that the early Christian scholar Origen (184–253 AD) tells us that Peter was crucified upside down because he felt himself unworthy of dying in the same manner as Jesus. Peter followed Jesus to the end.

† Lord Jesus, give us courage to serve you to the end and hold on to your promise: 'I have come that they may have life, and have it to the full' (John 10:10). Amen

For further thought

You may not know when or how you're going to die, but you do know it'll happen. How can you fully live for Christ today?

Into the unknown:
the spirit of discipleship –
6 God on the inside

Notes by **Deseta Davis**

Deseta is assistant pastor of a Pentecostal church in Birmingham, UK. Her main vocation is as a prison chaplain helping to bring hope to those who are incarcerated. Having obtained an MA in Theological Studies, she previously worked as a tutor in Black Theology bringing the study of theology to a range of people who had not considered such study. Deseta is married to Charles, and they have two grown-up children and a granddaughter. Deseta has used the NIVUK for these notes.

Sunday 21 March
Choices

Read Genesis 39:6–23

When his master heard the story his wife told him, saying, 'This is how your slave treated me,' he burned with anger. Joseph's master took him and put him in prison, the place where the king's prisoners were confined.

(verses 19–20a)

In my work as a prison chaplain, I see many prisoners who proclaim their innocence day in and day out. But if you get close to many of them, they would confess on the quiet that they really did commit the crime.

One Sunday in the prison chapel I preached on 'Choices', reminding the men that the choices we make can make or break us. The majority of the prisoners are in prison due to poor choices. I challenged them to a new beginning. A young prisoner came to me after the service and said he was going to change his plea to 'guilty' in court that week – dramatic change!

We start this week with the story of Joseph, an innocent man sent to prison. Joseph chose to do right. He chose not to sleep with his master's wife. He chose to live in prison without hatred, even though he was innocent. I have no doubt that in a prison of 1,200 people some are innocent. Some continue to appeal whereas others accept their lot.

Joseph's outcome, after many years, was to become the 'prime minister' of Egypt. Perhaps prison was a time of character-building for being prime minister. He made the choice to forgive both his brothers and no doubt his master's wife.

† Put yourself in Joseph's shoes, innocent and in prison – what choices do you think you would have?

Monday 22 March
Change of prison clothes

Read 2 Kings 25:27–30

So Jehoiachin put aside his prison clothes and for the rest of his life ate regularly at the king's table. Day by day the king gave Jehoiachin a regular allowance as long as he lived.

(verses 29–30)

After three months' reign, Jehoiachin, King of Judah, was forced to surrender to Nebuchadnezzar and exiled in Babylon where he was thrown into prison. Forty years later, Nebuchadnezzar's successor King Awel-Marduk released him. He was then given a place of honour, higher than those of other kings, and he sat and ate regularly at King Awel-Marduk's table for the rest of his life.

On release, Jehoiachin set aside his prison clothes and was accepted by the king and society. Today, even when a prisoner sets aside their prison clothes, sets aside the shame and the crimes, he or she may still not be accepted by society. Many leave the prison without accommodation or meaningful follow-up. Having come to faith in prison, many are even ostracised from the Church. Because of their convictions they cannot find a job, may end up in a hostel and eventually end up back in prison. It is easy for society to ignore those who have been released from prison. Many do not feel that prisoners deserve another chance.

A lot of prisoners eat at 'God's table' regularly whilst in prison but cannot find a human hand to help them upon release. We call them ex-cons and ex-offenders and identify them by their crime – but people can and do change. Sometimes all they need is a little help to put aside their prison clothes and become useful members of society. With a little extra help people can come to understand that their experiences do not identify them; their experiences make them!

† Compassionate God, I pray for those who are about to be released from prison. Please help them to make positive changes and use me as your hands and feet to assist them.

For further thought

Is there anything you can do to help a charity to assist those being released from prison? What could your church do?

82

Tuesday 23 March
Restorative justice

Read Isaiah 61:1–3

The Spirit of the Sovereign Lord is on me because the Lord has anointed me to proclaim good news to the poor. He has sent me to bind up the broken-hearted, to proclaim freedom for the captives and release from darkness for the prisoners, to proclaim the year of the Lord's favour ...

(verses 1–2a)

I have been asked on a number of occasions about the victims of crime. People sometimes feel that we have more compassion for prisoners rather than their victims.

I believe very strongly that God has a heart for victims. This text tells us that he comforts those who mourn and binds up the broken-hearted, which are the emotions of many victims of crime. Victims are just as important, but the fact is, if I spent a day talking about victims, not many people would ask about the prisoners' welfare. The victims would take centre stage and rightly so. Yet if we provide prisoners with appropriate decency and care, we could show them a new way of living. They could be rehabilitated which will also help victims of the past and avoid there being any more in the future.

Restorative Justice is a planned action that brings victims and prisoners into communication, enabling everyone to play a part in repairing the harm caused and finding a positive way forward. This aids rehabilitation.

Something to consider is that many years before Restorative Justice came about, Jesus came to release the prisoners from darkness. Being released from the darkness of crime will help to repair harm and foster a rehabilitative culture.

Luke 4, in which Jesus quotes from this passage in Isaiah, is now *our* mandate, to preach, release, recover and proclaim the year of Jubilee – the year of celebration where slaves were freed. The more prisoners that are freed and transformed, the more we can celebrate a decline in the number of victims!

† Pray for those harmed by crime. Ask God to give them comfort and peace.

For further thought
How does Restorative Justice work? Check online to find out.

Wednesday 24 March
He is in your hands

Read Jeremiah 38:1–13

Then the officials said to the king, 'This man should be put to death. He is discouraging the soldiers who are left in this city, as well as all the people, ...' ... 'He is in your hands,' King Zedekiah answered. 'The king can do nothing to oppose you.'

(verses 4a and 5)

As I write this, we have just finished a serious disturbance in one of our high-security prisons, with one officer hurt. This understandably was broadcast on the news. There were many comments regarding this on social media including:

> Who cares, let them rip lumps out of each other. Don't feed them for a couple of days they will then learn that brutal force achieves nothing.

In today's text the king told the officials, 'He is in your hands' (verse 5). Imagine if today's prisoners were in the hands of those on social media. Some said, 'Bring back corporal punishment,' which is what they wanted to do to Jeremiah. 'He should be put to death', they said (verse 4).

If a person has committed a crime, there is (and should be) punishment, but according to British law the person should be treated with respect and dignity. The law deems that being removed from society, family and friends is the punishment. It does not allow corporal punishment or starving people or treating them with disrespect. It decrees that people should be rehabilitated to re-enter society.

TV programmes about prisons are not always helpful. They form people's opinions and give them freedom to treat prisoners with contempt. Nevertheless, it takes one person to make a change to the life of a prisoner, just as Ebed-Melek saved Jeremiah's life. It took courage to go to the king but made a difference. With a change of mindset, one person can change a prisoner's life. Could that person be you? They are in your hands!

† Loving God, forgive me for my wrong thoughts about those in prison and help me to do what I can to help, remembering that they are in my hands.

For further thought

Could you put something on social media that could change mindsets about people in prison?

Thursday 25 March
Mental health

Read Matthew 11:1–14

When John, who was in prison, heard about the deeds of the Messiah, he sent his disciples to ask him, 'Are you the one who is to come, or should we expect someone else?' Jesus replied, 'Go back and report to John what you hear and see.'

(verses 2–4)

Prison makes you think differently. Things you were sure about do not seem the same when you're behind bars. After being in prison for a time, John started to doubt the things he knew. He could not find out information for himself, someone else had to report to him what they saw or heard.

With the rise in the prison population in the UK and beyond, we have seen a great rise in self-harm and suicide attempts. As some prisoners say, 'Prison has a way of messing with your head.' I have worked with prisoners who were never self-harming before but become prolific self-harmers in prison.

There are a number of prisoners who enter prison already under the care of a psychiatrist. I have heard many a parent, partner or child complain that prison is not the right place for their loved one; they should be in hospital. It is a sad state of affairs when the only real 'care' they can get is in prison because the mental health organisations have had funding withdrawn and there are not enough places to house those with mental health issues.

I wonder if John was going through a moment of mental distress when he sent the message to Jesus? But Jesus did not dismiss him, he showed him compassion and sent word.

For some prisoners their mental health and their very lives are dependent on the next word they hear from outside the prison. They live from day to day for that letter, that phone call or that visit!

† All-knowing God, I pray especially for those who have committed crime due to their mental issues. I ask that they will receive the care they need and that you will heal body and mind.

For further thought

Ever thought of writing to a prisoner or becoming an official prison visitor for those with no friends or family? Check online for your local prison.

Friday 26 March
Christ the prisoner

Read Matthew 25:31–46

'"I needed clothes and you clothed me, I was ill and you looked after me, I was in prison and you came to visit me." ... "whatever you did for one of the least of these brothers and sisters of mine, you did for me."'

(verses 36 and 40b)

I always wonder whether I would meet the criteria laid out here. I ponder this text many times and ask myself, 'When did I see you, Lord?' 'Where *do* I see you?' Do I only see you in my friends? Or did I see you in the faces of those who were sad, distressed and oppressed? Or in those that were unkempt? Do I see you in 'the least' of these?

The 'least' are the people we may hate to get our hands dirty for. They are the ones we can ignore or those that we feel are below us.

Jesus made it clear: as we serve others, we serve God. It is easier to turn a blind eye as we walk past the homeless on the street. But these are the 'least' as Jesus would have it. As we look into their faces, we see the face of Christ. As we feed them and love them, they are the embodiment of Christ.

As for prisons, many of us may have never even passed a prison and certainly not been inside one, but let us remember that Christ is in the prison. In every face of every prisoner is the face of Christ. These are amongst the 'least'. They are easy to ignore as we never really see them. But even the ones we turn our backs on because we feel they deserve all they get – these are also amongst them of whom Jesus said, if you did it for one of the 'least' of these, you did it for me (verse 40).

† Reflect on those who you think may be deemed the 'least' in your society, and pray for them.

For further thought

What role can you play in God's plan for these 'least'?

Saturday 27 March
Transformation

Read Acts 16:16–35

The jailer … drew his sword and was about to kill himself because he thought the prisoners had escaped. But Paul shouted, 'Don't harm yourself! We are all here!'

(part of verses 27–28)

As mentioned during this week, prison can be a very dark place, but it can also be a place of transformation. I often tell my prisoners that God may have brought them to prison to get their attention.

I remember a story of one of my prisoners who was a notorious gang leader, serving a life term. One night he dreamt that he was in the prison chapel and someone said, 'If you want to change your life, raise your hand.' He put his hand up and then awoke. Two weeks later he saw a load of men going to the chapel. He was told something was going to 'kick off' and he wanted to be in on it. At the very end of his talk the chaplain said, 'If you want to change your life, raise your hand.' He then remembered the dream – he lifted his hand and could not stop crying (men don't cry in public in prison!). His life changed from that moment.

Paul and Silas were put in the inner stocks after being beaten badly. Yet they never felt sorry for themselves; they prayed and sang songs. After the miraculous earthquake released them from prison, Paul could have allowed the jailer who held them in the inner prison to kill himself, but Paul helped him see the light and truth about himself, which brought about transformation. One of our roles as chaplains is to help those in prison to see from a different perspective, to sit with them and watch God bring about transformation.

† Pray that God will bring about transformation for those in prisons, that lives may be changed for the greater good.

For further thought

Do you know what chaplains do? Think of a way your church could support one.

Into the unknown:
the spirit of discipleship –
7 The cost of love

Notes by **Stephen Willey**

Stephen is a Methodist Minister who has been involved in mission to the economic world through industrial chaplaincies and work against human trafficking. Much of his ministry has been in areas of multiple deprivation. He is currently based at the city centre church in Coventry, England. Stephen is committed to seeing people's potential fulfilled inside and beyond the Church and is especially concerned for people who are young or vulnerable. Stephen has used the NRSVA for these notes.

Sunday 28 March (Palm Sunday)
Opening a new way

Read Psalm 118:1–2, 19–29

Open to me the gates of righteousness, that I may enter through them and give thanks to the Lord. This is the gate of the Lord; the righteous shall enter through it.

(verses 19–20)

I was digging a new plot to plant some vegetables. The heavy earth took many months to be transformed to good soil from grass and weeds. But this was a necessary first step. The initial digging and consequent bad back were indicative of my struggles with the earth involving spade and sweat. Creating new space for new possibilities often involves struggles, and can even involve a kind of violence and pain.

The psalmist uses different images for new beginnings: the day the Lord has made, the stone the builders rejected becoming the cornerstone, and opening the gates of righteousness. Jesus' journey towards his death is strewn not only with palm branches but also with pain and violence. This week many things are torn apart in order to open up a new way. Opening the gates of righteousness in order to reveal God's steadfast love is not easy in a world often entrenched against it. Knowing what he has to do, in Gethsemane Jesus struggles with his Father's will to open up a new way for humanity. Jesus is willing to struggle to open the gates, suffer the violence of being the rejected stone and thus begin humanity's new day.

† Lord, in this Holy Week, grant us courage to follow Jesus as we journey with him towards his crucifixion and burial.

The crisis caused by the Messiah

Read Mark 14:53–65

Then the high priest stood up before them and asked Jesus, 'Have you no answer? What is it that they testify against you?' But he was silent and did not answer. Again the high priest asked him, 'Are you the Messiah, the Son of the Blessed One?' Jesus said, 'I am.'

(verses 60–62a)

Ten years after my first sense of calling into ministry, which I resisted, I had a strong experience of God's presence in my prayer, and it seemed that God was laughing at me. I was considering being a brother of a monastic community but I felt, with certainty, that God was saying I would be a Methodist Minister! This meeting with God created a kind of crisis within. I could not see how the way would open up for me, but, well, here I am!

God's presence at the burning bush faces Moses with the difficult task of leading the Israelites away from slavery. The 'I am' opens up a way. Jesus' 'I am' in these verses opens up a way for a transforming relationship with the 'Blessed One'. The Israelites got to the Promised Land and the disciples got to Jerusalem, but the next step – a return to an unbroken relationship with God – was too hard. Many things got in the way. When Jesus came and said, 'I am,' the High Priest saw him. He heard Jesus' claim. And he needed no more proof. This man identifies himself with the Messiah, Son of the Blessed One. Seeing Jesus creates a crisis for the High Priest. He rips his garment – a ritual sign that blasphemy has occurred. In the religious eyes of the Pharisees this is blasphemy. However, with the eyes of faith, the eyes of hindsight, we can see that Jesus was no blasphemer. Truly, a relationship with Jesus creates a crisis, as his 'I am' opens the way to the Father.

† Jesus, Son of the living God, source and light of our lives, help us to see you as you are, even if that creates a crisis within.

For further thought

Could I see God's 'I AM' in some situation where I feel afraid or alone?

Tuesday 30 March
Peter sinks

Read Mark 14:66–72

But he began to curse, and he swore an oath, 'I do not know this man you are talking about.' ... Then Peter remembered that Jesus had said to him, 'Before the cock crows twice, you will deny me three times.' And he broke down and wept.

(verses 71, 72b)

As a child I remember seeing a painting in which Jesus seemed to look upon Peter with reproach and condemnation. Recently, when I had to deal with someone who had been caught stealing, I was reminded that it is often neither reproach nor condemnation that reduces people to tears, but compassionate forgiveness. As I quoted the Lord's Prayer, 'Forgive us our debts as we forgive the debts of others,' the tears that followed reminded me that a refusal to condemn and a determination to forgive can touch even the most carefully defended heart. On this occasion, new possibilities opened up. Is it possible that it was the knowledge of Jesus' understanding, love and forgiveness that broke Peter's heart?

Jesus knew Peter. He had seen that Peter was brave but impulsive. Jesus had experienced Peter buckling under pressure when things got too much for him, like the time he was walking on water (Matthew 14:29–31) and started to sink, needing Jesus' hand to lift him out of the water. Jesus had also discussed forgiveness with Peter. When Peter had asked how many times he should forgive, Jesus replied with an excessively compassionate answer (Matthew 18:21–22). And now, when things had got too much for Peter in the courtyard, pushed to reveal his discipleship, Peter lied. He repeated the lie in order to protect himself. Such betrayal must have caused Jesus pain. It emphasised Jesus' isolation as he was struggling to overthrow the ways of death and destruction in favour of the kingdom and life. However, he never stopped loving his disciple, Peter.

† Jesus, you know me and you have seen what I am capable of. Look upon me with compassionate love, even if it should break my heart.

For further thought

In the community around me, are there ways I can look on others who feel condemned, with love and compassion?

Wednesday 31 March
Nothing left to say

> **Read Mark 15:1–15**
>
> Pilate asked him, 'Are you the King of the Jews?' He answered him, 'You say so.' Then the chief priests accused him of many things. Pilate asked him again, 'Have you no answer? See how many charges they bring against you.' But Jesus made no further reply, so that Pilate was amazed.
>
> (verses 2–5)

Why does Jesus say so little in his own defence? Perhaps he is aware that it is pointless when the minds of those in the council are made up. Was not Pilate, who later on offers to release Jesus rather than Barabbas, offering Jesus a way out, in this moment when he asks him to say more? It appears that Pilate wants to hear Jesus' defence.

Perhaps Jesus' silence opens up a way for us to understand that sometimes we are condemned before we speak. No matter what we say, the judgement has been made. I have seen this happen with friends whose ethnicity has evoked prejudice and discrimination: a job which they will never be offered or a church in which they will never be made welcome! The Council has already agreed that the Messiah couldn't have come from Galilee (John 7:41, 52). Even Jesus' disciple Nathaniel asked, 'Can anything good come out of Nazareth?' (John 1:46). Just as it may have been Peter's accent that betrayed his origins in the courtyard when he spoke to defend himself, so Jesus has reached a point where he is already condemned because of prejudice and preconceptions. Nothing was going to protect him from the crucifixion determined by the religious and Roman authorities.

Jesus has spoken clearly about his identity. (The question in Greek is literally, 'You are the King of the Jews?') Pilate has said it, the High Priest has heard the 'I am'. There is nothing for Jesus to deny – he is who he is. There is nothing left to say.

† Jesus, your words are precious to us, but sometimes you are silent too. Pray within our silences and our absences and reveal your love and compassion in those places and times.

For further thought

When we have said all we have to say, what might silence reveal about our hearts?

Jesus, object of humiliation

Read Mark 15:16–20

[The soldiers] clothed him in a purple cloak; and after twisting some thorns into a crown, they put it on him. And they began saluting him, 'Hail, King of the Jews!' They struck his head with a reed, spat upon him, and knelt down in homage to him.

(verses 17–19)

In my work on human trafficking, I was often shocked and sickened by humans' behaviour towards other human beings. It seems the perpetrators had chosen to view the victims of their trade as less than human.

In this passage, Jesus is not only silent, but he no longer sets the agenda for what will happen. The action happens to him rather than at his direction. He has been flogged and is in the hands of soldiers. Nothing more will happen that might secure his release. In the hands of the soldiers, Jesus faces humiliation. They treat him like he is an inanimate doll or a scarecrow, goading him in a malevolent game, as they make the crown of thorns and kneel before him. His persecutors act out a macabre ritual which seemingly gives them permission to hurt and humiliate. Jesus' silence before Pilate and the Council is magnified. He is a person, but he is silenced and humiliated. Like a trafficked person, Jesus is at the mercy of his captors. It is as if he is there for their pleasure and benefit. The perfect human, Jesus – more human than the soldiers or anyone else in this all-too-human story – the one who is God, inside humanity, experiences objectification. Others deride him and he has no recourse. Perhaps the soldiers are enjoying using this man's humiliation to make themselves feel powerful.

So he waits, imprisoned in the governor's headquarters, for crucifixion.

† Christ, our brother, life and our way, help us never to see people as commodities or objects. Show us people who are ignored, lost or hidden that we may treat them as brothers and sisters.

For further thought

Have we ever elevated ourselves above others who are more vulnerable than we are in order to feel better?

Friday 2 April (Good Friday)
Seeing God on the cross

Read Mark 15:21–39

Then Jesus gave a loud cry and breathed his last. And the curtain of the temple was torn in two, from top to bottom. Now when the centurion, who stood facing him, saw that in this way he breathed his last, he said, 'Truly this man was God's Son!'

(verses 37–39)

The house I lived in as a young child had a strongroom with no windows and a solid door. I used to enjoy, as a small boy, being shut in this room. The complete absence of light changed my world. In the depths of the shadow I couldn't see anyone. It was like I was alone even if my brother was beside me. I knew I was safe, protected by a strongroom, but for Jesus, on the cross, there is an absence of light and he is not protected: no, he is exposed on the cross.

The one who is light, the light of the world, is entering the deepest shadows. Has God forsaken him? Will his life be restored? Will the light shine again? In the moment before he is immersed in death, a loud cry escapes him, and opens up new possibilities for us. Whatever that loud voice means, as it leaves Jesus' throat, it shakes the centurion on guard into a state of belief. For a moment in the gloom, it is possible to see who Jesus really is. Jesus is no longer on the streets or in the market squares, doing things and saying things which are marvellous. No, on this occasion, as the veil is ripped between heaven and earth, the centurion sees Jesus at his very most broken and vulnerable, and he glimpses heaven. As Jesus breathes his last, he is revealed to this Roman soldier, from the same place as those who mocked and spat on him. Today, now, we too look upon him, as he dies.

† Crucified Christ, rip the veil, raise your voice and reveal yourself to me by your presence. Through your vulnerability on the cross you open again the doors of hope and faith.

For further thought

In the shadows and gloom of Good Friday, the centurion sees Jesus. Where can I see Jesus today?

Into the unknown: the spirit of discipleship – 7 The cost of love

Saturday 3 April
Loving after death

Read Mark 15:40–47

[Joseph] taking down the body, wrapped it in the linen cloth, and laid it in a tomb that had been hewn out of the rock. He then rolled a stone against the door of the tomb. Mary Magdalene and Mary the mother of Joses saw where the body was laid.

(verses 46b–47)

On placement as a young trainee minister, I was asked to shadow a nurse in the Accident and Emergency department. One day a man came in by ambulance. He had suffered a severe heart attack. The doctors worked on him for several minutes after his arrival, compressing his chest, attempting to shock his heart back into life, but he was gone. They wrote the time of death on a whiteboard in the room and I was wondering what would happen next, when the young nurse stepped forward. 'I'll take it from here,' she said, allowing her colleagues to return to other patients. I stayed with her as gently she started talking to the man who had departed this world. Taking a cloth to clean the body, she quietly cleaned his hands, and wiped clean the damage from his fall. 'Poor you,' she whispered as she removed the shock pads and wiped over the marks they had made.

That day I discovered this: acts of love are possible in the bleakest places. Joseph of Arimathea and these women show us their way of loving Jesus that evening. Joseph wraps the body of a beloved teacher, rabbi and friend who has been cruelly mocked, beaten and crucified, in a simple linen sheet. The two Marys, watching, see where the body is laid. Their hearts tell them that they will come, after the sabbath is over, to anoint his body. They will return to show their gentle care and compassion, born of deep love.

† In the grave we look for you, O Christ, discovering that we still love you. May the Spirit's breath and the Father's love reunite us when dawn reveals the new day.

For further thought

Do I know someone who is trapped in shadows of sadness, grief and depression? How can I show a gentle love towards them?

The Bible through the seasons: spring

Notes by **Rt Revd Dr Peter Langerman**

Peter is a pastor in a Presbyterian church in Durbanville, Cape Town, and he is the Moderator of the General Assembly of the Uniting Presbyterian Church in Southern Africa. He is married to Sally and they have four daughters. Peter is passionate about the dynamic rule and reign of God. He believes that God invites all to be part of God's transformative mission through love, and that the most potent and powerful agent for the transformation of local communities is the local church living out faithfulness to God. Peter has used the NIVUK for these notes.

Sunday 4 April (Easter Sunday)
The silent witnesses

Read Mark 16:1–8

Trembling and bewildered, the women went out and fled from the tomb. They said nothing to anyone, because they were afraid.

(verse 8)

As we begin this spring season, we start at a wonderful place: the empty tomb, with the women who were the first visitors to the grave. But we come to this familiar place in Mark's version, which has caused problems for readers right from the time when people first began to read what Mark wrote. The oldest and most reliable versions of Mark's Gospel end after verse 8, with the women afraid and confused and silent. Why would the writer of the Gospel do this? Despite being told to share the good news, the women keep it to themselves, at least at first. Perhaps the writer understands what we all feel at times when confronted by change. Bewildered, unsure and too frightened to do anything at all.

Maybe after a long, hard and cold winter, you are feeling a little like this. The thaw of spring, the flowers and the hint of warmer weather should bring joy, but sometimes they do not. The thickness of winter doesn't disappear as soon as the weather begins to change. But be patient because just like the women who didn't stay silent forever, so you will find yourself gradually drawn to the wonder of a new beginning.

† Pray that you might find it easy to share some good news with a friend during the course of today.

Monday 5 April
The season of singing

Read Song of Songs 2:10–15

My beloved spoke and said to me, 'Arise, my darling, my beautiful one, come with me. See! The winter is past; the rains are over and gone. Flowers appear on the earth; the season of singing has come, the cooing of doves is heard in our land.

(verses 10–12)

As you head out this week, begin to notice the signs of new life around you. Whether you are walking in a country area or are able to take time off to sit at the beach or find yourself in a busy town or city, there will be signs of life. Blossoms on the trees, birds singing, the weather getting warmer, frost and snow melting, the sun peeking out from behind the clouds and bathing the earth in light. With the burgeoning signs of spring comes the sound of singing.

We seldom sing much anymore, in public anyway. One of the few places where we still sing together with others is in church. But spring is a time for singing. As you head into the helter-skelter of ordinary life, take time to hear the singing of the earth. One of the key insights of the writers of the Bible is that the whole of creation is singing in worship to our Creator. Sometimes we can catch a snatch of the melody, a few lines of the song, the rhythm of the great song of creation. Be encouraged to join in; hum along with the melody as you walk down the street; listen for the words as the waves crash into the beach; feel the rhythm as you enter the busy town or city. You will find the lingering heaviness of the winter lift off you as you do, for the winter is past and the season of singing has come.

† Creator God, please open my eyes that I might see and my ears that I might hear all that you are doing around me. Please help me to join in the great song of creation.

For further thought

Consider how you might help another person to experience the reality of new life today and encourage that person to see the signs of new life.

Tuesday 6 April
Forced to listen

Read Isaiah 42:5–16

'I am the Lord; that is my name! I will not yield my glory to another or my praise to idols. See, the former things have taken place, and new things I declare; before they spring into being I announce them to you.'

(verses 8–9)

We so easily become set in our ways. We drive the same way to work every day; we have the same routine when we get into the office; we eat the same things for lunch; and we head home at about the same time. Somebody has said that the only difference between a rut and a grave is the depth. That's a little harsh. We need order and routine in our day if we are to be productive. We don't want to have to make decisions on every small thing every moment of the day, because then we would not be able to make the really important decisions when we need to.

However, every now and then we have to be jolted out of our comfortable routine and compelled to do things differently. There are roadworks and we have to take a detour; there is a crisis that we have to deal with as we arrive at work; the lunch place closes down and we have to work late to finish a report. We find these inconveniences, but what if these were the ways in which God was trying to get our attention? When our lives are ordered and structured, it is difficult for God to get our attention. A little bit of chaos can shift our focus and, if we are alive to it, we might find that God is wanting to draw us away from our routine to speak a new word into our lives.

† Surprising God, please interrupt me today and help me to recognise you in the interruption. And when you do, please help me to listen to what you say.

For further thought
If your routine has been interrupted somehow lately, do you think God may have had anything to do with that? If so, what do you think God might be saying to you?

Wednesday 7 April
Spring cleaning

Read Hosea 6:1–6

'Let us acknowledge the Lord; let us press on to acknowledge him. As surely as the sun rises, he will appear; he will come to us like the winter rains, like the spring rains that water the earth.'

(verse 3)

I'm not sure how careful you are about spring cleaning, but traditionally spring is a time to clear the clutter that has accumulated during the long winter months. Sometimes we need to do spiritual spring cleaning and the thing to which we are forced to listen has to do with changes that we have to make in our lives. Together with the established routine and the familiar pattern often come practices and habits to which we seldom dedicate any thought or to which we seldom pay any attention.

The prophet/writer of the book of Hosea probably lived and spoke at a time when the Northern Kingdom of Samaria was going through something of an economic boom. People were doing well materially and financially, but the spiritual life of the nation was at a very low ebb. Things have not changed much. The more prosperous a people and a society become, the less they tend to look to God and vice versa. Hosea's challenge is a call to repentance; for the people to turn back to God. Hosea is certain that if the people return to God, they will find God faithful and true to God's promises and they will rediscover their spiritual centre.

Maybe it's time to do a spiritual spring clean in your life. Get rid of some of the habits and practices that have accumulated during the long winter and develop some new ways of doing things. One thing we can be sure of is that when we turn to God in real repentance, we find God waiting for us with open arms.

† Forgiving, gracious God, please forgive me for the times I have hurt others and help me to ask for forgiveness and to grant forgiveness to those who ask it from me.

For further thought

If you are able, ask those to whom you are closest and whom you trust most if they can help you identify habits that you need to break.

Left margin: April — The Bible through the seasons: spring

Thursday 8 April
Born of the Spirit

Read John 3:1–15

Jesus answered, 'Very truly I tell you, no one can enter the kingdom of God unless they are born of water and the Spirit. Flesh gives birth to flesh, but the Spirit gives birth to spirit. You should not be surprised at my saying, "You must be born again."'

(verses 5–7)

One of the more unfortunate things to have taken place in the 1970s and early 80s was a proliferation of products calling themselves 'born again'. A quick Google search revealed born again shampoo and beauty treatments, born again wedges (platform shoes!) and even a coffee mug inscribed with 'Born Again Buddhist'. The phrase entered popular culture through the incredible ministry and popularity of Billy Graham and many of those who have followed him in hosting large evangelistic crusades.

Whatever we may think of the effectiveness of those events, the phrase didn't originate with any modern evangelist of the nineteenth or twentieth century, but with a much more important figure in the first. Jesus, in conversation with a prominent religious figure, tells him that the only way a person gets to see the rule and reign of God is by being born of the Spirit, or born from above, or born again. Repentance is a necessary step if we are to see lasting change in our lives, but Jesus tells Nicodemus and us here that repentance, by itself, is not enough. Something else is needed. Turning to God in repentance is necessary, but there also has to be the submission of our whole life to God if we are to find new life. Many people have just enough religion to keep them on the straight and narrow, but when it comes to total submission of their entire lives to God, they are just not able to do it. Are you?

† Loving Lord Jesus, today I submit not just part of my life, but my entire life to you and ask you to fill me with your Holy Spirit.

For further thought
If you prayed this prayer, why not share what you have done with a trusted Christian friend and ask them to pray with and for you?

April

The Bible through the seasons: spring

Friday 9 April
The centre of our faith

Read 1 Corinthians 15:12–28

But Christ has indeed been raised from the dead, the firstfruits of those who have fallen asleep. For since death came through a man, the resurrection of the dead comes also through a man. For as in Adam all die, so in Christ all will be made alive.

(verses 20–22)

At the epicentre of our faith is the resurrection of Jesus Christ from the dead. Without a resurrection there is no Christian faith. While those who dispute the resurrection have tried to find alternative explanations, the most plausible and probable account of what happened to Jesus after his death and burial is that he rose again on the third day. We saw on Sunday that when the women came to the tomb it was empty. They had seen where he had been laid on Friday afternoon and the stone placed across the entrance. When they got there on Sunday the stone was gone, the tomb was empty and Christ was definitely alive.

Why is the resurrection so important to our faith? Paul says that if Jesus was not raised, then all those who claimed to see him after he rose are liars. The Christian faith is premised on a lie. If Christ is not alive, then those Christians who die have no certainty that they will be raised to new life. In short, our faith is futile.

However, if Christ has been raised then he is the first fruits. Just like the fruit harvested at the start of the season and given to God, so Jesus was the first to be raised from the dead and returned to God. The first fruit is followed by a much larger harvest and this points to the wonderful reality that all those who have faith in Christ will also be raised to new life to be with God forever.

† Thank you, risen Lord Jesus, that you are alive and that I can have true life in and through you, real life that begins now and is uninterrupted by death.

For further thought

Take some time to give thanks for the life, witness and impact of Christian friends and family members who have fallen asleep in the Lord.

Saturday 10 April
An imperishable body

Read 1 Corinthians 15:35–50

So will it be with the resurrection of the dead. The body that is sown is perishable, it is raised imperishable; it is sown in dishonour, it is raised in glory; it is sown in weakness, it is raised in power; it is sown a natural body, it is raised a spiritual body.

(verses 42–44)

One of the things that intrigues people sometimes is speculation about the kind of life we will live in heaven. Artworks of cherub-like angels sitting on clouds playing harps have caused some people to think this is what heaven will be like. Others, influenced perhaps by the fact that heaven is a spiritual place, have speculated that we will waft about like ethereal spirits. What we do know is that after the resurrection, we will have a body; we will have physical form. We know this because Jesus, who was the first to be raised from the dead and to receive his resurrection body, had physical form. He ate food with his disciples. They could see, recognise and touch him.

Although the resurrection body has physical form, it is different from our natural human bodies. There will be no gender or sexual identity, because Jesus says there is no marriage in heaven. Also, the spiritual, heavenly body will not be subject to decay, sickness or death.

While the Christian message is good news for this life, we must never forget that there is the sure and certain hope that we will be raised to life in and with Christ to be with him forever – to share his very life with God. This is an amazing promise that should keep us going when we feel like giving up. In the creed we declare that we believe in the resurrection of the dead – a reference not only to Christ's resurrection, but to our own.

† At the end of this week, ask God to renew your hope of what life will be like when we are with Christ.

For further thought
How does the hope of an eternity spent with God, with a new body, help you to live your life today?

Cosmonaut: first in space

Notes by **Heather Prince** and **Andrew Kruger**

Heather and Andrew were born and raised in South Africa and were married there in 2013. Andrew was ordained as an Anglican priest in November 2012 and holds a Master's degree in Theology from the University of Kwa-Zulu Natal. He served on the Secretariat of the Anglican Church of Southern Africa's Prayer Book Revision project and is an avid scholar of the liturgy. In 2016 Heather and Andrew moved to New Jersey, USA, where Andrew serves as Rector of Trinity Episcopal Church in Cranford, NJ. Heather is a graduate student in Astrophysics at Princeton University and a qualified yoga teacher. Heather and Andrew have used the NRSVA for these notes.

Sunday 11 April
Wisdom's part in God's creation

Read Proverbs 8:22–31

The Lord created me at the beginning of his work, the first of his acts of long ago … rejoicing in his inhabited world and delighting in the human race.

(verses 22 and 31)

On 12 April 1961, Yuri Gagarin became the first human being to enter space and orbit the Earth. Despite being from the then fiercely anti-religious Soviet Union there is some evidence to suggest that he may have been religious. Gagarin's local Orthodox priest recalled seeing the cosmonaut at Christmas and Easter services. While this is not overwhelming evidence for a life of faith, it is an invitation to take a closer look at Orthodox Christianity.

One of the great contributions of the Orthodox Church is the spiritual discipline of contemplative prayer. Western Christians typically understand prayer as talking to God. Eastern Christians are better trained in the art of listening to God. The method involves reciting a sacred word silently and faithfully to help let go of distractions and open the heart to God.

The first nine chapters of Proverbs vividly personify divine wisdom as a woman who was present with God at creation. Those who are willing to enter the silence of contemplative prayer are invited to hear the divine wisdom of God speaking to us through each element of the creation. Our task is to discern the pitch and rhythm of divine wisdom, which at first can seem unintelligible, and then to echo this divine music in our lives.

† Pray today the Jesus Prayer from the Orthodox tradition: Lord Jesus Christ, Son of God, have mercy on me. The prayer can be practised during pre-planned silence or during moments in your day where you might find yourself distracted or bored.

The star thrower

Read Psalm 147:1–11

Praise the Lord! ...
He determines the number of the stars; he gives to all of them their
names. Great is our Lord, and abundant in power; his understanding is
beyond measure.

(verses 1a, 4–5)

When God revealed Godself to the Israelites, they saw God as their own tribal God: the one true Creator of the universe seemed particularly concerned with one small group of people. In return for their worship and obedience they were given preference over different nations, granted victory in battle and given lush lands to live off.

The Jesus of the Gospels challenges this idea, as he challenges the religious leaders' views of who is favoured by God and who is on the outside. As the apostles spread the news about Jesus' death and resurrection, it is clear that God is bigger and more universal than even the most visionary Old Testament writers were able to imagine with the limitations of their perspective.

Yuri Gagarin's groundbreaking space flight expanded the previous limits of human exploration, and the other rapid advances of the space age shifted our human paradigm of what was possible. Have we allowed our view of God to expand as our knowledge of the Earth, humanity and even space have grown? Or have we retained a tribal, nationalistic sense of religion?

Naturally our mental picture of God is informed by our upbringing and our cultural beliefs, but Jesus' radical example demands that we interrogate these default attitudes. If God took on human form in our time, which of our beliefs about who is 'in' and who is 'out' might be upended?

† O God, your understanding is beyond measure: reveal our preconceived ideas and grant us the courage to embrace the values of your kingdom; through Jesus Christ our Lord. Amen

For further thought

According to recent research, stars, planets and galaxies make up just 4% of the visible universe. Scientists aren't sure what comprises the other 96%.

Tuesday 13 April
The earthling

Read Genesis 2:4b–9

... then the Lord God formed man from the dust of the ground, and breathed into his nostrils the breath of life; and the man became a living being.

(verse 7)

The two Voyager space probes were launched in 1977. Their original mission was to study planets in our solar system, but both probes have now left the solar system and entered interstellar space, the first objects of human origin to do so. A Golden Record, including images, music and spoken greetings, was placed aboard the Voyager spacecraft to communicate something about life on Earth to any intelligent extraterrestrial life form that may come across them.

Suppose for a moment that on a different planet around a different star, intelligent life has evolved. The God who created the entire universe is of course the source of life on this planet as well, although this life form may be vastly different to us humans in many ways. This race of extraterrestrials might develop their own religion in response to their experiences of God, possibly with some kind of holy literature or rich oral tradition, or maybe something completely foreign to us.

If we could communicate with these beings, could we tell them about Christianity in a way that would allow them to see that we ultimately worship the same Creator? If we heard their stories about God's revelation to them, would we recognise our God even in the context of a completely different culture? What things are universally true about our experience of God to the extent that we would expect to see those qualities in their descriptions of God, even if they were radically different from us? Perhaps it might be worthwhile to repeat this thought experiment for the religions of different groups of people around the world.

† O God, you created human beings in your own image: assist us by your Spirit to seek, discern and reveal the holy in every person we encounter; through Jesus Christ our Lord. Amen

For further thought
The Voyager 1 probe is currently the human-made object farthest from Earth.

Elijah's ascension and succession

> ### Read 2 Kings 2:1–14
>
> *... Elijah said to Elisha, 'Tell me what I may do for you, before I am taken from you.' Elisha said, 'Please let me inherit a double share of your spirit.' ... As they continued walking and talking, a chariot of fire and horses of fire separated the two of them, and Elijah ascended in a whirlwind into heaven.*
>
> *(verses 9 and 11)*

The first time I read Elisha's request for a double portion of Elijah's spirit, I assumed that he wanted to perform miracles that were twice as impressive or numerous as those of Elijah. However the language of 'double portion' is typically used in relation to the land an eldest son expects to inherit from a father; double the amount allocated to his brothers. In this sense Elisha is not asking for twice as much miraculous power as Elijah, but for twice as much as any other successor would receive.

Elisha is not only competitive in his personal life, seeking to be the best of Elijah's disciples, but is also ambitious on the national stage. He is sometimes referred to as the patriotic prophet because of his favourable disposition to the soldiers and kings of Israel. Competition is not necessarily a negative endeavour. The rivalry between the United States and the Soviet Union led to wonderful technological developments. However, the competition between these nations has also resulted in destruction, violence and competition for competition's sake.

Elisha did some truly amazing things; Jesus himself recalls how Elisha cured Naaman the Syrian of leprosy. And yet this same Elisha curses 42 boys with death-by-bear when they jeered at him (2 Kings 2:24). Competition and rivalry are often held up as virtues to be pursued but more often than not this attitude leads to pain and brokenness. Our culture's insistence to be better, or prettier, or more intelligent, or more athletic than others seems to be antithetical to the gospel of Jesus Christ.

† Vulnerable God, your Son taught us that the first shall be last, and the last shall be first: grant us the grace to embrace and nurture true humility; through Jesus Christ our Lord. Amen

For further thought
Does there have to be just one winner? Consider this in your interactions today.

April

Cosmonaut: first in space

Thursday 15 April
Alone with God

Read Mark 9:1–9

Six days later, Jesus took with him Peter and James and John, and led them up a high mountain apart, by themselves. And he was transfigured before them, and his clothes became dazzling white, such as no one on earth could bleach them.

(verses 2–3)

Mountains are considered sacred by many groups of people around the world. For example, in Native Hawaiian mythology the sacred mountain of Maunakea is the *'piko'*, or umbilical cord of the island of Hawai'i, the oldest child of the Sky Father and the Earth Mother.

Conflict often arises between indigenous people who want to maintain the sanctity of their holy mountains, and people who want to use these mountains for recreational purposes like rock climbing and ski resorts, or for scientific purposes such as astronomy. It is becoming more and more challenging to find places that are truly 'apart' from the rest of the world: even Mount Everest has become so crowded that climbers encounter human traffic jams on their way to the summit. We live in a time when humans dominate our natural world, imposing our will on the environment and recklessly sacrificing the health of our planet for the sake of convenience and consumerism.

The transfiguration story, together with the many times in the scriptures when Jesus retreats to the wilderness to pray, reminds us that it can be easier to become aware of God's presence when we step outside of the busyness of our daily lives and take some time to be alone in nature. How can we incorporate more times like these into our lives? And what steps can we take to protect the environment and ensure that future generations also have natural spaces to retreat to?

† Lord Jesus Christ, your life was marked by the pattern of contemplation and action: refresh us with times of solitude so that we will have the energy and inspiration to serve you. Amen

For further thought

There are approximately 20,000 artificial objects orbiting the Earth which are large enough to be tracked. Debris impact affects the safety and performance of space stations and missions.

Friday 16 April
Jesus' ascension

Read Acts 1:1–11

When [Jesus] had said this, as they were watching, he was lifted up, and a cloud took him out of their sight.

(verse 9)

As a young child growing up in South Africa I remember a time when Ascension Day was still a public holiday and many people would attend church. The ascension of Jesus is celebrated 40 days after Easter Sunday, and it always falls on a Thursday. Naturally church attendance declined when Ascension Day was no longer a public holiday and many churches ceased to hold services.

I suspect that many preachers breathed a sigh of relief when they were no longer required to make sense of Jesus' ascension 'into the clouds'. Modern congregations with even an elementary knowledge of geography and physics would have legitimate questions regarding Jesus' journey into the atmosphere: given what we know about the mechanics of space travel, wouldn't Jesus run out of oxygen, or become a frozen block in the cold of outer space?

The prayer for Ascension Day from the *Episcopal Book of Common Prayer* offers a clue as to how we might think about the ascension more fruitfully. This ancient collect begins with the ascription: 'Jesus Christ ascended far above all heavens that he might fill all things.'

During his earthly ministry Jesus was limited to a very small territory east of the Mediterranean and only lived for about 30 years. The ascension proclaims that Jesus is no longer bound by time and space, but rather 'fills all things'. Essentially, and most wonderfully, Christ is revealed as being present in all times and in all places; to you and me and not just the disciples of old.

† Almighty God, whose blessed Son our Saviour Jesus Christ ascended far above all heavens that he might fill all things: mercifully give us faith to perceive that, according to his promise, he abides with his Church on earth, even to the end of the ages; through Jesus Christ our Lord. Amen

For further thought

How would you explain the relevance of the ascension today?

107

Saturday 17 April
Praise the Lord

Read Psalm 150

Praise the Lord! Praise God in his sanctuary; praise him in his mighty firmament! … Let everything that breathes praise the Lord! Praise the Lord!

(verses 1 and 6)

Even in our postmodern world, many of us absorb the notion of a three-storey universe with the devil below and God above. Athletes who achieve great feats often lift their eyes skywards to acknowledge God, even though we know God is not sitting around on cotton-wool clouds with choirs of cherubs. Nikita Khrushchev, a Soviet statesman, said in an anti-religion campaign speech that, 'Yuri Gagarin flew into space, but didn't see any god there.' If God is not to be found in the clouds above or in outer space, where should we look for God?

Psalm 150 is not bound by our 'three-storey universe' worldview, but rather envisages a God who is present everywhere: an omnipresent God. Like so many of the preceding psalms the author uses the poetic device of parallelism to begin Psalm 150: 'Praise God in his sanctuary / praise him in his mighty firmament!' Parallelism is a kind of symmetry in which the idea in the first half-verse is developed or opposed by what is expressed in the second half-verse.

In the parallelism of verse 1 the poet considers the temple sanctuary and firmament to be synonymous; the earthly temple reflects God's heavenly dwelling. The pavement of the temple is the 'mighty firmament' which embraces the cosmos. For those who seek, it is possible to discern God's presence in the rhythm of the temple liturgy, and in the arc of a planet's orbit. Therefore, let us join the stunning concluding doxology of the Psalter, with its orchestral crescendo of praise to God.

† Omnipresent God: grant us the grace to witness your glory all around us and to add our breath to the song of your praise; through Jesus Christ our Lord. Amen

For further thought

Consider the 'sanctuary of God' the next time you look at the starry sky.

The Gospel of Mark (2) –
1 Jesus the healer

Notes by **Nathan Eddy**

Nathan is editor of Fresh From The Word, *a parent, chicken rustler and aspiring poet. He is ordained in the United Church of Christ (USA) and has served in the United Reformed Church (UK). Veteran readers of* Fresh From The Word *will be glad to know he has completed his PhD in psalms and graduated, and he now works in Jewish–Christian relations for the charity The Council of Christians and Jews. He lives in London with his wife Clare, a vicar in the Church of England, and their two daughters. Nathan has used the NRSVA for these notes.*

Sunday 18 April
Among the tombs

Read Mark 5:1–20

Night and day among the tombs and on the mountains he was always howling and bruising himself with stones. When he saw Jesus from a distance, he ran and bowed down before him.

(verses 5–6)

This week we consider healing in the Gospel of Mark, beginning with a dramatic story: Jesus' healing of a man possessed by evil spirits, a man cast out of his community because of his illness. Appropriately, he lives isolated in a cemetery, where he cries out day and night in anguish. When Jesus arrives, he runs to him. Is he eager for the life Jesus brings? Angry? Afraid?

Health in the Bible is not just something we 'get back' after we've been ill. It is the life force itself, the animating energy of God given by holy men and women. Life is not just the span of our days on earth, but our connection to God: our energy, personality and spirit. Human life is robust yet also fragile. Don't we all desire a healer who can bring life?

I invite you to look for the social aspects of health this week. Typical for his Judaism (as in Psalm 107:31–32, for example), Jesus commands the man to return to his community and tell his story. Healing is about friendship and community, not just pills and charts – and it is about our own initiative, too. I am struck by the clean clothes the man puts on (verse 15). Healing is the beginning of the man's story, not the end.

† God of life, I am grateful for my energy and spirit. Restore it within me today that I might reach out to those around me.

Monday 19 April
The fighter

Read Mark 5:21–34

She … came up behind [Jesus] in the crowd and touched his cloak, for she said, 'If I but touch his clothes, I will be made well.' Immediately her haemorrhage stopped; and she felt in her body that she was healed of her disease.

(verses 27–29)

The story of healing today and tomorrow is remarkable: it tells of two intertwined healings, woven into one story. A leader of a synagogue named Jairus, desperate for Jesus to help his daughter, implores him to come to her bedside, where she is at the point of death (verses 22–23). *En route* to Jairus' house, a woman afflicted with a haemorrhage (perhaps she suffers from ongoing vaginal bleeding) reaches for Jesus' cloak to be healed.

Although she is not named, the woman is a fully 'rounded' character. We hear her internal thoughts and can sense her despair and astonishment. Indeed, if not for Jesus' healing, she, too, would have been near death, just like the girl Jesus is going to heal. Despairing or not, her initiative is remarkable. No one brings her to Jesus. Her story suggests she is a widow, or divorced. She fights for her healing and for the attention of the healer. Purity laws would have kept this woman from temple worship (as in Leviticus 15:19–33); Jesus' healing means that she will be able to return there.

I wonder if you know any women like this one. I can think of several in my church: women who face medical issues and other setbacks without a family around them for support. The women I have in mind support the entire church, rather than the other way around.

Although we don't know what happened next to her, I imagine her in the temple, giving thanks.

† God of the isolated, never let us give up on life, or on the living.

For further thought

What does your church or community do for those suffering from social isolation?

Tuesday 20 April
Sleeper, awake

> **Read Mark 5:35–43**
>
> *He took her by the hand and said to her, 'Talitha cum,' which means, 'Little girl, get up!' And immediately the girl got up and began to walk about (she was twelve years of age).*
>
> *(verses 41–42a)*

Carrying on from our story yesterday, Jesus continues to Jairus' house, where a young girl lies on her bed, apparently dead. Jesus is mocked for even entering the house to heal her (verse 40). The links with the woman healed in yesterday's reading are intriguing: the woman suffered for 12 years with her bleeding; the young girl is 12 years old. Both are face-to-face with death, in seemingly hopeless situations.

Many interpreters of this story hear an echo of resurrection in the girl's story. 'Sleeping' is an ancient metaphor for death, and Jesus' command to her to 'rise' suggests life beyond death (verses 39 and 41). Yet this girl's life is a life in and for this world. The young girl stands, walks and even eats (verse 43). She is no spirit. She is ready for life beyond illness.

I confess I struggle with parts of this story. Unlike other healing stories in Mark's Gospel, it is slightly too neatly packaged for my liking. Not all 12-year-olds at death's door are lucky enough to have a healer in town.

Yet I also don't want to join the mockers in this story who laughed at Jesus' promise. We will see this week just how real and persistent illness and suffering are in this Gospel; Mark does not want to paper them over. What Mark does want is to encourage our trust in God's rule: to shape us as readers to desire it and even to make it real. Perhaps in my disbelief I can learn from Jairus. Jairus did not wait around or give up. He fought for the healing that Jesus freely gave.

† God of life, let nothing separate us from you. Help me be an agent of your life for all around me.

For further thought

Jairus had power and authority, and the woman suffering from haemorrhages had little. Yet Jesus considered both.

Bread at the table

Read Mark 7:24–30

[Jesus] said to her, 'Let the children be fed first, for it is not fair to take the children's food and throw it to the dogs.' But she answered him, 'Sir, even the dogs under the table eat the children's crumbs.'

(verses 27–28)

Church can be a place of sanctuary for all kinds of people. I think of a young mother under new pressure from social services, a man recovering from cancer treatment, a woman who recently lost her husband. We all come to church for different reasons, impelled by yearnings for health and wholeness of which we aren't always even aware. Once, when I was photocopying in the church office, a young man ran in to the small room, terrified, to hide from a group of boys chasing him! Sanctuary, indeed.

The Syrophoenician woman was no different. She wanted healing for her daughter, who was sick. She had heard of Jesus. She fell at his feet and begged him to help. Because we often forget Jesus' Jewish identity, this story can be quite shocking: Jesus at first pushes the woman away because she is not from Jesus' own people. In Matthew's version of the story, the disciples also help keep the woman away from Jesus (Matthew 15:23).

In part, the Syrophoenician woman reminds us of the importance of welcoming others. But she also reminds us to keep in touch with our own need for God, our own yearnings and terrors. As people gathered around Jesus, we are not primarily the gatekeepers. We are people like this woman: worried parents, cancer survivors, widows, even teenagers seeking a dark corner. In a mostly Gentile Church which often forgets its Jewish connection, it is not a bad thing to be reminded of our reasons for seeking Jesus. We are the outsiders who are graciously taken in – taken in, and welcomed by the one who gives us bread from his table.

† God of all, we are all beggars at your table. And you welcome us as a generous host. Help us always make space for others.

For further thought

In your community, who slips through the cracks and is in need of being welcomed?

Healing touch

> **Read Mark 7:31–37**
>
> *He ... put his fingers into his ears, and he spat and touched his tongue. Then looking up to heaven, he sighed and said to him, 'Ephphatha', that is, 'Be opened.'*
>
> *(part of verses 33–34)*

The church where I worship, where my wife is minister, passes the peace in a big way. Before the Eucharist each Sunday, we get up from our seats and share a 'peace' before we share in the bread and wine. In a community like ours in which many are isolated, it is possible that it's the only physical touch some people have for several days.

Touch is important to Jesus. This little story, recorded only here in Mark, portrays Jesus healing through touch and wordless prayer (looking up to heaven) and even a sigh or groan (verses 33–34). Perhaps his actions are sympathetic, mimicking the opening of the ears and the loosening of the tongue. It is a vivid portrait of a healer at work.

Mark portrays Jesus' healing as a symbol of the collective hopes of his Jewish people. Isaiah 35 tells of the return of Israel from exile, and a sign of that redemption is that the deaf hear and the mute regain speech (Isaiah 35:5–6). The crowd's exclamation in Mark, 'He has done everything well' (verse 37), suggests that they interpret Jesus' actions in this larger messianic context. Jesus is the one who, they think, will inaugurate a new age of redemption, healing and restoration. Their exclamation of 'well' even echoes God's speech looking on creation in Genesis 1:31, that everything was 'very good'.

Jesus' touch is a sign of God's rule of peace being made real on earth. For me, my church's passing of the peace is a sign of that rule, too. It shows me that God is real and alive among us, through our touch.

† God of healing touch, we praise you for your healing energy in Jesus. May that same power dance in our world today, joyfully and for all.

For further thought

For Mark, Jesus' healing miracles are not about his 'divine' nature, but rather his status as the long-awaited anointed one of God: the Messiah of Israel.

Friday 23 April
Seeing clearly

Read Mark 8:22–26

Then Jesus laid his hands on his eyes again; and he looked intently and his sight was restored, and he saw everything clearly.

(verse 25)

Like the story from yesterday, today's story is found only here. Although brief, it is a turning point in Mark; with another healing story, that of blind Bartimaeus in 10:46–52, it brackets Jesus' journey to the cross. Somewhat strangely, the story today tells of Jesus failing to heal. Jesus needs another try before the blind man can see clearly. In the very next passage, Peter rebukes Jesus for saying he must die on a cross (verse 32).

Perhaps Mark is suggesting that discipleship takes time: we don't understand everything right away. Some things only gradually swim into focus. The mystery of the cross seems to be one of those things.

The importance Mark gives this little story might also highlight the physical aspects of following Jesus. Like the man healed, we are to look for real signs of God's rule in the world around us. We, too, are to touch and heal (as in Mark 6:13). Our vision and our action are important; we've seen in these stories how Jesus uses more than just words to show God's reign.

My children are learning to play piano, and the sound of their playing echoes in the house most afternoons. Although they make many mistakes, I can also hear them gradually gaining proficiency and skill. Perhaps following Jesus is more about the mistakes we make, the bits we get wrong, than about getting everything perfect the first time around. Mark seems to think so.

† Lord, help me understand that I am central to your rule of justice and peace.

For further thought

Which of the senses or faculties would you use as a metaphor for your growth as a Christian?

Saturday 24 April
Glory and agony

Read Mark 9:14–29

When he had entered the house, his disciples asked him privately, 'Why could we not cast it out?' He said to them, 'This kind can come out only through prayer.'

(verses 28–29)

Among the healing stories in Mark's Gospel, only the story of the 'Gerasene demoniac', with which we started this week, is longer than the one today. Perhaps the boy suffered from epilepsy, as suggested in Matthew 17:15. For Mark and his audience, the boy is possessed by an unclean spirit so strong that the disciples are not able to cast it out.

Jesus' healing of this boy comes just after the Transfiguration, the story in which Jesus is raised up and glorified along with Moses and Elijah, two teachers from Israel's storied past. Perhaps this narrative order is significant. Coming down from the mountain of glory, Jesus doesn't encounter just the world's same old problems, but enters an intensified struggle with the sources of evil in the world. It is the same pattern that Jesus experienced after his baptism; he was immediately thrust into the wilderness and was tempted by Satan (1:9–13). Jesus manifests God's glory, but this glory is not merely otherworldly. It is firmly angled against the sickness and horrors of our world.

This story suggests that Jesus' glory is not a miracle cure for sickness and sin. Jesus' glory must not blind us to the suffering of so many in our world, especially those without easy access to modern medicine. Coming down from the mountain, Jesus attended to this boy, rigid with convulsions, and his terrified father. We must do likewise.

† God of all glory, be present today to those suffering in silence, without hope of a cure, or without access to modern medicine. And inspire us all to hope and help.

For further thought

Do churches do enough to help people cope with illness? A simple anointing with oil on the hand or forehead in worship, or just prayer, can help people heal.

The Gospel of Mark (2) – 1 Jesus the healer

The Gospel of Mark (2) – 2 Jesus the teacher

Notes by **Bruce Jenneker**

Before retiring in 2019, Bruce served as director of liturgy at Trinity Church Wall Street in New York City. He was formerly senior priest of the Diocese of Saldanha Bay and Rector of All Saints Church in Durbanville, a suburb of Cape Town. Worship and liturgy have been his lifelong passions. He served as precentor at Trinity Church on Copley Square, Boston, Massachusetts, and canon precentor of Washington National Cathedral and of St George's Cathedral in Cape Town. Bruce has used the NRSVA for these notes.

Sunday 25 April
Jesus' astonishing wisdom

Read Mark 6:1–13

On the sabbath [Jesus] began to teach in the synagogue, and many who heard him were astounded. They said, 'Where did this man get all this? What is this wisdom that has been given to him? What deeds of power are being done by his hands!'

(verse 2)

Mark's Gospel is testimony to the urgency of the person and message of Jesus: episodes of immediate encounter, a rapid trajectory to the climax of the cross and the salvation it offers.

Matthew's Jesus is the teacher; Luke's Jesus is the healer. And yet Mark's Jesus points the way with a prophet's insistence: 'The time is fulfilled, and the kingdom of God has come near; repent, and believe in the good news' (1:15). He instructs his hearers in the way with a teacher's wisdom that encompasses the past and harnesses the future: '"Hear, O Israel: the Lord our God, the Lord is one; you shall love the Lord your God with all your heart, and with all your soul, and with all your mind, and with all your strength." The second is this, "You shall love your neighbour as yourself." There is no other commandment greater than these' (12:29–31).

There is a simplicity to this astonishing teaching: an inviting focus, an alluring possibility. We are invited to focus on this simplicity this week, and follow.

† Open the eyes of my heart, unstop my spirit's ears that I may listen and hear the words of life you speak and claim them.

Monday 26 April
God's Law overrides tradition

April

> **Read Mark 7:1–13**
>
> *[Jesus] said to them, 'Isaiah prophesied rightly about you hypocrites, as it is written, "This people honours me with their lips, but their hearts are far from me; in vain do they worship me, teaching human precepts as doctrines."'*
>
> *(verses 6–7)*

The human spirit is determined always and ever to reduce mystery to certainty, making sublime truth humdrum banality. Good ideas become strategic first and habits ultimately. We are prone to codify numinous truths and render them predictable.

Control rather than surrender comes naturally to us. We seem constitutionally unable to risk an open curiosity to the wonder of things. We are drawn to trust only what is familiar and make familiarity the criterion for security. Unexamined devotion to tradition is the enemy of the liberating vision that alone makes the future secure.

Soon we are imprisoned in a conservative legalism that preserves the past but refuses to envision a new, brighter, freer future. We impose this hard and fast, black and white worldview not only on ourselves but demand adherence to it from all those around us.

Our vocation is to reach beyond the hold that the past can have over us and follow Christ into the bright future of the gospel. This is our calling: to turn the world upside down, making darkness bright, overturning sorrow with joy and injustice with freedom and peace.

Our calling demands the courage of a brave witness. As the American novelist Kate Chopin wrote in her novel, *The Awakening*, first published in 1899: 'The bird that would soar above the level plain of tradition and prejudice must have strong wings. It is a sad spectacle to see the weaklings bruised, exhausted, fluttering back to earth' (Random House, 2004, p. 217).

† Unsettle me, free me from the shackles that bind me to unexamined old ways and set me free to risk the new possibility of love, joy and peace Christ's gospel brings.

For further thought

Examine how you view the behaviour of those closest to you, the practices and rituals of religious devotion, the structure of society and its political life.

The Gospel of Mark (2) – 2 Jesus the teacher

Evil is a choice and a commitment

> **Read Mark 7:14–23**
>
> *'For it is from within, from the human heart, that evil intentions come: fornication, theft, murder, adultery, avarice, wickedness, deceit, licentiousness, envy, slander, pride, folly. All these evil things come from within, and they defile a person.'*
>
> *(verses 21–23)*

The wisdom of Jesus is love – love of God, love of neighbour and love of self. This vocation to love demands commitment to self-knowledge. It is only by knowing ourselves that we can love ourselves. Without honest self-love we can love neither God nor our neighbours.

When we refuse to acknowledge who and what we are, we live in denial, enter the realm of falsehood and self-deceit in which it is easier to criticise and condemn others, declare events and things taboo. Hyper-critical of others and scrupulously meticulous ourselves, we proscribe acts and actions, demanding that both others and we ourselves avoid them.

It is easier to monitor our acts and actions and judge those of others than to examine the depths of our hearts. It is there where our choice of evil can take up residence even if we rigorously avoid evil acts and actions. We can meticulously fulfil all the external obligations of the good life while nurturing festering evil in our hearts. With discrimination and prejudice, avarice and covetousness, hatred and spite, mean-spiritedness and irritability firmly rooted in our deepest selves, we can deliberately present a holier-than-thou presence to others.

Prejudice and criticism, censure and condemnation come easily to us, but words are cheap and posturing is easy. Those who follow Christ must examine their hearts, for it is there where sin resides.

† Search me and know me, in your mercy reveal to me what I am; then let your love restore me, your grace empower me to be what I was created to be.

For further thought

Examine the patterns of your loving, the choices you make, and take stock of the extent to which you love God, your neighbour and yourself.

Wednesday 28 April
Discerning what is human and what is divine

Read Mark 8:27–33

But turning and looking at his disciples, [Jesus] rebuked Peter and said, 'Get behind me, Satan! For you are setting your mind not on divine things but on human things.'

(verse 33)

Jesus was thoroughly misunderstood by his contemporaries, the disciples not the least among them. He broke into history at a time and in a place that was deeply wounded, torn and troubled: Palestine under Roman rule. Outrage and resentment festered among the people. They hoped for the deliverance promised by the prophets. Initially they thought Jesus was indeed the promised Messiah, but he proved to be a disappointment to them; in the end they abandoned him.

His contemporaries saw in Jesus a quick political fix for persecution, exploitation and injustice. They were focused on earthly, human things.

We fall into the same trap. We want Jesus to be a magician to charm away all that we fear. We want Jesus to be a puppeteer to manipulate and control people and events as we desire. We want Jesus to be a celestial Santa Claus to bring as presents all that we hope for.

Like his contemporaries we do not want Jesus to usher in a new way of being human, a fresh way of engaging the world, time, life and death. Not for us this big, divine picture. We want a cure now, liberation here, in the midst of life's harsh realities. In contrast to this, the main attitudes we must foster are openness and confidence that God's truth will find a way among us. It is this faith that God is working God's purpose out that will save us.

† Come, Lord Jesus, come. Lift my eyes to see the world around me clearly, inspire my mind to know your presence and understand your will. Then make me the channel of your redeeming work.

For further thought

Examine your relationship with Jesus, your understanding of his mission and your part in it.

The Gospel of Mark (2) – 2 Jesus the teacher

April

119

The way of the cross

Read Mark 8:34–38

'If any want to become my followers, let them deny themselves and take up their cross and follow me. For those who want to save their life will lose it, and those who lose their life for my sake, and for the sake of the gospel, will save it.'

(verses 34b–35)

Jesus, the Suffering Son of God, relaunches time and remakes history. In this re-creation of all things, his self-sacrifice of all-giving love becomes the substrate of the universe, opening forever a renewed way of being human. Time and history are reconstituted by love, in love, with love and for love. It costs no less than everything. By it we gain much more than everything. By his loving self-offering all is done, all is given, all is forgiven, all is refreshed, redeemed, renewed.

The way of the cross, a tortured, agonising and brutal execution of innocence, is not the end but a new beginning. By bearing his cross – from the first rejection to the final desperate cry of abandonment – love indeed conquers all. His final triumphant shout from the cross as he breathes his last (Mark 15:37) is the trumpet call announcing the new beginning of the universe. Reality is refreshed, redeemed, renewed by victorious, enduring love. No longer are pride, greed, envy, resentment and jealousy the parameters of the human condition. Sin is forgiven, wickedness is overturned, evil is destroyed and death is overcome.

This is the cross we are called to bear, nothing less than love. Not for us the torture, agony and death. For us love is the call, the way and the life.

† Take me with you, Jesus as in love you accept rejection as with love you take up the cross as for love you suffer cruel death – that moved by love I will become loving too.

For further thought

Examine the cross you take up – is it suffering, an agonising responsibility, or is it love that you are called to be and do?

Friday 30 April
True greatness

Read Mark 9:30–41

[Jesus said,] 'Whoever wants to be first must be last of all and servant of all.' Then he took a little child and put it among them; and taking it in his arms, he said to them, 'Whoever welcomes one such child in my name welcomes me.'

(part of verses 35–37)

Jesus holds up a child as the paradigm for fulfilled Christian living. Not self-sufficient independence but basic need, not arrogant confidence but risk-taking trust, not flaunted strength but accepted weakness, these are the building blocks of the good life.

This is not what the world advertises as success. Ours is a 'dog-eat-dog' world, all about Me – invincible, unassailable, towering over all. This is a message of deceit to lead us down the garden path to self-destruction. We are quite different.

Here is the paradox of the gospel: the first must be last and servant of all. The expectations of the world are overturned: God's foolishness is wiser than human wisdom, and God's weakness is stronger than human strength (1 Corinthians 1:25).

Vulnerability, the openness to injury and rejection, is the first step. Only vulnerability can inspire dependence and faith. True greatness is openness to living love, being love.

The choice is ours, but it is counterintuitive. Not superficially, as the world thinks or values, not Me-Me-Me. Rather, reaching for the deeper truth of each person's place in the divine scheme of things; to find in the web of life true meaning, profound fulfilment and lasting peace.

To choose self first is a quick fix merely, a shortcut through a fleeting pleasure to isolation, alienation and loneliness. The deeper choice of life and its web of connectedness locates us where we are meant to be: turning, turning, turning, till we come round right.

† Take all that I am, the pride that deceives, the arrogance that limits, the resentment that embitters and make me wholly yours – a child, ready, accepting, and open to love and loving.

For further thought

Examine your life: are you afraid of being vulnerable? Are you able to risk being defenceless so that love will triumph in and through you?

Saturday 1 May
Distraction, confusion, integrity

Read Mark 9:42–50

[Jesus said to the disciples,] 'If any of you put a stumbling-block before one of these little ones who believe in me, it would be better for you if a great millstone were hung around your neck and you were thrown into the sea.'

(verse 42)

We are part of a rich and diverse universe, the work of a single Creator. Every creature bears the Creator's fingerprints, part of the Creator's plan and design: created, nurtured and cherished. Nothing is left out, nothing is excluded and nothing is left behind.

While all that is, is one, there is an apparently unavoidable conflict at the heart of things. In the aftermath of the First World War, the Irish poet Yeats wrote: 'Things fall apart; the centre cannot hold; / Mere anarchy is loosed upon the world' (from his poem 'The Second Coming', published in his collection *Michael Robartes and the Dancer* in 1920).

Things fall apart: within us, between us, among us. Nothing holds together: the web of life pulls apart, nature spirals from order into chaos.

To restore all things to the perfection in which and for which they are created, God does the unprecedented and surprising thing of taking human form and entering into human history. To gather all things together in an enduring and mutual harmony, God-in-Christ makes a willing self-sacrifice.

Christ depends on our participation in this saving work. Made in God's image, we too must be creative, boldly imaginative in this project to redeem and restore the universe, and ourselves with it.

† Loving healer, speak your tender words to lift me from the mire of chaos around me. Lift my eyes to glimpse the vision of the universe restored. Then use me as you will.

For further thought

Examine your willingness to share in the saving work of gathering when all is scattered, binding up when all is wounded, illuminating the darkness.

Michal's story

Notes by **Ann Conway-Jones**

Ann is a biblical scholar, teacher and freelance writer. She is an honorary research fellow at the University of Birmingham and The Queen's Foundation for Ecumenical Theological Education. She is passionate about bridging the gap between academic scholarship and the Church, aiming to deepen and enrich people's understanding of the Bible. She is also involved in Jewish–Christian relations, and fascinated by how differently Jews and Christians read scripture. She is Chair of Birmingham Council of Christians and Jews. Ann has used the NRSVA for these notes.

Sunday 2 May
David, Jonathan and Saul

Read 1 Samuel 18:1–16

Saul was afraid of David, because the Lord was with him but had departed from Saul ... But all Israel and Judah loved David; for it was he who marched out and came in leading them.

(verses 12 and 16)

We tend to read the Bible in small chunks. But that doesn't do justice to the sweep and intricacy of some of its narratives. The story of David, from 1 Samuel 1 to 1 Kings 2, has been declared a literary masterpiece. It follows David from handsome youth to helpless old man, charting the forces that shape him, and the consequences of his decisions, both for the nation and for his family. He is talented, brave and resourceful, but susceptible to the seductions of exercising power. His public triumphs are contrasted with private tragedy. This is an in-depth portrait of a complex man.

This week we follow one thread of David's story – that of his first wife, Michal, Saul's daughter. If people have heard of Michal at all, it will be because of her disapproval of David's dancing. But to understand the end of their relationship, we need to go back to the beginning. So we start by observing the complications of David's relationship with Saul's family. David and Jonathan, Saul's son, forge a strong bond. But as Saul senses that his own hold on power is draining away, he becomes increasingly jealous of David – the new popular hero.

† We pray for those consumed by jealousy, whose bitterness cannot be soothed.

Michal loves David

Read 1 Samuel 18:17–29

Now Saul's daughter Michal loved David. Saul was told, and the thing pleased him. Saul thought, 'Let me give her to him that she may be a snare for him ...' Therefore Saul said to David a second time, 'You shall now be my son-in-law.'

(part of verses 20–21)

Before he fells Goliath, David is told that the person who does so will win the hand of the king's daughter (1 Samuel 17:25). This now comes to pass, but only as part of a plan to get rid of David. Saul offers him first Merab and then Michal. By the time of the negotiations over Michal, Saul is so mistrustful of David that he only communicates with him through servants as intermediaries. He counts on David not being able to afford the bride-price, so he makes his outrageous and deadly demand for a hundred Philistine foreskins. The plan backfires, however, and Saul is obliged to honour his promise, losing his daughter to David. Saul's motives are utterly transparent; but we are left wondering about David. Are his protestations of unworthiness a sign of genuine humility, or of diplomatic grovelling? Is he already becoming a shrewd operator – careful not to reveal his political ambition?

Michal, we are told, loves David. This is the only time in the Old Testament that a woman is explicitly said to love a man. But we learn nothing else about her. As for David, he 'is well pleased to be the king's son-in-law' (verse 26). For him, this marriage is a matter of social advancement – there are no hints of inner feelings. The final two verses sum up the situation: David's success, with God on his side, Michal's love and Saul's fear. And by noting the interplay between information given and information withheld, we see what a carefully crafted narrative this is.

† We pray for those who fear that their love is not reciprocated.

For further thought

How do we ever know the motives behind another person's words?

Tuesday 4 May
Michal rescues David

Read 1 Samuel 19:8–17

David's wife Michal told him, 'If you do not save your life tonight, tomorrow you will be killed.' So Michal let David down through the window; he fled away and escaped.

(verses 11b–12)

In today's reading, Michal gets the opportunity to prove the extent of her love and commitment to David. She takes a considerable risk for him. Having learnt somehow of her father's latest plot against David, she takes vigorous action, displaying resourcefulness and courage. There are some intriguing allusions to the story of Rachel, who also protects her husband and helps him escape by deceiving her father over the household gods (see Genesis 31:25–35). The same Hebrew word *teraphim* is used in both episodes; although in Rachel's case it seems to refer to multiple small objects, which she can sit on, whereas here there is one figurine, large enough to be taken for a sleeping man, at least at a glance. In neither story is there any note of condemnation for these objects, making the translation 'idol', with its pejorative connotations, misleading. They may have been statuettes of ancestors, rather than household deities.

When confronted by her father about why she has let David escape, Michal produces a quick-thinking lie, pretending that David has threatened her. And how does David, the heroic warrior, behave? He simply escapes as fast as he can. Not a single word of thanks. What a contrast to his tearful parting from Jonathan, another of Saul's children prepared to cover for him (1 Samuel 20:41–2).

† We pray for those who are never thanked for their efforts and resourcefulness.

For further thought

Is Michal justified in deceiving her father to save her husband?

Michal given to Palti

Read 1 Samuel 25:39–44

*Abigail ... went after the messengers of David and became his wife.
David also married Ahinoam of Jezreel; both of them became his wives.
Saul had given his daughter Michal, David's wife, to Palti son of Laish,
who was from Gallim.*

(verses 42–44)

David is now an outlaw, living as the leader of a guerrilla band.
In the course of a dubious scheme to support themselves, which
looks very much like a protection racket, he meets Abigail, the wife
of Nabal. She is described as 'clever and beautiful' (1 Samuel 25:3).
These adjectives are never applied to Michal, despite her ingenuity.
Abigail is then fortuitously widowed – Nabal suffers some kind
of stroke on learning of the threat posed by David (deftly averted
by Abigail) and later dies. David is thus free to marry her. And he
takes another wife, Ahinoam. All we know about her is her place of
origin. Both these wives will later be captured by the Amalekites,
and David will have to rescue them (1 Samuel 30:5, 18).

Michal, meanwhile, so active and resourceful when we read about
her yesterday, is treated as a pawn in male power games, passed
by her father from one man to another. Saul is ensuring that David
can no longer claim kinship with the royal family in a bid for the
throne. Michal is not consulted, and we are given no indication of
how she copes with her new situation. Has she received any news
of David? Does she even know about Abigail and Ahinoam? Given
these gaps, we can but fill the silence with our own imaginations.

† We pray for women who are pushed around by men, treated as status symbols or
objects of conquest.

For further thought

How do you imagine Michal is feeling?

Michal taken back

Read 2 Samuel 3:12–16

Ishbaal sent and took [Michal] from her husband Paltiel the son of Laish. But her husband went with her, weeping as he walked behind her all the way to Bahurim. Then Abner said to him, 'Go back home!' So he went back.

(verses 15–16)

The tension between Saul and David has degenerated into a bitter civil war, and David is gradually gaining the upper hand. By now Saul is dead, and his sole surviving son, Ishbaal, is clinging on to the kingship of Israel. But the tribe of Judah has gone over to David (2 Samuel 2:10). And the real power behind the throne is Abner, the commander of Saul's army. He has fallen out with Ishbaal over one of Saul's concubines, Rizpah – another woman caught up in male power games. Abner can also no doubt see the way the wind is blowing, and decides to change sides. As David seizes the opportunity of Abner's defection, he makes his move to get Michal back. There is no hint of any personal motive; she is a means of reinforcing his claim to the throne, and of persuading Saul's subjects to give him their loyalty.

And still we have no idea of how Michal is feeling – does she still think of herself as David's wife, or has she settled into being with Palti? For in contrast to David's calculating attitude, Palti suddenly emerges out of the shadows as a vulnerable human being with real emotions. We know almost nothing about him, not even the correct spelling of his name – Palti (1 Samuel 25:44) or Paltiel (2 Samuel 3:15)?

He doesn't say a word, but his tears speak volumes. He represents the human cost of political manoeuvres – his grief swept aside by a military leader obeying orders.

† We pray for those who weep, inconsolable in their loss.

For further thought

Palti springs off the page for a mere three verses. Why do his tears move us so?

May

Michal's story

David dances

Read 2 Samuel 6:12–19

David danced before the Lord with all his might; David was girded with a linen ephod. So David and all the house of Israel brought up the ark of the Lord with shouting, and with the sound of the trumpet.

(verses 14–15)

Now we come to the final scene between David and Michal. David is at the height of his powers, ruling over all Israel and Judah (2 Samuel 5:3). He escorts the ark, the symbol of God's presence, into his new capital city. He is popular and triumphant. His actions are described in detail. Dressed in a linen ephod, a priestly garment, he not only dances before the ark as it processes, but performs the priestly duty of sacrifice and blesses the people. He certainly knows how to fuel his popularity, with a distribution of food.

Michal is an unhappy spectator of the ark's grand entry. At the beginning of their story, she helped David escape through a window. Now she looks on at him from a distance through a window, in seething contempt. Her feelings of disgust are not simply caused by David's present exhibitionism – they are the result of the whole history of their relationship. She has loved him, and saved his life. But all she has ever been to him is the 'daughter of Saul' (verse 16), a useful asset in his designs on her father's throne. He has taken a harem of other wives – by now Ahinoam and Abigail have been joined by Maacah, Haggith, Abital and Eglah (2 Samuel 3:2–5) – showing her no gratitude or respect, let alone love.

† We pray for those whose relationship is at breaking point, whose love has turned to bitterness.

For further thought

How would you assess the gulf between David's public persona and the turmoil of his private life?

Saturday 8 May
Michal shamed

Read 2 Samuel 6:20–23

But Michal the daughter of Saul came out to meet David, and said, 'How the king of Israel honoured himself today, uncovering himself today before the eyes of his servants' maids, as any vulgar fellow might shamelessly uncover himself!'

(verse 20b)

David returns home to a confrontation with Michal. This is the first reported dialogue between them. And it is an explosion of angry sarcasm. Michal's love has turned to bitter scorn. She addresses David in the third person, using his public title, 'king of Israel' – not meant as a compliment. She is a king's daughter, and he has come from nowhere to usurp her father's throne. His behaviour is still vulgar – enjoying flaunting himself in his short ephod before the adoring female 'fans'. But David is unrepentant, secure in his sense of himself as divinely appointed king. He will define what counts as honourable. And he rubs Michal's nose in it, utterly humiliating her and her family. She has no answer – David is left with the last word.

The final sentence tells us that Michal, described as Saul's daughter rather than David's wife, remains childless. Is this simply an indication that David and Michal were never intimate again, or does it imply divine punishment? The biblical narrative of their relationship works on several levels. At times it reads like a historical novel. On the one hand, David is presented as God's choice of king, but on the other, his moral failings are clearly on display. He is no pious role model, but a complex manipulative leader, whose public image is at odds with the turbulence of his private life. Our sympathies are engaged by those with whom he is at odds. This undercuts simplistic notions about God's will, and forces us to ask probing questions about taking responsibility for the consequences of our fallibility.

† We pray for those longing to hold a child of their own, but fearing that it will never happen.

For further thought
Has reading Michal's story given you a new perspective on the depth and richness of biblical narrative?

May

Michal's story

Readings in the shorter Epistles – 1 Do good

Notes by **Revd Eric Rew**

Eric is a priest in the Church of England. He has served both in chaplaincies and in parish ministries and currently lives in Northamptonshire with his family. Leisure interests include art, poetry, science, science fiction and cooking. He has a blog at www.sundrytimes2.wordpress.com. He believes that faith, life and spirituality are 'all of a piece'. So, for example, trying to act according to God's will in a supermarket is just as real as when making life-changing decisions. Eric has used the NRSVA for these notes.

Sunday 9 May
More than words

Read Titus 1

To the pure all things are pure, but to the corrupt and unbelieving nothing is pure.

(verse 15a)

In one episode of the TV Sci-fi series *Star Trek*, Captain Kirk is set to overcome the robots which have taken control. His shipmate, Mr Spock, tells one of those androids that everything Kirk says is a lie. Once the robot has accepted that, Kirk says that he is lying. That sets the androids off in logical confusion which stops them in their tracks. The humans just laugh.

Paul wrote that, according to a Cretan, 'Cretans are always lying.' When you think about it, that piece of confusing logic must be a joke. It comes in the middle of the first chapter in his letter to Titus. Paul is coaching him in his work of leading other Christian leaders. Much of what he is writing here is serious: what to look for in a leader and the challenges of those whose idea of leadership puts making money before being authentic.

In making his joke, Paul shows that if you are always corrupt and lie, in the end you only bamboozle yourself while the rest of us are laughing. This is especially true for those of us who wish to lead. Character and behaviour matter: being good is more than just words.

† Dear Lord, help us to be people who live truthfully, so that we may lead others to the truth of the life-giving gospel. Amen

Monday 10 May
Do good for the sake of the gospel

Read Titus 2

Show yourself in all respects a model of good works, and in your teaching show integrity, gravity, and sound speech that cannot be censured; then any opponent will be put to shame, having nothing evil to say of us.

(verses 7–8)

I'm sorry, but I don't like this chapter. It seems to me to be full of anachronistic domestic relationships, against natural equality and contrary to human rights. Where is the complementary relationship between equals? Why are slaves basically told to behave themselves and do what they are told without complaining? Don't like it? Tough! Rant over.

Having said that, there is something to be said for being temperate, prudent, sound in faith and love. Good point about not being slanderous or 'slaves to drink' (verse 2). Self-control appears three times so I think that that must be important too.

Now, at the risk of appearing like a self-appointed busybody guardian of your morals, I ask you this: when was the last time you stopped to reconsider how much you imbibe alcoholic drink? Of course, there are those for whom their relationship with alcohol is an illness and who must give it up entirely. For others, however, it can also be a tricky relationship. If you are more inclined to say, 'I *need* a drink' than to say, 'I *would like* a drink' then that might be telling you something. A maxim I go by is that it is OK to have a drink when you are in a good mood to celebrate something. On the other hand, it only makes matters worse if you drink in order to try to cheer yourself up.

I once knew someone who was good company in the morning – before the pubs opened. As the day wore on, he became more stubborn and crass and I felt more and more uncomfortable. He said he could take his drink. Maybe. But I couldn't take his drinking. He died a few years ago and it left me with mixed feelings about him.

† Dear Lord, help us to build relationships with the people we live and work with. Help us to behave in a way that communicates the gospel of grace, which brings salvation to all. Amen

For further thought

For the sake of peace, Paul takes for granted the household order of his time. Should we ever disrupt the order for the sake of the gospel?

Tuesday 11 May
Cart before the horse?

Read Titus 3

But when the goodness and loving-kindness of God our Saviour appeared, he saved us, not because of any works of righteousness that we had done, but according to his mercy, through the water of rebirth and renewal by the Holy Spirit.

(verses 4–5)

We were holidaying in Suffolk one summer and had some spare time before arriving at the next B&B. So, we meandered through the countryside until it was time for a cuppa and a bun. I don't remember much about the tearoom, but I do remember the stables next door. Not every detail, but the horses – they were huge Shire horses whose duties once included working for a brewery, shifting a great many barrels over the years. They were retired now that modern vehicles had taken over.

I can't say I have ever put a cart before a horse. In fact, I am not sure how it would be done because either the horse would have to push the cart or somehow go backward – neither of these seem practicable. But with a horse in its rightful place, great loads could be moved and people could travel.

In this letter to Titus, a great deal has been said about Christian behaviour and conduct. I would suggest that that is the cart. Whether the cart has a heavy or an expensive load, a horse-drawn cart is not going very far without a horse. That, I suggest, is faith.

Let's not push the analogy too far: it would not do to boast about a heavier cart or a stronger horse. Statements like 'I work harder than you' or 'If you only had as much faith as I have' smack of pride. Let's remember that God saved us *for* doing good, not *by* us doing good.

† Dear Lord, in water we are reborn and by your Spirit we are renewed. Let us be inspired by our faith to do good things, trusting above all not in ourselves but in your mercy. Amen

For further thought

Can you think of ways in which Christians try to 'put the cart before the horse'? If you do not do 'X', are you not a Christian?

Thanksgiving and prayer

Read Philemon 1:1–7

Grace to you and peace from God our Father and the Lord Jesus Christ. When I remember you in my prayers, I always thank my God because I hear of your love for all the saints and your faith towards the Lord Jesus.

(verses 3–5)

Whether it's watching TV series like *Downton Abbey* or visiting historic stately homes, many of us have a fascination with the small communities which are based on class. There are the masters, the rich, the ones who reside 'above stairs' and then there are the servants, the poor, the ones who live 'below stairs'. Although their daily lives are connected and intertwined there is a definite separation between them. Many of those of the rich family are barely aware of how life is experienced by their servants. One plot theme is when that barrier between the classes is breached and the consequences that follow. For example, when a maid marries 'above her station'.

Paul is writing to his friend about one of his slaves. The contrast between master and slave is much more severe than the class distinctions in Downton, say. Philemon, the owner of Onesimus, has complete control over his slave. He would be within his rights to have him executed for running away. To him it could be little different to putting down a rabid dog. Paul is looking for a better outcome than that.

Paul chooses not to be confrontational but to appeal to Philemon's better nature. He begins by remembering his family and then tells him how much he appreciates him. 'Thank God for Philemon' is the gist of his prayer.

† Who are those people you could say 'refresh the hearts of the saints'? Have you met any? Thank God for them.

For further thought

When dealing with controversial issues, does being positive take centre stage – or is that approach just an afterthought?

Paul and Onesimus

Read Philemon 1:8–21

I am appealing to you for my child, Onesimus, whose father I have become during my imprisonment. Formerly he was useless to you, but now he is indeed useful both to you and to me. I am sending him, that is, my own heart, back to you.

(verses 10–12)

It's worth the effort to read this letter to Philemon out loud. I reckon a famous actor could do it wonderfully. The reason is, I think, that this letter is Paul being most himself. He is not telling someone off or expounding important spiritual truths. Here he is talking to one friend about another. I imagine a twinkle in his eye and warmth in his persuasive voice. In fact, he is saying, 'Do this old geezer a favour, will you?' (verse 9) and, 'By the way, I am coming to visit you when I can' (verse 22).

Paul says that he has become fond of Onesimus in much the same way that he is of Philemon and his family. It is his hope that the slave who has become 'useless' by running away, may become more than useful by being welcomed as a fellow brother in Christ. Paul is not saying that Philemon should free all his slaves; rather he is saying that fellowship with Jesus Christ supersedes any master–slave relationship.

We do not know why Onesimus ran away – did he steal something which now Paul says he will repay? Was he disobedient? If so, Philemon owes Paul obedience which he pointedly writes he will not insist on. Or maybe, I wonder, is it the price of a slave that is owed?

We don't know what happened next. We do know that Onesimus 'the faithful and beloved brother' is mentioned in Paul's letter to the Colossians (4:9) and someone had good reason to keep this letter safe. I believe it ended well.

† Almighty God, your risen and ascended Son Jesus Christ came to proclaim good news and set people free. Help us to accept his grace and to work for true freedom for all. Amen

For further thought

What does slavery look like in our time? When is it better to work around 'the system' and when is it better to work against it?

Friday 14 May
Faithful engineering

Read Jude 1:1–16

These are blemishes on your love-feasts, while they feast with you without fear, feeding themselves. They are waterless clouds carried along by the winds; autumn trees without fruit, twice dead, uprooted; wild waves of the sea, casting up the foam of their own shame; wandering stars …

(verses 12–13a)

When the pioneers of jet-plane travel first designed their passenger aeroplanes, they very much had the luxury market in mind. One feature was having windows that were at a convenient height and size to provide a good view. They were roughly rectangular, as you would expect. Unfortunately, after a series of crashes it was discovered that the windows had a design flaw: metal fatigue which built up unseen, particularly at the corners. They fixed the issue by changing the shape – more rounded – and the position of the windows.

The problem with hidden flaws is just that: they are hidden and you might not see them until it is just too late to avoid disaster.

Jude is alluding to something similar in the church he is writing to. There are people who on the surface seem as genuine as the next person, but who also represent a defect, a blemish (verse 12), which could break and divide the church at any time. He suggests some warning signs.

These people deny that Jesus Christ is Lord. They reject authority – as distinct from challenging authority which may be needed from time to time. They are the sort of people for whom ministry is a profit-making exercise (verse 11) – but show favouritism when it suits them (verse 16).

The take-home point I get from these verses is a warning to be alert to cracks beneath the surface of our church life, to keep an eye on our leaders but also to take care that I do not behave in the self-serving way described here either.

† Pray for all those with leadership responsibility in our churches. Pray that they may discern the difference between those who rightly challenge authority and those who destructively reject it, come what may.

For further thought

When I worried that 'keeping an eye out for anything suspicious' was leading to distrust, I was advised that 'respectful doubt' was called for. What do you think?

May

Readings in the shorter Epistles – 1 Do good

Saturday 15 May
Looking to the horizon

Read Jude 1:17–25

But you, beloved, build yourselves up on your most holy faith; pray in the Holy Spirit; keep yourselves in the love of God; look forward to the mercy of our Lord Jesus Christ that leads to eternal life.

(verses 20–21)

When I was first learning to drive, I was quite nervous. Above all else I wanted to avoid any kind of crash. Eventually my confidence would grow, and I would learn skills to enable me to drive safely. But in my first lessons I kept looking down at the car bonnet. I had not thought it through, but my instinct was that if I could see where the front of the car was, I could avoid bumping into things. That only worked if I drove rather slowly.

Fortunately, my driving instructor understood what was going on. He told me to lift my gaze towards the horizon. I would still be able to have the front of the car in my vision, but I would also be able to see what was ahead as well as where I was going. As in verse 21 in today's reading, he also warned me, 'Look where you are going because you will go where you are looking.'

I think it is true generally. If we have an eye to our destination, then we are more likely to go in the right direction to get there. So, if we believe our destination is eternal life, then looking to Jesus will point us in the right direction. Here the life on offer is full of mercy, not punishment. 'Looking forward' can mean 'expecting a good thing to happen and being happy about it now'. It also means facing forward, not looking backward all the time.

So, consider: are you looking forward to God's mercy?

† Now to the one who is able to guard you from stumbling, and to set you blameless before his glory with great joy, to the only God and Saviour, through our Lord Jesus Christ, be glory, majesty, might and authority before all ages and now and into eternity. Amen (author's translation of verses 24–25).

For further thought

Are you looking where you are going? Are you going where you are looking?

Readings in the shorter Epistles – 2 The way of love

Notes by **Kate Hughes**

Kate worked for the Church in Southern Africa for 14 years. Since her return to the UK she has worked as a freelance book editor, specialising in theology, including recently a number of books on Islam. She lives in a small council estate in Coventry with Looby, her Cavalier King Charles spaniel, is involved in her local community and preaches regularly at her local Anglican church. Kate has used the NRSVA for these notes.

Sunday 16 May
What we have heard and seen

May

Read 1 John 1

We declare to you what was from the beginning, what we have heard, what we have seen with our eyes, what we have looked at and touched with our hands, concerning the word of life.

(verse 1)

Scholars differ as to whether the writer of the Gospel of John and the writer of the three letters of John were the same person. There are similarities between their beliefs, but also differences, so it is perhaps safer to say just that the letters were written towards the end of the first century CE by someone who was a follower of Jesus from the beginning.

What the writer is passing on to those who receive his first letter is the assurance that what he has to say is genuine Christian teaching, heard from Jesus himself. God is no longer to be found only in the Jerusalem temple, which by this time had been destroyed. God appeared in a form that could be touched, looked at and listened to – the human person of Jesus who was also the Word of God, the Word that gives life. So what the letter is going to say can be trusted: to have fellowship with God is to be in the light, to have fellowship with each other and to be freed from our sinfulness (verse 7).

† Lord, help us through the reading of these letters to learn more clearly how to live in your light.

Monday 17 May
Living in the light

Read 1 John 2:1–17

… the darkness is passing away and the true light is already shining.

(part of verse 8)

We are offered a stark choice: we can belong to the darkness or we can belong to the light. To be in the dark is to be stuck in our sinfulness, bogged down in self-centredness, unable to enter into fellowship with others. We will be seen as people of the light when we allow Jesus to deal with our sin, and above all when we live in the Jesus way: 'Whoever says, "I have come to know him", but does not obey his commandments, is a liar' (verse 4); we have to 'walk just as he walked' (verse 6).

And the place where the light of God should be shown most clearly? The fellowship of those who know and obey God – the Church. The Church is not just a building (in John's day there were no special Christian buildings); it is not just a casual social gathering of those who happen to like that sort of thing. The Church is a fellowship of those who have allowed God to deal with their sin and who seek to follow his commandments. In them the light of God shines out in the darkness of the world. Someone once said that 'Christianity is caught, not taught', and a Christian congregation who love one another and whose love spills out to all with whom they come in contact is a shining light that draws others to it. 'But whoever hates another believer is in the darkness' (verse 11); a congregation torn by quarrels and hatred has ceased to be the Church, it has fallen back into darkness.

† Lord, help your Church to be a place of light, drawing others out of their darkness into fellowship with you and each other.

For further thought

How far is your own church a place of light that welcomes others to join its fellowship?

Passed from death to life

Read 1 John 3:11–24

We know that we have passed from death to life because we love one another. Whoever does not love abides in death.

(verse 14)

The ultimate place of darkness is the grave. Whether a body is buried in the earth, cremated, shut away in a cave or exposed in the open air, the light that was in it has been extinguished by physical death. But John is clear that the end of physical life is not the only sort of death that human beings can experience. Christians are called to follow Jesus by being channels of God's love in the world. The Holy Spirit is the spirit of love, always extending the boundaries of God's kingdom through those who are committed to Christ. This is what human beings are created to be – co-workers with God through the Holy Spirit. The love within the fellowship of the church will draw people in and overflow in service to others. Those who do not love may be physically alive, but they experience a kind of death – they are not being fully human. It is the love of God working in us that provides the continuity which is resurrection.

The local church I belong to is dedicated to St Francis of Assisi, and we use the so-called Prayer of St Francis as our community prayer (it was not written by St Francis but is very much in his spirit). I say it for all those (including myself) who are not behaving as the human beings God has created them to be – who are not 'instruments of his peace', who give way to hatred, who seek vengeance for injuries, who block the flow of God's love to the world, who are in darkness.

† Lord, may your Spirit love in and through us, so that we may live in your light.

For further thought

In what ways do you 'block the flow of God's love to the world'?

Wednesday 19 May
God is love

Read 1 John 4:7–21

We love because he first loved us.

(verse 19)

We sometimes sing a chorus at my church that begins by saying that the greatest thing for us is loving God – and it always irritates me! I want to stand up and say, 'No it isn't! The greatest thing is God loving us!' 'In this is love, not that we loved God but that he loved us and sent his Son' (verse 10). The love of God for every human being he has made – and for everything he has created – is the one unshakeable fact of life. We do not have to earn it; we can reject it; we can try to live as if it doesn't exist; we can treat God as a tyrant who will punish us if we take the smallest wrong step. But none of that will make the slightest difference to God. God is love. He cannot stop loving, because if he did he would stop being God. Whether we like it or not, we cannot prevent God loving us (and we all have moments when we wish God would leave us alone).

Even on the cross, God in Jesus never stopped loving us. In terrible pain, he forgave his torturers, he reassured the thief suffering beside him, he cared for his mother. As a real human being, he had a moment when he had to cling on in faith to the fact of God's love (Mark 15:34), but if we want to know how we can and should love, Jesus shows us the way. Secure in God's love, we can dare to love others.

† Thank you, Lord, that with all my failures and littleness you never stop loving me and enabling me to love others.

For further thought

Do you know how much God loves you? If not, make time to think about it!

Thursday 20 May
Conquerors of the world

Read 1 John 5:1–5, 13–21

Who is it that conquers the world but the one who believes that Jesus is the Son of God?

(verse 5)

The world often looks a pretty dark place. There are wars, refugees, terrorist bombs, harvests destroyed by climate change, earthquakes, plane crashes, Ebola and Covid-19 outbreaks – the pain and grief of human existence seem never-ending. And I don't suppose the world will look much better when you read these notes in 2021. And it certainly looked much the same when John was writing to the Christians of his time. So how can John talk about conquering this world?

Most of us are not called to be another Mother Teresa or an international peacemaker. But we still have to conquer the world – or it will conquer us. Here 'the world' means those things in life that oppose God, that impose upon us beliefs and ways of behaviour that are not those of God. Do we see other people as rivals for the good things of life – or as children of God? Do we work just to earn more money or get a promotion – or as an opportunity to serve others? How do we spend our money? Make use of our education? Deal with the difficulties and suffering of life? Spend our leisure time? Bring up our children? If we try to receive God's love as it is shown in Jesus and pass it on to others, then the world will have no power over us; we shall conquer it.

† Thank you that your love enables us to break the power of the world over us.

For further thought
What influence do 'the world' and its thinking have in your own life? What might you need to change in order to conquer the world?

This is love

Read 2 John

And this is love, that we walk according to his commandments; this is the commandment just as you have heard it from the beginning – you must walk in it.

(verse 6)

When I was younger, I struggled for a long time with the words of Jesus in John 15:14: 'You are my friends if you do what I command you.' It seemed to me that Jesus was saying, 'If you don't do what I say I won't love you anymore' – exactly the sort of thing that parents should *not* say to their children, or someone to their friends!

But now, more and more, I am discovering the depth of the love that God has for us. His love goes much further than simply a kindly attitude towards us. He has created us to be his co-workers, citizens of his kingdom, filled so full with his love that it will overflow to everyone we meet. And if we are responding to God's love, working together with him, we need to know what his plan is and where we fit into it – we need to 'walk according to his commandments'. Only if we do this will we be able to love others, especially those within the fellowship of the Church.

We cannot do this unless we first allow God to love us. That gives us the security from which we can reach out in love to others. This is where being a Christian starts, where it carries on as we learn to work with God in a fully human life, and where it ends (as far as this life is concerned) as the love of God goes with us into eternal life. This is what we have heard from the beginning. Walk in it.

† Lord, help us to discover more and more the joy of co-operating with your love.

For further thought

What does it mean in your life to 'walk according to [God's] commandments'?

Saturday 22 May
Do not imitate evil

Read 3 John

Beloved, do not imitate what is evil but imitate what is good.

(verse 11a)

I have seen parents blush when their young children come out with a phrase they have heard said at home that is not really suitable for public use – swearing is often involved! Humans learn by imitation, and an important part of parenting is to be good role models. We saw earlier in this week's notes that we can love because God first loves us – we imitate this love, helped by the Holy Spirit.

But it is important that we have good things to imitate, because we can also learn by imitating the wrong things. Teenagers start taking drugs because they want to be accepted by the other people in their class or the local gang. People fail as parents because their only experience of parenting is the bad example of their own parents. Our whole outlook on life can be bent if we try to imitate someone who will stop at nothing to be rich and successful.

It is important to deliberately imitate what is good. It helps if we direct our thoughts to what, in Paul's words to the Philippians (Philippians 4:8–9), is honourable, just, pure, pleasing, commendable, excellent and worthy of praise. It helps to look out for people who are worthy of imitation, perhaps members of our church. But above all, of course, our role model is Jesus, who embodies the love of God in all he says and does. We may not be called to imitate his exact actions, but we share his Spirit and, like him, can embody God's love towards his world.

† Spirit of Jesus, give us the wisdom to know what is good and the power to imitate it.

For further thought

What can you do in your own life to recognise and imitate what is good?

The underside of history – 1 Women of spirit

Notes by **Revd Mandy Briggs**

Mandy is a Methodist minister who lives in Bristol. She is the Education Officer at the New Room (John Wesley's Chapel), the oldest Methodist building in the world (newroombristol.org.uk), on Twitter at @NewRoomBristol and @mandbristol. Mandy has used the NRSVA for these notes.

Sunday 23 May
All change

Read Acts 2:1–21

All of them were filled with the Holy Spirit and began to speak in other languages, as the Spirit gave them ability.

(verse 4)

Everything changed at Pentecost.

Even though the disciples had been told by Jesus to wait in Jerusalem for the coming of the Holy Spirit, they had absolutely no idea what to expect. When the Spirit came, through sound, through flame, through language – they were changed forever.

As we read the familiar story again, here's a question you may never have asked – where were the women? It is easy to engage with the story of Pentecost and assume that it was just men who received the Holy Spirit. But going back to the preceding chapter, we read in Acts 1:14 that women were praying with the men in the upper room, including Jesus' mother, Mary. And when the Holy Spirit came, the verses emphasise that *all* were together throughout the event and *all* were filled with spiritual power. That means women as well as men – and we are encouraged to imagine all of them sharing the good news on the city streets.

The theme of this week's readings is 'Women of spirit'. We're going to be meeting strong, resourceful women who made a difference to the world around them. May their stories speak to us.

† God of equality, who loves all people, thank you for using both women and men in your work of sharing the gospel.

Tamar's dilemma

> **Read Genesis 38:6–26**
>
> *Then Judah acknowledged them and said, 'She is more in the right than I …'*
>
> *(verse 26a)*

Have you heard of the expression 'stuck between a rock and a hard place'? When we meet Tamar, she is in this kind of difficult position. Her husband has died, leaving her childless; but in this society, she has a right to bear children. Her husband's brother is legally required to help but will not, because he fears losing part of his own inheritance.

The next brother in line is far too young to be a father; so Tamar is left in limbo by her father-in-law, Judah. She is sent back to her father's house and left to live as a widow. Judah should take up the obligation himself, but he ignores the situation and Tamar is unable to remarry while he does so.

But Tamar knows her rights. We might struggle with the fact that she tricks Judah into getting her pregnant; but actually, under the law at the time, she was taking steps to claim her right to have a child. However uncomfortable her plan of action makes us, in the end Judah recognises that Tamar has forced his hand; she has been assertive enough to challenge his abandonment of her. When he attempts to blame Tamar and have her killed, her calm response leads to his confession: 'She is more in the right than I' (verse 26a).

In a patriarchal society, it was extremely difficult for a woman to take charge of a situation and claim her rights; but Tamar did so.

† Compassionate God, we pray for women we know who are facing difficult times right now; we ask that you would give them strength, hope and a way forward.

For further thought

In 2018, a charity was formed called 'Rights of Women – helping women through the law'. Find out more at www.rightsofwomen. org.uk.

May

The underside of history – 1 Women of spirit

Tuesday 25 May
Call the midwives

Read Exodus 1:15–21

But the midwives feared God; they did not do as the king of Egypt commanded them, but they let the boys live.

(verse 17)

I'm a big fan of the BBC TV show *Call The Midwife*. Set in the 1950s/60s, this popular drama series features a group of community-based midwives and trained nuns supporting families in the East End of London. As well as dealing with births, deaths and everything in between, the midwives and nuns cope with their own personal challenges amid a background of social change which is well documented by the programme's writers.

Call The Midwife could be classed as 'heart-warming nostalgia telly' but this would be a mistake. It also shows the harsh reality of women's lives in those eras and does not shy away from addressing difficult and sometimes harrowing subjects. The midwives and nuns are resourceful and tenacious and will often go 'above and beyond' to ensure the health of their patients.

Shiphrah and Puah would have fitted right in. They also showed resourcefulness and tenacity – as well as a healthy disregard for misguided instructions – which saved the lives of many Hebrew baby boys. Even as they carried out their jobs diligently, they had the spirit and the determination to be subversive, putting their faith in God before the orders of the king. The cast of *Call The Midwife* would be proud.

† God of birth and death, thank you for Shiphrah and Puah's faith and healthy disregard for misguided authority. Please encourage, strengthen and support all those who work in healthcare.

For further thought

When is it OK to disobey instructions?

Claiming their rights

Read Numbers 27:1–11

You shall also say to the Israelites, 'If a man dies, and has no son, then you shall pass his inheritance on to his daughter.'

(verse 8)

You may have never heard of the Succession to the Crown Act of 2013. Let me tell you a bit more about it. This is a law which changed the sequence of members of the British Royal Family who are in line to the throne. Before this law came into force in 2015, only male heirs were allowed to inherit the throne directly. So, a younger son could displace an elder daughter in the line of succession. After the act became law in 2015, women were allowed to become direct heirs too.

This change in the law has interesting parallels with the five daughters of Zelophehad – Mahlah, Noah, Hoglah, Milcah and Tirzah. They stood before Moses and asked for their inheritance – even though property rights, money and possessions would have traditionally only been inherited by men. This would have caused uproar – but Moses said yes.

Even if you've never heard of these women before, they are to be celebrated and remembered for taking a stand and calling for change. And a pat on the back for Moses too – he asks God for wisdom and acts on what God tells him. It would have been so easy for him to say, 'Sorry – we can't do this – it's just not done,' but he was willing to make a bold decision. Although much of the male inheritance line still existed in Moses' ruling, the women were able to take their rightful place and inherit from their father.

† Listening God, today we pray for all those who work in the legal profession, that you might give them wisdom to uphold the law and courage to know when to challenge it.

For further thought

How do we understand the word 'inheritance' in relation to our faith? Read 1 Peter 1:3–4 for one understanding of this.

May

The underside of history – 1 Women of spirit

I don't want jewellery!

Read Judges 1:12–15

As she dismounted from her donkey, Caleb said to her, 'What do you want?'

(verse 14b)

I have a small box at home where I keep the jewellery that I inherited from my mum. It's not much – a couple of rings, a necklace, some earrings – but I treasure them. They are special because they belonged to her.

Achsah is not a well-known character in the Old Testament but she is definitely a woman of spirit. Her name in Hebrew means a piece of jewellery – more specifically, 'an ankle bracelet'! She is Caleb's only daughter and he obviously dotes on her. After Caleb 'gives' Achsah to the soldier Othniel in marriage, Achsah tells Othniel to ask her father for some land, but for whatever reason he doesn't. So, she decides to go and make the request herself.

Traditionally, women were given jewellery or money as gifts, but never land. So Achsah is bold – and her father loves her so much that he doesn't just give her one piece of land but the 'upper and lower' lands which are fertile and full of wells. There's a powerful relationship metaphor in this short reading. A parent's love for their child leads to an extravagant gift motivated by love.

I treasure my mum's jewellery but I treasure the memory of her love and care much more. God our loving Parent longs to fill our lives with gifts of love – and that is something we can truly treasure.

† God of love, when I struggle to value myself, help me to know that I am your beloved child.

For further thought

Matthew 6:21 says: 'For where your treasure is, there your heart will be also.' What or whom do you treasure most in life?

Getting the message

Read 1 Samuel 25:4–19

But one of the young men told Abigail, Nabal's wife, 'David sent messengers out of the wilderness to salute our master; and he shouted insults at them.'

(verse 14)

There is a well-known TV advert in Britain which goes something like this. A camera pans around a richly decorated room where men and women in elegant gowns and tuxedos are talking, laughing and clinking glasses. The camera focuses in on a large tray of chocolates of a particular brand piled up on a table, or being handed around by a waiter. There is general appreciation, then someone exclaims, 'Ah, Ambassador … with (*the name of the chocolates*) you are really spoiling us!' The chocolates in question are not high-end or exclusive – but in this advert they are seen as the height of good hospitality and diplomacy.

Today's reading is like the beginning of an advert or a dramatic film. It sets the scene for an act of diplomacy in the face of high tension. The expected host, Nabal, turns out to be inhospitable and hostile to David's representatives. There are definitely no chocolates being passed around and the situation deteriorates until there is the threat of a potentially fatal face-off between the two men.

It is time for a different kind of diplomacy – and here Abigail steps in. She listens carefully and creates a bold plan to defuse the situation. She has to act quickly and carefully if her plan is going to work. And so, taking other gifts of food, she makes her way to see her husband's nemesis. She is taking a huge risk – and she has no idea if her plan to achieve peace will work. But in the name of peace, she is willing to try.

† God, we pray for peacemakers and diplomats who seek to maintain good relationships between countries and peoples.

For further thought
How far would you go to achieve peace?

May

The underside of history – 1 Women of spirit

Saturday 29 May
A woman of spirit

Read 1 Samuel 25:23–35

David said to Abigail, 'Blessed be the Lord, the God of Israel, who sent you to meet me today!'

(verse 32)

As we continue the story of Abigail in the book of 1 Samuel, it is clear that we are reading the story of a remarkable woman. Abigail is resourceful, intelligent, courageous and willing to take risks to step into the gap of mistrust created by her husband. She is a brilliant peacemaker between her household, and David and his men.

This story is remarkable for another reason. Abigail's speech, in verses 24–31, is one of the longest pieces of recorded speech by a woman in the Old Testament. In the patriarchal world in which she lived, it is rare that her name and her words have been recorded; we know of enough examples of women in the Bible whose names are not even attributed to them, let alone paragraphs of text.

Abigail's actions and words save her household; her bravery and wisdom diffuse the stand-off between David and Nabal (and if you want a happy ending spoiler, the selfish Nabal later dies and Abigail marries David).

Abigail steps out of her 'expected' role as a wife to also take on the roles of diplomat, go-between and counsellor. She is more than the role that her society has used to define her. She confounds expectations and makes a huge impression in doing so. Most importantly, she saves people's lives. She is a role model for women (and men) of spirit who refuse to be defined by the expectations and boundaries of society today.

† God of diversity, today we pray for people who challenge stereotypical ideas and roles in the world and in the Church.

For further thought

How do we keep our leaders accountable for their decisions and challenge them to change their minds – is it possible?

The underside of history – 2 Women of the word

Notes by **Barbara Easton**

Barbara is Head of Service for the Methodist Academies and Schools Trust. She started her working life as a secondary school teacher of religious education and wound her way to headship, taking in a number of interesting challenges on the way. A Local Preacher in the Methodist tradition, personal and professional life have given her the opportunity to follow interests in world religions, mysticism and worship; they have sometime detracted from her desire to finish more quilts. Barbara has used the NRSVA for these notes.

Sunday 30 May
Making a stand

> **Read 2 Samuel 21:1–14**
>
> *Then Rizpah the daughter of Aiah took sackcloth, and spread it on a rock for herself, from the beginning of harvest until rain fell on them from the heavens ... After that, God heeded supplications for the land.*
>
> *(verses 10a and 14b)*

At first reading, this is a simple story of boundless grief. Rizpah's sons' lives are sacrificed for the perceived greater good of a country plagued by famine and the guilt of past war crimes. Her story cries out on behalf of all those parents who carry the unimaginable burden of the loss of a child.

But Rizpah is more than this. In fighting the darkness of her children's deaths, she is also making a stand for what is right. God's Law forbids the ill-treatment of the dead and human decency demands that the bereaved receive dignity and respect. King David has chosen to overlook this, so Rizpah's public and rather dramatic mourning becomes a faithful protest against a ruler who is losing sight of God's ways.

She is incredibly brave. Alone in the wilderness, defending the bodies of her sons, she faces the wrath of the king, the elements and the wild animals. She does not give up until justice is done. In her faithfulness to the dead, Rizpah reminds us of the women who stood bravely with the dying Jesus and went early to the tomb to anoint his body. But I also hear echoes of courageous women throughout history whose private grief has cried truth to power.

† Hold, O Lord, all those who mourn today; lighten the darkness of those in the depth of grief. Give to us all your strength and peace.

A woman's silence

Read 2 Kings 4:17–22, 27–37

... the child opened his eyes. Elisha summoned Gehazi and said, 'Call the Shunammite woman.' So he called her. When she came to him, he said, 'Take your son.' She came and fell at his feet, bowing to the ground; then she took her son and left.

(part of verses 35–37)

A friend of mine organised a special service for women who had lost children in the earliest months of life. She wasn't sure anyone would come. But many did: some, familiar faces who had long carried an unacknowledged sadness; others, women who had not been near a church in years. Some joined in while others were more hesitant, sitting quietly to seek reconciliation with the past. People unfamiliar with church, yet believing they can be mended in God, in the company of God's people and in a holy place.

One of the strangest things about this second story of loss is the woman's silence. Like many people living their worst nightmare, she is reluctant to talk about it – she puts her son's body where it is unlikely to be found and doesn't even tell her husband why she is going out. She dashes alone to God, seeking out the prophet not, apparently, expecting a miracle but as someone to whom she can safely pour out all her bitterness and distress.

It's not just untimely bereavement. Our personal stories seem unfairly pierced by cruel grief and deep disappointment – circumstances which knock the stuffing out of us and make us doubt who we are or what the purpose is in our living. Like the woman of Shunem, we can take our unspoken anguish to the Man of God, who is swift to help, even if sometimes his healing seems to come slowly. And, as the People of God, we are called to be there for others, offering God's mending to a needy world.

† Jesus, Man of God, you came and lived among us. Be with me now in this silence, and let us share the world's griefs together.

For further thought
Look up Dietrich Bonhoeffer's poem, 'Men go to God when they are sore bestead', which holds together the crucifixion and human suffering.

Tuesday 1 June
A woman's word

Read 2 Chronicles 34:18–28

Those whom the king had sent went to the prophet Huldah … keeper of the wardrobe (who lived in Jerusalem in the Second Quarter) and spoke to her to that effect. She declared to them, 'Thus says the Lord, the God of Israel: Tell the man who sent you to me, Thus says the Lord …'

(part of verses 22–24)

'This is the Word of the Lord', we often declare at the end of our Bible reading in church. Huldah is considered to be the first recorded person to say that and mean it for real. Workmen restoring the Temple find a book of God's Law that no one has seen before. A deputation of the country's most senior men bring it to Huldah for verification. It falls to her to make the shattering pronouncement: this really is God's Word, this really is how God wants us to live.

It is thought that this newly discovered book was an early version of Deuteronomy, so if this were Huldah's only claim to fame, it might be enough. But it is not enough for Huldah, for whom the book on its own is insufficient. The Word of God needs not only to be acknowledged but also to be engaged with, reflected on and proclaimed. She does not let the king's advisers go before she has worked through with them what the scripture means and held it up as a plumb-line for their leadership of the nation's life. For Huldah, faith and morality are not simply private and personal – they speak to the systemic issues of how we live as a country and represent ourselves on the international stage.

Traditionally, Huldah is thought to have been a seamstress, busy with her own job and her husband's position in the royal household. She's not a full-time live-in-the-desert-eating-locusts sort of prophet. But this is no limitation either to her reputation for knowing God or to her confidence in speaking out about the God she knows.

† Still in your presence, I seek your light. Wherever life takes me today, let your light touch others through me.

For further thought

To us, the Bible is a treasure. To others, it's an ancient irrelevance. How, then, can we be like Huldah?

Wednesday 2 June
A woman awake

Read Judges 4:4–10, 5:1–12

Barak said to [Deborah], 'If you will go with me, I will go; but if you will not go with me, I will not go.' And she said, 'I will surely go with you …'

(verses 4:8–9a)

By any standards, Deborah is an outstanding figure in the history of ancient Israel. In the Old Testament, 'Judges' were the local rulers of Israel before the nation came together under one king, not the simple courtroom figures of today. Deborah's position reflected the respect and consent of her community but also an element of divine recognition. After all, her leadership was of God's people living under God's Law.

She must have been quite a remarkable woman. A talented leader, she is skilled at horizon-scanning, astute in judgement and decisive in action. She knows her limitations – she can't lead the army into battle herself, but she won't let that stand in the way of making things right for God's people. She knows how to compromise, to manage the cut and thrust of working with people like Barak – a recognised leader in his professional field but without the confidence and insight to act for God when the moment comes.

How does this ancient story speak to our times? A friend noted recently, 'I oftentimes despair of the times in which we live, but we are called to interpret them …' We read this story with the benefit of hindsight – we know how it ends and that Deborah was right. As history is made around us it is often difficult to discern what to do or how the people of God should act. We face uncertainty as a Church as well as in the wider world. We might not have Deborah's wisdom or Barak's command. But we can heed the call of their song, 'Wake up, wake up.'

† O still small voice, our world can be a place of whirlwind and fire. Lead us in your ways of grace and truth.

For further thought

Sit prayerfully with the news – TV, radio, internet or print. How do today's stories call for discernment and action?

Curating change, one day at a time

Read Luke 2:36–38

There was also a prophet, Anna … She was of a great age, having lived with her husband for seven years after her marriage, then as a widow to the age of eighty-four … At that moment she came, and began to praise God and to speak about the child to all who were looking for the redemption of Jerusalem.

(parts of verses 36–38)

As a young woman I found it difficult to see Anna's life as anything other than a dreadful waste. All those years spent waiting in the Temple for her moment in the limelight; she seems to find the thing that she is 'for' only when she is quite old. As an older woman, I find the story of Anna has a different resonance: even in the later part of her life, she discovers an active role in God's developing story. In fact, the nativity stories are full of old people: Elizabeth, Zechariah, Joseph, Simeon … God calls on the old to bring the new to birth. It is the job of the old to curate change.

And what of the years of waiting? Christians have sometimes dismissed earthly life as nothing but the waiting-room for eternity. That seems to me to deny both the gift of life and God's act in incarnation. After all, Anna wasn't just a 'waiter' – she was a professional prophet with a role at the heart of the faith. But it is true that our lives sometimes make more sense in God's time than in our own. Even the great churchman St John Henry Newman felt that, if God had a purpose for his life, he might not understand it until it was over. Things might make more sense in the perspective of God's eternity, but life comes to us to be lived one day at a time. While we are waiting to see our lives in God's, we can look for God's life in ours – changing the perspective of the everyday.

† Lord of life, I wait upon you. Open my heart to the mystery of your life in me, and mine in you.

For further thought

John Wesley is said to have prayed, 'Let me not be useless'. Is this a reasonable prayer for a Christian?

June

The underside of history – 2 Women of the word

Friday 4 June
Tabitha, disciple of the Lord

Read Acts 9:36–42

Now in Joppa there was a disciple whose name was Tabitha, which in Greek is Dorcas. She was devoted to good works and acts of charity. At that time she became ill and died. ... [Peter] gave her his hand and helped her up. Then calling the saints and widows, he showed her to be alive.

(verses 36–37a and 41)

Many people may be unfamiliar with this short story from the earliest days of the Church. But Tabitha has quite a claim to fame: there's only a handful of people raised from the dead in the Bible. Tabitha is the only adult woman – in fact, the only person – who was restored to life by Peter. It is interesting, then, that where she is commemorated it is not for this remarkable thing that happened to her but for the more 'unremarkable' things that she herself did.

Tabitha surely can't have been the only follower to have died during the early years of the Church. Yet her death, significantly, brings Peter all the way from Lydda to try to help her distraught Christian community in Joppa. The clue may lie in Tabitha's other claim to fame – she is the only woman in scripture of whom the word 'disciple' is used. And the main characteristic of her discipleship is not her erudition or her preaching but what she does with the skill she has. It seems Tabitha's gift is with her needle, and she uses this gift in the service of the poor.

A needle is a small thing yet, in the hands of a disciple, a small thing becomes an agent of grace. Through Tabitha's charity, some of the poorest people in Joppa find they are not only helped but cherished. She is at the heart of this early Christian community because the way she 'does' grace draws people into a new community of love. Her simple discipleship sets the tone of what it means to be 'church'.

† May my being in my world today be the presence of your grace and light for others, O God of all grace and glory.

For further thought

What powerful small thing do you have to share grace with today?

Saturday 5 June
A cloth dealer listens in

Read Acts 16:11–15

A certain woman named Lydia, a worshipper of God, was listening to us; she was from the city of Thyatira and a dealer in purple cloth. The Lord opened her heart to listen eagerly …

(part of verse 14)

Paul, you may remember, did not really plan to make this trip. A man from Macedonia appeared to him in a dream saying, 'Come and help us.' Paul always started his ministry amongst the Jews of any city. He must have been disorientated to arrive in Philippi and find, not the man of his vision nor even a proper synagogue, just a worshipping community of well-meaning women who weren't even properly Jewish. Yet, when he writes to the church in Philippi that began with this visit, he speaks of what grew there as the crown of his ministry.

God presses him into this service, almost against his natural inclinations. Many people consider Paul a misogynist because of statements he makes in his letters against women (as in 1 Corinthians 14:34–36). Yet here God calls Paul to grow a new Christian community in the home of a powerful woman and under her dynamic leadership. And her a Gentile as well! But God surprises Lydia, too. One minute she is a successful businesswoman. By the end of the chapter, her fine house is the first church in Europe and a valuable missionary base – and she has become the sister in Christ of the local gaoler. In this story, God turns all expectations upside down.

Commentaries often debate the plausibility of this story. Where, they demand, is the man? After two weeks studying the spiritual authority and leadership of these oft-overlooked biblical women, that need not be a question which troubles us. The first recorded Christian in Europe is a woman; the first person to tell of the resurrection is a woman. God turns all expectations upside down.

† You have called even me, Lord, to play a part in your story. Give me fresh eyes to be surprised again by your topsy-turvy ways.

For further thought

How have the last two weeks' study affected your perspective on biblical women? Which woman do you most want to tell others about?

Readings from Job –
1 Have you considered my servant Job?

Notes by **Wendy Lloyd**

Wendy is the worship and theology communications advisor for Christian Aid. This includes co-ordinating the worship resources for the Christian Aid website and facilitating 'Just Scripture' sessions, connecting groups across the world around the Bible. She studied an MLitt in Bible and the Contemporary World at the University of St Andrews after having a brief stint as a Geography teacher in Northern Ireland, from where she originates. Now she lives on a croft by the sea on the Isle of Mull. Wendy has used the NRSVA for these notes.

Sunday 6 June
The wisdom of Job

Read Job 1:6–22

Then Job arose, tore his robe, shaved his head, and fell on the ground and worshipped. He said, 'Naked I came from my mother's womb, and naked shall I return there; the Lord gave, and the Lord has taken away; blessed be the name of the Lord.'

(verses 20–21)

As a book of wisdom literature, the poetry and encounters within the book of Job are best approached with a creative imagination and an openness to mystery. This is particularly advised for this opening encounter between Satan and God which sets in motion the cascade of accusations and questions that fill the subsequent chapters.

It is a book that many turn to in the trials and tribulations of life and no less so for myself. I didn't turn to it during the cancer treatment I had in my late twenties – the most I could manage to read then were the gentle words of Henri Nouwen and the humorous insights of Calvin and Hobbes cartoons.

But in the years afterwards, seeking resolution and restoration, I found the Book of Job an incredible source of strengthening comfort. I still love how embodied Job's response is to such colossal loss: he rises, tears, shaves and falls, all before he worships.

And in the shaving of his head I find a resonance, that I expect I share with all who have had to shave their hair during chemotherapy. This sign of Job's bereavement becomes our own, a lament for all that went before.

† Almighty God, who counts the hairs of our heads, thank you for the wisdom that brings much comfort and encouragement to all who suffer. Amen

Monday 7 June
The power of presence

Read Job 2

They sat with him on the ground for seven days and seven nights, and no one spoke a word to him, for they saw that his suffering was very great.

(verse 13)

I cried from the depths of a place I don't think I'd gone before. Sobs that shook my body and washed over me in waves. The exhaustion that followed was what finally lulled me to sleep in the home of my friend. A friend who had been there through the hours of sobbing, staring and silence that preceded.

We'd followed through on our plans to go out for dinner on diagnosis day. The day when I heard those fateful words as so many people do: 'You have cancer.' But it was a very silent meal. I'm not sure I ate very much but I do remember staring out the window a lot. And she just sat there with me.

She didn't grasp for awkward platitudes or suggest superficial solutions. She didn't spew out her own shock and sadness all over my grief but just showed up with a willingness to sit with me in the pain and shock of having a rare cancer diagnosis at 28.

I was so grateful for the simple, silent power of presence. And this is what comes to mind when I read of how Job's friends both approached him and sat with him.

They practised good psychological hygiene by processing their own shock, sadness and grief from a distance; they didn't bring that to Job and heap on him the burden of their own pain. They practised the power of presence for seven days. And then they spoke.

† Thank you for the power of presence, gracious Father. For those friends who show up, sit down and remain silent. Thanks be to God. Amen

For further thought

Who in your circle of friends or acquaintances needs your 'good psychological hygiene' this week?

Tuesday 8 June
A loud and long lament

Read Job 3:11–26

*'Truly the thing that I fear comes upon me, and what I dread befalls me.
I am not at ease, nor am I quiet; I have no rest; but trouble comes.'*

(verses 25–26)

Job expresses honest words of lament; they are cathartic and raw, shocking and sobering. He gives voice to the pain and despair that many people experience across the world today.

A loved one caring for a husband in the late stages of pancreatic cancer, facing the future on her own. The widow left to face her later years on her own, her best friend and companion taken from her before they got to enjoy the restful years of grandchildren and holiday sunsets. A son suddenly faced with his father's death and tending a mother stricken ill with grief. These are just the stories I've encountered in my community this past week, let alone the countless stories I encounter on a daily basis in my work with Christian Aid.

The extreme hunger being suffered by the people of Yemen. The families stuck in campsites in Greece with no hope of moving on. The perpetual poverty and frustration of communities living under siege in Gaza. The victims of sexual violence in the protracted conflict in the Democratic Republic of Congo. I would expect that many of them might join in Job's refrain, 'I have no rest; but trouble comes' (verse 26).

Such honest lament is far from heretical; it indicates a willingness to turn to God even in the pain of life. It demonstrates a faithful knowing that God is big enough and gracious enough to absorb the pain and the suffering of all the world.

† Thank you, God, for the wisdom of your Word. That we have to hand honest accounts of how to handle the suffering of life. Strengthen us to always turn to you, whatever our lot. Amen

For further thought

What local, national and international situations would you add to those in the reflection above?

Wednesday 9 June
Silence is better than platitudes

Read Job 4:1–11

'Think now, who that was innocent ever perished?
Or where were the upright cut off?
As I have seen, those who plough iniquity and sow trouble reap the same.'

(verses 7–8)

If only it were thus, Eliphaz the Temanite, we might find more solace and understanding in the world. But it is far from true. The innocent perish on a daily basis, and all innocence is crushed with their lives. The upright face the same fate as the 'done-wrong' and in many cases those who 'plough iniquity and sow trouble' (verse 8) reap an abundance of riches and a luxurious, comfortable life. The worldview that Eliphaz occupies and peers through is not the real world and so his counsel is already called into question from the very outset of his lengthy speech.

His words could be heard with a note of comfort and reassurance or more likely they have a tone of judgement about them. Either way they bring to mind those many well-intentioned platitudes that are often shared, but rarely experienced by the one who hears them.

'What doesn't kill you makes you stronger': this was not my experience of chemotherapy. Kate Bowler explores such platitudes in her book *Everything Happens for a Reason and Other Lies I've Loved* (SPCK, 2018), where she combines her research of the prosperity gospel theology with her own lived experience of being diagnosed with an incurable cancer in her thirties. She understands the inclination towards such phrases: 'It would be nice if catastrophes were divine conspiracies to undo what time and unfaithfulness had done to my wandering soul,' but she explains, 'when someone is drowning, the only thing worse than failing to throw them a life preserver is handing them a reason' (Preface, p. xvi).

Would that you had remained in your silence, Eliphaz.

† Spare us, O God, from well-intentioned platitudes that are shared to salve another's discomfort or inability to meet us in our pain. Thank you for faithful friends who can sit in the mystery. Amen

For further thought

What platitudes do you need to throw away? Start a list and add to it this week.

Thursday 10 June
Learning from bygone generations

Read Job 8:8–19

'For inquire now of bygone generations, and consider what their ancestors have found; for we are but of yesterday, and we know nothing, for our days on earth are but a shadow.'

(verses 8–9)

There is a humility to be heard in Bildad's invitation to learn from previous generations. There are many insights to be gleaned from the cumulative wisdom of those who have gone before us, rather than disregarding the past as primitive and the present as progressive. How did they endure the trials of birth and dying and what can we learn of their lives inbetween?

Where I live, on the Ross of Mull, Scotland, the footprints of predecessors are everywhere. Just yesterday, on a little paddleboarding adventure, I discovered the remaining walls of a croft house.* It was hidden under grass on a headland protruding out into the sea. It was a precarious yet beautiful setting in which to have eked out a living.

These crofting generations endured much hardship amidst the beauty. The township of Shiaba is a place of particular pain on Mull, where the population plummeted from 350 to just a few families in the space of two years. The residents were evicted by the landowner in 1845 so the land could be used for more profitable sheep farming. It is a story that is replicated across the Highlands and islands of Scotland and today through forced migration around the world.

And as I sat on the headland sipping my coffee, I wondered what the ancestors of this land would make of our lives of leisure? Enjoying, more than working, the land. Although I imagine they might also say something along the lines of Frederick Buechner: 'Here is the world. Beautiful and terrible things will happen. Don't be afraid' (*Listening to Your Life*, Harper Collins, 1992, p. 289).

Crofting is a form of land tenure and small-scale food production particular to the Scottish Highlands and the islands of Scotland.

† God of all the ages, help us to listen to the wisdom of bygone generations, to learn from their mistakes and to heed the lessons of community care over individual concern. Amen

For further thought

What are the old, hidden stories in your community? How do they help you see your present community differently?

Friday 11 June
There is always hope

Read Job 11:7–19

'And you will have confidence, because there is hope; you will be protected and take your rest in safety. You will lie down, and no one will make you afraid; many will entreat your favour.'

(verses 18–19)

These words read in isolation make for comforting and encouraging reading. That is, only if they are read without the preamble of the verses before, that presume iniquity on the part of Job and the need for him to 'put it far away' (verse 14). Zophar's words, like those of Job's other friends, are devoid of grace or recognition of the unknowable ways of God.

To be fair, Zophar comes close in the opening words of this passage: 'Can you find out the deep things of God? Can you find out the limit of the Almighty?' (verse 7). He describes how the deep things are higher than the heaven and deeper than Sheol, and he almost gives space for God to be beyond our understanding.

However, it might have been better if he had stopped at verse 9 or just said these final words from verses 18 and 19 to Job. Words of comfort, security and unconditional hope. But regardless of Zophar's preamble there is always hope.

Hope for strength and support, hope for the suffering to pass, hope for sufficient grace to endure. Hope does not eradicate the pain of the world but it does enable a vision of how things can be. Hope inspires the tenacity to keep on keeping on.

Now faith, hope and love abide, these three, to quote 1 Corinthians 13:13; and while the greatest of these is love, hope is still a vital part of the trio.

† Hopeful God, grant us faith no matter what we face, give us hope to endure all adversity, fill us with love to overcome hardship, and in all these things help us abide in you. Amen

For further thought

Today, find a moment to rest in the God who is beyond all understanding.

Communion not consumption

Read Job 12:4–12

'But ask the animals, and they will teach you; the birds of the air, and they will tell you; ask the plants of the earth, and they will teach you; and the fish of the sea will declare to you.'

(verses 7–8)

It was a great wind that killed Job's children at the beginning of this book (Job 1:19), and the wind plays a significant role towards its end (spoiler alert! Job 40:6). Nature is both friend and foe to Job. And yet it is to nature that he turns to finds comfort and resolve in his troubles. There he learns the lesson that every creature on the Earth knows, that the hand of the Lord sustains all things.

Observing nature did not explain his suffering but reassured him he was not outside the will of God. This not only challenges the ideas of his friends but also the widely understood theology of those who first encountered this story. Hearers and readers who would have been trying to make sense of the suffering of exile.

Suffering from changes in nature is a present reality for those enduring droughts and storms as a result of climate chaos. Great winds continue to bring much sorrow for communities facing super-typhoons and stronger hurricanes across the world today. And even in these present challenges and struggles the ancient wisdom of Job has much to teach us today: pay more attention to the natural world.

Those living in the West need to return to a closer relationship with creation, one that goes beyond consumption to communion. Climate chaos will continue to inflict much undeserved suffering on those who have done the least to cause the problem unless we heed this simple yet profound wisdom of Job.

† God of all, forgive us for wandering from your ways and forgetting our place as creatures in your incredible world. Let us return to close harmony with you and all of creation. Amen

For further thought

What other connections do you see between Job and the current climate crisis?

Readings from Job –
2 Cold comfort

Notes by **Revd Norman Francis**

Norman, after spending over two decades in congregational ministry in Africa, England, Scotland and his home country, Jamaica, now serves as Co-ordinator of the Eldership and Lay Training programme of the United Church in Jamaica and the Cayman Islands – an exciting and relatively new initiative, designed to equip and empower laypersons to realise their full potential in building God's kingdom. He is married to Karen and has two adult sons. Norman has used the NRSVA for these notes.

Sunday 13 June
Life is stronger yet!

Read Job 14:1–17

'If mortals die, will they live again?'

(verse 14a)

In our text, Job raises the age-old question: is there life after death? Many people are terrified at the prospect of dying, fearing that death brings *everything* to an end.

Job, too, seems to believe this (verses 7–13). His rhetorical question in verse 14 – 'If mortals die, will they live again?' – anticipates a negative response, because Job, like everyone in the ancient world, did not have a developed theology of resurrection. Nevertheless, hope emerges. At the end of verse 14, Job states, '… I would wait until my release should come.' In the Septuagint (the Greek translation of the Old Testament), these words are translated: 'I will wait until I exist again …' Amid Job's struggle with the finality of death, we see what now appears to be an emerging understanding that there is, after all, *hope of resurrection*! Only resurrection can make sense of the meaninglessness of life. Job's struggle with death leads to an understanding that death is, in fact, not a full stop, but a comma – a pause that ends when we rise to new life!

† Living God, may we be assured that death is not the end, and that afterwards, we will be raised to new life with you forever. Amen

June

Readings from Job – 2 Cold comfort

165

Monday 14 June
Discomforting comforters

Read Job 16:1–5

'... miserable comforters are you all.'

(verse 2b)

How often we are callous and unsympathetic in the face of tragedy! Human life itself at times seems expendable, and many feel free to offer judgement instead of sympathy.

We see this common tendency to be thoughtless in our words in the story of Job – a man who suffers unimaginable tragedy without knowing why. As he struggles to find answers, he is joined by three of his friends who, instead of providing comfort, offer nothing but pious platitudes. 'If you're suffering,' they say, 'it's because you're guilty of wrongdoing.' Unable to accept his friends' insensitive platitudes, Job lashes out. Have you ever felt like doing that? I know I have. I can still remember how, at my mother's funeral service many years ago, several speakers kept saying: 'This is not the time to mourn!' After a while I felt like just telling them all to shut up! If I can't mourn at my mother's funeral, then where can I? Job's encounter with his friends reminds us that the well-meaning platitudes we speak in people's times of distress are often meaningless to them.

Let us guard against ill-conceived, insensitive words, so that, like Job, we too can say, 'I could encourage you with my mouth, and the solace of my lips would assuage your pain' (verse 5). Truly, life and death lie in the power of our words (Proverbs 18:21). Let us speak life!

† Gracious and compassionate God, may my words of encouragement be more than just empty clichés. Instead, may they always speak life into the despair of those whose lives are in turmoil. Amen

For further thought

Are you willing to speak a word of comfort and encouragement today to someone you know who might be facing distressing circumstances?

Tuesday 15 June
Is there a deliverer?

Read Job 19:19–27

'For I know that my Redeemer lives, and that at the last he will stand upon the earth.'

(verse 25)

In the verses leading up to today's text, Job sees God as the cause of his suffering (verses 1–22). And so, Job seeks to be rescued not so much *by* God but *from* God's adversarial presence (verses 25–27). Amidst his excruciating agony, Job expresses his deepest longing: 'I know that my Redeemer lives, and that at the last he will stand upon the earth' (verse 25). By this he means that there is someone out there who will one day rise up as his defence attorney to plead his innocence before God, whom Job thinks is treating him unfairly.

Do you sometimes get angry at God because you feel God has treated you unfairly, and that no one understands? Like the lone widow bending over a recently dug grave, who, between her flood of bitter tears, lashes out in anger: 'This isn't fair' ... 'Why wasn't the drunk driver the one who got killed in the accident instead of my husband?' ... 'Henry never deserved this' ... 'Where is God now that I need him most?'

The good news is that we do have a Redeemer when the going gets rough – his name is Jesus Christ. He intercedes before God on our behalf (Romans 8:34), pleads our case in the courts of heaven (1 John 2:1) and successfully defends us against the accusations of the adversary (Revelation 12:9–11). We must therefore *choose* to trust that our Redeemer – Jesus Christ – knows what we are going through and will never abandon us in our time of need, even when we feel forsaken.

† Loving Lord, the next time I feel I am being treated unfairly and that you have turned a blind eye to my suffering, help me to trust your heart. Amen

For further thought

Think about a time when your anger towards God challenged your faith. Did you emerge with a stronger faith? Why or why not?

June

Readings from Job – 2 Cold comfort

When God is silent – 1

> **Read Job 23:1–12**
>
> *'Today also my complaint is bitter; his hand is heavy despite my groaning. O that I knew where I might find him, that I might come even to his dwelling!'*
>
> *(verses 2–3)*

Job's struggle is one that all people of faith, at some point, struggle with: 'If God desires to have such an intimate relationship with us, why does God appear to be absent amidst our desperate struggles?' (verses 2–3). Could it be that God allows us to experience feelings of abandonment so we may adopt a more mature outlook on life and on our relationship with him? Let me explain.

There was once a man whose puzzling behaviour attracted the attention of his pastor. This man kept scurrying from behind the trees that lined the sidewalk, as if trying to avoid being spotted. The pastor, on seeing this, shouted to the man, who quickly motioned to him to pipe down. The man then hurried across the road to his pastor and said, 'I realise you're baffled by my odd behaviour. I'm keeping an eye on my six-year-old boy, but I don't want him to catch sight of me.' This father had permitted his boy to go to the nearby convenience store for the very first time all on his own. In other words, he was helping his boy to grow up by taking responsibility for doing something new all by himself. But at no time was his son ever really on his own. His father was close by, even though his son was unaware.

In a similar way God's apparent absence gives us room to grow as we step out into the unknown, unaware of the outcome. This is faith: '… the assurance of things hoped for, the conviction of things not seen' (Hebrews 11:1).

† Ever-present God, when you seem far from me during my times of greatest need, help me to know that you see me, care about me and are giving me room to grow. Amen

For further thought

Why do you think it is so devastating when people think that God has forsaken them? What could you say to such persons?

Thursday 17 June
Unimpeachable!

Read Job 27:1–12

'Far be it from me to say that you are right; until I die I will not put away my integrity from me.'

(verse 5)

In the beginning we see that Job was amazingly steadfast in his faith, even after he suffered unimaginable losses (1:20–22; 2:9–10). However, by the time we get to chapter 27, Job is now disheartened, crushed and driven to despair, all because of God's prolonged absence in his hour of greatest need. Yet, Job remains incredibly confident in his personal integrity before God despite his friends' harsh and incessant criticism of him. This reminds me of a Jamaican proverb: *'Dawg wid to much massa sleep widout suppa'*: 'A dog with too many masters will go hungry.' In other words, we must trust our own convictions when making decisions, and not rely unduly on the opinions of too many other persons.

Job's stance challenges the conventional wisdom of his day, which said that when people suffer, it is because they have sinned. That's what his friends told him. But Job's tenacious grip on his integrity has debunked such thinking, even when his friends continued to condemn him. He shows us that the righteous are not exempt from pain and suffering, and that even during our turmoil, we can still be assured of our status before God. Conventional wisdom isn't always an accurate indicator of God's purpose behind the experiences we sometimes undergo. We must therefore be very wary of those, like Job's friends, who hastily criticise us, claiming to be speaking on God's behalf. Let us not be swayed by popular opinions about, or easy answers to, our life experiences. Let us remain resolute in the strength of our integrity.

† Lord, help me develop an unswerving conviction that, even in the face of harsh criticism, I will rest in my position in Jesus Christ, which is eternally secure. Amen

For further thought
Which has the greater effect on you: knowing your personal integrity before God is intact, or a friend's criticism of you? Explain.

The expensive, but free gift

> **Read Job 28:12–28**
>
> *'"Truly, the fear of the Lord, that is wisdom; and to depart from evil is understanding."'*
>
> (verse 28b)

The focus of today's text is wisdom: that elusive quality that many people seek after, but few ever find. As Rabbi Jonathan Sacks points out, 'Wisdom is free, yet it is also the most expensive thing there is, for we tend to acquire it through failure, disappointment, and sometimes grief.'[1] We see this in Job's experience. He certainly had more than his fair share of disappointment and grief, but at some point in his ordeal he was able to say, 'Truly, the fear of the Lord, that is wisdom' (verse 28)! From this we see that God, wisdom and suffering are all interrelated.

The connection between God and wisdom is self-evident (verse 28b). But when it comes to the connection between God and suffering, we often ask, 'Why does God allow suffering?' But we often fail to recognise that when God created us, he gave us freedom to choose to do good or not. For God to respect that freedom, God must limit his response when we make bad choices … even if they lead to suffering. For God to do otherwise would be to violate our free will. Finally, there is the relation between wisdom and suffering. Sadly, wisdom often results from suffering, as we see from Job's. His suffering provided deeper intimacy with God (Job 42:5), leading to greater wisdom (verse 28b). We can become wiser from suffering, but only if we allow God room, even when, like Job, there's much we don't understand.

† All-wise God, may you grant me a perspective beyond my present trials, so that I can see your eternal purpose of transforming me into a wiser, more empathetic and mature person. Amen

For further thought

Reflect on a time of great adversity you've endured. How did that experience help you grow closer to God and thereby become a wiser person?

---

1 From Rabbi Sacks' website: rabbisacks.org/things-judaism-has-taught-me-about-life

When God is silent – 2

Read Job 29:1–17

'O that I were as in the months of old,
as in the days when God watched over me;

when his lamp shone over my head,
and by his light I walked through darkness;

when I was in my prime,
when the friendship of God was upon my tent;

when the Almighty was still with me,
when my children were around me;

when my steps were washed with milk,
and the rock poured out for me streams of oil!

(verses 2–6)

In our text, Job remembers 'the good old days', when the wisdom in his counsel was sought after; when he championed the cause of the disadvantaged; and when he was a respected figure in the community. But now, reduced to a shadow of his former self, Job pours out his heart, hoping that somehow God will either respond to his claim that he's innocent (31:35) or condemn him if he's not (31:38–40). But up to this point, God is shrouded in silence. I wonder if you ever felt the silence of God in the midst of troubles. Have you ever felt like this at a time of deep distress?

Job did. Consequently, both his hope of rescue by his redeemer (19:25) and his confidence in wisdom's redemptive value (Job 28) seem to have disappeared. However, this passage doesn't tell the whole story. God eventually spoke (Job 38–41), and for the first time, Job realised that he had been speaking without knowing the whole story (42:1–6). From Job's experience we learn that God is *always* good and just, even when circumstances may say otherwise. We must *choose* to believe this.

† Mysterious God, whose ways are past finding out, help me to know you are always working behind the scenes to ensure that, no matter what happens to me, my future will always be better than my past. Amen

For further thought

What practices will help you believe in the words of the prayer above?

Readings from Job –
3 Out of the storm

Notes by **Pevise Leo**

Pevise is an ordained minister in the Congregational Christian Church of Samoa. He graduated from Malua Theological College, Samoa in 2004 with a Diploma in Theology and is currently the minister of a church in Brisbane, Australia, named **Setima O Le Ola** *– Brisbane Central. He is also a songwriter who has penned more than 100 Samoan contemporary and gospel songs. He lives in the small town of Inala, 40 minutes from Brisbane City, with his three children. Pevise has used the NIVUK and the NRSVA for these notes.*

Sunday 20 June
Right living in the storm

Read Job 31:1–15

*'Is it not ruin for the wicked, disaster for those who do wrong?
Does he not see my ways and count my every step?'*

(verses 3–4, NIVUK)

Tropical Cyclone Heta was a powerful Category 5 tropical cyclone that hit the South Pacific islands of Tonga, Niue and Samoa during late December 2003 and early January 2004. It was during the school holidays, and I was attending Malua Theological College in Samoa at the time. A handful of pupils and I stayed on in the compound doing our fa'amuli – where we became the caretakers of the whole compound for a week. Getting out of that storm was all I could think about, as my family were already in New Zealand.

Nobody likes to get caught in a storm. Job lived in the most-fierce storm of life. His story is so painful, his name has been linked to suffering itself. In his continual self-examination Job looked at his life. He felt that he had never committed any injustice. He had remained faithful to his wife. Job is so confident of his innocence that he pronounces a series of conditional curses upon himself.

The story of Job is a book about life as it really is; where good, bad and just plain confusing things happen; where there is grief and agonising and asking why; and where there is God whose ways we don't always understand. As we read through the remaining chapters of Job this week, let us be mindful of how we live in the storms of life.

† Gracious God, guide my ways in the storms of life. Amen

Knowing your place

Read Job 32:1–9

'I thought, "Age should speak; advanced years should teach wisdom."
But it is the spirit in a person, the breath of the Almighty, that gives
them understanding.'

(verses 7–8, NIVUK)

Samoan life has been divided into different structures. *Fa'aSamoa*, or the Samoan way, guides the way the Samoans live their lives, and has three key structural elements: the *matai* (chiefs), *'aiga* (extended family) and the church. A *matai* is the head of each *'aiga* where there are elders and children. Although the elders are deemed to be wiser, *Fa'aSamoa* has given the *matai* more power and wisdom to hold over the elders and the *'aiga*. Within the church context, the roles are reversed. The minister is more respected, honoured, has more guidance and wisdom.

Perhaps Elihu is working with the traditional model. He thinks that the elders are wise enough to resolve the problem. Unfortunately for Elihu, trying to get Job out of the storm is too complicated. He realises that age does not equate to wisdom. He is younger and therefore should not speak first. But the elders did not produce the wisdom he thought they may have, hence his reasoning in verses 8 and 9. He claims that wisdom does not come with age. It is God the Almighty that gives it. It doesn't matter how old or how great you are; if God does not give you wisdom, then you will just be an old person without wisdom. Maybe this is why the Samoans rely on their clergy for wisdom and guidance and respect and honour them more: because God Almighty has given it to them.

† God Almighty, I ask you today for your divine wisdom so you may illuminate my way when I'm confronted with the dark storms of life. Amen

For further thought

Where might you need to heed the wisdom of the elders? Where might God's wisdom conflict with this?

June

Readings from Job – 3 Out of the storm

The game or the player?

Read Job 35:1–8

Then Elihu said:

'Do you think this is just? You say, "I am in the right, not God."

Yet you ask him, "What profit is it to me, and what do I gain by not sinning?"

'I would like to reply to you and to your friends with you.

Look up at the heavens and see; gaze at the clouds so high above you.

If you sin, how does that affect him? If your sins are many, what does that do to him? …

Your wickedness only affects humans like yourself, and your righteousness only other people.'

(verses 1–6 and 8, NIVUK)

We know that God will punish the wicked and bless the righteous. Is this why we do things for God? For a reward? Or is it because we love him with all our hearts, and we want to please him?

Elihu tells Job that he is completely without understanding of God's ways and what Job has said up to this point is lacking wisdom. In Elihu's mind, because Job has not acknowledged his sin, the punishment has multiplied. God does not punish unjustly, therefore Job is wrong, he is a sinner. Job's words are empty, in Elihu's view. There must be a reason God is punishing Job! Elihu's viewpoint is unshakeable.

But is it really true, as Elihu argues, that sin and righteousness affect human beings more than God (verses 6–8)? Sin and disobedience cannot injure God, but can hurt his heart. God loves his children and hates the sin. God's heart is affected, too, by our sin and arrogance.

† Loving Father, I come to you humbly, that you look kindly upon me while playing the game of life. Amen

For further thought

What do you do when the unjust sleep soundly, and the just suffer?

Wednesday 23 June
Stormy justice

Read Job 36:1–12

If they obey and serve him, they will spend the rest of their days in prosperity and their years in contentment.

But if they do not listen, they will perish by the sword and die without knowledge.

(verses 11–12, NIVUK)

There is a certain time of the year that is called the *palolo* (sea worms) season. The palolo worm is a polychaeta or 'bristle worm' species from the waters of the Pacific islands around Samoa. Reproduction involves mass spawning at night in October and November. We enthusiastically gather the palolo worms with nets, and they are either eaten raw or cooked in several different ways. This is a delicacy like no other, as it is only harvested or caught once a year.

I grew up with the understanding that several factors caused the palolo worms to rise: when the *moso'oi* tree is in full blossom, the *palulu* flower (a morning glory) closes, toxins occur in reef fish, and there are abrupt weather changes or there is bad weather such as thunderstorms or lightning, then the best palolo worm rising will follow. This is the cause and effect that I understood about the *palolo* season. I also grew up knowing that when bad things happen, there was always a reason why. Cause and effect. Stormy justice is a conflict between cause and effect.

In our reading today, Elihu is somehow acting as a spokesman for God. He is claiming that God is just and always right. For him, Job must be guilty of an awful sin. Yet we know that Job did nothing wrong in the eyes of God.

We sometimes get stormy justice from our peers and colleagues. Job knew himself, trusted God and was willing to stand firm in his conviction. We must do the same, because the storms of life are not always related to cause and effect.

† Merciful God, help me cope with the stormy justice of life. Amen

For further thought
What resources do you have to cope with life's storms?

June

Readings from Job – 3 Out of the storm

Thursday 24 June
Listening during the storm

> **Read Job 38:1–18**
>
> *Then the Lord answered Job out of the whirlwind:*
> *'Who is this that darkens counsel by words without knowledge?*
> *Gird up your loins like a man, I will question you, and you shall declare to me.'*
>
> *(verses 1–3, NRSVA)*

For almost 90 percent of his book, Job has struggled with God's apparent absence, distance and silence. And now God answers him, not telling him what he did wrong but explaining his creation. This answer refers to Job's despairing cry that he wishes he could disappear and 'vanish in darkness' (23:17). God's words make it clear that Job speaks in ignorance. No matter our circumstances, God can still speak to us. If we don't listen, we will never hear. God may even choose an unpleasant circumstance as a platform from which to speak.

In August 2018, I lost my wife of 28 years to a heart attack. And being a church minister of the Congregational Christian Church in Samoa, it is mandatory that I remarry to carry on as a parish minister. Four months on, I left my parish vowing never to be parish minister again. I didn't want to remarry; it was hard to lose a life partner and I didn't want to go through it again. I gave up, but I also left it to God's will. If God's will was for me to continue, then only God could make it happen. I remember clearly as if it were yesterday that during our final goodbyes with the congregation my tab collar broke in two. I knew then that it was God's answer to my wish, or so I thought. Exactly three Sundays later, God explained his answer when he sent me another partner to carry on in the ministry.

There are so many storms of life, and if we don't stop and listen, we won't hear God's silent voice.

† Loving Father, thank you for speaking to me during my storm. Help me to stop and listen often so I know your will. Amen

For further thought
Sometimes God speaks with words, and sometimes with the simple sustaining of creation around us.

Friday 25 June
Stormy silence

> **Read Job 40:1–14**
>
> *Then Job answered the Lord:*
> *'See, I am of small account; what shall I answer you?*
> *I lay my hand on my mouth.'*
>
> *(verses 3–4, NRSVA)*

Legend has it that there was a Samoan man named 'Ae, who went to Tonga and became the king's talking chief. He felt homesick and begged the king for a leave of absence. The king gave him two turtles on which to ride to Samoa. When he arrived, the people killed one of the two sacred fish and ate it. The other escaped to Tonga and told the king what had happened. The king was so angry at 'Ae that he prayed to his gods to send him back so that he could punish him. He got his wish. When 'Ae awoke and found himself in his master's house, he was speechless with terror. All he could say was: *'Ta te nofo atu nei, a o a'u o 'Ae.'* ('Here I sit; I am 'Ae.') This saying became a proverbial expression, used as a request for pardon.

Thinking that God would punish him for questioning his goodness and justice, Job says the same thing: 'I am of small account; what shall I answer you? I lay my hand on my mouth' (verses 3–4). Job was speechless, dumbfounded and unable to comprehend the majesty of God.

Job recognises how insignificant he is. He is unable to answer any of God's questions, and remains silent. He is not stewing in anger; this is a humble and submissive silence in the presence of God.

Stormy silence is knowing when to be quiet. We pray and ask for so much and forget that God knows our situations, and knows what we need.

† Dear God, forgive me for not being sensible with what I ask of you. Amen

For further thought
Sit in silence with God today.

Readings from Job – 3 Out of the storm

Saturday 26 June
Through the storm

The Mau was a nonviolent movement for Samoan independence from colonial rule during the first half of the twentieth century. *Mau* means 'opinion', 'unwavering', or 'testimony' denoting 'firm strength' in Samoan. The Mau movement culminated on 28 December 1929 in the streets of the capital Apia, when the New Zealand military police fired on a crowd which was attempting to prevent the arrest of one of their members. The day became known as Black Saturday. Up to 11 Samoans were killed, including Mau leader and high chief Tupua Tamasese Lealofi III. Many others were wounded. The Mau movement's efforts would ultimately result in the political independence of Samoa in 1962. Thousands and thousands of Samoans went through a political storm.

Job went through a storm of faith. The overwhelming vision of God's questioning has put Job in his proper place before God. Hearing about God all his life had not prepared Job for the reality of God. When he finally saw God in all his glory, Job knew that he had fallen short of the glory of God.

In life, we have to go through the storm. If we avoid the storm, we may never see God as Job did, and we will always stay the same. If the Mau movement hadn't gone through the political storm, there would have been no independence. If Job hadn't gone through the faith storm, his life would have been still the same, and he would have missed out on the lessons of the storm. Is it possible that we will see the goodness and justice of God through the storm itself?

† Father God, help me go through the storm so I can learn from its lessons, and to know you fully in faithful eyes. Amen

For further thought

As we conclude the Book of Job, ask yourself, what were you like before you entered the storm? And what are you now after the storm?

The Bible through the seasons: summer

Notes by **Paul Nicholson SJ**

Paul is a Roman Catholic priest belonging to the Society of Jesus, a religious order popularly known as the Jesuits. He currently works in London as Socius (assistant) to the Jesuit Provincial. He edits The Way, *a journal of Christian spirituality, and is author of* An Advent Pilgrimage *(2013) and* Pathways to God *(2017). Since being ordained in 1988 he has worked principally in ministries of spirituality and of social justice, and was novice-master between 2008 and 2014. Paul has used the NRSVA for these notes.*

Sunday 27 June
Know that summer is already near

Read Luke 21:29–31

Then he told them a parable: 'Look at the fig tree and all the trees; as soon as they sprout leaves you can see for yourselves and know that summer is already near. So also, when you see these things taking place, you know that the kingdom of God is near.'

(verses 29–31)

June

Fresh From The Word is read worldwide. This can make it difficult to write about the seasons. This week is near midsummer in the northern hemisphere, but midwinter in the south. So some of you might need to draw on memory of, or look forward in hope to, the summer experiences these texts present for prayerful reflection.

Jesus describes an experience common in temperate countries. In late spring, trees sprout new leaves. Seeing this, you know winter is truly over and summer is just around the corner. If you're lucky, this evokes pleasant images of holidays, warm days and long evenings, a chance for rest and relaxation. Early summer can be a time of joyful anticipation.

The parable suggests we can look forward to the coming of God's kingdom in the same way. For Jesus, the idea of the approaching kingdom does not focus on a fearful judgement, but a time when this world will be reshaped as God wants it. Jesus believes that, if we look around us, we can see signs and places of that happening already. In Christian communities, for example, you should already be able to notice people living out the values of the kingdom of God.

† What are the things going on around you in the world at the moment that could suggest that 'the kingdom of God is near'?

Monday 28 June
Toiling under the sun

Read Ecclesiastes 2:18–25

What do mortals get from all the toil and strain with which they toil under the sun? For all their days are full of pain, and their work is a vexation; even at night their minds do not rest. This also is vanity.

(verses 22–23)

If you don't enjoy the benefits of modern air conditioning, there is no guarantee that summer weather will be pleasurable. This is especially true if your work involves hard physical labour, out of doors. This seems to be the kind of picture conjured up for the writer of Ecclesiastes when he hears the word 'summer'. Nine times in this short passage he uses the word 'toil' to describe a central aspect of the human condition. Toil is not just any kind of work, but the hard, back-breaking type. Not only that, but such toil is, in his view, ultimately fruitless, it is 'vanity'.

If you are fortunate, your own work may feel productive, something that you look forward to and can count as a blessing. But Ecclesiastes gives a voice to those who don't feel this way. That probably includes most of us, at least some of the time. Not all toil is obviously productive, even if it cannot be avoided. The image of working hard under a baking summer sun captures that feeling of futility well.

What is your response to times like that? Do they lead you to turn away from God, at least temporarily, until you are feeling better? Or are you able, like the writer of today's passage, to speak openly with God about the situation in which you find yourself? The fact that such a passage found its way into the Bible suggests that it represents an important aspect of our own response to God, and perhaps one that we need to practise and grow into.

† I pray today, Lord, for those whose work is hard and unrewarding, for those who must work in baking heat or freezing rain. Bless their efforts and offer them your reward.

For further thought

Recall a time when you've had to do work that felt unproductive. Read this passage again while thinking of that, and see what you notice.

Tuesday 29 June
In God I trust

Read Psalm 121

The Lord is your keeper; the Lord is your shade at your right hand.
The sun shall not strike you by day, nor the moon by night.

(verses 5–6)

Nobody looks for shade in winter. Shelter maybe, protection from driving wind, snow and rain. But looking for shade is a summertime activity, seeking relief from the heat and the glare of the sun, a place to rest and even luxuriate. Any kind of shade will do: a welcoming tree, an overhanging building, even a parasol. It is this kind of comfortable, and comforting, protection that is the basis of the image in this psalm. It is suggested that this was a psalm sung on the way to Jerusalem on pilgrimage. If so, its original audience would have been well aware of what it means to urgently seek shade in the noonday heat.

Reading this psalm, I am invited to share the experience of the psalmist. Initially, he and I are looking for help, without being sure where that help will come from. Almost immediately, however, an awareness dawns that only God can be relied upon to offer the support that is being sought.

From that point on, the psalm becomes a prayer of great confidence. Not only is God able to offer all that is required, but the psalmist is convinced that God will in fact do so, and I, in reading, am invited to share that confidence. The gift of a summer's shade is just one example of God's care for me, a care that is promised not just for today, but for evermore.

† Notice how you react to the psalmist's great confidence in God. If you share it, give thanks; if you don't, ask for some share of that confidence as a gift.

For further thought

Read this psalm again in the context of what you know about the current climate change debate. Does it sound any different?

June

The Bible through the seasons: summer

Gathering in the harvest

Read Proverbs 6:6–11; 10:5; 30:24–28

Go to the ant, you lazybones; consider its ways, and be wise …
it prepares its food in summer, and gathers its sustenance in harvest.

(6:6 and 8)

Where I live, in southern England, grey squirrels are the animals most obviously engaged, in late summer, in gathering in the harvest. They run back and forth on lawns, seizing acorns and beech-nuts, and scrabbling small holes to bury them for a winter food supply. Left to themselves, the ones they overlook will grow into new forests. Yet the squirrels always seem to remember enough of their storage sites to tide them over the harshest winter.

The ant seems to occupy the same position in the mental imagery of the writer of this part of the Hebrew Bible. The ant ensures its own security in challenging times by its earlier hard work. The invitation of the reading is to be like the ant, and not like the lazy child who dozes in the summer sun. Later in the book, badgers, locusts and lizards all have lessons to teach the observant human being.

These are not complicated lessons. But they are ones that will only become apparent to the one who takes time to observe the world round about. If your only reaction to ants is to spray them with insecticide to protect your food, or squirrels are no more to you than pests digging up plants you have carefully tended, these proverbs will mean little. Scripture writers lived closer to nature than many of us who inhabit today's cities. One value of prayer can be to lead you back to an appreciation of the simple lessons of God's creation.

† Lord Jesus, who invited us to contemplate the birds of the air and the flowers of the field, help us to appreciate more fully all that you have created, and to learn from it.

For further thought
Take a few minutes today simply to look at a tree or a pot plant, a pet or a wild animal. And thank God for it.

Thursday 1 July
Generosity in a time of scarcity

Read 1 Kings 17:1–16

'For thus says the Lord the God of Israel: The jar of meal will not be emptied and the jug of oil will not fail until the day that the Lord sends rain on the earth.'

(verse 14)

In the lands where the Bible was written, drought was, and remains, a frequent feature of summer, a time when little rain falls and water courses dry up. The drought in this passage, however, is not simply a consequence of the season. It is a punishment sent by God on an evil king, Ahab, bringing his land to its knees.

The concern of the writer, nevertheless, is not as much on the drought itself, as on those whom God chooses to protect from its worst consequences – first Elijah the prophet, and then the widow of Zarephath, rewarded for her generosity to the prophet, and her young son.

It is natural, maybe, to ask first what happened to all the other blameless people who were around at the time. Jesus himself faces this challenge in chapter 4 of Luke's Gospel. But perhaps your own prayer today might take you in a different direction. Can you recall times when God has protected you in difficult situations, sending people with the help you need, just at the time when you need it? Or alternatively do you find yourself at present in need of just this kind of help? The summer drought can stand as a symbol of all sorts of difficulties that a person of faith encounters in the course of Christian living. What is it that enables you to relate directly to this passage today?

† Lord, you invited all who thirst to come to you for refreshment. Bring your living waters today to the parched and drought-stricken areas of my life.

For further thought

Recall places and situations where you, or members of your church, have shown the people around you the generosity that the widow of Zarephath showed to Elijah the Tishbite.

Friday 2 July
Breaking the silence

Read Psalm 32

While I kept silence, my body wasted away through my groaning all the day long. For day and night your hand was heavy upon me; my strength was dried up as by the heat of summer.

(verses 3–4)

Ignatius of Loyola, the sixteenth-century founder of the religious order to which I belong, compiled some advice about dealing with anything that might lead you away from God. One of his suggestions was that whatever was wanting to lead you in this direction – he called it the 'bad spirit' – would want its promptings to be kept secret. This was best dealt with, then, by finding someone with whom you could speak freely about the temptations you were facing.

The psalmist here has an image for this same experience. Keeping a drawing towards sin secret, it is suggested, is like being out in extreme summer heat. It saps the energy and dries up your strength. Only by acknowledging the assaults of the evil spirit can you hope to return to being able to draw on the ample support that God offers.

Think, then, as you pray this psalm, of all that is the opposite of its summer heat: a cool drink, a refreshing breeze, a welcome shade. These are the experiences that can be compared with God's forgiveness, freely made available to all who seek them.

It is natural, when confronted with behaviour of which you are ashamed, to want to keep it secret. Nor is there any suggestion here that your temptations and sins need to be broadcast. But at least the first step, of admitting them openly to God, can begin that move from drained energy to rejoicing in the Lord.

† Lord Jesus, help me to be open to you about my faults and my failings, my temptations and sins, speaking to you as openly as I would to a trusted friend.

For further thought

What helps you to overcome a natural reluctance to acknowledge your faults, even to God?

Saturday 3 July
All shall be well

Read Revelation 7:9–17

They will hunger no more, and thirst no more; the sun will not strike them, nor any scorching heat, for the Lamb at the centre of the throne will be their shepherd, and he will guide them to springs of the water of life.

(verses 16–17b)

This passage takes us beyond the reach of the earthly seasons. The great multitude gathered around the throne of God can no longer suffer from hunger or thirst, or the burning heat of summer. It is no longer the sun that is their source of light and energy, but God himself. The first thing to do in praying with a passage like this is to make sure that you really hear the great promise it makes, and notice how you react to it.

Maybe you find within yourself the kind of hope that enables you to face difficult times even now. Perhaps you'd really like to believe that this is the future that you're called to, but find it difficult to trust in that. You may even be frankly sceptical, seeing this as little more than 'pie in the sky'. Whatever your spontaneous reaction is, don't censor it. Our God of truth can deal with whatever response you make, provided that it's an honest one.

In the end, though, we're brought back to comparisons taken from our own human experience, here and now. It is, after all, the only thing we truly know. No more hunger, no more thirst, no scorching heat, but the light and joy of a pleasant summer's day. God leading a rejoicing people to the springs of the water of life. Pray that you are able, with all the angels gathered around the throne, to say 'Amen' to that.

† Lamb of God, you take away the sins of the world; have mercy on us.

For further thought

What one thing could you do today to make this world here and now just a little more like the world described in this reading?

The words of the wise

Notes by **Michael Jagessar**

Michael is a writer and researcher 'at large'.
More on Michael's biography and writings can be found at
www.caribleaper.co.uk. Michael has used the NRSVA for
these notes.

Sunday 4 July
A handbook for living

> **Read Proverbs 1:1–7**
>
> *'Let the wise also hear and gain in learning, and the discerning*
> *acquire skill …'*
>
> *(verse 5)*

All cultures and religious traditions have their array of 'wisdom sayings'. It serves as a sort of handbook for life and living. The Book of Proverbs is not intended to merely tickle the ears; it seeks to teach 'wisdom' – the attitude and means by which to live well. My grandparents called it 'common sense'. I can still see the glint in their eyes as they would then proceed to say that, though 'common', much of the wisdom is lacking today. This will only continue to get worse if we do not give greater agency to experience and observation. With most of us glued on some form of online media gadget, taking in loads of (mis)information, reality can quickly become far removed, manipulated and confused. Our observation skills can become dull. And we wonder why 'things fall apart'.

How do we reclaim wisdom that begins with a reverence for the Divine, that is about character formation, accountability, the common good and qualities such as honesty, integrity, self-control and the 'fear' of being held to account for distorting the way of the economy of full life for all? There is an urgent need to recentre on the Divine and rediscover some of these timeless insights on how we can together manage our life together as nations. It is foolish to do otherwise as the consequences are devastating.

† Whether personal or communal worship, consider using silence and only very few words to recentre or focus on God and what God in Christ may be saying to you at this moment.

Monday 5 July
In search of dreamers ...

Read Genesis 40:1–15

They said to him, 'We have had dreams, and there is no one to interpret them.' And Joseph said to them, 'Do not interpretations belong to God? Please tell them to me.'

(verse 8)

Every one of my peers in my village in Guyana had dreams that, at the time, seemed like wishful thinking. We never expected them to be realised. It was our way out of a small and restricted village world. We served as interpreters for each other's dreams. While all of us left that small place we knew as home, our dreams took directions we never expected.

We were not alone in our dreaming. History is replete with dreamers. Some would say that today we need more dreamers. Our religious texts are also filled with dreamers. God often communicated with God's prophets through dreams. Vision and direction often came through dreams. Dreams may be visions, fantasy and exploration – glimpses of past, present and future. Some dreams need interpretation whereas others offer insights into hopes and aspirations. And dreaming may be a blessing: yet not all of us have the luxury of spending time attending to dreams. Some are robbed of the ability to dream and fulfil their dreams as life continues to be a nightmare. Some of us are rightly dismayed that even churches are more apt to go for business plans with profitable growth outcomes, rather than listening to the dreams and desires of the community. We can manage and control business plans. Dreams are too challenging, especially when it has to do with envisioning a better world and calling into question the distortions of the Jesus economy of abundant life for all. We need dreamers to rise up so that oppressive, restrictive, exclusive, life-denying practices may crumble. We need dreamers to rise up for a better world for the whole of creation.

† Consider praying for the gift of the imagination, and especially that dreamers and visionaries for a just and peaceful world may rise up from our communities.

For further thought

Who and where are our current dreamers? What kind of a world do you dream of? How can this dream take concrete shape? Where is it taking shape?

The words of the wise

July

187

Tuesday 6 July
Beyond riddles

Read Judges 14:5–18

'Out of the eater came something to eat.
Out of the strong came something sweet.'

(part of verse 14)

There is more than what meets the eyes of the reader in this text. Samson the hero, the one with extraordinary strength, is also witty! The story of this special-birthed Nazarite pushes religiopolitical boundaries at multiple levels. It includes loving Philistine women, spending his time in wine country, handling dead carcasses and eating unclean food. These break the rules of purity as well as any neat national narrative or plot. Ironically, Samson's exploits and penchant for breaking rules offer a way out for Israel from domination by the Philistines. Can it be that Samson's violation of his Nazarite vows are symptomatic of Israel's violation of its covenant with *Yhwh* – the downward spiral of Israel and its leaders? Some felt that the leadership had sunk a long way from Moses. The people would rather live under the rule of the Philistines than come to *Yhwh* for deliverance. And so, a question was: how will God deliver a people not wishing for it?

Riddle aside: the violence against women in the Book of Judges is mindboggling. There seems to be no place for women in the land. One can reasonably ask: is there much difference between the Israelites and Philistines when it came to violence against women, vengeance and personal interests? Perhaps, the riddle here is a call to consider the death and sacrifice of women while men run around with their various 'tools' of destruction. What has changed today?

† God who releases and frees: deliver us from growing despair, touch our brokenness with your balm of love, cure our designed unawareness and forgive us of our constant tendency to destructiveness. Become, in our lives, the way to what we need, to what we can become and to what we can do.

For further thought

Reflect on the fact that in the Book of Judges, God is often represented as passive while women (many unnamed) are left to the excesses of men.

Wednesday 7 July
Prophetic entrapment

Read 2 Samuel 12:1–15

'There were two men in a certain city, one rich and the other poor. The rich man had very many flocks and herds; but the poor man had nothing but one little ewe lamb, which he had bought.'

(verses 1b–3a)

He is rich and has everything he wants. Yet, his greed is insatiable. It is an old story as the Samuel text highlights. Nathan tells David a story that cleverly got him to implicate himself. Nathan did what prophets do: speak truth to power. We do not need resolutions from Church Assemblies or Synods to prompt us; nor 'risk assessment' to curtail us from doing so. David was outraged and swore that the rich man deserved to die and ought to make reparation. It is amazing how power made him so insensitive that he was not even aware until Nathan pointed out: 'you are the one!' David does not see his indictment coming. The readers and audience can begin to make connections right away: Uriah is the poor man, Bathsheba is his one little ewe lamb and David is the rich man with a sense of entitlement.

David's designed unawareness is a consequence of absolute power and privilege. People of privilege tend to become accustomed to a world that conforms to their desires and hence they operate with impunity. When this then becomes entrenched into something systemic that robs people of sharing in abundant living, then prophets like Nathan need to come forward. Our current economic system can serve as one example. When we can see the greed (and our complicity) at the heart of this model of our current economic relationships, we may then start to see how David's murder of Uriah may be connected to the consequences of such a world driven by greedy self-interest. Would a recognition and understanding of such connections offer some openings into the change needed for a different economy to be at work?

† Lover of justice, shape our conscience and heart according to your way of just, peaceful and loving lives. Move us to speak with compassionate courage and to act with conviction and humility. Through your Spirit sustain us.

For further thought

Does the story favour David too much, so that he gets away with adultery and murder? Does our justice system favour or privilege the wealthy and powerful?

The words of the wise

July

Thursday 8 July
The Divine watches

Read Jeremiah 1:11–12

'You have seen well, for I am watching over my word to perform it.'

(verse 12b)

The next time you delight in your almonds or almond-flavoured products, do think of the prophet Jeremiah. Picture the scene: God showing Jeremiah a branch of an almond tree and then saying to Jeremiah, perhaps with a wink: 'I will be sticking around to watch my word come true.' What was the Divine after?

For scholars suggest that there is a play on the Hebrew words for 'almond tree' and 'to watch' in verses 11 and 12 (both sound like '*sha-ked*'). Hence, the almond tree has been referred to as the 'watching' or 'awakening' tree. In the region it is the first tree in the year to bud and bear fruit. In fact, the blooms preceded the leaves and perhaps it is from this we have the idea of the branch representing God who is watching for the bloom or the flourishing of God's word.

Putting the insights of scholars aside: I warm to the idea of God keeping watch over our own deploying of what we may perceive as words from and about the ways of the Divine. God must be fully aware of all the human ambiguities we embody, hence the need to ensure that God's desire for life and love will come alive and bear fruits that will transform lives. So let us ask ourselves: are our words (and actions) life-giving and faithful to the way of the one who offers full life for all?

† God-always-with-us, we pray that your Spirit will bring freshness to our thoughts and words and actions, so that we can dream new and creative possibilities, discern the challenges before us, find life-giving ways to care and embrace, and dare to take risks in the adventure of walking your way.

For further thought

What are the words we offer amid the harsh realities around us? Would these bear fruit? What new words should we contemplate?

Friday 9 July
Wear and underwear

Read Jeremiah 13:1–11

This evil people, who refuse to hear my words, who stubbornly follow their own will and have gone after other gods to serve them and worship them, shall be like this loincloth, which is good for nothing.

(verse 10)

It is common for prophets to teach with signs, mimes and parables, drawing on imageries that people will connect with. We often speak of the imperative of reading the signs of the time. What then comes forward, though, from such current readings may not necessarily be performed in symbolic acts. We seem to have lost this part. The closest we may get to prophetic symbolism like that of the biblical prophets may be a hunger strike, a sit-in or a demonstration against some issue. I cannot imagine one of us walking around the Houses of Parliament (UK) in dirty underwear. The security services would be all over us.

In this passage, God picks out the sign and basically has Jeremiah act out this object lesson to make a point. And what a strange one: underwear! Hardly something we display for public viewing and here it is in the Bible. But it is certainly an object we can all intimately relate to and perhaps have a good laugh about. It would certainly be a crowd-puller. Imagine a themed conference on 'wear, underwear and rebellion'. But, here the intimacy of underwear is compared to the close relation between God and God's people: a rather disturbing comparison for more prudish Bible readers. The episode, though, compares the evil of a people who would not listen to God with the soiled underwear which is of no use. Artfully crafted, here is a parabolic comment on Israel's identity: for how long will Israel continue to reject her covenant relationship, and when will she grow up rather than messing it all up?

† May the word of God, the Divine Lover empower our thoughts and words; may the love of Jesus inhabit our hearts; and may the breath of the Holy Spirit inspire our lives today and every day.

For further thought

Reflect on the importance of prophetic symbolism for today: what would be one such symbolic act that a faith community may engage in?

The words of the wise

July

Imagining a different future

> **Read Ezekiel 4**
>
> *Then he said to me, 'See, I will let you have cow's dung instead of human dung, on which you may prepare your bread.'*
>
> *(verse 15)*

What would people make of a person like Ezekiel today? He and his weird prophetic imagination and symbolic acts would be viewed as wacky. Imagine the scene: a preacher told to act out the message by working with Lego – taking a brick, drawing a city – and then God saying, 'Go further: put battlements, walls, ramps and heavy security around the city.' In other words, the city must look like a fortress. Now depict the enemy by putting in soldiers with battering rams and more. This is how the city will be depicted on the pottery. And then Ezekiel is told by God to take that tile and shatter it into pieces, depicting the inevitable destruction of the city.

And the list of actions continues from lying on his sides to cooking bread with cow dung. In the face of coming danger, Ezekiel is called to serve as that 'watching conscience' over the people of Judah. It is now past pleading time on behalf of the people, the usual task of the prophets. Ezekiel is now acting out the part of God who is wholly fed up with the rebellious, stiff-necked and hard-hearted lot. To call a people to accountability will never be a comfortable task. Ezekiel is part of a long tradition of deploying a 'prophetic imagination': communicating God's word or message in the context of the people's reality in ways that would stir the imagination to new possibilities, to imagine an alternative despite the situation in which people find themselves.

† Spirit-who-gives-us-breath, hold and shape us so that we can reflect the love of God and the compassion of Christ. Open our hearts and minds to imagine new possibilities that draw us away from apathy, selfishness and comfortable corners to walk your way of full life for all.

For further thought
Imagine being called to act out our message like Ezekiel – how would we know what we are asked to do? Does it matter?

Bible riddles

Notes by **John Proctor**

For John's biography, see p. 10. John has used the NRSVA for these notes.

Sunday 11 July
Contested ground

Read Matthew 13:24–30

'"Where, then, did these weeds come from?" He answered, "An enemy has done this." The slaves said to him, "Then do you want us to go and gather them?" But he replied, "No … Let both of them grow together until the harvest …"'

(from verses 27–30)

Jesus loved telling parables, and the Gospels bring us many of these. A parable is a story with a meaning. Yet often the meaning is a mystery. It takes work, time, and thought to get at. Then even when we do unwrap the parable, we find that the parable has unwrapped us. It has taught us something about ourselves and our living and opened us up to God in a new way.

Matthew 13 begins with four parables about growth. Natural growth, of seeds, plants and yeast, points to the growth of God's kingdom in the world. Yet progress is not always straightforward. In the parable of the sower (13:1–9) success is patchy. And here, with the wheat and the weeds, a promising crop is impeded by the work of 'an enemy'.

God's work in the world can appear untidy. You can't always tell what (or who) is good or evil. Mistakes, compromises, selfishness and sin will camouflage and tangle what God is doing. So don't try, says this parable, to be too sure, precise and decisive in our opinions and judgements. We do better to acknowledge the untidiness, contribute what we can to the good growth, and leave the final judgement to God.

† Do you know of any church work where progress and difficulty have run side by side? Pray for persistence and trust for the people involved.

Monday 12 July
Miniature and mighty

Read Matthew 13:31–33

'The kingdom of heaven is like a mustard seed that someone took and sowed in his field … The kingdom of heaven is like yeast that a woman took and mixed in with three measures of flour …'

(parts of verses 31 and 33)

Here are two compact little parables – really just pictures rather than full-scale stories. One is typical of a man's daily work (in that ancient society), of sowing and tilling the land. The other is a woman's parable, set in the kitchen. As if to say that God works with equal power and purpose through men and women alike.

Both parables tell of surprising growth from unimpressive beginnings. Though the mustard seed is tiny, the shrub it produces reaches out to provide safety and shelter for the birds. Yeast is fine as dust, but it can lift and leaven a hefty lump of dough. So with the Jesus movement: it started small, and now spans the world. Yet the growth happens in hidden ways – buried in the soil, kneaded into the flour. Only as the kingdom takes effect do we recognise its strength.

There was no great prestige in mustard. It was a very ordinary sort of shrub. Nor was yeast always welcome. It was a pollutant, an impurity, at some seasons in the Jewish calendar. People scoured their kitchen to get rid of it. Jesus' kingdom too, despised and resented by many, grows from the margins, among the poor, without prestige, beneath the radar of official religious ceremony.

So despite their brevity, these two parables have a rich array of insights to offer. Parables are often like that. What you learn from them may depend on the questions you ask, the experience you bring, the road by which you have travelled, and the particular tuning of your ear to the harmonies of God.

† God of purpose and surprise, please help me to notice your kingdom growing, and to rejoice, even in places I might not have expected. In Jesus' name. Amen

For further thought

Can you remember a moment when a parable that you thought you knew well suddenly taught you something fresh and new?

Tuesday 13 July
Treasuring the kingdom

Read Matthew 13:44–52

*'The kingdom of heaven is like treasure hidden in a field ... Therefore
every scribe who has been trained for the kingdom of heaven is like the
master of a household who brings out of his treasure what is new and
what is old.'*

(from verses 44 and 52)

Today's reading brings us four more little parables, of treasure and
a pearl, of a fishing net, and finally of treasure again.

The first is a tale of commitment. The treasure seems to be
unearthed by accident, turned up by the labour of plough or
spade. Perhaps it was buried long ago: who knows? This is not a
story about ethics, about the feasibility or rightness of tracing the
original owner. It is about those moments in life when you need
to be wholehearted. Discovering God's kingdom is one such. You
need to grab it, and let it grab you. Heaven's purpose claims our
life, not just our curiosity.

Treasure surfaces again in our reading, a few verses later. The
picture is of a careful householder, who keeps the family valuables
in a safe place, to be brought out when they are wanted. Such
a person is like a learned teacher, says Jesus, who deploys hard-
won insight as occasions and needs require. And if a Jewish scribe,
versed in the Hebrew scriptures, was then gripped by the fresh
vision of the Jesus movement, there would be treasures new and
old to share. The old would help to explain the new; the new would
enliven and energise the old.

Some people think this last picture is Matthew's autograph – a
cameo portrait of the Gospel-writer within the Gospel. As a film
director may appear as an actor in one short scene, so Matthew
shows us himself in Jesus' words. He is a scholar of ancient
scripture, and herald of the good news. For him the two roles
belong together.

† Think about commitment, and pray for courage to grasp the opportunities and
challenges God puts in front of you.

For further thought

New and Old. For us, two testaments. How, for you, do they shed
light on one another?

Church expectant

Read Luke 12:35–46

'Be dressed for action and have your lamps lit; be like those who are waiting for their master to return from the wedding banquet, so that they may open the door for him as soon as he comes and knocks. Blessed are those slaves whom the master finds alert when he comes ...'

(verses 35–37a)

It has been said that we only meet two kinds of event in our lives – those we expect and those we don't. Yet perhaps this passage tells of events that are both expected and unexpected, certain and uncertain. When servants wait for their boss to come home from a wedding (verses 35–38), they may have many questions in mind: how long will it go on; how late will he be; will he come back in high spirits; might he bring guests to stay? But the one sure point is that he is expected, so they must be ready.

Similarly, you may not have an appointment with a burglar tonight (verses 39–40). But surely criminals are out there, and one day they may visit you or me. If we knew the moment, we would be ready. And obviously there is a kind of readiness that expects the unexpected – locks, fences, insurance and so on.

Then in verses 41–46 we see again a household of waiting servants. Now the impression is of a longer absence than before, but the point is the same. Be ready for the certainty that the householder will return, amid all the uncertainties about how or when.

The main point of these parables is Christian accountability. God will reckon with us, surely and knowingly, and perhaps at moments we had not expected. Certainly we wait in hope for the final coming of Christ. Meanwhile there are the uncertainties of the years to negotiate. Be faithful, be consistent, be trustworthy, is the message in these verses.

† God of all my days, if I meet something unexpected today, it will not surprise you. Help me to meet the day's events and people faithfully and without fear. For Jesus' sake. Amen

For further thought

To what extent does the thought of being accountable to God motivate your Christian life?

Bible riddles

July

Thursday 15 July
Cryptic Christ

Read John 16:16–30

'I have said these things to you in figures of speech. The hour is coming when I will no longer speak to you in figures, but will tell you plainly of the Father.'

(verse 25)

John's Gospel portrays a Jesus who is difficult to understand. At least, people who talk with him often find him so. Opponents, enquirers, disciples – all of them stumble over his words, and only gradually come to terms with the meaning he has in mind. 'I have said these things to you in figures of speech' (verse 25) – in riddles, in code, in pictures, in words that contain more than one layer of truth.

It was surely a deliberate method on Jesus' part. The process helped to lodge his teaching in his hearers' hearts. The hiccupy learning, false starts, insight by instalments and gradual realisations – all of it gave the message grip and grounding in their lives. The misunderstandings were stepping-stones, to discovery and often to faith.

In today's reading the cryptic Christ repeats three words many times over. 'A little while' comes seven times in verses 16–19. We can see, although the hearers cannot, how this refers to the fast-moving events of Holy Week – from table to trial, trial to tomb, and tomb to the triumph of Easter. Then the words 'joy' and 'rejoice' appear six times in verses 20–24. This is the end-product of Easter – joy for the friends of Jesus, joy that is heartfelt (verse 22), lasting (verse 22) and full (verse 24).

Eventually Jesus will speak more directly (verses 25–28). Surely this refers to the Holy Spirit, coming to live among his followers, sharing his truth and life with and within them. But it has been important, along the way, for these followers to cross the stepping-stones of misunderstanding to the solid ground of personal trust.

† Pray for someone you know who is genuinely interested in Jesus, but puzzled by him too. Ask that the uncertainty may not be a barrier but a point of growth and learning.

For further thought

When Jesus is involved in a situation, never think that grief and pain have the last word.

Bible riddles

July

Opening up the future

Bible riddles

July

Read Revelation 6

... the souls of those who had been slaughtered for the word of God and for the testimony they had given ... cried out with a loud voice, 'Sovereign Lord, holy and true, how long will it be before you judge and avenge our blood on the inhabitants of the earth?'

(parts of verses 9 and 10)

Pictures of destruction. The first four seals show us a world at odds with itself, suffering deeply and bitterly from its own anger. Four riders make their way among peoples helpless to resist. War, death, famine and disease ravage the Earth. Lands are ruined and wrecked. 'But do not damage the olive oil and the wine!' (verse 6). Guard the luxury goods, that the wealthy of the nations may still prosper. So often the world works that way. The weak are wounded, exiled, starved, bereaved and forgotten, while the powerful manage to insulate and protect themselves.

Then from beneath the altar – from a safe and holy place in heaven – comes the voice of faithful martyrs. 'How long, Lord?' They are heard. Their voice counts. It is echoed and amplified in the future that Christ unveils.

For as the sixth seal opens, we hear of 'the wrath of the Lamb' (verse 16). Beyond all the pains and tears, the judgement of Christ stands, placing a limit on the hardships of time, calling to account the anger of the nations, intervening for justice and truth. The horsemen do not have free rein. The witness of the martyrs is honoured. Sin and suffering do not write the whole script.

The 'Lamb' – the crucified and risen Jesus – has opened the seals. He holds the future, and he will gather it into his purpose. He has lived among the frailties and defeats of dust and time, and he will gain the victory, for his people, for a hurting world, for ever.

† Lord Jesus Christ, may my life count for you. Let me speak and serve in faith, and if need be, give me strength to suffer for you without fear.

For further thought

In a destructive world, how can you act for mercy and justice?

Saturday 17 July
Borrowing the story

Read Revelation 12:1–17

*A great portent appeared in heaven: a woman clothed with the sun,
with the moon under her feet, and on her head a crown of twelve
stars. She was pregnant and was crying out in birth pangs, in the agony
of giving birth.*

(verses 1–2)

The Book of Revelation is not a stand-alone vision. It is a tightly
woven tapestry. Many a thread carries themes and motifs from the
Old Testament, and from stories and lore of the writer's own times.
The patterns in this chapter come from both scripture and wider
culture.

'A woman giving birth' is surely, we might think, Mary with her
son Jesus; or mother Zion and Israel's promised Messiah; or the
Church and her Saviour. The dragon, the ancient serpent, is the
snake in Eden, the devil of all the ages. Yes; but more than this.

The Greco-Roman world told of the birth of the god Apollo,
child of the great Zeus and his lover, Leto. The newborn child was
threatened by a dragon, Python. Yet he managed to kill the dragon
and usher in an age of hope and prosperity. Roman imperial
publicists used this story to tell of their Emperor as the conqueror
of chaos. The Empire's success would embody and continue the
story of Apollo. No one, said Rome, can threaten or defeat us. Our
peace and power are here to stay.

Now Revelation borrows the story and appropriates it as part of a
Christian vision. As if to say, the blessing that Rome attaches to the
name of Apollo is most truly found in the Messiah, the Lamb, Jesus
Christ. Mary's son is hope for the world. Testifying to him, tough
and testing though it will be, is a burden and battle worth tackling.
Do not fear. Even the angels of heaven will be on your side.

† Do you know anyone who faces really serious opposition for being a Christian?
Pray for that person, for courage, discernment, confidence and patience.

For further thought

What slogans and stories have most influence in our wider culture
today? Do they help or hinder the witness of the Christian Church?

Bible riddles

July

Family tensions in Genesis – 1 Husbands and wives

Notes by **Helen Van Koevering**

After living in Southern Africa for most of her adult life, Helen, raised in England, moved to the USA in 2015. Helen is a Rector of St Raphael's Episcopal church in Lexington, Kentucky, where her husband serves as bishop. She has previously served as a parish priest and as Director of Ministry for the rapidly growing Anglican Diocese of Niassa in northern Mozambique during a decade of extensive and transformative church growth, and now, with the lens of missionary spirituality gathered in those formative years in Africa, is discovering new perspectives for life-giving faithfulness in her new context. Helen has used the NIVUK for these notes.

Sunday 18 July
Bone of my bone

Read Genesis 2:18–25

That is why a man leaves his father and mother and is united to his wife, and they become one flesh. Adam and his wife were both naked, and they felt no shame.

(verses 24–25)

Back at the beginning of all time, human beings were created to live in relational cultures: living intimately, breathing deeply, walking alongside one another, working beside one another, eating together and sharing one another's lives. God created us for companionship, support for one another, honest friendship, mutual regard.

But the reality of broken relationships, hurt, betrayal and dishonesty has caused abuse, suffering and shame. Tension between the dream of God and the reality fills the pages of the Old Testament, beginning in Genesis, and the brokenness of all societies is reflected in conflict, violence and domination. The reality caused by humanity disregarding God's dream has personal, familial and societal repercussions. God's promise needed God's self to show us how to be healed and return to God's way of love as our hope for life. As the apostle Paul later wrote, 'hope does not put us to shame, because God's love has been poured out into our hearts through the Holy Spirit, who has been given to us … God demonstrates his own love for us in this: while we were still sinners, Christ died for us' (Romans 5:5, 8).

† God, may your power continue to transform and bring unity, hope and life. Amen

Monday 19 July
A curse

Read Genesis 3:14–21

The Lord God made garments of skin for Adam and his wife and clothed them.

(verse 21)

The story of God's confrontation with the man and woman in Genesis 3 is about choice: listening to God, or listening to other voices. Or, in other words, listening to the voices of good and the voices of evil.

When reading this passage today, we are struck by the image of a deity with human characteristics. The Hebrew word translated in English as 'sound', also means 'noise', 'voice', 'thunder' and even 'message' or 'proclamation'. We are hearing the sound of God in the garden, in an intimacy with Adam and Eve that should surprise us. This passage implies that the sound of God seeks out communion with humans who hide themselves from God's approach. And this in the garden created for them. The Hebrew term *gan* for 'garden' was translated from the Hebrew into Greek as *paradeisos*, 'paradise'. This approach and this hiding contribute to the sense of Genesis 3 as paradise lost.

As verse 14 tells us, the creature that is cursed is the serpent. Yes, the woman's decision to listen to the serpent has dire consequences for the couple, yet she is not responsible for the origin of sin in the world or the 'fall' of humankind. Those words don't appear here. The narrative is about whose voice should be listened to amongst those heard around us. And the reminder that, beyond all that, God's loving care for Adam and Eve was made apparent in the covering, guiding and settling that end this chapter. Beyond the curse, there remains a choice to listen to God's presence and care in a new place. We are not abandoned.

† Lord, open the eyes of our hearts to truly know you are with us. May we be surprised by you today, and praise you for your loving care and life given for us. Amen

For further thought

What sound might remind you of God's presence and kindness today – a flowing stream, a thunderstorm, the wind in the trees?

Tuesday 20 July
A denial

Read Genesis 12:10–20

'Say you are my sister, so that I will be treated well for your sake and my life will be spared because of you.' … she was taken into [Pharaoh's] palace. He treated Abram well for her sake, and Abram acquired sheep and cattle, male and female donkeys, male and female servants, and camels.

(verses 13, 15b–16)

Here is one of those passages not so often read in our lectionaries. It is an example of the ancient world's involvement in slavery, in what we call human trafficking today. Familial trafficking is one form of this slavery, where families join in with the lucrative trade in humans that is happening on a global scale today. In our world today, there is evidence that around 25 million are involved in this trade, and that 70% are girls and women trafficked by an intimate partner.

Yet, even in dire circumstances and obscurity, there are places of hope and healing. Like a small house in Lexington, Kentucky, where women can stay for two years to recover and renew their lives, be heard at a local church, shop, walk and live in a safe environment. They may have seen the worst, had their dreams shattered, and given up on intimacy, but are finding themselves again. And in the faith that motivates the givers and in the sisterhood that is rebuilding their environment, they speak gently of finding grace. God's grace that stands between, around, behind and ahead.

† Loving God, to walk in the shoes of another, we need the grace that only you can give. Pour out your loving grace and heal us. Amen

For further thought

Find out about human trafficking and organisations in your area. Follow God's grace-filled lead.

The God who sees

Read Genesis 16

Now Sarai, Abram's wife, had borne him no children. But she had an Egyptian slave named Hagar; so she said to Abram, 'The Lord has kept me from having children. Go, sleep with my slave; perhaps I can build a family through her.'

(verses 1–2a)

Again, today's reading is shocking. Wrapped up in the earlier story of God's promise to Abraham (the one who in chapter 15:6 is deemed righteous for putting his faith in God), Abraham knew he was to have a child and yet ten years had passed. Sarai takes matters into her own hands by giving Abraham her personal servant Hagar to bear a child. Sarai's initiative is narratively seen in her prominence – her gesture, her feeling of being slighted, her treatment of Hagar. The second half of the story is about Hagar and the angel's announcement of her child's fate. Seeing God, trusting in God's gracious care, she gains courage. In a culture that values motherhood, like many developing countries today, women are vulnerable. Without childbearing, women are not treated equally with the mothers around them. Sarai is suffering loss of esteem; Hagar is suffering from persecution. The husband and father is to show justice within the cultural context. He doesn't.

Yet the story foregrounded in this is that of Hagar. She gains courageous insight from the God who sees. An angel messenger from God meets her and tells her that, through her son Ishmael, she will be a mother of a great nation at the margins of the land promised to Abraham and Sarai's son. Sometimes, God's grace is simply in being seen and heard because, sometimes, the culture awaits transformation. And, sometimes, many times inexplicably, being seen and heard is enough for now.

† Gracious Lord of our fathers and mothers of the faith, may we rest in the knowledge that wherever we may flee, you are there.

For further thought

Hold in your prayers any that you know are struggling. Pray that they may know themselves seen and heard.

Thursday 22 July
Overthrown

Read Genesis 19:15–29

Thus he overthrew those cities and the entire plain, destroying all those living in the cities – and also the vegetation in the land. But Lot's wife looked back, and she became a pillar of salt.

(verses 25–26)

Remember the story of Genesis 18 and Abraham and Sarah's generous hospitality to three visitors who came to them by the oaks of Mamre in Canaan? The semi-nomadic desert life carried with it a social obligation to welcome strangers. Christian tradition has read that passage as being a revelation of the mystery of the Holy Trinity, elevating even more the social practice of hospitality.

Lot, Abraham's nephew, was also hospitable to angels. Lot invited these strangers to spend the night in his house, but others, Sodomites, wanted Lot to hand them over in accordance with the city's practices of hospitality. Lot, in a confusion of the culture of hospitality/inhospitality, offered the Sodomites his two daughters instead.

Why was Lot's wife turned into salt? Possibly as a statement against inhospitality. Salt is a fundamental necessity of life, a seasoning, a preservative, a disinfectant, a component of ceremonial offerings, a unit of exchange and part of religious sacrifice in the Temple. Eating salt together was a sign of friendship around the Mediterranean.

Lot's wife, they say, was a Sodomite herself. Hospitality was not her custom, and to become a pillar of salt was symbolic of a desolated land (Psalm 107:34; Job 39:6; Jeremiah 17:6). Since it was hospitality that led to Abraham and Sarah having a son and prospering, the denial of hospitality (not only Lot's wife, but the entire city of Sodom) led to destruction and a wasteland.

† Lord, may we practise hospitality and welcome friends and strangers. Show us how to be gracious hosts. Amen

For further thought

Where do the cultures in which we live collide with biblical imperatives? Where can we show the graciousness of God?

Friday 23 July
Devastation and new life

Read Genesis 19:30–38

So both of Lot's daughters became pregnant by their father. The elder daughter had a son, and she named him Moab; he is the father of the Moabites of today. The younger also had a son, and she named him Ben-ammi; he is the father of the Ammonites of today.

(verses 36–38)

This is just one more story of Genesis' theme of destruction and devastation before new life. This bizarre and foolish story of incest as the birthing of the lines of Moab and Ammon, genealogically related to Israel and later to become enemies, is just one more story of contrast between Abraham and Lot. One more story of dysfunctional family tension, poor judgement and lack of consideration for family that expands out into sexual immorality and violence against girls and women that our world suffers from today. Maybe this is a story of the origins of sexual abuse. Maybe this explains Israel's long history of hostile relations with the Moabites and Ammonites. Maybe the last glimpse we have of Lot, destitute and drunk, lying senseless in a dark mountain cave, is to be a warning.

Or maybe it is truly to show us the contrast of the graciousness of God's light overcoming darkness. Remember the story of Ruth, of her relationship with Naomi, her mother-in-law, and marriage to Boaz in the Promised Land? Ruth became the great-grandmother of King David, in the family tree of Jesus. Ruth was a Moabite. She grew up in a culture that hated the children of Israel, yet her life is a wonderful instance of God's light and grace overcoming the darkness of sin, evil and hatred.

Light overcomes the darkness. God's grace is promised.

† Father, you change dark into light, bring new life out of devastation. We praise you for that and ask that you may use us to shine your light in dark places. Amen

For further thought

What are the dark places that our society struggles with today? What might it mean for the Light of Christ to bring change there?

205

Saturday 24 July
A boy named Laughter

Read Genesis 21:1–7

Now the Lord was gracious to Sarah as he had said, and the Lord did for Sarah what he had promised … Sarah said, 'God has brought me laughter, and everyone who hears about this will laugh with me.'

(verses 1, 6)

In the form of an unfolding television mini-series, and with whispers of the birth of Jesus, the story of Abraham and Sarah moves from announcement (or 'annunciation') to consummation – from promise to fulfilment. The central fulfilment of the Abraham tradition, the birth of Isaac, shows God in action as God keeps promises, turns darkness into light, changes mourning into dancing, transforms weeping into joy. Here we are afforded a glimpse of God's very heart – as God transforms Sarah's mocking laughter of disbelief in chapter 18 into a joyous laughter of faith's fulfilment in this chapter.

The child Isaac is born – the child whose very name means Laughter. When God renewed the promise to Abraham in chapter 17, the old man laughed (17:17). When God renewed the promise yet again in chapter 18, the old woman laughed, too (18:12). So when the child was born, it was God's turn to laugh. The child was named Laughter and Sarah said, 'God has brought me laughter; everyone who hears about this will laugh with me' (verse 6). God is faithful to Sarah, as the text notes. Whom is the story of God's faithfulness in Genesis 16–21 primarily about? Abraham? Or Sarah? In an ancient, patriarchal society, to note that the emphasis in these verses is on Sarah is counter-cultural. God's promises and grace were not just for Abraham, but for Sarah, too. The Lord's covenant was wonderfully big enough not just for the old man, but for the old woman, too.

† Lord, threaded through the stories of family tensions and breakdowns, we see that you are there, drawing all people, all broken and broken-hearted women and men towards your promise. We give you our hearty, joyous thanks. Amen

For further thought

The journey this week has taken us to some dark places that are as relevant today as ever. When you hear the news today, hear about disaster and devastation, look for the signs of God's life at work to bring God's love. And be thankful.

Family tensions in Genesis – 2 Brothers and sisters

Notes by **Terry Lester**

Terry has been an Anglican priest in the Cape Town area for over thirty-eight years. Having experienced first-hand the racial discrimination of apartheid, he has focused his efforts on justice and reconciliation through storytelling. Victims tell their own stories referencing their sorrows and joys as people of colour. Today he serves in Constantia where he was born. His three adult children live in Cape Town and he has a granddaughter, Frances. Terry has used the NSRVA for these notes.

Sunday 25 July
Caring not killing

Read Genesis 4:1–16

Cain said to his brother Abel, 'Let us go out to the field.' And when they were in the field, Cain rose up against his brother Abel and killed him.

(verse 8)

Our readings over the next few days take us into some more of the 'darker' texts of the book of Genesis where readers were first introduced to the originator of Light, God Almighty! Chapter 2 describes with intense intimacy how God put man and woman together by 'taking', 'forming', 'blowing breath into' and 'putting to sleep'. It also describes how man co-creates with God in naming and shaping Eden – heady heights indeed! Then these shattering words about Abel's death at the hands of his brother Cain. How did they get from the one to the other in just a few short steps – from life in Eden to death in a field?

If the first story in Genesis is about overcoming the darkness that broods over the waters of chaos, the second story is about the chaos that broods within and accepting what we are like as humans. The story of Adam and Eve and of Cain and Abel tells us that this is how we are and how things unravel for us. Maybe Paul understood this too well when he wrote: 'Wretched man that I am!' (Romans 7:24). Cain's response to God's enquiry about where his brother is, is cheeky: shall I shepherd the shepherd? But Cain does not have the last word, the Good Shepherd does, the keeper of the vulnerable and the silenced. God will be God. But God is also Father and Shepherd to the perpetrator and the victim – the story of grace has begun.

† God, I pray you that you consider the hopes and hurts of all families, including mine. Send your Spirit over these stories this week, for the good of all. Amen

Monday 26 July
Far, far more unites than separates

Read Genesis 21:8–21

And God heard the voice of the boy; and the angel of God called to Hagar from heaven, and said to her, 'What troubles you, Hagar? Do not be afraid; for God has heard the voice of the boy where he is.'

(verse 17)

My dad was born in the 1930s, the third son born to his white father and coloured mother. They were raised on a vegetable farm in the Constantia Valley where my grandfather was foreman to the white farm owner. Growing up with the farmer's son, they played, hunted, squabbled, teased, chased, rode bicycles, fought and laughed together. They were like brothers.

That changed around their teenage years, however, when my dad recalls being summoned to the main house by the farmer's wife. Leaning over her back door, she instructed him that no longer should he address her son by his first name, as he always had, but to address him as 'Master Ivan'. Things had changed! In societies where distinctions of gender, class, status and 'breeding' still hold sway, these things are considered normal. No hard feelings! It is the way it is.

But not for Hagar. She wouldn't have it. She had named her son Ishmael, meaning 'God has heard'! She lifted her voice and wept till God heard the boy! The text attempts to soften the harshness Hagar and Ishmael suffer by suggesting she is partly to blame through her conduct towards Sarai. And Abraham makes a timid attempt to prevent this injustice, but relents. But God hears the slave girl who cries for justice for her son. Her son does not speak in the story, yet we are told that God has also heard the boy! And so, through her efforts, a new path of grace is opened and God's vision for the world broadened, too.

† Lord God, you hear the cries for those who cannot cry anymore or whose tears no longer come because they are so used to not being heard. Thank you. Amen

For further thought

It is devastating when cries for help and justice go unheard. How can I be a listening ear to them?

Faith and trust

Read Genesis 22:1–19

After these things God tested Abraham. He said to him, 'Abraham!' And he said, 'Here I am.' He said, 'Take your son, your only son Isaac, whom you love, and go to the land of Moriah, and offer him there as a burnt-offering on one of the mountains that I shall show you.'

(verses 1–2)

Mukuni Village was abuzz that morning as the news spread that a man was going to walk across the Victoria Falls on a tightrope stretching from the Zambian to the Zimbabwean side! No one believed that anyone would, let alone could, cross Mosi-oa-Tunya (or 'The smoke that thunders' as it was known locally) – it would be utter madness. The villagers watched in awe as he made his way across. It was something to behold. 'Do you believe that I can push a person across in a wheelbarrow?' the man asked. *'Kwete! Kwete!!'* they all shouted. 'Never!' So he put some rocks the weight of a person in the wheelbarrow and wheeled it across to their utter amazement and disbelief. A young man, Takudswa, who had left his usual chores to view the spectacle, looked like he had seen a ghost as he stood awestruck and speechlessly gazing. 'Do you now believe that I can wheel a person across these falls in a wheelbarrow?' 'Yes!' Takudswa blurted out, 'Yes, I believe!' 'Good,' said the man, 'Then you can be first!' Like Abraham, Takudswa was about to have his faith in the man tested. He was suddenly reminded of the chores he had to do and what awaited him if he didn't do them. Yet, how could he not trust what he had just witnessed with his own eyes?

† Dear Lord Jesus, letting go and letting God is easier said than done. I trust your love; help me to believe more. Amen

For further thought

Trust and belief are so necessary in everyday life, yet often people break trust. How can I be more trusting in what I say and do?

Wednesday 28 July
All have a place in God's story

Read Genesis 25:21–34

When the boys grew up, Esau was a skilful hunter, a man of the field, while Jacob was a quiet man, living in tents. Isaac loved Esau, because he was fond of game; but Rebekah loved Jacob.

(verses 27–28)

The story of Jacob and Esau is told in bland tones with little joy or gratitude – even for the miracle of Rebekah conceiving twins! The 'miracle' is overshadowed by the comedic but mostly sad detail of the story. Maybe it is this that makes it such a human story, for often we too are captivated more by the distasteful drama and fail to see the miracle that brought things into being.

As a South African, I am often reminded of the miracle that marked our transition from apartheid in the 1990s. The project of nation building has proved a much more difficult task though. Difference, in all its shapes and forms, has proven much harder to navigate. This is often true in families, too, where smoothing over the friction caused by strong personalities often detracts from the oneness desired, even prayed for. Sometimes our stories offer comedic relief, as does this one in some of the descriptions; mostly, though, we are left holding the sadness and disappointment and learning to live with it, no matter how painful. Yet God doesn't love one more than the other, and neither are people written out of God's plan just because of the choices they make. That is so for the Patriarchs and it certainly is so for us.

† Lord God, you created variety and difference. Help me celebrate and accept all with whom I am blessed to share. Amen

For further thought

Where can I help in initiatives that reach across divides of differences so that community bonds are strengthened?

Fresh From The Word 2022

It's never too early, *Fresh From The Word 2022* is now available to order.

Order now:

- direct from IBRA
- from your local IBRA rep
- from the Lion Hudson website: www.lionhudson.com
- in Christian bookshops
- from online retailers such as Amazon, Eden and others

To order direct from IBRA

- website: **shop.christianeducation.org.uk**
- email: **ibra.sales@christianeducation.org.uk**
- call: **0121 458 3313**
- post: **using the order form at the back of this book**

Fresh From The Word is available for Kindle, and in ePub and PDF format from online retailers such as Amazon and Eden.

Become an IBRA rep

Do you order multiple copies of *Fresh From The Word* for yourself and your friends or people in your congregation or Bible study group?

When you order three or more copies direct from IBRA you will receive a 10% discount on your order of *Fresh From The Word*. You will also receive a free promotional pack each year to help you share IBRA more easily with family, friends and others at your church.

Will you consider leaving a legacy to continue IBRA's legacy?

A gift in your will to IBRA's International Fund will help continue the legacy of over 139 years. Every penny of your donation goes directly towards enabling hundreds of thousands of people around the world to access the living Word of God.

> *Indeed, the word of God is living and active, sharper than any two-edged sword ...*
>
> **Hebrews 4:12 (NRVSA)**

It was the vision of Charles Waters to empower people in Britain and overseas to benefit from the Word of God through the experiences and insights of biblical scholars from around the world. The goal was to develop people in their homes and situations, wherever they were. His legacy lives on today, in you, as a reader, and the IBRA team, across the globe.

Our work at IBRA is financed by the sales of the books, and since 1882 we continue to ensure that 100% of donations to the IBRA international fund go to benefit our local and international readers. We are blessed every year by those who leave a legacy in their will – ensuring that their hopes are continued to be fulfilled by IBRA, when they have gone onto eternal life with our Lord. To continue this important work, would you consider leaving a legacy in your will?

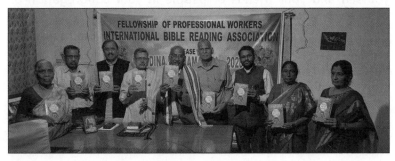

To find out more please contact our Finance Manager on 0121 458 3313, email ibra@christianeducation.org.uk or write to International Bible Reading Association, 5–6 Imperial Court, 12 Sovereign Road, Birmingham, B30 3FH.

- To read more about the history of IBRA go to page 28.

- To find out more about the work of the IBRA International Fund go to page 370.

Thursday 29 July
A full and total embrace by God

Read Genesis 27:30–45

Esau said, 'Is he not rightly named Jacob? For he supplanted me these two times. He took away my birthright; and look, now he has taken away my blessing.'

(verse 36a)

The English idiom 'warts and all' is an invitation to describe and accept a person for what they are, including their faults. It is credited to Oliver Cromwell, who in the 1600s was Lord Protector of the Commonwealth of England, Scotland and Ireland. It is said that when it came time for the artist Sir Peter Lely to paint his portrait, Cromwell told him to render his likeness 'warts and all'. We do not know if the editors of these stories in Genesis about the Patriarchs were issued a similar instruction, but they certainly do not hold back in their portrayal of Isaac, Esau and Jacob. Neither does Rebekah come off lightly!

We live in an age where image matters so much, where your story is custom-made to suit a particular audience market and where every little wart or blemish can be airbrushed and removed figuratively but also literally! In a world where people can (nearly) design the genetic makeup of babies, this story of Esau and Jacob is a breath of fresh air. Like Matthew who, in his genealogy of Jesus, mentions three women with less than 'pure' credentials (in Matthew 1), so too here we are presented with a patriarchal lineage far from perfect which tells the story of all our origins, our faith beginnings and the grace which saves.

† Lord Jesus, in you we see pain and weakness, sorrow and brokenness. Help me to see what you see and to be what you are to all. Amen

For further thought

Check in with yourself today and note how often you shun the unattractive, the not-so-pleasant and ugly.

Friday 30 July
Sisters with silenced voices

Read Genesis 29:15–31

Jacob loved Rachel; so he said, 'I will serve you seven years for your younger daughter Rachel.' Laban said, 'It is better that I give her to you than that I should give her to any other man; stay with me.'

(verses 18–19)

We have a tradition at our church for the reader to announce at the end of a reading: 'The word of the Lord' – to which the congregation responds: 'Thanks be to God.' Maybe we should say: 'The work of the Lord!' For despite the sordidness of the detail of our story, it speaks of God at work. Using far-from-perfect, deeply flawed and rarely holy people, God builds God's people.

Here, love is in the air for Jacob! Things are beginning to come together for him. Love and the prospect of marriage help him forget for a while what he is running away from even though his future is yet unclear. But not for long! Laban inflicts a deception on him that rivals the one he inflicted on his brother Esau. It is a sad and heartless deed perpetrated on Jacob – not to mention this father's treatment of his daughters and slave girls! Laban had opportunities to explain the local marriage customs to Jacob, but didn't. Our story suggests that, in the end, Jacob doesn't do so badly after all and receives some balm for his bruised and battered ego.

To fully 'get' what God is doing, we need to stay with our flawed forbears. We also need to place ourselves fully in the narrative of being God's people through understanding of our own flaws and our need of God's love and grace.

† Lord Jesus Christ, help me to see what and whom you see and then to do as you would do. Amen

For further thought

Is there a shelter or safe house for battered and abused women near you that could use your support?

From fear to freedom

Read Genesis 33:1–17

But Esau ran to meet him, and embraced him, and fell on his neck and kissed him, and they wept.

(verse 4)

I have often found that imagined scenarios which can torture the mind hardly ever turn out as expected. When we stop dithering and confront our fears, they are not nearly so bad. So much energy and time are spent running away from what we fear most in order to avoid the proverbial 'elephant in the room'. In our story today, Jacob had to confront his fear of Esau. He also had to confront his part in the sorry and shameful saga of it all. So he fled the safety of his exiled existence and Laban, crossed the Jabbok, a tributary of the Jordan and gateway to the Promised Land, and he put things in place to ensure that his household was safe should things turn rough in his meeting with Esau.

Freedom from past hurts benefits both victim and perpetrator. We can only all be free together. But for that to happen we need to turn from running away to running towards each other. We will be surprised because often we discover that God has already prepared the ground for our meeting. We must know what our fears are and own our part in why they are necessary for our journey back across our Jabboks. Then we, too, reach the promised land.

† Lord God, give me courage and strength to quieten my fear so that I may be truly free. Amen

For further thought

What are the things you fear most and how can you stop running from them and start your journey back, especially in your relationships?

Pastimes and pleasures in the Bible – 1 Time to relax

Notes by **Simei Monteiro**

Simei is a Brazilian poet and composer. She has worked as Worship Consultant at the World Council of Churches in Geneva, Switzerland. She is interested in worship and the arts, and her book The Song of Life *(ASTE/IEPG, 1991) explores the relationship between hymns and theology. As a retired missionary from the United Methodist Church, USA, she lives in Curitiba, Brazil, with her husband, Revd Jairo Monteiro. They have two daughters and three grandchildren. Simei has used the NRSVA for these notes.*

Sunday 1 August
A need for rest

Read Exodus 20:8–11

But the seventh day is a sabbath to the Lord your God; you shall not do any work – you, your son or your daughter, your male or female slave, your livestock, or the alien resident in your towns.

(verse 10)

It is such an amazing thing to have a pause in a week of work, studies and errands. We know our body needs a pause from time to time. A sabbath pause is not just a gap or an empty time but, like in music, a meaningful pause. This week we will be exploring the pauses in our life as a gift, a holy time to be spent meaningfully. It can be a whole month, a week, a day or just a short break. What matters is the quality of time and not only the amount of time – a holy time to be kept in our memory!

Since the institution of the sabbath, we have known we can have this holy and wholly time at our disposal. God the Creator paused to enjoy his masterwork, creation. That is why we also must enjoy a time to see the world as a gift from God!

Life is like music: we have sounds and pauses to give a clear meaning to musical phrases, to strengthen a melody or a rhythm. It is important to consider this time for leisure. We have so many possibilities. Let us enjoy this holy time with gladness!

† Eternal God! Set our time by your time so we will work and rest with pleasure. Give to our breaks a timeless quality. Amen!

A future with hope

Read Jeremiah 29:4–11

But seek the welfare of the city where I have sent you into exile, and pray to the Lord on its behalf, for in its welfare you will find your welfare … For surely I know the plans I have for you … plans … to give you a future with hope.

(verses 7 and 11)

We humans seem to be a little lost in this world. At times we are strangers and wanderers; uprooted, looking for a shelter we could call home. We have to find a purpose for our lives whether in our homeland or abroad. We need to feel good, have a house, food and free time!

It is incredible how human beings always are longing for a place, a garden and time just to be quiet and rest. Even on a tourist trip we look for spaces where we can enjoy the nature around and contemplate the view. It seems the impulse to find the Eden garden is still in each of us when we visit a city or a small village. God has planted a garden for us as a sign of his care and love. There he put the Tree of Life as a sign of the full life desired for us.

Social peace and stability demand the basic needs of potable water, housing, food and space. In the city of São Paulo, we can find places named Angela's Garden, Europe's Garden etc. But if we go to see these places, we soon realise that they are just shams. There is no garden, but people keep naming them '*Jardim*' (Garden). Is there hope for our city? According to the Bible, surely yes! 'For the Lord will comfort Zion; he will comfort all her waste places, and will make her wilderness like Eden, her desert like the garden of the Lord; joy and gladness will be found in her, thanksgiving and the voice of song' (Isaiah 51:3).

† God, Creator of space and king of Earth! Have mercy on us because our wars transformed so many cities in the world into places of desolation; gardens into waste; lives into death.

For further thought

Do you have a favourite garden or a peaceful place to relax in your city? Do you go there frequently?

Tuesday 3 August
Showing hospitality

Read Genesis 18:1–7

He said, 'My lord, if I find favour with you, do not pass by your servant. Let a little water be brought, and wash your feet, and rest yourselves under the tree. Let me bring a little bread, that you may refresh yourselves ...'

(verses 3–5a)

Nowadays, in some countries, we are wary and even fearful of foreigners. Children are raised to avoid people they do not already know. The strangers: newcomers, immigrants and refugees.

Hospitality is a gift. It means living openly and generously towards others. It is to be sure they feel welcome, included and loved. We feel blessed not only when receiving hospitality but also when giving it to others.

I lived for a while in Recife, in the northwest of Brazil. Sometimes after Sunday service, we were invited to have lunch at one of our parishioners' homes. I recall visiting a local family and being amazed at their hospitality. Later I discovered it was a common practice in this region.

As soon as we arrived at the house, they offered us a bath, slippers and even clean and light clothes! With this gesture they wanted just to say, 'Feel at home!' and after the wonderful meal, we could enjoy a siesta in hammocks under the trees. Never in my entire life have I had such a strong feeling of being really 'received', as Romans 15:7 says: 'Welcome one another, therefore, just as Christ has welcomed you, for the glory of God.'

As Christians, we are blessed by a God full of hospitality, and this spiritual gift must be part of our normal life on earth. It is a privilege and a joy to serve others without expecting any returning favour.

These verses in the Bible brought me good memories of a simple and beautiful life and from my dear sisters and brothers in Christ I will never forget.

† Dear travelling God! Thank you for the gift of hospitality. May it be a common practice in our lives, especially towards the strangers.

For further thought

Remember with gratitude a special moment of enjoying a meal with strangers.

Wednesday 4 August
Celebrating a holiday

> **Read Esther 2:17–18**
>
> *Then the king gave a great banquet to all his officials and ministers –*
> *'Esther's banquet.' He also granted a holiday to the provinces, and gave*
> *gifts with royal liberality.*
>
> *(verse 18)*

Celebrations are milestones in our life's rhythm and also in our country's history. We use them to mark our birth, our passages in life, our achievements and victories.

Do we enjoy the celebrations? What is the meaning and purpose of a holiday? Why do countries have such special commemorations? It is part of our social life and its main purpose is to bring people together. It can be in a small or a big family, with friends, village, city, country and the whole world! Even on occasions where we remember past tragedies or the loss of a loved one, friends and family come together as a group to remember, celebrate and support one another.

The Christians in the early times used to celebrate the deaths of martyrs, the saints. In some countries, the Roman Catholic Church has established a great number of such holidays.

In Brazil, during the time of slavery, the majority of slaves became Christians. Beyond the religion there was another reason to be so faithful: on the days dedicated to the saints, the slaves were allowed to go, well dressed and together with their master's family, to the main church and take part in the festivities.

Some of them became very good musicians and were requested by the priests to play in the street bands and processions. These were days of freedom and the slaves took advantage of each holiday to dance and enjoy life.

We can also celebrate our future freedom on earth or in heaven, even in the middle of our troubles and heavy work!

† Dear God, you are the Giver of Life; help us to give thanks for our entire life – when we are happy and healthy or when we approach the closing scene of our life.

For further thought

Which day is your favourite holiday?

Picnic on the beach

Pastimes and pleasures in the Bible – 1 Time to relax

Read John 21:4–13

When they had gone ashore, they saw a charcoal fire there, with fish on it, and bread. Jesus said to them, 'Bring some of the fish that you have just caught.' ... Jesus said to them, 'Come and have breakfast.' ... Jesus came and took the bread and gave it to them, and did the same with the fish.

(verses 9–10, 12a and 13)

The disciples, led by Peter, returned to be fishermen. The beautiful and complete communion with their Master was broken and they felt disappointed, dismayed and abandoned. What had happened? Why had all their expectations become frustrations?

Now they have spent all night trying to fish, without success. At dawn, tired and disappointed about their unsuccessful work and themselves, all they want is to relax and have a good breakfast.

Jesus took the initiative and searched for his disciples at the shore. Jesus would like to restore his communion with them and is now preparing a meal for them. Peter was sad about his behaviour towards Jesus. He was feeling the heavy load of his betrayal, he wanted desperately to feel again that Jesus still loved him.

We know from the Gospels that soon after the meal at the shore Peter would have been reassured that although Jesus knew in advance of his betrayal, it did not disqualify him from being his disciple.

Jesus asked them to bring also their fish as a visible sign that the communion has been restored. In some cultures, like the Chinese, when a couple's relationship is broken or threatened, the spouse arranges the Tea Ceremony and invites the husband to come. This is a silent meal but the gestures have the purpose of restoring the couple's communion. After they drink tea together, all can be fine again.

A healing meal can be prepared to restore broken relationships. In Brazil we call it 'breaking the ice' and it works!

† Let us pray for broken hearts and broken families, communions and communities.

For further thought

Notice the meals prepared during international peace conferences or summits between nations. Do you think there is a healing purpose to them?

Enjoying nature

Read Psalm 104:10–18

By the streams the birds of the air have their habitation; they sing among the branches. From your lofty abode you water the mountains; the earth is satisfied with the fruit of your work.

(verses 12–13)

The earth is satisfied with the fruit of your work. The creation is perfect! There is fullness everywhere, the soil is saturated with rain, the seeds germinate and bear fruit, there is plenty of water for the animals; there are water and food for all living beings!

But if we were to address these same words to us humans, what would be the answer? Is the Earth satisfied with the fruit of our work? Are civilisation, progress, development, technology and welfare the good fruits of our work as partners in God's creation? Are we doing good to our creation, a gift from God?

Brazil is a beautiful country, full of places to go and spend a holiday appreciating its beauty. Unfortunately, I fear this is changing now! Recently, we have been threatened by several disasters: the rupture of two dams in south-eastern Brazil, the fire in the huge Amazon forest, and a massive oil spill affecting many places along our coast! Are all these natural disasters? I do not believe so!

God's work is to be enjoyed and caring for creation is our responsibility. We have to take care of creation to have the right to enjoy it. Is it possible to have sustainable development in our world? Do we still have time?

I recently heard on the news that we are already reaching the point of no return in global warming. This scares me so much, mainly when I think about the kind of world I am leaving to my grandchildren and their descendants.

God have mercy!

† Creator God, thank you for the beauty of creation and the time to enjoy it. Help us to care and protect the Earth so that it continues to be a place that sustains life!

For further thought

What can you and your community do to care for our shared creation?

Finding space and refreshment

Read Psalm 23

He leads me in right paths for his name's sake.

(verse 3b)

At the beginning of this psalm, all seems to be in the right place, with good pastures and still waters. Nevertheless, we know that our journey is not always easy and peaceful.

Wandering around, sometimes we do not use the main road; normally we will try to use the small paths and there is a danger, despite the beauty of the place, because we can choose the wrong path and get lost. To be sure we are on the right path we will need a guide. A loving guide will take care of us even at the risk of his own life. The Good Shepherd suffers violent death for the sake of his flock and works to save us!

The idea that God might be leading me along the right path in my life for his own name's sake sounds strange at a first glance. But this expression is not uncommon in the Old Testament; we see that God calls, creates, judges, leads and saves for the sake of his name. What does 'for his name's sake' mean?

God determines to preserve his reputation. God will never give up on our life, our destiny, even when we are not able to find the way. It is for the sake of life that the God of life will always drive us to the right path. God will always direct us and lead our lives on the right path, even when we go down twisting paths. God watches over our pilgrimage on this earth; he is our 'traveller unknown', our fellow on the way.

† Dear God, you are our shepherd and guide. We give thanks for your gracious care, mercy, faithfulness and goodness. We believe you will never let us go astray or into danger for your name's sake!

For further thought

If we go alone we cannot go so far, but if God is our guide we will go all the way safely.

Pastimes and pleasures in the Bible – 2 Feeding mind and body

Notes by **Pete Wheeler**

Pete leads St Peter's, an Anglican church plant in a deprived 1960s estate in Aylesbury, UK, hosting two very different 'fresh expressions' of what being church looks like. Having spent the 20 years prior working as a musician – composing, producing and licensing music for film and TV – he trained at St Mellitus Theological College, London. He is married to, and leads church with Ali, a graphic designer. They have two children. As well as music, Pete's creative downtime involves not enough golf and lapsang souchong tea. Pete has used the NIVUK for these notes.

Sunday 8 August
Like music to your ears

Read 2 Chronicles 5:2, 11–14

Then the temple of the Lord was filled with the cloud, and the priests could not perform their service because of the cloud, for the glory of the Lord filled the temple of God.

(verses 13c–14)

It's the big day. They've been practising for weeks. As musicians play and singers sing, God's glory fills the temple. In fact, the presence of God is such that the priests decide it's probably best to abandon the service order (verse 14) – they would have to 'play it by ear'!

Music is a wonderful gift of God that helps us to give him his worth. It reflects, participates in and points us to the beauty of God. Its implicit qualities are hard to describe. It can trigger remote areas of the brain, soothing and relaxing or invigorating and activating us.

When I was five, my big sister helped me play the piano. I let my ears guide me. My first teacher berated my inability to read sheet music, but I continued to play by ear. I went on to make music a career. Music remains a keystone of my spirituality, woven through me, always pointing me back to God. It feeds my mind, body and spirit.

This week we will discover other restorative ways to feed our minds and bodies. As you journey with the Holy Spirit today, try letting go of the sheet music and start playing by ear.

† God of grace, thank you for music and gifts that feed and refresh my mind, body and spirit. As we walk together this week, show me more.

Monday 9 August
Music as therapy

Read 1 Samuel 16:15–23

Whenever the spirit from God came on Saul, David would take up his lyre and play. Then relief would come to Saul; he would feel better, and the evil spirit would leave him.

(verse 23)

Music speaks to us. Its transcendent quality can speak to the very deepest fabric of our souls and being. Isn't it fascinating though that for some of us it's the beats of grime or hip-hop that does this; for others folk or rock; and for others classical or world rhythms?

I like the implication that David's instrumental music (without worship lyrics!) can be used in a worshipful godly way – in this case, to quell the harmful spirit that is upon Saul. Music here is not worshipful in the proclamatory sense or through an outpouring of emotion, but curative – calming, soothing and healing. The fact that Saul's servants turn to music as a solution for his troubles, reveals music's power to affect us positively.

David's skills as a lyrist are apparently well known (verse 18). David serves his king with the gifts he has been given – creativity, skill, dexterity – to make music as a therapy for Saul. Soul music, perhaps? This also helps us understand music's therapeutic value as a stimulant for our own well-being. It is subjective – yes – but music undoubtedly lifts our spirits, our outlook, and can therefore have a positive effect on our mental health. God is Creator and provider and music is a healing, restorative part of that creative provision.

Music teaches us to listen. And herein lies a paradox – it's often the pauses, silences and breath spaces between notes that communicate the loudest. As we live (sing) out our story (melody), these spaces help us to make sense of the story the Holy Spirit is telling through us.

† Creator God, thank you for melodies and rhythms that restore my soul. Help me to listen and know that you are working in my waiting, through the pauses and the silences.

For further thought

Pause to listen to an instrumental music track (or maybe on your way to work?). Pray as you listen, letting God speak. Have a Bible handy too!

Tuesday 10 August
Make a song and dance out of it

Read Exodus 15:19–21

Then Miriam the prophet, Aaron's sister, took a tambourine in her hand, and all the women followed her, with tambourines and dancing. Miriam sang …

(part of verses 20–21)

I love a song with a story. I enjoy listening to 'New Country' – a US music genre that reflects many cultural values and idiosyncrasies, sometimes with an amusing degree of self-deprecation. Songs that illustrate life as a drama, rocky relationships, the pickup truck, fried chicken and how I miss my dog.

Of course, Christians also have a long history of using music to communicate doctrinal truths in our hymns and worship songs, telling God's story, communicating the gospel. Whilst I confess that tambourines have fallen out of favour somewhat in my circles of church, the *tof* or *timbrel* with its wooden frame and metal *zills* was the principal percussion instrument of the Israelites. It's what you pick up when you've got something to celebrate!

Moses has made a real song and dance out of a real-life drama. Joining in, Miriam picks up her tambourine to celebrate her people's salvation. God has done it all! The chains of slavery are broken and freedom in God's promised land awaits. And so they dance and sing! Their freedom in movement expresses their freedom from slavery – their song and dance reflects the restorative work of a God who saves.

In the sport of golf, the 'green' is often described as the 'dancefloor', and it's where I like to do some of my 'dancing'! For me, sport is a way to recuperate. Playing football and golf releases endorphins that keep my mental health in check. It's restorative movement, just as singing and dancing can mirror our inner freedom. Tomorrow we'll think more about the importance of our bodies to God.

† Thank you, God, for stories, songs and dancing – the opportunity and privilege to worship you through our movement. What a Saviour! You who, through Jesus Christ, restore us to true freedom.

For further thought

Joy is often a remedy for tiredness. How might you use your body to worship, and express inner freedom? What's your 'restorative movement'?

Wednesday 11 August
Fit for life

Read 1 Corinthians 9:24–27

Therefore I do not run like someone running aimlessly; I do not fight like a boxer beating the air. No, I strike a blow to my body and make it my slave so that after I have preached to others, I myself will not be disqualified for the prize.

(verses 26–27)

In many UK estates with high levels of deprivation, boxing clubs have often been a story of successful youth work, helping young people become physically active and improving their well-being. The discipline required to train hard, box with integrity and win or lose well is a transferable life skill that stays with young people their whole lives.

The apostle Paul is talking about the self-discipline required to live a spiritually whole life and live it well. Looking after our bodies through physical activity, healthy eating and good discipline is part of the journey of our being made whole in Jesus Christ.

Being fit for life means taking care of the temple that the Holy Spirit chooses to live in and minister through! Not for the sake of conforming or looking good – our identity in Christ doesn't require a certain body size, shape or ableness – but being fit for our calling!

God's endorsement of the human body is Jesus. Like everything God has made, our bodies are fundamentally good. But, like our minds, they're fallen, resulting in a distorted image of ourselves. Our mistake is to assume they aren't worth redeeming (1 Corinthians 6:19), or to think this doesn't matter and that they can somehow bring us to fullness of life anyway (1 Corinthians 6:12).

Feeding our minds and bodies therefore means handling them with care and discipline – Paul determines to bring his body under his leadership, making it 'his slave'. How might you do the same, to keep running the race that God has called you into?

† Jesus, thank you for being born to us in a human body. Help me to enjoy running the race you set before me. As I am raised to new life with you, renew in me your image.

For further thought

This runner is not aimless but focused on the finish line. What's your focus? This boxer keeps their body in check. Time for a check-up?

Thursday 12 August
Feeding the mind

Read 1 Kings 4:29–34

God gave Solomon wisdom and very great insight, and a breadth of understanding as measureless as the sand on the seashore.

(verse 29)

I have a friend, Phil, a vicar in Aylesbury, who loves to spend time lovingly restoring VW camper vans. It has not escaped my attention that as these vehicles are given loving care and attention, week by week, month by month, they are not the only thing being restored. Phil's mind is energised, renewed and sustained in his ministry by spending creative time in his garage! When he speaks about and drives one of his vans, you can see the energy it brings him.

Similarly, if you're a songwriter or author, the solution to 'writer's block' isn't to work harder, but less. To write creatively requires one to get out into the world and experience creation and creativity first-hand. Without any creative activity, you won't have any new experiences to write about.

Our minds need a healthy diet of input, rest, variety and creativity amongst other things. Solomon obviously took this seriously, as he was a prolific song and proverb writer, emanating from his gift of his wisdom. I have been writing music and songs most of my life, but I daresay my total works number well short of 1,005 (verse 32)!

Most notably though, we get a hint that Solomon's creativity flowed from being in relationship with creation. His legendary depth of wisdom – as measureless as grains of sand on the beach – spanned from plant life to the animal kingdom (verse 33).

How do you feed your mind, such that it is restored and renewed? It is the constant renewal of our minds that leads to our transformation (Romans 12:2).

† Holy Spirit, would you come and do a new creative thing in me today? Inspire me. Broaden your horizons in me. Show me your wonders. Use me for your glory and teach me your wisdom.

For further thought

Making bread. Going for walks. Reading. Gardening. Identify the creative activities that sustain you and bring you energy.

Friday 13 August
Social media

In her spare time, my friend Gwladys enjoyed watching pastors preaching on TV shows. If she was to give monetarily, they told her, she would certainly be blessed with God's favour, wealth and prosperity.

The real blessing however is that Gwladys, a new Christian in her nineties, sought my advice on this, to which I voiced, in authority as her pastor, my certain disagreement.

Sometimes it's hard to recognise that we are feeding ourselves (or being fed) unhealthily. We might all agree that the internet and particularly social media can be a gateway to the creation of idols that, presenting a false authority in our lives, can either engage us in unhelpful practices and ways of thinking, or draw us away from that which is holy and righteous. We do well to pause and pray before we hit comment or reply.

The apostles' open letter to the believers in Antioch was a great use of social media. Its distinguishing mark was its extremely careful wording. Having gently established their authority, they affirmed the Gentiles in refusing to observe unnecessary Jewish practices (such as circumcision). This was followed with firm encouragement to ignore the predominant cultural worship of created idols for gods (with related sexual practices), and instead turn their worship to the uncreated One.

It's generally accepted practice to poke the produce in a market to test its quality. We do well, then, to give our recreation time (particularly if we use social media) a poke, to discover if it is a truly healthy practice, asking ourselves, 'What's the quality of its fruit?'

† Father, give me your daily bread. I choose today to live under the authority of your name, and I turn my worship to you only.

For further thought

Does your use of social media encourage others, or undermine them?

Saturday 14 August
Using time to leave a legacy

Read Acts 4:32–37

For from time to time those who owned land or houses sold them, brought the money from the sales and put it at the apostles' feet, and it was distributed to anyone who had need.

(verses 34b–35)

I heard a story recently about a struggling entrepreneur who was twice given a free newspaper whilst at the airport when he was without any money. After the entrepreneur became extremely wealthy, he remembered the friendly vendor and offered him virtually anything as repayment for his kindness.

The newspaper vendor, though, decided to teach what the entrepreneur described as his most valuable lesson yet, by pointing out that when he had offered him a free newspaper it was from a place of poverty. He had responded in kindness when he had little to give. The entrepreneur, on the other hand, was now offering charity from a position of immense wealth.

Reflecting on this story, the entrepreneur humbly realised the vendor was probably the richest person he had ever met.

To truly practise altruism – the selfless concern for the well-being of others – the believers needed to be 'one in heart and mind' (verse 32), centred on the person of Jesus Christ as the perfecter of their faith (Hebrews 12:2). Their calling was to share everything faithfully and selflessly, to leave a legacy of love as the first church.

You don't need to be wealthy to be generous. Using your spare time wisely and healthily is a great way to leave a legacy of love.

Have you heard the phrase, 'You can't take it with you when you're gone'? Well, I'm not sure that I agree! The apostles knew that spending everything on building the kingdom of God meant they would leave a legacy that they would get to enjoy in eternity! We can do the same!

† Help me to use my spare time wisely, healthily and generously. Feed my mind and body. Grow in me a spirit of generosity that builds your kingdom.

For further thought

Who around you might most benefit from an act of unexpected or outrageous generosity today?

Numbers in the Bible –
1 How many?

Notes by **David Lees**

David is a minister in the British Methodist Church, and currently serves in the Shetland Islands, living there with his wife Becca, son Barnaby and tortoise Cracker. He has particular interests in biblical translation and the book of Esther. In his spare time he enjoys wildlife photography and hiking the hills, coastline and small islands of Shetland. David has used the NRSVA for these notes.

Sunday 15 August
What's your number?

Read Genesis 2:1–4a

And on the seventh day God finished the work that he had done, and he rested on the seventh day from all the work that he had done.

(verse 2)

Living on an archipelago that lies on the 60th parallel, numbers seem to be a common way of identifying life in Shetland. From Aberdeen there is a 12-hour ferry ride that will bring you to our collection of over 100 islands, of which 16 are inhabited, and in which can be found 281,644 sheep, 200,000 puffins, 23,200 people, 8,066 archaeological sites and 87 pigs. Or thereabouts.

The first of these numbers has particular significance – the number 60 is etched into Shetland minds. Being 60° North makes this the only corner of the British Isles to be labelled 'sub-arctic', and level with Greenland and St Petersburg, with 19 hours of sunlight at midsummer and views of the Northern Lights in the winter. The number 60 shapes the Shetland identity, and is familiar to islanders for what it represents.

The number seven likewise takes on particular significance in the Bible. So much of the identity of the people encountered in this week's readings is related to the number seven, for the rest, order and sacredness in this passage, but for more as the pages are turned. Seven is familiar throughout the Bible for what it represents.

† God, grant us regular periods of rest, and help us see your holiness in the rhythm of life.

Recreation each day

> **Read Genesis 7:1–10**
>
> *'For in seven days I will send rain on the earth for forty days and forty nights.'*
>
> *(verse 4a)*

God has brought order from chaos in separating the water from the land, but here chaos is set to return as the land is reclaimed by the rising seas, all except for the microcosm of order that is the ark. Noah and family move over the waters of chaos and remain separate from this during the 40-day deluge. Here is the first period of 40 whereby the righteous are separated from normality and routine in preparation for something new.

You may be experienced on the sea and can contemplate whether 40 days feels orderly. I can't fail to note how the ark's dimensions are a close match for the passenger ferry that links Shetland with Aberdeen. Familiarity with 12 hours on the North Sea in a modern vessel fitted with stabilisers does not fill me with enthusiasm for a 40-day stormy voyage, plus the time taken for the water level to drop.

Throughout the Bible it can seem that God's standards are often at odds with human ones. In this passage God chooses to present order, safety and provision in a way that might not be our first choice. Nevertheless, the timescale of 40 days prepares Noah and family for the resetting of creation, and prepares us – as readers – for the significance of periods of 40, to reset our minds to what God is doing, and the time God takes. Resetting, recreating, refocusing cannot be rushed.

† Lead us, Lord, through the changing seasons and help us reset our minds on you, that we might evermore give you thanks for your presence with us.

For further thought

Look back on the last 40 days, months or years. Make a note of the ways you can perceive God's reworking in your life.

Tuesday 17 August
God's family – who and where?

Read Numbers 1:1–16

Take a census of the whole congregation of Israelites, in their clans, by ancestral houses.

(verse 2a)

Around the world family names are often indicators of geography, sometimes historically so, but sometimes in a way that reflects the present. These names might be identified with large geographic regions, or whole countries, but can also identify smaller areas or specific towns. There are family names that are identifiably Shetlandic. Within the isles, however, many of these traditional family names are geographically restricted further, and it is curious to find a surname appear somewhere other than the smaller island or district with which it is most associated. Shetlanders know where the Taits, Gears, Goudies or Pottingers come from (the West Mainland, Isle of Foula, South Mainland and Burra Isle, respectively). As a result, the family history society is strong and able to do histories of these families. Similar setups no doubt exist elsewhere.

The ancestral families of the congregation of Israel are used as a basis for equitably choosing warriors, with 12 men assisting the census. The named individuals represent 12 families, but in this they represent the 12 different geographical locations in which the family of the people of God could be found. The whole congregation of people is thus held in mind, with no corner forgotten.

† Thank you, God, for the family of your people. Help us remember your family wherever it is found and that in our different locations it is you we serve.

For further thought

Which places locally or worldwide are on your mind and in your prayers, and which places have you not prayed for recently?

Wednesday 18 August
Clarity of vision

Read Exodus 24:3–18

*The glory of the Lord settled on Mount Sinai, and the cloud covered it
for six days; on the seventh day he called to Moses out of the cloud.*

(verse 16)

Ascending a high hill can take effort, but the reward of a clear and
impressive vista can be the drive needed to keep on walking up.
As part of a celebration of the Christian presence in one corner of
Shetland I guided a group between two churches over the highest
hill in the region, which rises above all the surrounding landscape.
This was a route taken by ministers in days gone by. For us, a four-
hour walk came with the anticipation of fine views over the North
Atlantic coast. The day arrived but the cloud was thick and low. We
went, sometimes unable to see any further than 20 yards through
the fog, but with a clearer focus on the saints of the past who had
travelled this route in response to God's call.

Moses has no clear view from the mountain over the landscape
below, but is given a clarity of vision, hard to put into words; a
vision of God and of how to live with God. For this clarity and
focus Moses needs time on the mountain to prepare his mind and
being for this moment, time to refocus, time to appreciate the
significance of this encounter with God. What is not clear for the
congregation below is in fact a help to Moses to be free from visual
distractions, to adjust his eyes to a greater vision than the one
offered by the height of the mountain.

† God of Moses, thank you for the wonders of your creation we can encounter; help
us not to lose sight of you as we stand in awe of your works.

For further thought

Are there activities that you need to step out of for a short while to
have a clearer vision of God?

Thursday 19 August
Pressing the reset button

Read Leviticus 25:1–17

That fiftieth year shall be a jubilee for you: you shall not sow, or reap the aftergrowth, or harvest the unpruned vines.

(verse 11)

Rest is a gift that is to be regularly received. Rest is good for people, and the rest of the created order. This summer we followed advice and left half of our lawn unmown as butterflies and other insects need the wild flowers and grasses. Relentless work at the expense of rest does not produce healthy people or societies. The commands of God here are not just for rest from work at set intervals, but a full reset every 50 years.

Rest is not laziness, rest is not sitting around twiddling thumbs. Societal rest can be hard work. These commands acknowledge that within the Law of God, some people may still find ways of overworking, or over-accumulating. Both of these affect not just the individual but can be detrimental for the society at large, and God sets out a system to reset, to start over. In these words is communicated something of God's heart: some should not accumulate more than is needed at the expense of the neighbour who begins to lack what is necessary for life. Human nature is frail and broken, and without regular check-ups these cracks can widen.

It can be hard work to prepare for the generational rest, for the generational reset, for the generational evaluation of, 'How is it with our community?' We might find it easier to keep going through the motions than to stop and consider where the cracks are forming and to change tack and to address them. Rest is not necessarily the easy path, but it is essential for the health of individuals and of communities.

† Pray that God would help you find a balance of rest and activity, and to know what tasks to lay aside for a while, or which new ones to focus on.

For further thought

If you have a lawn, give the land some rest and leave a section to grow wild.

Can God's compassion be quantified?

Read Jonah 4:1–11

'And should I not be concerned about Nineveh, that great city, in which there are more than a hundred and twenty thousand people who do not know their right hand from their left, and also many animals?'

(verse 11)

On the small island of Papa Stour, which lies to the west of Shetland, can be found the ruins of a small Methodist church. These days the island hosts a population of no more than 15 people, yet when the Methodist church was built the island was home to nearly 300 people, a number that is almost hard to believe when visiting the island today. The ruins are a result of depopulation and the stones of the walls being used for other purposes.

Nineveh, on the other hand, boasts a far more astonishing number of people, all contained – like an island on the land – within the walls of the city. Significantly it does not fall to ruins when the Book of Jonah ends. There is some ambiguity, however, whether it is preserved because of Jonah's proclamation there, or regardless of it. Jonah complains that he needn't have bothered and God claims at the end that he has a right to be concerned about this vast quantity of people who do not know right from wrong, or at least right from left. The concern God has for the world, and the people in it, is bewildering in its limitlessness. This is a concern that cannot be contained by the boundaries of the city walls of Nineveh, by the coast of Papa Stour or by us. The vast numbers and extreme distances put words to what cannot truly be said, the quantity of concern God has for our lives and how we live.

† Gracious God, help us know your concern for us in our difficulties and to share that concern in living it out with regard to others.

For further thought

Offer some time, gifts or resources to a charitable cause whose aims are not those that you would normally support.

Counting our days

Numbers in the Bible – 1 How many?

August

Read Psalm 90

So teach us to count our days that we may gain a wise heart.

(verse 12)

A nineteenth-century grave in Cross Kirk Cemetery in Eshaness, in the North West of Shetland, remembers the life of Donald Robertson, who was 'a peaceable, quiet and to all appearance a sincere Christian'. The memorial memorably continues in unashamedly stating that, 'his death was much regretted which was caused by the stupidity of L. Tulloch who sold him nitre instead of Epsom salts …' I wonder how the psalmist would have responded to this event, a life that ends in a sigh, that soon flies away, and another which was in need of a wise heart.

Psalm 90:9–10 may sound a bit like Ecclesiastes' pessimistic laments of, 'What's the point of it all, when all is but a mere breath?' Nevertheless, in verse 12 the psalmist does not follow through that all is lost, but injects some enthusiasm; our days may be short relative to God's existence, but let us learn wisdom because we can. There is sufficient time in life to gain a wise heart, to experience gratitude and gladness, and to know God's favour.

The psalm is not an individual one, it is not about my life, its brevity and what I might do with it. It is a communal psalm; it is our lives together. The wise heart (singular) is somehow a joint expression of us counting our days. The psalm looks forward to those who follow us, that they might experience goodness in God because we have found goodness in God. We live as God's people not as isolated individuals, but as a community gathered in God, and our lives likewise reach other people, including those who will outlive us.

† Holy God, may others remember the goodness we have known in you and our lives stand as a testimony to your steadfast love.

For further thought
Write a letter to someone younger than you, sharing some testimony and advice that you have from your walk with God.

Numbers in the Bible –
2 How many more?

Notes by **Karen Francis**

Karen is the Council for World Mission's Mission Secretary for the Caribbean and co-ordinator of CWM's Partners in Mission. A commissioned minister in the United Church in Jamaica and the Cayman Islands, Karen served in various roles including Director of Communication. Karen holds a degree in mass communication and a Masters in theology. In her local congregation she is a worship planner, co-ordinator and trainer. Karen has used the NRSVA for these notes.

Sunday 22 August
Numbers to live by

Read Acts 1:15–26

And they cast lots for them, and the lot fell on Matthias; and he was added to the eleven apostles.

(verse 26)

In Jamaica, there is a game called 'Cash Pot', a lottery in which numbers have special meaning. Consequently, prospective gamblers feel compelled to purchase tickets based on numbers they encounter repeatedly over a short time.

In the Bible, numbers also have special meaning, and we will see this as we journey through this week's reflections. Today we focus on the number 12 which, in the Bible, represents governmental perfection.

Why do you think the disciples took steps to replace Judas after he betrayed Jesus? Perhaps it would have restored the governmental perfection of the Jesus movement to build the kingdom of God. In today's passage, the remaining disciples 'cast lots' to select his replacement: a tradition in ancient Israel which was used to make decisions without fear of accusations of nepotism or favouritism and was felt to be divinely led.

What guides your decision-making? Mood? Opinions and expectations of others? Tradition? A deep-seated conviction or 'feeling'? For Christian believers we are encouraged to be guided by the Word of God in all we do and to examine our motives before acting. In a world of competing voices, methodologies, fads and even opinion-leaders within the Christian community, decision-making is still not a simple matter.

† Lord, help me to make the right decisions and to always rely on your guidance above all else.

August

Monday 23 August
Who's got your number?

> ### Read Matthew 4:1–11
> *He fasted for forty days and forty nights, and afterwards he was famished. The tempter came and said to him, 'If you are the Son of God, command these stones to become loaves of bread.'*
>
> (verses 2–3)

I understand that the number 40 in the Bible signifies a very long time. Indeed, when I practise the spiritual discipline of fasting, if even only from one meal, it does seem like a very long time without food. Jesus went without food for 40 days and nights, and so have many people I know today. Denying oneself of something vital to the body such as food is quite a formidable task, at the end of which one would be excused for wolfing down any kind of food one encounters.

It was at that moment of intense vulnerability that Satan showed up offering Jesus a way to get the food, which by now, he was craving. But that way was in fact enticement to display power for self-gratification. Well, what's the danger in that? Jesus had a need which was in his control to address. Go for it.

However, let's consider a few details. Jesus had just spent a very long time preparing himself for the important mission he had been given by his Father – to redeem humanity. Jesus' focus would be on meeting *their* needs and sacrificing for *others*. Now he is faced with a temptation which, if he yields, would put self at the forefront. Contradiction? Definitely! Moreover, Satan felt he 'had Jesus' number' as we would say in Jamaica, meaning, he knew the very thing that would appeal to Jesus. He knew Jesus' tremendous power, so his proposal would be enticing for Jesus because it involved the exercise of power. But Jesus did not yield.

† Think of a time when yielding to a temptation would have placed you in a position which conflicted with values you esteem. Reflect on how you responded.

For further thought
The challenges we face are insidious. In the coming week be alert to the pitfalls which could distract us from our purpose and calling.

Who counts for you?

Read Matthew 15:32–39

Those who had eaten were four thousand men, besides women and children.

(verse 38)

Two experiences come to mind when I reflect on this portion of scripture. Firstly, I once heard a well-respected and highly effective leader in a church in Jamaica say, 'We count what matters to us.' He was referring to the obvious contradiction in the Church between being willing to count the offering and set a target for income and also being reluctant to set a target for evangelism. Secondly, I am also aware that both traditional and social media are such influencers of opinion and action that the version reported or published is often the version which is believed, largely because it is the only version which is known. In other words, what is counted (reckoned, taken into consideration, recorded) reflects that which matters.

When Jesus fed the multitude who heard his Sermon on the Mount, the number of persons reported as having been fed were men; the women and children were not counted. My twenty-first-century filter has influenced my opinion that by the standards of the reporters, the persons who were important to count were the men; the women and children were not important. I am aware that the stories in the Bible reflected a cultural context which was highly patriarchal, so that method of reporting would not have been unusual.

However, note that Jesus instructed his disciples to serve everybody. Everybody was fed – regardless of gender and age. Isn't it a blessing that Jesus counts everyone? In this action Jesus did not reflect the wider patriarchal context which would have excluded the women and had little regard for children. What or who counts for you?

† Spend some time thinking about those whom Jesus welcomed: persons who may have been excluded by the religious community at the time. How did this challenge their norms?

For further thought

What acts of injustice are carried out in your own context which favour one group over another? How can you model a different approach?

Numbers in the Bible – 2 How many more?

August

Wednesday 25 August
No magic in the numbers

Read John 2:1–12

His mother said to the servants, 'Do whatever he tells you.' Now standing there were six stone water-jars for the Jewish rites of purification, each holding twenty or thirty gallons. Jesus said to them, 'Fill the jars with water.' And they filled them up to the brim.

(verses 5–7)

If you are offered a shortcut to figuring things out, wouldn't you embrace it? Why do the hard work of experimentation and investigation? If someone else has figured out the formula, then let's follow it: 'Seven steps to success', 'Five ways to build self-esteem'. As we reflect on numbers this week, do you think there was significance to the numbers in this story? What contributed to Jesus' miraculous conversion of water into wine? Was it the six water jars, or the 20 or 30 gallons each could hold? Would the miracle have happened if there were eight water jars or 40-gallon quantities? It might seem an affront to believers that these questions could be asked.

Let's go deeper. It is reasonable, isn't it, to want to know the exact steps to take to achieve a specific end? This is applicable to so many goals – owning a home, getting an education, buying a car. However, shouldn't we be careful about scrupulously applying the same approach to our relationship with God? Do we trust the formula someone offers, or the path someone else has taken and neglect to seek God's guidance for ourselves? In doing so we may miss what God wants to do in our lives by expecting him to do what he has done for someone else.

There is no magic in the 6, 20 or 30 in today's passage. (Otherwise, I am sure the hosts of other parties would try to replicate the miracle!) On the contrary, the key to achievement was the servants' obedience in doing what Jesus told *them* to do.

† Reflect on God's ways, described in Psalm 25:4–5a, and ask for God's guidance.

For further thought

Do we fixate on replicating the circumstances and approaches used by others in order to resolve our own issues and concerns?

When your number is up

> **Read Luke 10:1–12**
>
> *'But whenever you enter a town and they do not welcome you, go out into its streets and say, "Even the dust of your town that clings to our feet, we wipe off in protest against you. Yet know this: the kingdom of God has come near."'*
>
> *(verses 10–11)*

The numbers seven and ten are known to have special significance in the Bible. Seven is said to represent perfection and ten God's completion, or God's Law. The number on which we focus today is 70 which is the product of seven and ten. Seventy has meanings of its own – a period of judgement and a period of restoration.

How can the meaning of these numbers help us to reflect on God's mission which is the focus of the passage today? If we look closely at the passage in Luke 10, we will see that among Jesus' instructions to the 70 (verses 10–12) was a directive which may have been considered harsh. This directive reflects judgement. (Interestingly he gave similar marching orders to the 12 disciples in Luke 9.)

But 70 is also associated with restoration. In sending out the 70, Jesus provided opportunity for them to share the gospel which would restore relationship between God and humanity. These opportunities represented moments of hope. It all depended on the choices of those to whom the 70 (and the 12) were sent.

The mission of the 12 was the same as the mission of the 70, and it is also the mission of all of us who are believers in Christ. We are sent with the gospel of Christ in the hope that people will choose to receive him and to have restored relationship. May it be our prayer that those to whom we go will make the choice which will not lead to death at the point of judgement.

† Lord, we pray for the salvation of all who hear the gospel of Jesus Christ. May they choose to receive you as Saviour and Lord.

For further thought
How do you feel about the finality of Jesus' instruction to the 70 to shake the dust from their feet?

Numbers in the Bible – 2 How many more?

August

241

A number too large to count

> **Read Revelation 7:1–9**
>
> *After this I looked, and there was a great multitude that no one could count, from every nation, from all tribes and peoples and languages, standing before the throne and before the Lamb, robed in white, with palm branches in their hands.*
>
> *(verse 9)*

Carpooling was common in Jamaica when I was growing up. I dreaded journeys with one mother who made us do our multiplication tables. Such abuse! One day it dawned on me that the best way to reduce my stress was to learn my tables. I felt the thrill of victory when I ascended the 12 times table scale to reach the pinnacle: $12 \times 12 = 144$!

When I read today's scripture, the first three numbers of 144,000 reminded me of victory. The great tribulation (recorded in Revelation 6) may have signalled the triumph of evil as many were killed. However, for those of us who are believers in Christ we know that true victory lies in the fact that death is not the end. Those who were persecuted for righteousness' sake had their names written in the book of life in the indelible ink of the blood of Jesus Christ and have eternal life. No one can reverse that. Nothing can reverse that. They have eternal life. Jesus Christ won the ultimate triumph over death and his finished work of redemption can never be obliterated.

The number which matters here is 144,000 sealed (marked off, preserved by God): an unimaginably large number in addition to the great multitude too large to count who waved palm branches of victory because they had overcome by the blood of the Lamb.

† Lord, we pray for those who suffer persecution because of their faith. We also pray for those who have witnessed the death of their family members or friends because of their faith.

For further thought

Many people fear death. Think about your perspective on death. What are your thoughts on Revelation's description of victory for those who had been persecuted?

Whom do you include?

> **Read John 10:11–18**
>
> *'I am the good shepherd. The good shepherd lays down his life for the sheep. … I have other sheep that do not belong to this fold. I must bring them also, and they will listen to my voice. So there will be one flock, one shepherd.'*
>
> *(verses 11 and 16)*

One of the evils with which we struggle in Jamaica is poverty, and in some communities one person becomes the provider or 'Godfather', meeting many physical needs. Unfortunately, this 'Godfather' also makes nefarious demands, requiring unquestioned allegiance. Many poor families are caught in that trap. This individual is referred to as the 'One Don'.

In the passage for today we also see a cavalry of one: one shepherd. Picture him – not Hollywood's Rambo or Terminator, but a shepherd. When Jesus spoke of the inadequacy of the hired hand to protect the sheep it would be reasonable to expect that the opposite would be an ultimate fighting machine, a 'superhero' of sorts. It may be hard for persons living in the twenty-first century, especially if not in a largely agrarian society, to imagine a shepherd as the one who saves the day. Hardly the depiction with which millennials would connect.

Jesus' salvific work contradicts our human expectations of a provider, saviour or 'Don'. Not only does Jesus suffer brutality without exercising might to quash violence, his work of redemption is inclusive. We may ponder his reference to 'other sheep'. I use this reference to contemplate that this one shepherd made a sacrifice which was for those considered to be within the flock (e.g. acceptable by association, birth, race, gender, denomination) and for those many of us would think are not worthy.

Jesus challenges our perception of who is included. For sure, we are clear that he is the one who brings salvation, he is the one who loves to the point of death, and that includes everybody.

† God, you are one. There is none beside you, none greater than you, none before you, none coming after you. Unite us as one in the beauty of your unity. Amen

For further thought

What measurement do we use to determine the worthiness of others to receive blessings? How does Jesus offer us an example of grace?

Letters to the churches

Notes by **John Birch**

Based in South Wales, John is a Methodist Local Preacher, writes prayers, worship resources and Bible studies for his website, faithandworship.com, and is constantly amazed at where in the world these are being used and how God has used and blessed lives through them. Some of the prayers have been adapted for use within choral and more contemporary worship settings. John has several published books and in his spare time plays guitar, sings and enjoys gardening and exploring the beautiful Welsh coastline. John has used the NIVUK for these notes.

Sunday 29 August
Royal mail

Read Revelation 1:4–11

'I am the Alpha and the Omega,' says the Lord God, 'who is, and who was, and who is to come, the Almighty.'

(verse 8)

Studying Revelation can be like paddling in the sea: pleasant to do for a while, then you're suddenly out of your comfort zone and looking for the lifeguard!

Don't worry, this week we are firmly in the shallows, so off with the shoes and socks and let's walk together to the water's edge!

The opening chapters of Revelation are like a group text to seven churches where everyone can read each other's message. The theme, 'He is coming!', is a source of joy to the Church and a challenge to the world. John, exiled for his faith, is merely the secretary, retelling God's revelation in words and images. Here, it is Jesus Christ returning in glory in the clouds so that all will see him, and either worship or tremble!

I've never endured more than mild ridicule or sarcasm for saying I'm a Christian, yet I know as I write that there are people of faith like John suffering physically and economically for their beliefs. In times such as these it can be a great comfort to remember that God's strength, which has been unfailing in the past, is no less so now. That is where our journey begins this week.

† Remember all Christians meeting together for worship today in your local area, that in their prayers and singing they might sense God's presence and voice.

Monday 30 August
A love that's lost?

Read Revelation 2:1–7

'Yet I hold this against you: you have forsaken the love you had at first.'

(verse 4)

In its heyday, Ephesus was the greatest harbour in Asia Minor, positioned on the major trading route to Rome. I've walked through this ancient city and even in a crowd of tourists it feels like a place of importance. Within its narrow streets are remains of shops, cafés, brothels, a huge amphitheatre and temples to the gods of those times, particularly Diana, whose temple was one of the Seven Wonders of the Ancient Age. The risen Christ compliments its Christians on persevering for so long when faced with temptation, opposition, hardship and false teaching.

But something was not quite right, and maybe we can empathise with those Christians, exposed to the exotic mix of beliefs and temptations passing daily through their busy streets. Look back, Jesus says, and see how you've changed over time as people of faith.

If we were all to do that, to remember the time when a spark became a flame as we embraced so eagerly our new-found brothers and sisters in faith, and then compare that moment with the present, what would Jesus say to us?

I've never lived in a city, but I am exposed to the influences of a world which, if not antagonistic towards Christianity, has many thoughts on what really makes for happiness and contentment. These can seem both tempting and reasonable. It's not that faith is lost so much as softened, the flame dimmed. Stop, says Jesus. Remember, repent, relight the flame and move on in faith!

† Prayerfully think about your daily walk of faith and how it compares with a time when it was new. Has it matured and grown, or is it in need of refreshment?

For further thought

Increase your knowledge of persecuted Christians worldwide, and where possible keep abreast of, and support, campaigns raising awareness of their plight.

Letters to the churches

August

A phoenix people

Read Revelation 2:8–11

'I know your afflictions and your poverty – yet you are rich!'

(verse 9a)

Smyrna was a beautiful Aegean seaport (now called Izmir), destroyed in 600 BCE and rebuilt by the successor to Alexander the Great. The image of the phoenix, the legendary bird that rises from the ashes of its destruction, was applied to the city and is seen in these words to the believers there. There's no criticism at all for these faithful Christians in their hardship and suffering, and if they can endure a little longer then, like the phoenix, they will rise victorious and know the true richness of God's love and mercy.

My family has known times of hardship as well as plenty. When life was hard it seemed, perhaps strangely, to strengthen rather than knock our faith, because we were sure that the God who had shepherded our lives to that point would not leave us, but lead us (as Psalm 23 suggests) to greener pastures. Maybe not as spectacular an image as the phoenix, but just as rewarding, as it has meant we can witness to God's goodness based upon our own experience over many years.

It is easy to become discouraged when life starts dragging us down, and for Christians it can be perceived as God's judgement and a feeling of betrayal. But the message from today is that strength can come from weakness, and times of suffering are not ones that should cause us to walk away from God, but rather draw us closer. Be faithful to our faithful God and be blessed!

† Remember those times when, looking back, you can see God's hand was at work in your life, and give thanks.

For further thought

Is there a way in which you can help people in need locally, perhaps by offering your time to the nearest Food Bank or a similar organisation?

Wednesday 1 September
Holding on

Read Revelation 2:12–17

'To the angel of the church in Pergamum write:
These are the words of him who has the sharp, double-edged sword.'

(verse 12)

I am amazed by the amount of information available via the internet. Be it recipes, politics, religion or car engine faults, someone will have expressed their opinion on web pages or discussion boards. It's like having a library the size of a small town at your fingertips. And yet there are dangers in having so much information not actually in print. It changes, and although that can be a good thing, it also means that what might be considered truth one day can subtly change the next.

I'm looking at pictures I took on a visit to Pergamon as I write this. It's a city on a steep hill with spectacular views, renowned in its day for a library containing 200,000 parchment rolls. There were also temples to several pagan gods, but was that enough for it to be called a place 'where Satan lives'?

Perhaps that was because the city was also the regional centre for Caesar worship, the place where you were forced on pain of death to take the name of 'Lord' and give it to Caesar rather than Christ.

How easy when living in a centre of learning, pagan belief and political pressure to wonder what is true and worthy of belief. Some Christians were holding firm and even dying for their faith, others were drifting away. Be sure of what you believe, is Jesus' message. His word is that double-edged sword of truth, so hold on to it!

† Pray for discernment to find, within the news and comment that come through newspaper, TV and internet, the truth.

For further thought

Does your church have a regular Bible study and are you a part of it? Have you considered volunteering to lead it?

Letters to the churches

September

Neveltheless ...

Read Revelation 2:18–29

*'I know your deeds, your love and faith, your service and perseverance,
and that you are now doing more than you did at first.'*

(verse 19)

I've never been keen on workplace reviews. They are often well-meaning, but after faint praise about your contribution to the team there often follows the word 'nevertheless ...' where points for improvement are listed, most of which you know should already have been addressed. Or is that just me?

I picture the Christians in the small garrison city of Thyatira fidgeting as they started reading this appraisal. It begins well, very well in fact, and there are improvements to shout about, but there's also a 'nevertheless ...' to bring them back down to earth.

This wasn't a particularly religious place. Christians weren't threatened by persecution as in some cities, but there were plenty of trade guilds, often holding common meals in temples, with plenty of drink and meat offered to idols. Maybe Jezebel had been encouraging church members to get too involved with the darker side of city life?

As a young Christian I was so involved with church life that I didn't have the opportunity to do much else. Then I realised this holy bubble was not where God wanted me full-time, as I needed to take my faith into the world. Out there I soon realised there were difficult choices to make, and I made both good and bad ones!

God's Word focuses our minds. It reminds us that 'nevertheless ...', although painful, allows for us to repent, turn around and get back on track with our lives as believers.

† Take time to prayerfully think about the balance in your life between church and culture.

For further thought

Is there scope and mission opportunity for the churches in your area to get more involved with community activities?

Wake up!

Read Revelation 3:1–13

'I know your deeds; you have a reputation of being alive, but you are dead.'

(verse 1b)

Have you ever had the feeling that everything is going along swimmingly, and for once in your life you feel pretty much in control … and then suddenly everything falls apart?

If so, welcome to the world of Sardis! The city was once under siege by the Persians, and the army inside were so convinced it was impregnable, perched 500 m up atop a steep cliff, that they didn't even bother to post guards on the battlements. But that cliff-face was porous, and cracks allowed a raiding party to find their way into the city, open the gates while the population slept, and let the enemy in!

And isn't that a message and wake-up call to the Church in every generation? How easy is it, when membership is high, to think that everything is wonderful, and maybe in that time of comfort it's outreach or mission that takes a back seat, and suddenly the young people have all gone? Or when church membership is low, how easy to believe there's nothing we can do other than sit back and enjoy fellowship together until it's time to call it a day.

The church in Philadelphia was small and weak, but that hadn't caused them to lose hope and give up. They got full marks for faith and endurance! So, wake up, says Jesus, to the church in Sardis – but also to us as individuals. There's unfinished work to be completed here, and together we can get this done!

† Pray for a faith that stays watchful and active, and never becomes too comfortable.

For further thought

How might your own church reach out and offer support to another that is maybe struggling?

Letters to the churches

September

249

Saturday 4 September
Knocking at the door

Read Revelation 3:14–21

'Here I am! I stand at the door and knock. If anyone hears my voice and opens the door, I will come in and eat with that person, and they with me.'

(verse 20)

How strange that one of the most-loved verses in the Bible should come from a passage which has nothing good to say about a group of Christians!

One abiding memory I have of a church mission project was talking to the husband of one of our members. He was not a Christian and could see no reason to be one, because in his eyes all the things that he owned, the big house, great job and flash car, were the result of his own efforts. He was totally in control and had no need of God. Now, that did change, I'm pleased to say, but Jesus had plenty to say on the problems of wealth and greed, because the love of money can blind us to the true riches in life which come from God alone.

Ironically, problems with eyesight brought money into Laodicea, then a great banking, financial and manufacturing centre. It had a medical school famous for an eye ointment, or 'salve', which they exported all over the world. Now they are told to put this 'salve' on their own eyes, so they might see their problem – they had been spiritually blinded by their greed and neglected the call of the gospel on their lives.

But lives can turn around, I know that only too well, and Jesus does stand at the door and knock, waiting for it to open, and to enter our lives as both friend and Saviour.

† Search online for Holman Hunt's famous picture of *The Light of the World*. Spend time in prayerful meditation with this image.

For further thought

How can the Church speak more effectively into a society that is so focused on money, possessions and self?

Letters to the churches

September

250

Galatians –
1 All one in Christ

Notes by **Noel Irwin**

Noel is a Belfast boy and a Methodist Minister. In 2000 he moved to Sheffield: firstly working for the Church of England as a community outreach worker, then as Superintendent of the Methodist Mission in the city centre. After working as Director of the Urban Theology Unit in Sheffield, he is now Tutor in Public Theology at Northern College Manchester and trains Church Related Community Workers for the United Reformed Church there. In his spare time he enjoys running in the hills and Brazilian jiu-jitsu. Noel has used the NRSVA for these notes.

Sunday 5 September
Not happy

Read Galatians 1:1–10

I am astonished that you are so quickly deserting the one who called you in the grace of Christ and are turning to a different gospel.

(verse 6)

When I was a ministerial student and working as a hospital chaplain, my boss, when he was annoyed about something, would compose one letter – stating EXACTLY what he thought. Then he would tear it up and write a more measured response. In the age of email and social media it is easier to just click 'send' in anger without going through the helpful thought process of my old senior chaplain.

Now, while it would be fascinating to know what Paul's process of composing a letter was, it is clear, in terms of both form and content, he is angry. Firstly, the opening part of the letter is more abrupt and brusque than his other letters, with no nice things at all being said to the recipients. In verses 8 and 9 you see how annoyed he is, as he even pronounces angels 'accursed'!

Why the annoyance by Paul? Our best guess here is that Jewish Christians came after Paul and were able to convince the Gentile Galatian Christians that to be 'proper' Christians they had to be circumcised and keep the Jewish Law. For Paul this is not a small change but actually it constitutes a totally different gospel.

† Paul's letters would have been read aloud in the churches they were written for. In preparation for our thinking, prayer and action over the next two weeks please read Galatians straight through; preferably aloud!

Monday 6 September
All change

Read Galatians 1:11–24

They only heard it said, 'The one who formerly was persecuting us is now proclaiming the faith he once tried to destroy.'

(verse 23)

I am firmly convinced that one of the most difficult things for us to do as human beings is to change our minds on a major issue – perhaps especially as we get older. As a teenager growing up during the 'Troubles' in Northern Ireland, I struggled to change my views (which I gained in church, community and family) about Roman Catholics. Nowadays with the internet, in theory we should be exposed to a myriad of perspectives, but in practice much of life has become an echo chamber discoursing with those who are just like us.

In the Bible we have some wonderful accounts of changes of heart and mind: Jesus and the Syrophoenician woman (Mark 7), the conversion of Peter (Acts 10) and of course Paul on the Damascus Road (Acts 9). We think of the account of Paul's conversion in Acts as 'lights', 'camera', 'action', a total instant change of perspective. Perhaps it was all that. But I am intrigued with what Paul was up to for three years (verse 18) before he went to Jerusalem. Did he straight away move from one way of life to another? Was that three years a time of study, prayer, conversations, encounters? We are told that change involves both 'learning' and 'unlearning'. Did Saul becoming Paul actually happen earlier than the experience on the Damascus Road, when he witnessed the martyrdom of Stephen? How stuck in our ways are we? In his poem 'The Age of Anxiety', W.H. Auden observes that we have a tendency to prefer ruin over change. Sadly, I have heard this sentiment in a few churches.

† Pray that God will show you what you need to 'learn' and 'unlearn' in your life and church.

For further thought

Try to engage with the perspective of someone with whom you vehemently disagree on something. See if you can understand at all why they think what they think.

Tuesday 7 September
Oh, freedom!

Read Galatians 2:1–10

But because of false believers secretly brought in, who slipped in to spy on the freedom we have in Christ Jesus, so that they might enslave us …

(verse 4)

Here Paul continues his autobiography, which raises almost more questions than it answers, due to the difficulty in matching together the chronology given here in Galatians and the chronology of Acts.

He also introduces the terms 'slavery' and 'freedom' which provide an important part in arguments he will advance later in the letter. If you look at the commentaries on Galatians you will see that within the New Testament, it contains a large proportion of the words 'freedom' and 'free' within its six chapters. Freedom is a hugely important and emotive word for human beings of all political persuasions, but does 'freedom' mean the same for Paul as it does for young people protesting in Hong Kong, for example, as I write these notes?

We tend to think of freedom in a negative (freedom from) and a positive (freedom for) sense. Here in Paul's view of freedom we see a bit of both aspects. It is clear he rejects the idea that says Christian freedom means I can do anything morally that I want – we see this particular problem in Corinth and his problem with it is outlined in 1 Corinthians 6:12 and 10:23. Paul also wants the Gentile Christians in Galatia to resist being enslaved by additions to what was needed for them to be Christ followers: on this occasion, the requirement to be circumcised and food laws. They are free from those requirements, which allows them to be free for the Christ who gives himself to live through them, enabling them to serve others, particularly remembering the poor (verse 10).

† Pray for those struggling for freedom in our world today.

For further thought

What is absolutely essential for you to be called and known as a follower of Christ?

Practical divinity

> ### Read Galatians 2:11–21
>
> *For through the law I died to the law, so that I might live to God. I have been crucified with Christ; and it is no longer I who live, but it is Christ who lives in me.*
>
> *(verses 19–20a)*

It has often been said that Paul's letters are like listening to one side of a telephone conversation! Here particularly it would be nice to hear Peter's part of the discussion. However, as far as we know, Paul and Peter never worked together again after this. This incident provides a bridge into the theological meat of the letter. Before Paul summarises his understanding of the gospel in verse 16, which I love, I must say verse 15 puzzles me greatly – 'We ourselves are Jews by birth and not Gentile sinners' – as I thought that Paul held that Gentiles by faith ceased to be sinners in the eyes of God? Or is he being ironical here? Or, as we often do, are we retrospectively underestimating the Jewishness of Paul through our later Christian eyes?

John Wesley when he spoke of theology always referred to it as 'Practical Divinity'; that is, it should not be about abstract speculation but relevant and useful in the life of the Church and the world. In our passage today we see Paul's concern for 'Practical Divinity' as he takes a difficult personal encounter and uses it to create one of his deepest personal reflections on his faith in Christ. He concludes on a personal level and bequeaths us one of his best-known declarations of his faith in verses 19 and 20. One of the things I particularly like about Galatians is the passion with which Paul expresses his theology. Here we see a faith which holds together both head and heart in a commitment to the person of Christ.

† Give thanks for the Son of God loving you and giving himself for you.

For further thought

What does it mean to be crucified with Christ?

Being biblical

Read Galatians 3:1–14

Did you experience so much for nothing?

(verse 4a)

One of the best footnotes I have ever come across in a sermon said, 'Argument weak, shout loudly!' Our first five verses today are quite 'shouty' before the tenor of the letter changes when Paul, from verse 6 to chapter 5 verse 1, comments on around a dozen passages of scripture. Now, I am not saying Paul's argument is weak, though verses 13 and 14 are notoriously obscure and difficult to interpret. I am more interested in the broader picture of how Paul begins with autobiography, then moves on to the exposition of scripture. Why that order? Why not do it the other way around? Or why not mix autobiography and scripture in together?

I see myself as a contextual theologian, so that although scripture and tradition are important, it is the concrete situation and experience now that I see as key and with which I want to begin and end. I am sure Paul's opponents are quoting scripture and indeed perhaps had the stronger arguments from it (much like those who argued in favour of slavery in the nineteenth century) and I am interested how he begins with current experience – people receiving the Spirit without all of these 'extras' to their faith which others were encouraging them to adopt. While scripture is vital to understand what is going on in Galatia now, he is clearly putting front and centre in this letter the recent past, rather than the distant past. Here my argument may be weak, though I am not shouting loudly ... well not too loudly! But I do think there is something to it.

† Pray through the issues front and centre for you, your church and your community.

For further thought

Saying that something is 'biblical' is the beginning, not the end, of the discussion.

Galatians – 1 All one in Christ

September

Alive to the Law?

Read Galatians 3:15–22

Is the law then opposed to the promises of God? Certainly not! For if a law had been given that could make alive, then righteousness would indeed come through the law.

(verse 21)

One of my favourite songs is 'I Fought the Law' by Sonny Curtis, made famous by the Clash. It has had quite a revival lately, being the chosen tune to a number of videos relishing the recent difficulties, with Parliament and the courts, of the current Prime Minister (as I write) Boris Johnson! At first sight Paul, like Boris, has a difficult relationship with the law he is concerned with: the Jewish Law, the Torah. There is no doubt Paul says difficult things about the Law here which a Jewish person would find upsetting. There is also no doubt that Paul's arguments about the Law seem/are both tenuous and tendentious to us today.

In defence of Paul he of course has no sense at all that he is writing 'scripture', and we tend to forget that. The things he says about the Law are for his Gentile Galatian audience, who are being persuaded by other apostles and their followers to accept at least circumcision and food laws. In that context he says some pretty angry and difficult things about his apostolic colleagues! Elsewhere and indeed in Galatians (5:14) the Law is affirmed. So we need to understand Paul's context before we jump to declare the letters of Paul as a 'law-free' zone.

Saying all that, I still would want to affirm Paul's juxtapositions which certainly apply to Christian churches today. They are a focus on freedom rather than restrictions, a living person rather than dead tradition and hopeful promises rather than laws and rules.

† Pray for good relationships, mutual understanding and service to one another between Christians and Jews.

For further thought

Find out what some Jewish views on Torah are.

Saturday 11 September
One

Read Galatians 3:23–29

There is no longer Jew or Greek, there is no longer slave or free, there is no longer male and female; for all of you are one in Christ Jesus.

(verse 28)

Our passage today is one of the few places where Paul speaks about baptism. He focuses on the new clothes which someone who has just been baptised is dressed in. These symbolise the new identity which a person now has in Christ which overrides all other identities. When God sees those who have just been baptised he sees his Son! Baptism abolishes divisions in the eyes of God. This then leads to what is surely the most well known verse in Galatians – verse 28.

While the verse reflects the major divisions in Paul's world, the important division for the Galatians was of course between Jew and Greek. The message is that the Spirit of God does not actually adhere to society's rules. In terms of these three areas, with the benefit of hindsight, we can say Paul did pretty well in abolishing the distinction between Jew and Greek and not so well at all in abolishing the other two major distinctions. But to be fair, at least Paul did something about one of them. It was many centuries before Christians campaigned in a concerted way to abolish slavery and there are still large parts of the Christian Church who continue to discriminate against women.

This verse has been key in inspiring campaigns for the abolition of slavery and the equality of women. It has been central to the argument that there are times to go beyond the letter of scripture, which is largely pro-slavery and anti-women, to the spirit and heart of scripture reflected primarily and best in Galatians 3:28.

† Loving God, by your Spirit, help me not to make distinctions between people, but to see them through your eyes.

For further thought

Write a contemporary version of verse 28.

Galatians – 2 Freedom in Christ

Notes by **Noel Irwin**

For Noel's biography, see p. 251.
Noel has used the NRSVA for these notes.

Sunday 12 September
Imagination

Read Galatians 4:1–11

Now, however, that you have come to know God, or rather to be known by God, how can you turn back again to the weak and beggarly elemental spirits? How can you want to be enslaved to them again?

(verse 9)

It never ceases to amaze me how many people I know who are dismissive of Christianity as 'superstition' are incredibly superstitious themselves. Horoscopes, crystals, angels and spirit guides all get a fair crack of the whip, alongside a total faith in science to solve every problem, and they do not see there is any issue with this at all! This is quite a good connection with what is going on in Galatians. Here, Paul is speaking to people who have experienced liberation from superstition and are wanting to go back into captivity while theologically wanting to have their cake and eat it.

As I have said last week, we need to be careful about seeing Galatians through a lens of anti-Law and anti-Judaism. I would want to apply Paul's disquiet about the Law in this letter as being about people just fitting in with the prevailing worldview around them. In my context I see a thoughtless theism (believing in God) being replaced by a thoughtless atheism and I am not sure which is worse. The Galatians have tasted a new world and possibilities through the grace of God, Paul despairs: why would they want to go back?

† Pray that we will have a foretaste of the heavenly glory prepared for all God's people.

Monday 13 September
Airbrushing

Read Galatians 4:12–20

You know that it was because of a physical infirmity that I first announced the gospel to you; though my condition put you to the test, you did not scorn or despise me, but welcomed me as an angel of God, as Christ Jesus.

(verses 13–14)

I really struggle with all the scriptural arguments in Galatians. If one of my students wrote an essay taking biblical texts out of context and used strange allegories they would not get great marks! But then I am not a first-century Jew and so it is not surprising I argue and make my case in a very different way to Paul. What I do like is how in the midst of his scriptural reasoning he connects in his own real life experiences.

One of the things you always get with Paul is a brutal honesty about himself and with others. In this passage there is a real struggle within Paul between love for and annoyance at these congregations which obviously meant a lot to him. The Galatians knew that Paul's life had totally changed. He had moved from being a persecutor of the followers of Christ to being an apostle – one sent from Christ. In our era people are airbrushed to look 'flawless' on film and social media; in Paul's time there was religious airbrushing where you were only thought to have the blessing of God if you were completely healthy, so that if you had any infirmity at all you were considered to be under God's disapproval or even curse. So, Paul was not a good 'influencer' for a first-century faith and yet the Galatians had really received the Spirit through his preaching and ministry. They had, to their credit, recognised the crucified Christ in this sick apostle and because of their openness they had been blessed.

† Pray for those, known to you, who are struggling with sickness today.

For further thought

Think about whose ministry and life enabled you to receive the Spirit of God.

Subversion

> ### Read Galatians 4:21 – 5:1
>
> *For freedom Christ has set us free. Stand firm, therefore, and do not submit again to a yoke of slavery.*
>
> *(verse 5:1)*

Paul is very clever here. What he does is subvert the standard Jewish way of looking at Genesis 16, which basically stated that the Jews are the freeborn heirs to the promise whereas the Gentiles are seen as the slaves. Here he paints a picture where Jews are enslaved to the Law, while Jerusalem is enslaved to the Romans and so Christians are actually those who are the freeborn heirs.

Paul reads scripture in the light of his Christian experience. If Paul can reverse a standard way of looking at a passage due to experience and the influence of the Spirit, does this open up the Bible for us to find new insights? I suppose the question is, who or what sets the parameters for the reinterpretation of passages?

An interesting and important 'fresh' perspective on Genesis 16 came in the 1990s from African-American women who saw in the story of Hagar (which of course is about slavery, race, sexual exploitation and poverty, but also meeting with God) close parallels with their history and their present experience. This movement called 'womanist theology' (the term comes from the author and poet Alice Walker) has provided a vital critique to both a black theology which was based on the experience of black males and a feminist theology focused on the concerns of white, middle-class females.

So both with Paul and with womanist theology we see a reading of their own contextual experiences into a Bible story and thus the demonstration of the freedom of Christ in action in relation to scripture and the promptings of the Spirit.

† Lord, thank you for freedom. Help me to exercise it responsibly in the context of your body the Church.

For further thought

Go back through Galatians and see how much you can follow Paul in reading into scripture from your experiences.

Wednesday 15 September
The only thing

Read Galatians 5:2–15

For in Christ Jesus neither circumcision nor uncircumcision counts for anything; the only thing that counts is faith working through love.

(verse 6)

Here we are now in what some commentators see as the third part of the letter, which is concentrated on issues of how to live as a Christian, or what we might term morals or ethics. Paul has outlined the key to salvation as being faith in Christ and not trying to observe all the demands of the Law all the time. But there is a danger if you suddenly find all of your restraints and inhibitions removed: you might feel you can do anything at all you want (verse 13), no matter how destructive and inappropriate. In fact the Galatians were doing OK (as a runner I do like verse 7) but then they got stopped in their tracks!

The first safeguard Paul gives is love – so that we do not binge on junk food and find it impossible to walk anywhere, never mind run! Verse 6 is a wonderful expression of that truth. He loves paradoxes; somehow explaining the gospel actually demands them. So in the new life in Christ, to be free is actually to be a slave to others because of love (verse 13).

One of the odd things about Paul is that he does not often connect his letters in with the teaching and life of Jesus. But here we do have a correspondence between verse 14 and the teaching of Jesus that the central commandment was the love of God and neighbour in Mark 12:30–31, while the working out of what that means is famously expressed in Luke 10:30–37 with the parable of the Good Samaritan.

† Who is my neighbour?

For further thought

What is the relationship between the love of God and love of neighbour?

You in your small corner and I in mine

Read Galatians 5:16–26

I am warning you, as I warned you before: those who do such things will not inherit the kingdom of God.

(verse 21b)

So, the first safeguard Paul gives us is love, and the second one is 'Spirit' which, as you can see in our reading today, is opposed to flesh, which is basically living just for yourself. Paul gives us examples of both ways of living. There is a mixture of social sins and religious sins, but the list is not exhaustive; he finishes it by saying 'and things like these' (verse 21a). The nine items on the list of the fruit of the Spirit are the sort of qualities you would want for a group of folk to have in order to live and work together. I am sure Paul would be appalled at our contemporary individualism. In his two lists, we have one which is all about self-centredness and the other about the Spirit bringing people together to build community and fellowship. In other letters, Paul will use the image of the body and it is interesting that here he brings in the central corporate image of Jesus' teaching: the kingdom of God.

All of those who have caused dissension and difficulties for the Galatians have split the fellowship. The divisions need to be healed, and I am sure many of us know how painful and difficult that can be in the life of the Church. The wonderful thing for Christians is that we have resources to do what may seem impossible, because the Spirit working in and through us can give us those as a community. These gifts will enable us to be salt and light for God.

† Pray for the fruit of the Spirit.

For further thought

Think of issues which divide the Church. Apply Paul's list of the fruit of the Spirit and creatively imagine how their application might transform what seems insurmountable.

Friday 17 September
Faith and works

Read Galatians 6:1–10

So then, whenever we have an opportunity, let us work for the good of all, and especially for those of the family of faith.

(verse 10)

It is interesting that, as we reach the conclusion of the letter, there has not been any mention of any ministry in the churches to which Galatians is addressed. The focus seems to be very much focused on the congregations, not their leaders. Is that a deliberate ploy to go over their heads? But verse 6 does speak of a 'teacher'. As we have mentioned, Paul very rarely refers to the words of Jesus, but in 1 Corinthians 9:14 he says, 'In the same way, the Lord commanded that those who proclaim the gospel should get their living by the gospel.' Here it is the same message, though with a teacher not a preacher.

In a letter which is so much about faith I am intrigued by how, in the last words dictated to a scribe, before Paul writes the final part of the letter in his own handwriting, he says, 'let us work for the good of all' (verse 10). Over the centuries there has been so much conflict about the relationship between faith and works; this is sometimes expressed as a row within the New Testament between Paul and James (or more precisely the Letter of James, which was probably not written by James, the brother of Jesus). But Paul is certainly a 'doer'; he was always clear that walk must match talk, so the contrast between faith and works is between works which are those commanded by the Law (circumcision, dietary laws etc.) and those which are overflowing responses to God's grace and thus expressions of love and faith.

† Pray for all who teach the Christian faith, whether in schools, churches, universities or theological colleges.

For further thought

How can I better be a doer of the word?

September   Galatians – 2 Freedom in Christ

Saturday 18 September
Awkward!

Read Galatians 6:11–18

May I never boast of anything except the cross of our Lord Jesus Christ, by which the world has been crucified to me, and I to the world.

(verse 14)

At the end of a letter, Paul often recaps his earlier arguments. Here, though, it is rather awkward for the Galatian communities, as here he would normally include personal greetings, which does not happen. The lack of the expected cordiality speaks volumes about his rather strained relationships with them! If we return to the beginning of the letter Paul spoke about the resurrection; at the conclusion he talks about the cross, particularly beautifully expressed in the words of verse 14. The cross and resurrection, not keeping the Law, are the source of our salvation.

As well as the summary of what has gone before, he refers to Jesus Christ as 'Lord'. This simple title is actually political and theological dynamite, because without pointing it out explicitly, it is expressing the view that even the Roman emperor (not Lord) is subordinate to Christ (Lord). This is a very important statement not just then, but also now for Christians, whether they identify with the right, middle or left politically. Our primary allegiance and the one who judges all of our allegiances is the Lord Jesus Christ.

Remember as well that when Paul speaks of 'a new creation' in verse 15 he is not just talking about any sort of personal renewal, but the renewal of the whole of creation (Romans 8:19). This is such a vital message for the times we live in, where there is huge yearning for the Earth to be renewed from our abuse of it. So with hope may we join joyfully with the last word of the letter, *Amen* – LET IT BE!

† Pray through the words of the hymn *When I Survey the Wondrous Cross* as an expansion of verse 14.

For further thought
Reflect on your political views and how they relate to the Lordship of Christ in your life and over creation.

The Bible through the seasons: autumn

Notes by **Shirlyn Toppin**

Shirlyn is a presbyter in the Methodist church in Ealing, London. She believes passionately in the preaching of the Word of God without compromise or fear, and exercising a pastoral ministry of grace. She enjoys various forms of leisure and relaxation and her favourite pastime is shopping. Shirlyn has used the NRSVA for these notes.

Sunday 19 September
Harvest offering

Read Deuteronomy 26:1–15

You shall take some of the first of all the fruit of the ground, which you harvest from the land that the Lord your God is giving you, and you shall put it in a basket and go to the place that the Lord your God will choose as a dwelling for his name.

(verse 2)

Worship, dedication and obedience are a few words to describe the duties to be fulfilled by the people of Israel in the celebration of the harvest festival. The instructions for this ceremonial act asked for faithfulness on the part of the people, for the offering of their harvest to God in the temple was not simply a way of honouring God, but a recognition of his blessings past and present.

Dedicating our harvest to God first, be it the fruits from an allotment or a portion of our salary, conveys that what we have is not ours but God's, with a mindfulness of not adopting the rich fool's ideology in Luke 12. What we give to God is not meant to be a kind of payment for God's future provision; rather, the faithfulness of obedience ensures God's blessings, not the offering itself. Therefore, as we journey this week exploring the autumn festivals in the Old Testament, we are challenged to rely on God's graciousness and offer back what he has given to us. Additionally, may we see how our lives and not only our gifts are to be offered to God in obedience and faith.

† Jehovah Jireh, God our provider, thank you for your abundant blessings and may we offer back to you in sacrificial faith and obedience. Amen

The goodness of God

Read Jeremiah 31:10–14

I will turn their mourning into joy, I will comfort them, and give them gladness for sorrow.

(verse 13b)

Celebrating God's faithful promises and generous blessings is paramount regardless of the situation. Today's reading continues with another aspect of bringing an offering to God: not harvest produce, but our lives themselves. Jeremiah reminds us that God's restoration led to rejoicing as the people of Israel who were once exiles in a foreign country were given a renewed hope and future. Joy, comfort and gladness were the fruits of his reward as the people were called to return to worship, which was at the centre of their life. Restoration led to celebration – most of all the celebration of God's goodness to a people who were not always faithful.

We tend to speak of God's goodness when the result is what we want or consider good. Yet life experience reveals that bad things occur, and rarely do we celebrate the goodness of God when confronted with pain and suffering. It seems unlikely that God's goodness would be aligned with what is seen as the opposite of good. However, we celebrate God's goodness not because of what he does, but who he is. Was God not good during the exilic period of his people in Babylon? The words recorded in the reading say that there was a certainty in God's ultimate promise of deliverance, which should engender confidence for those who are struggling to visualise a change in the bleakness of their circumstances. For God's goodness is not dependent on great outcomes, doom or emotion.

† Lord, help me to celebrate your goodness, not being indifferent to the suffering of others, but having a confidence that comes from knowing that you are good. Amen

For further thought

Do you only celebrate the goodness of God when the outcome is what you want?

Tuesday 21 September
Reaping with shouts of joy

Read Psalm 126

May those who sow in tears reap with shouts of joy. Those who go out weeping, bearing the seed for sowing, shall come home with shouts of joy, carrying their sheaves.

(verses 5–6)

Hope amidst hopelessness echoes from this jubilant but realistic psalm. It comes with a message of encouragement for anyone struggling to make a difference in the lives of others, whether engaged in ministry or societal reformation. There is a clear realisation that the psalmist was pointing out that joy is often preceded by tears, where the process of sowing is long and arduous, requiring patience and perseverance. There will be times of disappointment, hurt, uncertainty, fear and even a desire to give up, because circumstances seem to conspire against your efforts, but the reward is worth it, as sweat and tears become rapturous shouts of joy.

Farmers get into a frenzy of activities when harvest time arrives and the memory of long laborious work necessary to guarantee a good produce seems to fade in the distance. There's a sense of pride and fulfilment at seeing the finished result of what may be considered as 'sowing in tears'. Jesus said in John 16:21, 'when a woman is in labour, she has pain, because her hour has come. But when her child is born, she no longer remembers the anguish because of the joy of having brought a human being into the world.' The concept of sowing and reaping is not just confined to farmers. Each of us has experienced harvest times in our life, demanding hard work towards our goals, whether spiritual, professional or emotional. But the psalmist reminds us that with persistence and diligence we will reap rewards of joy.

† We thank you, Lord, that one day there will be no tears, but everlasting joy. Amen

For further thought
Reflect on Psalm 30:5b. Are these words of comfort or challenge?

Holiness and trumpet blasts

> **Read Leviticus 23:23–25**
>
> *The Lord spoke to Moses, saying: Speak to the people of Israel, saying:*
> *In the seventh month, on the first day of the month, you shall observe a*
> *day of complete rest, a holy convocation commemorated with trumpet*
> *blasts.*
>
> *(verses 23–24)*

A day off from work! Yes, but not a day of rest as highlighted in verse 25. Although they ceased from engaging in their livelihood, a special duty unto God was requested: a presentation of their sacrifices. The offering to the Lord was a meaningful and momentous occasion as it enabled the celebrant to look back in time to God's miraculous deliverance. The festival of trumpets was appointed at a certain time so the offering made by fire to God could be commemorated. Ecclesiastes 3:1 says, 'For everything there is a season, and a time for every matter under heaven'; this solidifies the call of the people of Israel to an appointed time for their offering, which demanded a full dedication to God.

The call for holy convocation – a call to holiness – is practised in the Diaconal Order of the British Methodist Church. It reminds us that complete rest of body and mind is vitally important for spiritual renewal. A backbone member of the congregation shared with me her practice of sabbath as a way of enabling her to stop and focus on God. As a result, she feels rested, re-energised and renewed for the Lord's day and the rest of the week. This formula may not work for most people, but its biblical principle of observing a period of rest is deemed essential as a way of honouring God.

† God of eternal rest, give us wisdom to seek rest in your presence for renewal each day. Amen

For further thought

How can you adopt a version of the Diaconal Order's practice of holy convocation?

The Day of Atonement

Read Leviticus 23:26–32

Now, the tenth day of this seventh month is the day of atonement; it shall be a holy convocation for you: you shall deny yourselves and present the Lord's offering by fire.

(verse 27)

In Hebrew, the word for atonement means 'covering'. The blood of the Passover lamb on the lintel and two doorposts of the homes of the Israelites during their liberation trials in Egypt was a covering from death (Exodus 12:7). Therefore, the purpose of the sacrifice was to bring reconciliation between the people and God by covering the sins of the people. This is the most holy of the Jewish festivals, celebrated annually to remind the people that their daily, weekly or monthly ritual sacrifices and offerings were not sufficient to atone for their sins. The festival also stipulated that all the people must deny themselves and fast from food and drink (verses 29 and 32). Why the emphasis on self-denial? Maybe as a way for spiritual strength; renewal; honouring God with their bodies (a spiritual temple); a sign of repentance; sensitivity to hear God's voice.

Christianity does not celebrate this solemn festival (it is observed in Judaism as Yom Kippur, in a form much changed from biblical times). However, I'm aware of many Christians who fast on the Sunday of Holy Communion, as an act of repentance, dedication and preparation to receive the sacraments. The Book of Hebrews, chapters 8 and 9, explains how Jesus Christ became our High Priest and entered the Holy of Holies, not through the blood of a sacrificed animal, but through his own blood on the cross. As a result, Hebrews suggests that Jesus Christ's sacrifice is a fulfilment of the Day of Atonement, covering our sins.

† Thank you, Lord, for becoming the sacrificial lamb once and for all and covering our sins. Amen

For further thought

How does the study of Old Testament festivals help add meaning to the Christian faith?

The Bible through the seasons: autumn

September

269

Friday 24 September
The high priest makes atonement

Read Leviticus 16:2–10, 29–34

This shall be an everlasting statute for you, to make atonement for the people of Israel once in the year for all their sins.

(verse 34a)

Yesterday's reading focused on the celebration of the Day of Atonement and its impact and emphases. Today we turn to the role of the high priest, who must follow the necessary protocol instructed by God when he performs the elaborate ritual to atone for the sins of the people.

First, the priest was required to bathe and dress in the holy priestly garment. Second, to dedicate a sin offering for himself and the other priests by sacrificing a young bull and a ram as a burnt offering. Third, Aaron would enter the holy of holies and use his fingers (not hyssop) to sprinkle the blood of the bull on the mercy seat for the sins of the people. Fourth, the high priest was commanded to cast lots between two goats and the chosen one would be presented before God as a sin offering, atoning for the holy place. Finally, the grand ceremony came to a climax when the high priest placed his hands on the other goat, confessing the sins of the nation of Israel. The goat would be released into the wilderness 'for Azazel', symbolising the scapegoat carrying away the sins of the people.

Each act of atonement by the high priest was meaningful, with far-reaching implications. The instructions confirm that careful obedience is crucial for the manifestation of God's grace. The imagery has meaning in the New Testament, as well. For Matthew, as Christians we are privileged to enter the holy of holies through the sacrifice of Christ, exemplified in the tearing of the veil in the temple in Matthew 27:51.

† Heavenly Father, help us to come before your presence in reverence and humility. Amen

For further thought

What are the lessons to be taught in these ancient stories about the way we approach God today?

Saturday 25 September
The festival of Booths (Tabernacles)

Read Leviticus 23:33–43

You shall live in booths for seven days; all that are citizens in Israel shall live in booths, so that your generations may know that I made the people of Israel live in booths when I brought them out of the land of Egypt: I am the Lord your God.

(verses 42–43)

The climax of this week's reading notes ends with the celebration of the last of the festivals the Lord commanded the people of Israel to observe. The festival of Booths, also known as the feast of the Ingathering or the feast of the Tabernacles, occurred five days after the Day of Atonement. The Bible describes Booths as a time of jubilation as the people celebrate God's continued provision in the current harvest and remember with thanksgiving his protection of their ancestors in the wilderness for 40 years.

All Jewish males were required to make pilgrimage to Jerusalem for the festival, and it was also the time they brought their tithes and offerings to the temple. However, with many people gathered for the festival, erection of temporary booths/shelters was part of the requirements of the festival, which is still practised in different ways by Jews today. It made for interesting viewing and conversation during Bible study at the church where I was appointed.

God's deliverance of the people of Israel was seen in his provision and protection during their wilderness wanderings; this holds true for Christians, too, as God protects and provides for us when we go through life in the wilderness. Like the Israelites who desired to enter the promised land, we may also be longing for the promised land (heaven), desiring to be in the presence of God. We are reminded to wait for the day of his redemption, when Jesus Christ shall return and come and dwell among us.

† As you provided for and protected the people of Israel in the wilderness, loving God, may we always be thankful for your continual provision and protection. Amen

For further thought

Reflect on your own moments of wilderness experiences, where you've felt God's presence providing and protecting – and give thanks.

Mercy –
1 The mercy of God

Notes by **Jane Gonzalez**

Jane Gonzalez is a Roman Catholic laywoman. She is at work on a Professional Doctorate in Pastoral Theology, looking at new approaches to adult faith formation. She has a keen interest in studying scripture and occasionally pops up on local radio reviewing the Sunday papers. Other interests include singing and gardening and spending time on the narrowboat that she and her husband have a time share in. Now that she is retired she hopes to visit all the English cathedrals and walk the Camino de Santiago. Jane has used the NRSVA for these notes.

Sunday 26 September
A grateful heart

Read Lamentations 3:22–33

The steadfast love of the Lord never ceases, his mercies never come to an end; they are new every morning …

(verses 22–23a)

Nowadays, our preferred methods of communication seem to be texts or messages on social media. But the art of writing is not completely dead … While most people no longer write letters, we still love to send and receive cards – at Christmas, for birthdays, while on holiday and as thank-you notes. I collect postcards and notecards on my travels and keep them as a resource for the future. It is a delight to send one that suits the recipient. Sometimes the picture reflects their character, personality or interests; sometimes the words say it all.

There is one card, however, that remains in my box – I don't think I will ever send it. It says, 'Start each day with a grateful heart.' This has, in fact, become the first prayer of my day. I wake to give thanks because whatever the day brings, or the night has left behind, I can be sure that I am surrounded by God's love. The author of Lamentations, in the midst of destruction and desolation, finds comfort and consolation in the certainty of the steadfast mercy of the Lord and his loving kindness. In our everyday trials, we too can be certain of this.

† Father, help me and inspire me to reflect your loving kindness in every thought, word or action of the day.

Monday 27 September
As streams in dry land ...

Read Deuteronomy 4:25–31

Because the Lord your God is a merciful God, he will neither abandon you nor destroy you; he will not forget the covenant with your ancestors that he swore to them.

(verse 31)

As I write this, around the world, people are preparing to demonstrate, peacefully, about the biggest challenge facing the human race: climate change. Global warming manifests itself in many ways: rising sea levels, icecaps melting, desertification and wildfires. This summer has seen exceedingly high temperatures, parched landscapes and dried-up rivers and lakes. Deserts look set to become part of the landscape for many of us, if we continue to ignore warning calls to put the brake on our relentless over-exploitation of the planet. The pitiless, merciless harshness of the desert will be the experience of many.

The landscape of the heart can be as unforgiving. When we are hurt or wounded by others it is often very difficult to find room in our hearts for forgiveness or to emulate God in our treatment of those who have wronged us. We seek retribution – what we call justice – forgetting that mercy is 'God's creative and fertile justice' (Cardinal Kasper, *Mercy*, The Paulist Press, 2013, p. 54). The all-encompassing mercy of God is the central message of our scriptures, and at the heart of the God who never abandons us or seeks our destruction. Scripture exhorts us not to harden our hearts against God (Psalm 94) but how often do we do so against our fellow creatures?

Portia, in Shakespeare's *The Merchant of Venice*, speaks of an unrestrained and unlimited mercy that falls, like rain, from heaven, bestowing blessing on the giver as well as the recipient. Showing mercy helps us to flourish and grow, like the desert after rain. Have we the courage to be merciful?

† Father, help me to find room in my heart for forgiveness and reconciliation, even in the face of great hurt.

For further thought

Read and reflect on Psalm 51. Is there someone in my life whose transgressions I need to blot out? Where do I need to forgive?

Tuesday 28 September
My ways are not your ways

Read Psalm 25:1–10

Make me to know your ways, O Lord; teach me your paths. Lead me in your truth, and teach me, for you are the God of my salvation; for you I wait all day long.

(verses 4–5)

Although I was brought up as a Catholic Christian, I didn't own a Bible until I joined a prayer group in my thirties. There was a Bible at home but it was never opened. My religious instruction and formation came mainly via the catechism and the stories of the saints. When I looked to buy a Bible, I was astonished to find that there were numerous translations and versions available – to suit all pockets and tastes. Since then, I have expanded my library and own several different ones. Different editions from different traditions allow us to appreciate more fully what often gets 'lost in translation' and the nuances that we may miss if we stick rigidly to one version. Of course, the central message does not change but it is as well, now and then, to challenge what may have become safe and comfortable for us and to allow the Lord to teach us his ways anew.

Take the word 'mercy' for instance. In Hebrew, the most important expression for this is *hesed*. *Hesed* is multifaceted – it has a myriad of connotations: undeserved loving-kindness, friendship, grace, compassion and more. The single word 'mercy' cannot encompass all these attributes. It is a word containing a wealth of meanings which we must strive to find every time we encounter a situation which requires mercy. Our world sees mercy as, perhaps, a soft option that allows the 'other' to 'get away with it'. Christians, too, can fall into this trap if we cease to ponder endlessly the word of God in its (sometimes) elusive yet profound significance.

† Father, give me strength to challenge my prejudices and entrenched opinions. Let me be open to new understandings of your eternal word.

For further thought

Tradition identifies seven *Corporal and Spiritual Works of Mercy*. Which of these can you reflect upon and put into practice this week?

The look of love

Read Psalm 123

As the eyes of servants look to the hand of their master, as the eyes of a maid to the hand of her mistress, so our eyes look to the Lord our God, until he has mercy upon us.

(verse 2)

My mother came to England in the 1930s to work 'in service'. The economic situation in Ireland obliged her, and many of her contemporaries, to seek employment a long way from home, in domestic service. She was employed as a maid of all work in a variety of posts. Her recollection of the jobs was good – fortunately she was well-treated and, had the war not intervened, she would have been sponsored in college by one set of kind employers. My mother was fortunate. The lot of the domestic servant throughout the ages has often been poor. As a class they were powerless and frequently at the mercy of unscrupulous and exploitative employers. Circumstances changed post-war and it is now rare to find modest households with maids and cooks. But servitude still exists – in spite of the abolition of slavery two centuries ago, we know that modern slavery persists – in homes, sweatshops and factories both here and abroad.

Scripture often speaks of the relationship between God and ourselves as one of master/servant. 'Speak, for your servant is listening …' (1 Samuel 3:10). How do we ourselves see this relationship? Do we see God as a tyrannical master determined to catch us out in some dereliction of duty? As a mistress who runs her fingers over the furniture to find dust and dirt we have not noticed or dealt with? Or do we approach God conscious of his tender, loving gaze, the eyes of mercy with which he sees us and our frailty? To be at the mercy of God is a wonderful blessing.

† Father, your gentle gaze gives me strength and hope. May I always look on my sisters and brothers with compassion and tenderness.

For further thought

Modern slavery is well disguised – it can be nail bars, car washes or fruit-picking. What are your local churches doing to combat this blight and help the victims?

Mercy – 1 The mercy of God

September

Standing in the shadow of love

Read Hosea 14:1–7

They shall again live beneath my shadow, they shall flourish as a garden; they shall blossom like the vine, their fragrance shall be like the wine of Lebanon.

(verse 7)

This year autumn has been spectacular – a riot of reds, yellows, russet and gold. From my window I observe the changing seasons as the horse chestnuts go from bare branch to 'sticky buds', from white candle-shaped flowers and conkers, to bareness again. But trees are not just significant because of their beauty – we know how essential they are to the well-being of life on Earth. They are the lungs of the Earth; they prevent soil erosion; they provide shelter for birds and animals; they are the source of food and wood for fuel and carving. Not the least of their attributes is that of providing shade. In hot countries, they give merciful coolness, rest and respite.

It is surely this beneficent and merciful shade that Hosea refers to as 'shadow' in our reading. Shadows may sometimes have sinister overtones – nobody wants to live in somebody else's shadow and we fear the valley of the shadow of death (Psalm 23). Who can fail to share Mole's distress as he wanders and stumbles through the looming dark danger of the Wild Wood in Kenneth Grahame's beloved novel *The Wind in the Willows*? But shade and shadows are as necessary for life as light is, giving life and space to the more fragile and less hardy flora and fauna. We too, frail creatures that we are, can find in the merciful embrace of God's shadow a place of refuge, growth and solace.

† Father, when life is difficult and my courage fails, help me to find joy in the 'shadow of your wings' (Psalm 63:7).

For further thought

God's creation needs our protection. Consider planting a tree in memory of a loved one or as a gift: visit www.nationalforest.org or www.woodlandtrust.org.uk.

Friday 1 October
Blessed are the merciful

Read Matthew 9:10–13

'Go and learn what this means, "I desire mercy, not sacrifice." For I have come to call not the righteous but sinners.'

(verse 13)

What does it mean to be a Christian? Or a good Christian? This is a question that I sometimes ask in formation groups or on days of reflection. I'm not suggesting that I have a blueprint or know all the answers – I ask it because I am all too aware how easily I can fall into a rut or mere routine in my own spiritual life. I need to remind myself of the demands of discipleship to avoid becoming safe or complacent. Sometimes, I just tick the box … If they put me on trial for being a Christian, would there actually be any evidence to prove I was?

When I was growing up, the evidence would have been the account of my attendance at church and the obedience shown to the rules and regulations. But the demands of discipleship are not merely about communal worship and the tradition. Jesus asks us to take the gospel to a needy world – to preach through words and action. We are asked to live holy lives that will inspire others to follow Christ: to be as perfect as God is (Matthew 5:48). The evidence we can offer at our trial is just that: holiness.

What does it mean to be holy, therefore? To be perfect as the Father is? Surely mercy is the key. The Benedictus prayer, prayed every morning in the Catholic tradition, speaks of the 'loving kindness of the heart of our God'. Mercy defines God – it is his heart – and it is mercy that must define a truly Christian life. It is all the evidence we need.

† Father, help me to be a witness to your love and kindness today. May I preach your presence through all I do or say.

For further thought

Read Zechariah's prayer in Luke 1:67–79. Give thanks for the occasions when you have felt God's merciful and loving embrace.

Mercy – 1 The mercy of God

October

Saturday 2 October
Without mercy, where is goodness?

Read Ephesians 2:1–10

For we are what he has made us, created in Christ Jesus for good works, which God prepared beforehand to be our way of life.

(verse 10)

They say that, 'Your schooldays are the best days of your life.' Not everyone would agree, but I have nothing but fond memories of both my primary and secondary education. I had some inspirational teachers and made some good friendships that have endured for over 60 years. Most of us had to travel to school on the bus and an abiding memory of the journey is testing each other on our catechism or times tables on the top deck. I wonder what the other passengers made of it all! Some of the questions from that time are indelibly printed on my brain. *Who made you? Why did God make you?*

The catechism taught me that God made us to 'know him, love him and serve him in this life and to be happy with him forever in the next'. Getting to the next world would be the result of being good in this one! And that is the quest and goal of the Christian life – to be good. Goodness is not merely about being nice, however, or just avoiding sin. It is a hard and difficult road to take as a disciple. Mercy is one of the most difficult challenges and perhaps the one where we fail most often. We resist mercy as a choice in our relationships. But without it how can goodness exist? God made us to know him – as merciful Creator; to love him – by extending his love and generosity to others; and to serve him – by choosing to show mercy and forgiveness to others as he chooses to do so to us.

† Father, I thank you for the gift of life. May my life choices reflect your goodness and my decisions be based on your ways.

For further thought

In quiet moments today, pray the Jesus Prayer: 'Lord Jesus Christ, son of the living God, be merciful to me, a sinner.'

Mercy –
2 Called to be merciful

Notes by **Dafne Sabanes Plou**

Dafne is a social communicator who works on issues of gender, technology and internet policies. She has recently retired but is still active in her contributions and participation in workshops, seminars and conferences. She is a member of the Methodist Church in Argentina and in her local church, in Buenos Aires' suburbs, she works in the area of community building and liturgy. She has a big family and enjoys baking cookies for her grandchildren. She's also a women's rights activist and participates in the women's movement in her country. Dafne has used the NIVUK for these notes.

Sunday 3 October
Defeating hostility

Read 1 Samuel 24:1–7

With these words David sharply rebuked his men and did not allow them to attack Saul. And Saul left the cave and went his way.

(verse 7)

After watching the BBC show *Peaky Blinders* for five seasons, one would think David's decision was not the wisest one. For sure the gangster Tommy Shelby, the star of the show, wouldn't have lost his chance to get rid of such a mighty enemy! Why go on hiding in caves, in fear and humiliation, when David could get his enemy on his knees, grab him or even kill him? David's men must have felt disconcerted. Why lose this chance?

But David was listening to a stronger mandate, not one coming from hate or revenge. He even repented of having cut the corner of Saul's robe, an action that undoubtedly showed his courage and power over his enemy. Was it just obedience and respect for the Lord's anointed one? Was it fear of confronting Saul and his army? Or was it the power and strength of one who trusts God and knows that everything is possible for one who believes (Mark 9:23), even sparing his enemy's life?

David held his faith in God and in God's plans for his future in a powerful and creative way. He would go on confronting Saul, but his position was now much stronger because he had shown that mercy could defeat hostility in a life-giving way.

† Jesus, strengthen our faith so that we become brave believers and followers, with the power to heal and transform, filled with your life-giving Spirit. Amen

Not only kindness ... but God's kindness

Read 2 Samuel 9

David asked, 'Is there anyone still left of the house of Saul to whom I can show kindness for Jonathan's sake?'

(verse 1)

It's not so difficult to show kindness: a welcoming smile, a warm handshake, a gentle greeting, a cordial gesture, a friendly invitation. But would setting a place for Mephibosheth at the king's table every day be enough to show recognition to a much beloved friend, his father Jonathan who had become 'one in spirit with David' (1 Samuel 18:1) and even made a covenant of trust with him? It's interesting that David first speaks of his wish to show kindness, but then he goes beyond and points out he wants to show 'God's kindness'. Is there any difference?

Just gentle recognition was not enough for David, not if he truly wanted to show God's kindness. Because God not only wants us to be nice, but urges us to put justice into practice. Mephibosheth considered himself a 'dead dog' (verse 8): disabled, no land, no riches, no future. Eating at the king's table everyday was a great honour, no doubt, but would that do away with the burden of feeling insignificant, no longer important, dispossessed?

Implementing God's kindness and making it true and visible meant restoring what had been taken away in hostility and denial. David decided to do justice and his enmity with Saul was defeated by his strong bonds of brotherhood with Jonathan. He not only gave back to Mephibosheth all the land that had belonged to his grandfather but he also provided him with workers who would farm the land and look after him. There is a point when showing mercy is not enough. Forgiveness, generosity and justice speak of what it means to reflect God's love.

† Inspire us and our faith communities, dear Lord, so that our witness may let others know that your kindness is abundant in grace and justice. Amen

For further thought

Is it possible to achieve reconciliation if there is no justice?

Tuesday 5 October
Making others invisible

Read Zechariah 7:8–14

'But they refused to pay attention; stubbornly they turned their backs and covered their ears. They made their hearts as hard as flint ...'

(verses 11–12a)

It's hard to travel by train in Buenos Aires nowadays. So many vendors line up in the wagon's corridors to sell their goods. They are quite polite with each other and take turns to offer their goods. Sometimes they pronounce long speeches, trying to get possible buyers' compassion. Others sound smarter and just talk about their merchandise's good value and possible uses. Or they just sing or play small instruments to catch passengers' attention. They all look so poor, distressed, tired ...

Where do they come from? Do they live here, nearby? Were they in town before? Yes, they have always been around, though we hadn't seen them, as they stayed in their shanty towns. But now the economic crisis is big, they can't make ends meet, and so they come to town to seek for our attention and help to overcome their hunger. We knew the economic and social situation was shaky in the suburban areas, and so did our politicians and those in government, but most of us refused to pay attention. We turned our backs, thinking poor people would find their way to survive. And they have! They are calling us!

Economic plans, plans that were never centred on people but on profit and accumulation of riches in a few hands, have made our pleasant neighbourhoods desolate. Abandoned factories and workshops, shaky warehouses, empty streets ... people feel scared when walking down those roads. Will we listen to the Lord Almighty's call? Let his Holy Spirit inspire us to action now!

† God, don't let our foot slip; watch over us and help us make the right decisions so that our world becomes a place where we can all share its goods and gifts in abundance. Amen

For further thought

Is there anything your community could do towards people hanging around a nearby train, subway or bus station?

Mercy – 2 Called to be merciful

October

Wednesday 6 October
Seeking liberation

Read Matthew 18:21–35

'"Shouldn't you have had mercy on your fellow servant just as I had on you?"'

(verse 33)

It is so difficult to forgive an offense, an insult, the breaking of family rules, a transgression, a deceitful relationship, or a debt that takes too long to get paid back. Our hearts and minds get hard as if people were already sentenced to be in debt with us for good. Most times we're not ready to listen to any excuses. We avoid settlements and show no understanding. We even think Peter sounds crazy when talking of forgiving someone seven times (verse 21)!

When we lock mercy out of our lives, we get stuck in a circle of anger and selfishness. But the first servant in the parable was lucky. His boss was open to listening and being moved, even cancelling his debts. But why is it that his master's action of deliverance and grace did not touch his heart when his fellow servant begged him to be patient and consider his situation? He was not only denying his fellow servant an opportunity that would change his life, but he was trampling on a new way of looking for solutions, based on understanding, solidarity, empathy … The master had paved the way, but the servant's arrogance betrayed him and stopped him from following new rules, new behaviours, based on love and mercy, God's kingdom's pillars.

French theologian Suzanne de Dietrich affirmed that Jesus' 'actions of liberation' that he carried out when healing, teaching, assuring justice and securing reconciliation were visible signs of the kingdom to come and of Jesus' victory over sin and death. Unfortunately, the servant followed his own way and turned down any act of liberation.

† Encourage us, Jesus, to be bold and engage in 'actions of liberation' wherever there is need for solidarity, justice and reconciliation. Help us to announce in actions your everlasting grace. Amen

For further thought

Try to list some of Jesus' actions of liberation in the Gospels and tag them. In how many ways does he set us free?

Urban enemies

Read Luke 6:32–36

'... he is kind to the ungrateful and wicked. Be merciful, just as your Father is merciful.'

(part of verses 35–36)

The boy knew he was considered an 'urban enemy'. Living in a big city, full of social and economic gaps, where differences in ways of living and expenditure are bluntly exposed, many consider that petty thieves are their worst enemies. 'They should be locked away for life,' one can hear people saying, even if they are talking of a pickpocket, someone who just grabbed their cell phone. A circle of fear of each other enwraps us, based mainly on fear of fear and on an almost neurotic need for security.

After a few weeks in custody, a probation period started. The boy was expected to do maintenance work in the premises of a human rights organisation. At first, staff members would hardly speak to him and they would never leave any valuables around nor out of their sight. But as time went by, the circle of suspicion and fear, on both sides, started to melt and the boy felt he wasn't seen as an enemy any more.

During the day he witnessed people coming to denounce discrimination, hate, bullying at school or at work, abuse, police brutality. He saw people crying, shocked, in anguish, and the staff members always ready to listen, to find a way out, to take action.

Probation ended and the staff organised a small farewell gathering. 'If I had met you before, I would have never gone astray,' said the boy. 'Thanks for making room for me.' When he left, he was confident he could start a new life.

† Jesus, help us to overcome barriers and prejudices. Encourage us to be brave enough to break down the circles of fear and build new relations based on justice and inclusion.

For further thought

How can your church or community welcome those whose life is going astray and who need support and understanding?

Mercy – 2 Called to be merciful

October

Online neighbours

Read Luke 10:29–37
'And who is my neighbour?'

(verse 29b)

How was your internet today? Intensive use of the internet and social networks has shown us that there are no boundaries between the real and the virtual. Though many still think that what happens in the digital world is not as important nor has the same level of impact as what happens in the streets, at school or work, or at home, we know for sure that a little heart or a smiling face can make us happy and a 'thumbs down' can hurt, be upsetting and cause pain.

Do we consider people we connect with online are our neighbours? Working on issues of online violence with a group of teachers and trainers, a young radio journalist told us she had closed her Twitter account because of the amount of insults, threats and aggressive comments she received online every day by people she had never met. She lost her freedom of expression, and the constant harassment weakened her emotionally. An older secondary school teacher mentioned frankly he had stopped using Facebook after an online quarrel over political issues with a group of friends that lasted several hours. He felt so embarrassed he never opened this platform again and has lost touch with these acquaintances.

In present urban societies, being connected is the rule. But does this 'connection' engage us truly with other people's humanity, their needs, their feelings and emotions, their thinking, their beliefs or religious inquiries? Are we willing to care for them as our neighbours, or do we just pass by on the other side when we find them injured, devastated or in pain? Mercy must have a place online too!

† Let us recognise your presence, dear God, in this connected world so that we accept others not only as virtual friends, but as true people who need love and acceptance.

For further thought
Think of meeting with your church or community group to debate about the new challenges of virtual relations and activities.

Remain free and win life

Read James 2:1–13

Speak and act as those who are going to be judged by the law that gives freedom.

(verse 12)

At the time of the coup in Bolivia, in November 2019, most people couldn't believe their eyes when TV and social networks showed the image of a rightist rich businessman and local political leader entering the presidential palace with a huge Bible in his hands. He lay the national flag on the floor of the central hall, placed the Bible on it, and then kneeled and prayed, saying that Christian religion and values would stay there for ever. Then violence in the streets and persecution of opposition leaders started.

His symbolic move expressed the rejection of racial inclusion and religious and cultural diversity, values held very dear in a country where 40% of the population is made up of indigenous people coming from different ethnic groups. Bolivia had been declared a secular, plurinational state in a new constitution in 2009, and this had brought peace and development. Now everything was shaking.

Putting the Bible in the middle of a power confrontation was a huge challenge to Christian churches and their faithful in this country and in neighbouring countries, too. Some spoke of the present times as a 'new apocalypse', when Christians need to witness the gospel's message of love and care, confronting power and standing in solidarity with those who suffer unjust impositions and discrimination.

'You will bear testimony to me,' says Jesus in Luke 21:13–15. 'I will give you words and wisdom that none of your adversaries will be able to resist or contradict.' May his Holy Spirit sustain us to remain free, stand firm and win life.

† Give us courage at difficult times, dear God, to give witness to the new life we have in Jesus that liberates us from authoritarianism and discrimination. Amen

For further thought

What might this 'new apocalypse' mean? Are we Christians ready today to stand firm?

Mercy – 2 Called to be merciful

October

The Gospel of Mark (3) – 1 Seeing more clearly?

Notes by **Edel McClean**

Edel is a facilitator, trainer, spiritual director and retreat leader living in Bury, just north of Manchester, UK. She is currently employed as a learning and development officer for the Methodist Church in Britain, having previously worked at Loyola Hall, an Ignatian spirituality centre, and Fisherwick Presbyterian Church in Northern Ireland. She has a particular interest in prayer, discernment and in helping people meet with God in all the ups and downs of life. Edel has used the NRSVA for these notes.

Sunday 10 October
A fallen world, deeply loved

Read Mark 10:1–12

And crowds again gathered around him; and, as was his custom, he again taught them.

(verse 1b)

Something about Jesus draws people to him, and he responds, he chooses to be with the crowds, he wants to help, to guide, to reach out. The Pharisees, however, come to test, not to learn. They want a black and white answer that will decide who is 'in' and who is 'out'.

Jesus' response reminds us of the fallenness of creation. We are made for wholeness, but we are touched by brokenness, our own and others'. He points out that divorce is less than what is willed for us. He does not, however, take the next step that the Pharisees hanker after.

It's worth remembering Jesus' engagement with a group of religious leaders and Pharisees nursing stones in John 8. Again they try to trap Jesus. Again they seek a black and white answer. Jesus' response doesn't condone adultery, but neither does he condemn. The world is less than it should be. Sin and brokenness are realities. But if we're looking for an excuse to judge our fellow sinners, we will not find it in him.

This week we see how Jesus responds to the brokenness in the world and we can choose how open we will be to what he shows us.

† Jesus, friend and brother, let me be drawn to you again this week, and open to what you teach.

Monday 11 October
Welcomed at our most vulnerable

Read Mark 10:13–16

'Let the little children come to me; do not stop them; for it is to such as these that the kingdom of God belongs. Truly I tell you, whoever does not receive the kingdom of God as a little child will never enter it.'

(verses 14b–15)

I'm not convinced the purpose of this passage is to romanticise childhood and children. People were bringing these children along to meet Jesus. The initiative came from the adults. Why? In a world where life was so viciously vulnerable to illness, war and natural disaster, who could blame a parent for wanting their children to have as much protection, as much blessing as possible?

It is at the moment when we realise the acute vulnerability of our existence, our dependence on chance, on luck or fate or grace, that we become most open to God. As we grow older we inoculate ourselves against the terrifying unpredictability of life by clinging to health or possessions or power or influence to avoid having to consider the riskiness of life.

We see some trace of that in those who most vocally condemn migrants coming to their country. They refuse to believe that they could ever find themselves desperate, hungry, unsafe, without the means to provide for themselves and their family. They have built up their defences against realising that they might one day find themselves in similar circumstances.

It is to those aware of their vulnerability and need that 'the kingdom of God belongs' (verse 14). Children are instinctively aware of their need for their parents' love and care. We adults instinctively seem to avoid our own need. But it is when we are ready to admit our need of God that we find God already reaching out and welcoming us.

† Jesus, friend and brother, help me to recognise the vulnerability in myself and in others, and to welcome your compassion there.

For further thought

Where in your own life do you have the greatest sense of need? How does Jesus respond when you bring this need to him?

The Gospel of Mark (3) – 1 Seeing more clearly?

October

287

Tuesday 12 October
Looked upon with great love

Read Mark 10:17–22

Jesus, looking at him, loved him and said, 'You lack one thing; go, sell what you own, and give the money to the poor, and you will have treasure in heaven; then come, follow me.'

(verse 21)

When I was a teenager there was an elderly man who we occasionally saw hitching a lift by the side of the road. Sometimes we spotted him in town, or outside the local priest's house, always ragged, bearded and frequently drenched. One day some lads in our class were making fun of him when our teacher, the marvellous Sr Anne Marie, stopped them. 'That man', she said, 'was once very rich. And someone he loved died, and he was broken-hearted, and he gave everything he had away and made himself homeless.'

I didn't know the man's name. I don't know how many still remember his existence. But I remember being startled into realising that some people actually took these words of Jesus seriously.

The thing that bugged me then, as a good Catholic schoolgirl, was that it wasn't sensible. I had somehow reckoned that Christianity was the religion of common sense, modesty and not drawing attention to yourself. And here was this strange fool standing in the rain on the edges of our awareness.

I owe that old man a debt of gratitude, for startling me into the realisation that Christianity wasn't just a lovely idea for nice people. Jesus, I believe, asks us to be willing to walk away from those things to which we're most attached, if they get in the way of following him. And it helps to remember that all of those who choose to walk sadly away, and don't we all at times, continue to be looked upon with great love.

† Jesus, friend and brother, help me to loosen my grip on those things that get in the way of following you and to open myself to what you are offering.

For further thought

What helps you to remember that Christianity is not a 'lovely idea for nice people', but a radical call to a transformed life?

Wednesday 13 October
For God all things are possible

Read Mark 10:23–27

They were greatly astounded and said to one another, 'Then who can be saved?' Jesus looked at them and said, 'For mortals it is impossible, but not for God; for God all things are possible.'

(verses 26–27)

The impression of wealth as a sign of God's favour was common enough in Jesus' time that, for the disciples, hearing that the wealthy struggled to enter the kingdom of God must have been bewildering. It continues to be a popular lie today – it's not unusual to encounter Christians who believe that our financial, career or life successes are a reward for a well-lived life. Although few would be so crass as to say that God gives you money if you pray enough, yet there is a tendency to assume that we somehow get what we deserve in life. A few years ago after I was involved in a car accident, a deeply committed Christian asked me with concern if I thought that the accident could have been avoided if I had shown greater obedience to God. The illusion of control is comforting, even if untrue.

Jesus, however, is telling the disciples that the kingdom of God does not conform to their notions of worthiness or deservedness. He recognises how tempting and reassuring it is for us to want to be in control, to earn our way into the kingdom (through wealth, or 'being good'), to somehow prove ourselves worthy. But for Jesus, the kingdom operates by a completely different dynamic that we cannot entirely grasp. When Jesus becomes the one who offers our life orientation and safety, he doesn't promise ease of life, or wealth, or health, or safety in any conventional form. He promises belonging, and a place where those who cannot possibly earn their way into the kingdom encounter God's impossible promise.

† Jesus, friend and brother, help me to trust that the things that seem impossible to me, in my own life and in the world, might become possible with you.

For further thought

Where do you encounter the idea that people somehow earn their way into the kingdom of God? How can that idea be challenged by the Church?

Thursday 14 October
Planting seeds of hope

Read Mark 10:28–34

'They will mock him, and spit upon him, and flog him, and kill him; and after three days he will rise again.'

(verse 34)

Jesus is striking amazement and fear into the hearts of his followers. On the one hand he offers reassurance – that those who loosen their grip on the things of this world will be rewarded – while at the same time taking that reassurance away, adding 'with persecutions'. He is clear that the comfortable certainties and tidy assumptions of how life and faith are orientated will be turned on their head.

Seeing the 12 frightened, he takes them aside and tells them that he is going to suffer, to be mocked, vilified and murdered, and then will rise again. Like many of us, I suspect all they heard was 'mock, spit, flog, kill'. Jesus reminds them of this future several times, perhaps to allow it to begin to sink in, hoping that somehow enough of what he says will be remembered in the midst of the crisis.

We all need the same reminder. When life is going well, we assume this is how it will always be. Jesus' life says otherwise, that we may well find our lives caught up in pain or sadness or storms we could never have imagined.

'After three days he will rise again' (verse 34), Jesus reminds his followers. Here is hope, listen to it! Let it find a place somewhere inside you so that it will breathe hope within you when you feel there is no hope. We might want a more comfortable promise, but Jesus doesn't offer false comfort. Instead he promises that the darkness is not a full stop, but a place where he joins us and leads us towards light.

† Jesus, friend and brother, help us to treasure your promises of hope so that we can be reminded of you when life seems dark.

For further thought

Can you integrate your most treasured promises of Jesus into your life so that you can easily find them when they are most needed?

Friday 15 October
The status of disciple

Read Mark 10:35–45

'… but whoever wishes to become great among you must be your servant, and whoever wishes to be first among you must be slave of all.'

(verses 43b–44)

We've spent much of this week looking at the things that we all tend to hold onto for security. For James and John, their concern is not primarily with possessions. Instead they want status, to be seated in the positions of influence so that everyone can see their importance.

When Jesus says, 'whoever wishes to be first among you must be a slave of all' (verse 44), surely everything we have been taught tells us to do the opposite. Be the first, not the last, be the served, not the servant, be the great, not the little. Even though the world we live in shows the failure of that – where psychological illness soars and individuals implode under the self-imposed pressure to be the first, the served, the great – we are still also told that we must aspire, must compete, must come out on top.

Jesus tells his disciples not to desire greatness or to lord it over others. Deep down, when our mind tells us it's madness to listen, our hearts tell us it's madness not to. We know that we can be our best and truest selves when we are simply being the people God calls us to be. We don't need to worry that without status we'll be forgotten, that we are not safe. Our starting point, our solid ground, the rock on which we stand is this. We never have to compete for Jesus' attention or approval. We do not need to earn his love. Our most important status is simply belonging to him.

† Jesus, friend and brother, help me to pay attention to the love you have for me and to trust it in my daily life.

For further thought

Where do you notice the temptation to be first, or served, or great? How does Jesus respond to you when you feel that way?

Saturday 16 October
Adjectives and action

Read Mark 10:46–52

Then Jesus said to him, 'What do you want me to do for you?'

(verse 51a)

The New Testament isn't generous with its adjectives. Jesus doesn't make his way laughingly, or determinedly, or playfully. He looks at people with love, but we're never told the colour of his eyes or whether he had dimples. We are almost never told his emotional state or the expression on his face.

We're left to imagine how Jesus' face changes as he moves through a busy crowd, when he hears someone calling for him and when he finally comes face to face with this beggar demanding his attention. Similarly we can only imagine the tone of his voice when he asks, 'What do you want me to do for you?'

It's an intimate question to be asked – what do you want? Under all the different wants in your life – for good weather, a different politics, a better car, a hip that doesn't ache, an end to global warming, a decent sleep, the safety of those you love – what do you want most of all?

I believe that both sets of wants matter to Jesus. He cares for the day-to-day hopes and worries of our life, and he cares about the deep stream of desires that flow beneath the surface turbulence. We build our friendships by sharing both the small things and the large, and the same is true with Jesus. Bartimaeus wanted to see again, and the first thing he sees is Jesus looking back at him. Can you tell Jesus what it is you want? And can you imagine the look on Jesus' face as he looks back at you?

† Jesus, friend and brother, help me to open myself to an ever-deepening friendship, a greater understanding of who you truly are.

For further thought

How has how you imagine Jesus changed as you've grown older? What has caused your image to change?

The Gospel of Mark (3) –
2 Who is this man?

Notes by **Michael Jagessar**

For Michael's biography, see p. 186.
Michael has used the NRSVA for these notes.

Sunday 17 October
Movement

The Gospel of Mark (3) – 2 Who is this man?

Read Mark 9:1–13

As they were coming down the mountain, he ordered them to tell no one about what they had seen, until after the Son of Man had risen from the dead.

(verse 9)

I wonder what the three expected when they followed Jesus up that mountain. They got much more than they bargained for: an encounter with the holy – a glimpse of God's kingdom and God's affirming voice; and perhaps seeing each other and Jesus in a new way – humanity wrapped up in divinity. Mountains are indeed 'thin places' where the Divine can be experienced! No wonder the sense of disorientation.

This mountain climbing may look like a diversion from Jerusalem. It may be, though, a reminder that transfigured and transfiguring communities and lives need to stay open to the movement of the Spirit. As if the disorienting encounter on the top was not enough, the friends of Jesus on the way down were told to keep 'silent' about it all. Is that a clue about the importance of silence and listening in our life together, when the instinctive thing to do is to rule out the encounter? Can it be that those of us who are wordy Protestants have missed a clue here? That Christ invites us to stop listening to our own voices and start listening deeply to be transformed, to hear and respond to those voices silenced over the years?

† God-of-past-present-and-future, may your Spirit take hold of our lives and raise us up to walk your way of truth and sincerity, so that our witness is brought alive to reflect your way.

October

293

Monday 18 October
Save us!

> **Read Mark 11:1–11**
>
> *Then those who went ahead and those who followed were shouting,*
> *'Hosanna!*
> *Blessed is the one who comes in the name of the Lord!*
> *Blessed is the coming kingdom of our ancestor David!*
> *Hosanna in the highest heaven!'*
>
> *(verses 9–10)*

This is more than an astute act of political theatre. Here was a crowd in desperate need for a liberator. Today this group would be quickly represented as discontents and anarchists – like Extinction Rebellion blocking up traffic. Then as now, they would have been perceived as troublemakers. Blessed, though, are such troublemakers in their counter-procession, mimicking an imperial procession perhaps entering the other side of Jerusalem at the same moment. The grandeur of Empire's (Pilate's) procession was directed at the occupied to let them know who is in control – and should they consider 'stepping out of line', to expect the full force of the state military machinery. The donkey entry and parade deployed weakness by way of taking power from the imperial forces that would seek to stifle it. The act was a public display of denying the Empire's defining of the occupied. They needed a saviour/deliverer and here he is riding into the heart of imperial occupation. They are celebrating their own hero rather than genuflecting at the feet of political power.

Down the centuries the chants may have changed but the sentiments remain: 'Save and deliver us!' That word 'hosanna' reminds us of the psalmist's cry, 'Save us, we beseech you, O Lord! O Lord, we beseech you, give us success!' (Psalm 118:25). Here is one way of disrupting empire: rewrite the script and make those things that impose themselves upon us our own, in a countering way.

† May Mark's account continue to haunt us, to challenge us and to inspire us as we discern how God is calling us today, in our time and place, to follow Jesus' risky way of non-violent activism, loving-kindness and gracious compassion.

For further thought

Consider joining an upcoming protest march or writing a letter to your local political representative.

Tuesday 19 October
Fig tree, temple and justice

Read Mark 11:12–19

He said to it, 'May no one ever eat fruit from you again.' And his disciples heard it.

(verse 14)

How do we read the cursing of the 'fig tree' in the context of climate and eco-justice? Should the fig tree ask for justice in relation to an unfair judgement, what would be our response? Interpretations over the years have highlighted that the inability of the fig tree to bear fruits relates to the faithlessness of the temple leadership. If the temple is not the house of prayer, then it will suffer the fate that all non-bearing fig trees will suffer. That may be the case. Some scholars suggest that in cursing the fig tree Jesus was pronouncing judgement on the religious, economic and political order of his time which had lost its anchor from its covenantal moorings.

At the same time, I wonder if Jesus was guilty of putting his immediate needs in front of his natural world and its ecological relationships. Having cursed that fig tree, where would people and the birds shelter? And, the idea that the tree's purpose is to produce raises questions about the commodification of a gift and our dependence on 'fruits' linked to a system of growth. Then there is the small matter of barren and fruitful and the link to what is then cursed or blessed!

The mindset here at work is that when a tree grows, the natural consequence of growth is to produce fruit which one can commodify immediately. Growth is related to fruits that must be commodified for personal use. Consider the link with the current economic model premised on debt and growth! An economy of 'full life for all' must include this fig tree waiting for an apology and restorative justice.

† Giver of life, kindle in our hearts your way of living so that shoots of hope spring forth in and around us.

For further thought

Reflect on some of our inherited, traditional matters of faith that you have for some time put a question mark (?) around or continue to wrestle with.

Generosity and empire

Read Mark 14:1–9

'Truly I tell you, wherever the good news is proclaimed in the whole world, what she has done will be told in remembrance of her.'

(verse 9)

Extravagance – pure extravagance – excessive and beyond the bounds of reason. This is what this story is about. Can it be that what we have here are two different ways of being in the world, two examples of how one might confront scarcity? The religious *status quo* and the Roman authorities sensed their stronghold threatened, and in the face of such a threat they choose to tighten their grip. So the woman's act of extravagance, sensuality and beauty is surrounded by brutality: the system and its agents plotting to kill Jesus (14:1). Empires will not tolerate any disruption to their power base and *status quo* so will quickly use every means available to reassert control. That maverick and upstart of a rabbi must be co-opted, and if not neutralised.

I would invite us to consider the response of the system, of empire. The system immediately commodifies both the act and the tangible tool (perfume) to carry out the act. The baffling act of generosity without greed or a profit motive will always trouble systems based on these. The lifestyle of a give-away ethos (to gain is to lose) for the common good troubles a system with greed and profit at its core. In the end, empire's reach, and religion and colonial power in partnership, had its way. Judas was bought out and Jesus was nailed for threatening the economic base of the system.

But back to the woman and her act of extravagant subversion: wherever the good news of full life for all is lived out, the fragrance of that act will shout out a collective and loud 'NO' to all that deny full life.

† God who caresses, kisses and dries feet, help us not to calculate the cost of or hold back our love for you. May all we think and do this and every day grow out of abundant and fragrant love.

For further thought

Reflect on the ways we respond to 'overflowing' generosity: what are our usual reservations? What prevents us from embracing such outpouring?

Thursday 21 October
Bread and betrayal

Read Mark 14:10–16

When they heard it, they were greatly pleased, and promised to give him money. So he began to look for an opportunity to betray him.

(verse 11)

Here are two curiously juxtaposed narratives: an agreed sell-out or betrayal and a key meal in the life of Jesus and his friends. The table fellowship which used to be that space where much was shared now becomes a fractured space where Jesus declares that one among his close team will betray him. Yes, it will be one 'eating bread' with him. Judas, part of a larger picture, often gets a very bad press. There is a conflict going on here. The dominant one is between Jesus and the religious, economic and political establishment. This upstart rabbi was too radical in wanting debts written off, flagging up the year of Jubilee, questioning rituals and practices that were generating good income for the priestly class, keeping and eating with a whole array of dodgy company, and was generating a large following who saw him as their liberator.

Jesus' mission demonstrated that it is possible to take on the big power through alternatives to empire. Hence, Judas' selling out is about more than money and deflated expectations around an imagined liberator. Empire co-opts and buys out Judas. Bread here, then, is both a physical and a spiritual matter. Scholar Richard Horsley reminds us that Rome managed to maintain her power and hold on her citizens through the provision of bread (grains) and circuses (entertainment) at the expense of its colonies whose resources were drained away. So, the matter of bread for Jesus is about more than sitting around a table and dipping chunks in honey and olive oil. It is a counter-statement in the suffocating embrace of empire.

† Bread-making, bread-sharing God, may we continue to sense and experience your presence among us this new day. May the yeast of your Spirit raise us up to become bread and wine of your way of full life for all.

For further thought
Reflect on the role of 'bread' in Jesus' ministry, connecting it with the Lord's Prayer for 'daily bread' and 'forgive us our debts'. Who controls bread and debts? Why?

The Gospel of Mark (3) – 2 Who is this man?

October

Eucharistic shape – a new economy

> **Read Mark 14:17–25**
>
> *While they were eating, he took a loaf of bread, and after blessing it he broke it, gave it to them.*
>
> *(part of verse 22)*

It has been suggested that there is a fourfold shape of our life together as people of the Jesus way: Jesus taking, blessing, breaking/pouring and sharing. This eucharistic shape contains Good Friday and Easter together. The table meal points to a different economy at work, one of abundance that is enough for all.

Imagine what a difference our world can become when viewed from the perspective of God's generosity and abundance. We become more open, less negative and thrive on life-giving relationships. In a world of plenty and at the same time scandalous scarcity, this meal-habit that we have received from Jesus comes as both a countering challenge to the disparities that plague us and an assurance of something different from what the world offers as 'bread'. Around this table, we cannot eat of this bread and forget. We cannot eat of this bread and walk away. We cannot eat of this bread and go on with life as usual. When we eat and drink, we too are saying that God's will for all of us and all the world is to be restored, saved, healed, made whole! When our lives are fed by the living bread, something happens to us: there are certain habits of heart and mind that we inhabit. In the bread blessed, broken and shared and the cup blessed, poured and shared there is a new kind of economy at work around this table. When bread is broken and shared, loaves will abound and there will be more than enough for all. And it is free. There is no expropriation of labour here or commodifying of anything.

And the invitation is clear: do this and it will make you remember me!

† God who spreads a table in unlikely places, thank you for love that touches our deepest needs, and for calling us on a walk of memory and hope. Filled with your Spirit, may we go out in love to be bread and wine for all.

For further thought

Reflect on the ways we have spiritualised this table habit of Jesus into a tasteless ritual. In what ways are you walking the way of the bread of life?

Saturday 23 October
Praying in anguish

Read Mark 14:32–42

He said, 'Abba, Father, for you all things are possible; remove this cup from me; yet, not what I want, but what you want.'

(verse 36)

The reach of systemic evil via its agents is long and persistent. The intent is to cause weariness and a sense of being beaten. It is geared to cause us to question our motivations. How about seeing the text for today as Mark's take on the killing of love, a glimpse of the real of evil and the agony of love? In this sense this garden episode is not merely an account of something in the past. Here is something we can identify with and live out in multiple ways. This is very human: to be tormented, to be upset and to have fears and doubts. Jesus was no exception. It is human to reach these points of struggle about our course of action. It is here, as one example, we can feel the humanity of Jesus. It is both a vulnerable and a courageous moment.

The outcome of the moment could have turned out differently. It takes courage, a sense of purpose and commitment, to make the decision Jesus eventually took that resulted in love being sacrificed. He was nailed to a cross. The *status quo* found a 'full life for all' economy a dangerous challenge to their privilege, so Jesus will not be allowed to live. In this sense, my understanding is that God who wills life for all would wish Jesus to live. It was the *status quo* that brought down its full force on him. In the end life triumphed.

† Give us, this day, Holy One, new hearts, minds and spirits to live lives of holiness that will bring honour to your name as we continue to grow in your image.

For further thought

Think of those you know who are on the 'front-line' of activism against policies and systems that continue to marginalise and impoverish many. Consider a couple of practical ways you can support them.

The Gospel of Mark (3) – 2 Who is this man?

October

The Gospel of Mark (3) –
3 Controversy in Jerusalem

Notes by **Eve Parker**

Eve is a Postdoctoral Research Associate at Durham University, focusing on inclusion and diversity in theological education. She holds a PhD from St Andrews University in Scotland that explored a Christian theology with sacred sex workers in South India. She has previously worked for the Council for World Mission and the United Reformed Church, and is passionate about intercultural ministries and liberationist theologies. She is married to James, and they have two daughters, Minerva and Iris. Eve has used the NRSVA for these notes.

Sunday 24 October
Land and exploitation

Read Mark 12:1–12

'A man planted a vineyard, put a fence around it, dug a pit for the wine press, and built a watch-tower; then he leased it to tenants and went to another country. When the season came, he sent a slave to the tenants to collect from them his share of the produce of the vineyard. But they seized him, and beat him, and sent him away empty-handed.'

(verses 1b–3)

This parable speaks instantly to class conflict in Jerusalem. The upper-class landowner appropriates peasant land, planting a vineyard to make profit from the labouring tenants, creating a system of dependency. He builds a fence and a watch-tower around it, signifying the boundaries of his claim. The boundaries that later become battlegrounds where it is the voiceless slaves who are caught in the crossfire.

Jesus' parables often expose the unjust systems of oppression and offer glimpses into another way of being. The wealthy elites continue to own, control and distribute the world's land and resources. And as is the case in the parable, it is often the characters that remain nameless that perhaps have the most prophetic stories to tell. In this story we read of slaves that were sent by the rich landowner to collect from his tenants and reclaim his capital, but the slaves one by one are beaten and killed.

Why is it that some lives matter more than others? Who is it that puts up fences and watch-towers denying equal access to God's creation? Why must labourers violently demand rights, land be destroyed and slaves be caught up in the crossfire?

† God of the exploited, the worker, the land and the slaves, help us to create systems of equality.

Monday 25 October
Justice over greed

Read Mark 12:13–17

And they came and said to him, 'Teacher, we know that you are sincere, and show deference to no one; for you do not regard people with partiality, but teach the way of God in accordance with truth. Is it lawful to pay taxes to the emperor, or not?'

(verses 14)

Mark's Gospel speaks at a time in which tax collectors were despised. In speaking out in favour of taxation, Jesus risked offending his followers. But if he spoke out against it, he would be accused of treason by the Roman Empire. Instead, he does both, calling on the people to, 'Give to the emperor the things that are the emperor's, and to God the things that are God's' (verse 17).

If the role of the state is to help provide services to the people, including health, education, welfare and other such necessities, then taxes must be paid in order to meet the needs of the people. The system fails, however, when the richest within society refuse to pay their taxes. This is visible today in the growing divide between the rich and the poor, where the 26 richest billionaires own as many assets as 3.8 billion people, and where multinational corporations get away with paying little or no tax. Many people argue that political systems are geared against the poorest in deference to the wealthy. Christ, however, 'show[s] deference to no one' (verse 14); he does not submit to the corruption of the rich or the ruling elites but calls on all to live justly.

Christ here tells us that earthly systems need to offer protection and sustainability particularly for the oppressed. To give to God's what is God's, in other words, to give ourselves to God, demands of us actions in the here and now that we seek greater truth and justice in the systems of power. As God's people on earth, we are duty-bound to hold earthly systems to account when they are dominated by greed, deference and partiality.

† God of peace, love and justice, help us to live in the light of your truth to not regard people with partiality but to seek the fullness of life for all, as we are all one in Christ Jesus.

For further thought

Building on yesterday's reading, imagine a vineyard where there are no fences or watch-towers, where people have equal rights and access to the land, and instead of labourers, we are all stewards equally sharing and caring for the crop.

Tuesday 26 October
God of the living

Read Mark 12:18–27

Jesus said to them, 'Is not this the reason you are wrong, that you know neither the scriptures nor the power of God? For when they rise from the dead, they neither marry nor are given in marriage, but are like angels in heaven.'

(verses 24–25)

The Sadducees were the High Priests and religious elites during Jesus' time. Here, they sought to trap Jesus by using the scriptures in order to test the authenticity of faith in the resurrection, and Jesus' response is blunt: he declares them 'wrong'. Jesus opposes the Sadducees' literalist reading of the scriptures and presents them instead with the *living word*, declaring that God is the God of the living not the dead.

As Christians we can often get lost in a moral battleground, testing one another in the authenticity of one's faith based upon what we believe the Bible to say and using it to then cast judgement on others. We sit in churches, study groups, synods and assemblies, declaring who has the right to serve Christ in ministry, the right to love in marriage, the right to represent at the altar. Like the Sadducees we test each other with scripture, we deny people of their right to live and love Christ freely in who they are; we see this in the ways in which our scriptures have been used to justify slavery, racism, xenophobia, homophobia and violence against women.

If the Sadducees had been paying attention to Jesus' teachings, perhaps they would have reconsidered their questioning, and asked how better they could have supported the poor woman who was widowed seven times, was childless and later died? The God of the living calls on us to challenge such realities, to take the side of the widow and to do so without ignorance or prejudice.

† God of the widow, be with her as she mourns, as she marries, as she grieves, as she hungers and as she dies, and is born into new life.

For further thought

What can we do in our communities to better serve those who are pushed to the margins of society?

The Gospel of Mark (3) – 3 Controversy in Jerusalem

October

Wednesday 27 October
Love with all your soul

Read Mark 12:28–34

'"Hear, O Israel: the Lord our God, the Lord is one; you shall love the Lord your God with all your heart, and with all your soul, and with all your mind, and with all your strength." The second is this, "You shall love your neighbour as yourself." There is no other commandment greater than these.'

(verses 29b–31)

Roman soldiers upheld the boundaries of the colonialised lands of the Roman Empire and demanded loyalty and love for the emperor from its subjects. The emperor was given divine status and deemed lord of the world. Christ, though, calls on the people to love God our Lord with all our heart and soul. This was a provocative statement, calling for a radical love that required the people to put God and neighbour before self, empire and emperor.

The world is full of walls and boundaries, some figurative, some literal. They separate us as nations, as individuals, as families, as religions and as institutions. The boundaries can prevent us from seeing our neighbours in their wholeness, they can create feelings of isolation, marginalisation, and fear and hatred of the other. The walls and boundaries can lead to hate and intolerance that lead to violence, and the neighbour whom we are commanded to love as ourselves becomes the enemy. If we turn on the news today, we will likely hear stories of war, knife crime, gun crime, and of antisemitic, Islamophobic and racist hate crimes. We will read about the refugee crisis, the rise in homelessness, global poverty and violence against women. All such realities point to humanity's failure in truly loving our neighbours as we love ourselves.

To love God with all our heart and soul requires living our lives as Christ loved, by taking the side of the oppressed, the widow, the refugee, the poor, the sick and the marginalised and refusing to succumb to the injustices of empire that lead to a fear and hatred of our neighbours.

† Lord our God, what a glorious love you have revealed to us, let us live such a love in all our thoughts, words and deeds.

For further thought

How can we resist the oppressions of today's empires that build walls between us and our neighbours?

The Gospel of Mark (3) – 3 Controversy in Jerusalem

October

Thursday 28 October
The prophetic widow

Read Mark 12:35–44

A poor widow came and put in two small copper coins, which are worth a penny. Then he called his disciples and said to them, 'Truly I tell you, this poor widow has put in more than all those who are contributing to the treasury.'

(verses 42–43)

In Jesus' era the widow was representative of the poorest and most vulnerable in society, yet it is the silent and marginalised widow that humiliates the powerful temple elites. Despite the widow remaining nameless and voiceless, her actions are prophetic as they speak of resistance against empire. She has been left in a state of poverty, yet with the only two copper coins she has, she gives them back. On the one hand this could be considered a humble and submissive act to the religious authorities, but to see it simply as this would be to patronise this woman's existence, as she risks starving to make her point. She gives all that she has, which is so little, and in doing so we can witness the failures of the political and religious systems of power that have left her struggling. She gives to Caesar what is Caesar's and to God what is God's, as she gives herself as witness.

The actions of the widow, like the actions of Christ, are shaped by a radical love that exposes the injustices of empire. Christ calls out the scribes who walk around in expensive robes, take 'the best seats in the synagogues' (verse 39) and demand respect whilst 'devour[ing] widows' houses' (verse 40). The hypocrisy of the religious elites who take from the poor whilst enabling the rich opposes all that the kingdom of God represents. It would be like a church that runs a food bank whilst propping up a state that has brought about food poverty; such acts are no different than those of the hypocritical scribes.

† God of the poor, help us to have the courage to act against systems of oppression, to speak up for the marginalised and to beware of the scribes who demand deference.

For further thought
With whom do you most identify in this passage?

Friday 29 October
End of earthly empires

Read Mark 13:1–13

Then Jesus asked him, 'Do you see these great buildings? Not one stone will be left here upon another; all will be thrown down.'

(verse 2)

Imagine watching as the temple buildings crumbled before you. It would be terrifying, but Mark's Gospel speaks here to the coming of the end times where we will witness the upheaval of all earthly empires. During the time when Jesus spoke these words, some considered the temple to be a reflection of the injustices of the corruption of empire that was dominated by greed, power and exploitation. Whilst the disciple praises the grandeur of the building, Christ makes it clear that he is not impressed, but that the power of God will bring about the downfall of the imperial ambitions that have caused so much inequality and oppression for those at the underside of the imperial regime. When Jesus goes on to warn the disciples that there will be people who will try to lead them astray, he speaks of the religious elites and political regimes that build these grand temples as statements of power.

Throughout Mark's Gospel Jesus speaks directly against those who demand power and privilege in the name of God but do so hypocritically whilst ignoring the needs of the poor. Jesus forewarns the disciples of the Lord's coming where all such earthly empires will crumble. Today we see the grandeur of earthly empires in the face of consumerism that distracts us from the damage we are doing to the Earth's resources, and the poorest within society. Have we been led astray by the apparent grandeur of products and over-consumption that is causing the Earth to crumble?

† We pray for the courage to not be led astray by competition and consumerism.

For further thought
How can we better protect the Earth from crumbling?

The Gospel of Mark (3) – 3 Controversy in Jerusalem

October

305

Son of Man

> **Read Mark 13:14–27**
>
> *'Then they will see "the Son of Man coming in clouds" with great power and glory.'*
>
> *(verse 26)*

Jesus knows his time in his earthly mission will soon be coming to an end, and he therefore speaks with great urgency to his disciples, noting that he has 'forewarned' them and they must stay focused. The language used is prophetic and apocalyptic. We hear of a great persecution that will take place, where 'no flesh would be saved', and where we must not be fooled by 'false messiahs and false prophets' (verse 22). Christ knows his earthly death is imminent; the disciples must carry on his mission and so they must be sure to listen (how could one not listen to such graphic descriptions of what is to come?!).

And yet we often don't listen. We can turn on the news and hear about global poverty and malnutrition that causes the deaths of 2 million children a year, about the violent wars where so many innocents are dying, or about the refugee crisis where children's bodies are left to drown in the oceans as they are forced to escape the horrors of the land. But do we listen? The destruction of the 'temple' will bring about the end of the earthly regimes that permit such vile injustices. The Son of Man's coming will guarantee liberation for the oppressed, but that does not permit us to escape into a future utopia; we must 'look!' and 'listen' to the signs of the times, and as Christ did, we must speak truth to power, because it is in the Son of Man, both living and coming, that true glory is found.

† Son of Man, Son of Peace, love and hope, we call on you to help us listen to the cries of the suffering and to be witnesses to your mission on earth.

For further thought

Do we listen well enough and do we act bravely enough in response to the oppressive signs of the times?

On eagles' wings

Notes by **Deseta Davis**

For Deseta's biography, see p. 81.
Deseta has used the NIVUK for these notes.

Sunday 31 October
Soaring above the storm

Read Exodus 19:1–6

'"You yourselves have seen what I did to Egypt, and how I carried you on eagles' wings and brought you to myself."'

(verse 4)

This theme looks at the surprisingly rich image of the eagle in the Bible. The Bible sees the eagle as one of the strongest and most resilient birds and uses the image positively and negatively.

In some countries, the eagle is seen as the father of birds of prey. It is a fascinating bird representing speed, strength, security and care, each of which is borne out in the Bible. This week we look at the array of characteristics afforded to this magnificent bird.

In today's text, Israel has just camped at Mt Sinai and Moses goes up the mountain to receive the commands of God. But before this happens, God tells Moses to remind the people where he has brought them from. Using the metaphor of the eagle, he emphasises to the people that God carried them on eagles' wings and brought them to himself.

The very large wingspan of the eagle enables it to fly at very high altitudes, high above the clouds, where no other bird can fly. The eagle welcomes the challenge of the storm and flies above it. God sees himself as the eagle carrying his people Israel soaring to greater heights, using the current of the storm of Egypt and Exodus.

This metaphor still works today. During times of trials and difficulties, God carries us as if on eagles' wings, not only above the storm but bringing us to himself.

† Creator God, help me to remember that through my difficulties you carry me to yourself, as if on eagles' wings, above the storm.

Monday 1 November (All Saints' Day)
The discipline of the Lord

Read Deuteronomy 28:1–7, 47–51

The Lord will bring a nation against you from far away, from the ends of the earth, like an eagle swooping down, a nation whose language you will not understand, a fierce-looking nation without respect for the old or pity for the young.

(verses 49–50)

The opening verses of today's text tell of all the blessings of obedience, such as defeating of enemies who 'come at you from one direction but flee from you in seven' (verse 7). Yet in life, positives and negatives walk side by side, and so we also see the result of disobedience: 'the Lord will bring a nation against you ... from the ends of the earth, like an eagle swooping down' (verse 49). These blessings and curses are both conditional on obedience or disobedience.

Today we look at the power of sustained flight and the speed that the eagle can attain. Some can move in excess of 30 mph with a mighty force, especially when swooping to catch their prey.

In a prophetic interpretation of today's reading, the eagle might represent the Roman army capturing Israel, although some believe it to be the Babylonian invasion. The force and swiftness with which both these armies invaded Judea, besieged Jerusalem and attacked the Jews could be metaphorically seen as the eagle. It is also quite telling that the ensign of the Roman army was an eagle.

We see here God attempting to instil the discipline of obedience into his people, which feels sometimes like the force of an eagle. The thought of such harsh discipline can be difficult to accept from a loving God, but Hebrews 12:11 tells us, 'no discipline seems pleasant ... however, it produces a harvest of righteousness and peace for those who have been trained by it.' Try to remember this the next time you feel you are in a period of God's testing.

† Ask God to give you spiritual insight when you are going through what seems like a time of discipline.

For further thought

When it feels like you are on the wrong side of God's wrath, remember he disciplines those he loves not to harm but to give a future and a hope.

On eagles' wings

November

308

Cruel to be kind

Read Deuteronomy 32:10–12

like an eagle that stirs up its nest and hovers over its young, that spreads its wings to catch them and carries them on its pinions.

(verse 11)

Left to her own devices, my granddaughter, like many of her age, would eat nothing but sweet things. When told she cannot have anything until after dinner, she moans and complains, 'It's just not fair.' As adults, we know you cannot live on cakes and sweets all your life, and life does not seem fair at times. As it is said, sometimes 'you have to be cruel to be kind'.

Being fair does not always come into play, and we note in today's text how a mother eagle prepares her young for flight. After making her nest in a very high cliff or tree, she prepares it by making it soft and downy for the comfort of the newborn eaglets. After fiercely caring for them she knows that for them to survive they need to learn to fly and swoop.

When the time comes, mother eagle starts to remove all the comfort layers from the nest, exposing sticks and pricks. The eaglets become uncomfortable but still won't leave the nest. She then bounces up and down on the twigs, allowing the eaglets to fall, or she throws them out of the nest. As they are about to hit the floor, she swoops down and carries them back to the nest. This is repeated many times until the eaglets, shrieking and bleeding from the pricks in the nest, eventually start flapping their wings, gaining strength each time and soon learning to soar. It may not have seemed fair but the outcome is a strong, soaring eagle who could not survive otherwise.

† Loving God, please give me wisdom to know the difference between being cruel to be kind and being cruel for the sake of it.

For further thought
Does life feel unfair at the moment? What do you think God is trying to teach you for this season?

On eagles' wings

November

Eagle's vision

> **Read Job 39:26–30**
>
> *Does the eagle soar at your command and build its nest on high?*
> *It dwells on a cliff and stays there at night; a rocky crag is its stronghold.*
> *From there it looks for food; its eyes detect it from afar.*
>
> (verses 27–29)

I really enjoy TV programmes where the baker makes magnificent images out of cakes or other edible ingredients such as chocolate. I remember marvelling at one where the baker made a massive eagle lifting its prey (a big fish) out of the sea, all made out of cake. Fascinating!

Eagles are known for excellent vision and concentration. An eagle is said to have two centres of focus which allows it to look to the front and the side at the same time. It may perch on its high cliff, somewhat hidden from view, focusing on its prey with laser-like intensity. Known for its patience, it is willing to wait for its hiding prey, no matter how many hours. Then it swoops and grabs it with its sharp talons, able to lift up to twice its own weight. As it flies high, the eagle continually looks for opportunities. It is alert to what is going on in the environment, and takes its opportunity with courage and fearlessness. It knows when to pounce and when to ascend.

Job's life had changed dramatically and as he complained, God challenged him about his own power and discernment. Looking at the changing life of society today, we could be asked the same question: are we discerning of our environment? Do we have laser-like vision both for what is happening in front of us and also for a vision of the future, or do we sit and complain? Are there opportunities that you are missing because you are not looking for them?

† Ask God to open your eyes to the opportunities around you in your environment and for the courage to take them.

For further thought

What does it mean to have a discerning spirit?

On eagles' wings

November

310

Sense of renewal

> **Read Psalm 103:1–5**
>
> *who redeems your life from the pit and crowns you with love and compassion, who satisfies your desires with good things so that your youth is renewed like the eagle's.*
>
> *(verses 4–5)*

How does an eagle renew its youth? There are many stories and interpretations about this, but I read one view below which made me very excited.

There is a popular story about eagles' lives which, although it might not be strictly biologically true, can teach us about human resilience. Eagles, the story goes, can live up to 70 years, but to reach this age the eagle must take action. In its 40s, its talons and beak are no longer as strong and sharp as they once were. Its feathers become heavy and thick, impeding its flying. The eagle is left with two options: to die or to go through a painful process of change.

So, the eagle flies to a mountaintop. There the eagle knocks its beak against rocks, plucks it out, and then waits for a new beak to grow back. It does the same to its talons, and then it starts plucking out its old-aged feathers. After five and a half months the eagle takes its famous flight of rebirth and lives on.

Life itself is full of change which can be very difficult. Nevertheless we all have to go through this tough and painful process. However, in his renewing God said he redeems your life from the pit, crowns you with love and compassion and satisfies your desires with good things. You will then be renewed like the eagle.

† Gracious God, help me to be like the eagle and go through change with patience and dignity.

For further thought

Are you going through a process of change? Seek help where necessary but reflect on the process and the renewal it can bring.

On eagles' wings

November

He rested

Read Proverbs 23:4–5

Do not wear yourself out to get rich; do not trust your own cleverness. Cast but a glance at riches, and they are gone, for they will surely sprout wings and fly off to the sky like an eagle.

(verses 4–5)

One holiday I was staying with a couple who were birdwatchers. We went to see an eagle flying over the rocks which caused the whole place to stand still. No one moved, everyone was watching closely, afraid for it to disappear. What I remember that day was the way that bird stood still in the air. Its wings were outstretched and it did not seem to be moving at all. It did not exert any energy, just stayed as if it was stuck in the air. Soaring without flapping its wings, resting on the wind.

Today's proverb warns us about trusting in riches, which are constantly sought in the West. The balance between work and life can be an illusion that people pursue but find difficult to attain. With so many programmes encouraging celebrity cultures or reality TV, people continue to seek fame and fortune even though very few succeed on the global stage of riches. The majority of seekers continue to flap around, wearing themselves out to get rich. Life today is full of busyness, no time for rest or relaxation, just a consistent 'need' to seek and make money.

Rest is a very important aspect of life; it keeps us healthy in mind and spirit. Like the eagle resting on the wind, God rested on the seventh day of creation. As he rested, so *we* need to rest. Rather than flapping around for riches, let us consider that we are made in God's image and we, like the eagle, are made to rest as well as work!

† God of rest, help me take adequate rest daily. Remind me that I work to live and do not live to work.

For further thought

When was the last time you took time out to really rest and reflect?

On eagles' wings

November

Saturday 6 November
Strength for the weary

Read Isaiah 40:29–31

Even youths grow tired and weary, and young men stumble and fall; but those who hope in the Lord will renew their strength. They will soar on wings like eagles; they will run and not grow weary, they will walk and not be faint.

(verses 30–31)

In 1968 'Only the Strong Survive' was a very popular classic soul song. Yet Paul the apostle turned this idea on its head in 2 Corinthians 12:10 – after accepting God's grace for his situation, he said, 'for Christ's sake, I delight in weaknesses, in insults, in hardships, in persecutions, in difficulties. For when I am weak, then I am strong.'

In today's text, after going through the struggle of exile and captivity and receiving prophecies of doom and gloom, the people were tired and disillusioned. They were now told, however, that they can find strength and hope for the future, from a God who never grows tired or weary.

But to receive renewed strength necessitates action on the part of the recipient, specifically to hope in the Lord (verse 31). To hope in the Lord is not just sitting around passively, but patiently waiting on him and trusting in him. As the eagle patiently waits for its prey and trusts in the power of its wings, its sharp talons and laser-like vision, so we need to wait patiently and expectantly on the Lord with confidence that he will give us strength in our weakness.

As we end this week on eagles, we reflect on their strength, speed, patience and soaring above the storm. We remember all God has taught us regarding this magnificent bird and the hope and perseverance they represent. Like Paul, we can say that God's power is made perfect in our weakness.

† Thank you, loving God, that it is no shame to be weak, for then you show your strength. Help me to hope in you and trust in your strength rather than that of the world.

For further thought
Reflect on what God has taught you this week regarding the eagle. Is there anything you can replicate in your daily life?

On eagles' wings

November

Beginning at the end: readings from the Minor Prophets – 1 At the watchpost

Notes by **Pevise Leo**

For Pevise's biography, see p. 172. Pevise has used the NIVUK for these notes.

Sunday 7 November
Chaos from the watchpost

Read Micah 7:1–7

'But as for me, I will look to the Lord, I will wait for the God of my salvation; my God will hear me.'

(verse 7)

Is God really a merciful God? In 2019, my beautiful island of Samoa declared a state of emergency due to a measles outbreak which killed more than 70 people, mostly infants. It is possible that the outbreak came about after the parents of young children in Samoa lost their trust in the health system. Immunisation, which was usually a routine in Samoa, where parents would be seen lining up desperate to have their children immunised, had dropped to a low of 30 per cent. The health department had been pleading with people to bring their children to be immunised, but parents refused out of fear. And then the measles outbreak!

I know that God was there, suffering with them. He was in pain. He was not just standing there saying, they deserve to suffer. He was at the watchpost. He was watching and suffering with them. People from all over the world volunteered to go to Samoa to help vaccinate the people. They left their homes and gave up their jobs to help. I believe they were the saints in this epidemic, because they offered to go knowing that they could become victims themselves. Being a saint is when one does not think of oneself, but others. Today, I think of them, and give thanks.

† Lord! Watch upon me kindly at the watchpost. Amen

Justice at the watchpost

Read Habakkuk 1:1–15

'Look at the nations and watch – and be utterly amazed. For I am going to do something in your days that you would not believe, even if you were told.'

(verse 5)

Justice can be defined as the way people are treated fairly, or being impartial. In our reading today, Habakkuk is 'speaking out' or complaining to God that God's people are full of injustices and yet God is not doing anything about it. At the beginning of 2019, several church ministers in Samoa were taken to court for their rejection of the government's new law which imposes taxes on all church ministers. This decision took effect in January of 2019. Ever since I grew up, church ministers had never been taxed. Their incomes were donations from parishioners to help the ministers and their families to be able to bring up a family and still be able to preach the word of God. In Samoa, both the minister and his wife work full-time.

We can easily critique those who have been given the power to make decisions, but God is at the watchpost … watching … with so much grief. We sometimes think that God is not responding to our cries, our questions and our complaints. We sometimes think that God is heartless when we are in the midst of epidemics and chaos. In my opinion, how else could God convey an important message to some of the most powerful people?

It is important to listen to God's response. Learn from his response. He is watching.

† O merciful God, don't let my shortcomings bring harsh circumstances. Amen

For further thought

What is God looking at, with grief, in your community?

Beginning at the end: readings from the Minor Prophets – 1 At the watchpost

November

315

The gatekeeper watches

Read Habakkuk 2:1–14

For the revelation awaits an appointed time; it speaks of the end and will not prove false. Though it linger, wait for it; it will certainly come and will not delay.

(verse 3)

The Congregational Christian Church in Samoa has strict rules about its church ministers when their wives depart this earth. To be precise, the grieving church minister has three months to find a suitable wife to continue with the ministry. When Habakkuk complained to God, God's response was to wait for the right time. His time. God's time. When my wife passed away in 2018, reality started to crawl in. The thought of having to remarry was completely out of the question. I knew I could not find anyone that would be suitable. So, what did I do? I resigned from my ministry. I could not wait for God's calling. Habakkuk, on the other hand, had all the time in the world. He was willing to wait. To wait for God's answer, no matter how long it would take. God's response to him was, the time will come. Habakkuk had to wait for God's timing.

Exactly three Sundays after I resigned, I met my wife who was willing to walk with me. We had known each other previously and we had not seen each other for 33 years. For a year, we prayed and waited on God to guide and direct us, then finally got married.

Sometimes, our plans and God's plans are not the same. Our timing and God's timing are not the same. We just need to trust him wholeheartedly that he will guide and direct us to his plan. God is the gatekeeper, watching and working to direct us on the right path. Making sure that his servants do not give up easily. Making sure we do not give up on him altogether.

† Loving Father, thank you for all you have done for me. I pray you keep watch as I go through this journey called life. Amen

For further thought

Where in your life do you sense God might be inviting you to wait and watch?

Silence at the watchpost

Read Habakkuk 3:8–19

Though the fig-tree does not bud and there are no grapes on the vines,
though the olive crop fails and the fields produce no food,
though there are no sheep in the sheepfold and no cattle in the stalls,
yet I will rejoice in the Lord, I will be joyful in God my Saviour.

(verses 17–18)

In this final chapter, we the readers expect to read more confusion from Habakkuk; however, we read about his prayer of praise and exalting God. In chapters 1 and 2, we read how Habakkuk was full of questions, confusions and prayers. God answered him and, in this chapter, we read that Habakkuk has finally learned that the only answer to everything is to trust in God, so in his prayer, he exalts God. He rejoices in God and says that he believes in him and he trusts him.

Why? Because God is worthy of this praise. He is the maker of everything. He rules. Sometimes we complain against a trial and say, 'Why me? I don't deserve this!' But, if we stop and pause for a moment, and allow the Spirit to minister to us, we will find that God is watching. In the midst of all the chaos, God is watching.

So, like Habakkuk, we learn that God is worthy of praise. Despite all the chaos and many deaths, during the tsunami in the year 2009 the Samoans still continued to give praise to the Lord Almighty. A special day is held to commemorate this sad day for the families that lost loved ones. Although a sad occasion, the Samoans on this day sing songs of praises and send thanksgiving prayers.

† Majestic Almighty, you alone are worthy of all praises. Help me so I can praise your holy name in the good and the bad times. Amen

For further thought

Rewrite the verse quoted above, using examples appropriate from your life and context. Will you still praise God even if electrical power cuts out and your car breaks down?

Beginning at the end: readings from the Minor Prophets – 1 At the watchpost

November

The righteous watchman

Read Zephaniah 1:1–13

'At that time I will search Jerusalem with lamps and punish those who are complacent, who are like wine left on its dregs,
who think, "The Lord will do nothing, either good or bad."'

(verse 12)

I grew up in Samoa, where every day was a day of worship. In the early hours of the morning I heard the sound of my parents chanting a morning hymn of praise, and then a prayer. Every evening during the hours from 6 pm to 8 pm there was a village curfew, announced by a bell or the sound of a conch shell being blown: the whole family's worshipping time.

Family worship consisted of a hymn of praise, Bible reading and then a prayer. The prayer was divided into three parts and was shared by family members. It was a time when the families bonded in the name of God. There were lots of benefits of this specific time. Not only did the children learn the structure of what an evening *lotu* (worship) looked like, but they also learnt to pray and read the Bible in Samoan. It was also a time of reflection. Things that did not go so well in the day, and things that went well in the day were discussed, celebrated and forgiven. Some families use this time to discipline their children and give them advice, or redirect them to the right path if they have fallen or are starting to fall off the wagon.

Zephaniah, like Habakkuk, is describing the people around him engaging in dishonest practices and enjoying doing violence. It's no wonder we see God's wrath and anger! While this is happening, God is watching. Although we read of the promise of destruction in Zephaniah, we know that God is the righteous watchman. He is merciful and righteous. He waits for people to repent.

† Loving Father, help me to repent, so I won't be the recipient of your wrath. Amen

For further thought

Do you have regular prayer times during the day, including the middle of the day?

Friday 12 November
Take heed

Read Zephaniah 2:1–7

Gather together, gather yourselves together, you shameful nation, before the decree takes effect and that day passes like windblown chaff, before the Lord's fierce anger comes upon you, before the day of the Lord's wrath comes upon you.

(verses 1–2)

'E tata logo atu pea Masefau' is a Samoan saying used to warn people about things to come. Legend has it that this story came about because of a beautiful girl named Sina and her brother, Masefau. Tagaloaalagi, who was the Samoan god in ancient times, proposed to Sina for her hand in marriage. But the Tuifiti, the Fijian king, set sail from Fiji to Samoa and proposed to Sina as well. Masefau, Sina's brother, pleaded and advised Sina to accept Tagaloaalagi's proposal; but Sina rejected Tagaloaalagi's proposal and accepted the Tuifiti's. Tagaloaalagi was furious and used his power to turn Tuifiti and his crew into stones. When you go to Tuana'i, one of the villages in Samoa, the stones can still be seen in the ocean, especially during low tide.

I suppose this story illustrates what Zephaniah is doing as well. Zephaniah is pleading with the people, especially the unbelievers, to repent before God's wrath falls upon them; pleading with them that although the day of judgement is coming, the day of destruction is coming, there is still time to repent and turn back to God. He is a merciful God and the good news is that God sent his son Jesus Christ to suffer judgement in our place. Jesus endured the judgement of God that should have been ours. He was the sinless Lamb. Take heed before it's too late.

† Lord, do not let me perish for my iniquities, judge me with your mercy. Amen

For further thought
What societal sins are affecting the health of your community?

Beginning at the end: readings from the Minor Prophets – 1 At the watchpost

November

The watchman restores

Beginning at the end: readings from the Minor Prophets – 1 At the watchpost

> **Read Zephaniah 3:8–20**
>
> *'At that time I will gather you; at that time I will bring you home. I will give you honour and praise among all the peoples of the earth when I restore your fortunes before your very eyes,' says the Lord.*
>
> *(verse 20)*

Fa'aSamoa is simply described as the Samoan way of life. Every village has its own salutations, dignities, honorifics and genealogy which embody the history of the village. They also have their own village governance, where each villager has to abide by the village rules. When a villager offends or does not follow the rules, they will be punished. Punishments can be in the form of presenting the village council with a certain amount of pigs, taro root, boxes of mackerel or corned beef. If the offence is serious, exiling from the village either for a certain time period or for good is administered. In some instances, the village council may consider an *ifoga*. An *ifoga* is simply a plea for pardon, done in a manner of remorse. If the plea is accepted, the punishment is overruled; if not, the punishment is carried out. This is a form of restoration done in the villages. When it is done well, it prevents the escalation of offences and more disputes.

In this final section of his book, Zephaniah turns from a theme of anger to a theme of restoration. God will dwell in his people. He will make past wrongs right. God will restore the rights to his people.

As we conclude the theme, 'At the watchpost', let us be reminded of our way back to God, and that is only through repentance. God does not want to punish us, but he cannot also let us get away with our offences. Let's be mindful of God's grace, but not take it for granted.

† Father God, restore me in your mercy, so I may serve you wholeheartedly. Amen

For further thought

What would the restoration of fortunes look like in your community?

Beginning at the end: readings from the Minor Prophets – 2 Rejoice, O daughter Zion!

Notes by **Anthony Loke**

Dr Anthony Loke was formerly an ordained Methodist minister and Old Testament lecturer in the Seminari Theoloji Malaysia for many years. He is now a layman with an itinerant teaching, preaching and writing ministry. He has a PhD in Old Testament from the University of Wales, UK, and serves as an adjunct lecturer in two Bible colleges. His wife is a recognised trainer in a private international college. They have two adult children, Charis and Markus. Anthony has written 12 books and is currently writing on the Book of Ruth. His latest book is Esther Made Simple *(Pustaka SUFES, 2019). Anthony has used the NRSVA for these notes.*

Sunday 14 November
Consider how you have fared

> **Read Haggai 1**
>
> *Now therefore, thus says the Lord of hosts: Consider how you have fared.*
>
> (verse 5)

The people of God returned home from Babylonian captivity in 538 BCE and started laying the foundation of the Jerusalem temple. But then work stopped due to many factors. The rebuilding did not resume until 520 BCE when God raised two prophets, Haggai and Zechariah, to inspire the people to complete what they had started. Haggai's first two messages are recorded in chapter 1. Speaking on God's behalf, he challenged the people to consider how they have fared. The answer was not good: the temple lay in ruins while the people were busy beautifying their own homes. They thought that their personal priorities were more important than finishing God's house. But they reaped what they sowed: their half-hearted commitment brought in less yield and profit. Even the heavens and earth were obeying God to withhold the dew and produce.

God gave the people a wonderful promise of 'I am with you' (verse 13b). And he stirred the hearts of the two leaders, Zerubbabel the governor and Joshua the High Priest, as well as the remnant of the people. Encouraged by the word, the people put their hearts and minds into the rebuilding programme.

† Lord, help us to put our priorities right. Let us seek first God's kingdom and the rest will fall in line. Amen

Beginning at the end: readings from the Minor Prophets – 2 Rejoice, O daughter Zion!

November

Take courage ... do not fear!

Read Haggai 2

My spirit abides among you; do not fear.

(verse 5b)

A month later, the rebuilding work on the temple stalled as the people lost heart. We are told that some of the returnees who had seen the glory of Solomon's temple were clearly disappointed with the current building, which was no match for the former. Still suffering from the long effects of the devastating war and currently facing a drought (1:11), there were few available resources to build a splendid temple to match Solomon's. Disappointment, if not adequately dealt with, could be disastrous for the people's low morale. Haggai's third message sought to encourage the people with promises that God will one day shake the nations and fill his temple with splendour.

The people had failed to see the paralysing effects of the unfinished temple. It stood out like an eyesore, resembling an unclean thing in their midst. God could not bless his people if they continued to live in such a state of being. Finish rebuilding the temple and God will open the heavens. Haggai's final message was a personal one for Zerubbabel (verses 20–23). Leaders, too, need to hear an encouraging word so that they can effectively lead their people forward.

† Lord, you promise your presence will be with us in all our endeavours. May the 'I Am' strengthen our hands for every good work. Amen

For further thought

At crucial junctures, God speaks to the leaders: 'Take courage! Do not fear!' (verses 4 and 5b).

The divine horsemen

Beginning at the end: readings from the Minor Prophets – 2 Rejoice, O daughter Zion!

Read Zechariah 1:1–17

I have returned to Jerusalem with compassion …

(verse 16b)

Zechariah was the second prophet raised by God to encourage the people to finish rebuilding the temple. A question that would have been asked during the Babylonian exile was the reason why their forefathers had gone into captivity. Zechariah's answer was their failure to repent and return to God (verse 4). Now that the exile was over, the people were questioning God why he seemed to be withholding mercy from Jerusalem and from the cities of Judah (verse 12). Should God not be blessing his people instead?

The answer came to the prophet in a night vision where he saw God's divine horsemen who patrolled the Earth. Like the Persian king who had his 'spies' who carried messages on horseback to him from all over the empire, God had his own network of riders and horses covering the whole Earth. Judah suffered terribly under Babylon and her allies but God will soon change that. He will cause the temple to be rebuilt; Judah's cities will overflow with prosperity; and the Lord will again comfort Zion. It is not that God is unable to act or powerless to act in the face of formidable foes; for God has his own timing and his people should learn to trust in him.

† Lord, your eyes see the whole world and nothing escapes their sight. Your eyes are on each sparrow which falls to the ground. Amen

For further thought

God's ways are higher than our ways; his thoughts higher than our thoughts (Isaiah 55:9b).

Return to Jerusalem

Beginning at the end: readings from the Minor Prophets – 2 Rejoice, O daughter Zion!

Read Zechariah 2

Sing and rejoice, O daughter Zion! For lo, I will come and dwell in your midst, says the Lord.

(verse 10)

In the third night vision, Zechariah saw a man with a measuring line going to measure the restored and rebuilt Jerusalem. Two angels appeared to the prophet to explain the meaning of the vision. In the second vision (1:18–21), the nations that had defeated Jerusalem and Judah were themselves defeated which paved the way for the city to be rebuilt. But the scope of the rebuilding and restoration of Jerusalem is larger than what we know from history. Most commentators treat this prediction of the growth and prosperity of the city as something belonging to the future: namely, the messianic kingdom era. Jerusalem will become so large that her inhabitants will spill over beyond her walls. But God will protect the city by setting a wall of fire around it.

The people living in exile in Babylon were called to leave the doomed city to return to Jerusalem (verse 7). God will bring about a reversal of fortunes: those who enslaved God's people will themselves be enslaved. God will do all these things because he will dwell among his people again like in the days of the wilderness where God dwelt in the tabernacle.

† Lord, come and dwell again in the midst of your people. May all our actions flow from this centre, which is God. Amen

For further thought

'Be silent, all people, before the Lord; for he has roused himself from his holy dwelling' (verse 13).

The lampstand and olive trees

In the fifth night vision, Zechariah saw a golden lampstand with seven lamps on it. On each side of the lampstand were two olive trees. The purpose of the vision was to encourage the two key leaders in the rebuilding project, namely, Zerubbabel the governor and Joshua the High Priest. Joshua received a full oracle in the fourth vision in chapter 3 and here Zerubbabel receives his oracle as well. The fourth and fifth visions were to remind the two men of the divine resources available to them. The rebuilding project may seem difficult and slow going but they were reminded that it was not by might, nor by power, but by God's Spirit that the project will eventually be completed. One day Zerubbabel will place the final capstone on the temple to signify its completion (verse 10).

There were scoffers who derided the project right from the beginning ('the day of small things' in verse 10). There were also others who thought that the project was too insignificant. Leaders can become discouraged by persistent negative attitudes from the people they are serving. Likewise, Zerubbabel and Joshua, the two olive trees representing the royal and priestly offices, needed encouragement to persevere so that the finished temple could be a witness and testimony to God's power to the nations around them.

† Lord, we as your people are called to be a light to the Gentiles and to serve as God's witnesses to the nations. Amen

For further thought

In the last days, God will also raise two special witnesses (Revelation 11:3–12).

Beginning at the end: readings from the Minor Prophets – 2 Rejoice, O daughter Zion!

November

Coming peace and prosperity

Read Zechariah 8

Jerusalem shall be called the faithful city, and the mountain of the Lord of hosts shall be called the holy mountain.

(verse 3b)

In the previous chapter, the people of God were called to learn from their exile and therefore to repent and to live righteously in order not to fall back into their sins. Here in chapter 8, the people are called to do the same but in the light of what the future will hold for them. God had promised to bless his people ten times, each beginning with the messenger formula 'Thus says the Lord of hosts' (verses 2, 3, 4, 6, 7, 9, 14, 19, 20 and 23). Thus, the entire chapter is an oracle of salvation or deliverance. Not only will God return and dwell with his people, he will grant them long life, peace, prosperity and security. What may seem impossible in the eyes of the people living at that time, God said it is not impossible for him. To the people, it looks like a mountain but in God's eyes, it is only a molehill.

What God promised to do in these verses is yet to be completely fulfilled. There is a future dimension in God's promises, a 'now' and a 'not yet'. Again, the purpose of these promises was to encourage Zechariah's listeners not to lose heart in the rebuilding project. 'Do not be afraid, but let your hands be strong' (verse 13). One day, nations and peoples will throng in pilgrimage to Jerusalem to worship the Lord (verse 22).

† Lord, it is easy to take our eyes off you and see molehills as mountains. Set our eyes on you always so that we see as you see. Amen

For further thought

'Come, let us go up to the mountain of the Lord, to the house of the God of Jacob; that he may teach us his ways and that we may walk in his paths' (Micah 4:2a).

The coming king of Zion

> **Read Zechariah 9:9–17**
>
> *Lo, your king comes to you; triumphant and victorious is he, humble and riding on a donkey.*
>
> *(part of verse 9)*

Chapter 9 is located in the second part of the Book of Zechariah, which contains prophecies mostly of the future. Most commentators think chapters 9–14 are exclusively eschatological, referring to the future messianic age. Chapter 9 is certainly about a coming messianic figure who delivers the nation from her enemies (verses 1–8). The people of Jerusalem are called to rejoice at the advent of their king who will come riding upon a colt, the foal of a donkey (verse 9). Christians are right to see in the text a reference to Jesus who also made his triumphal entry into Jerusalem in a like manner (Matthew 21:1–9).

The character and mission of this messianic Davidic king are described in verses 9–10. This king is righteous and will bring salvation to all. He is humble, unlike other ancient kings. His mission is to end wars and proclaim peace to the nations. In order to do this, he will defeat his enemies first (verses 11–13). Then he will appear in a glorious theophany (verses 14–15) just like in the days of old at Sinai. He will bring deliverance and blessing upon his people, ushering in the messianic age where peace, security and prosperity will occur.

† Lord, may our hearts be glad to welcome the coming messianic king. Our Lord, come. *Maranatha!* Amen

For further thought

'Blessed is the one who comes in the name of the Lord' (Matthew 23:39).

Beginning at the end: readings from the Minor Prophets – 2 Rejoice, O daughter Zion!

November

Beginning at the end:
readings from the Minor Prophets –
3 Strong in the Lord

Notes by **Clare Nonhebel**

Clare is a published author of 14 fiction and non-fiction books (website: clarenonhebel.com), including one co-written with a Death Row prisoner. Her most recent book, Flourish! – A Gentler Way to Grow People, *is about mental well-being, nature and community. She lives in Dorset, UK. Clare has used the NIVUK for these notes.*

Sunday 21 November
Strong in love

Read Zechariah 10

*'I will restore them because I have compassion on them …
I will signal for them and gather them in.'*

(verses 6b and 8a)

What's your idea of a strong Christian: an active, dynamic person always quoting scripture, planning programmes, righting wrongs and saving souls?

The God who says, 'My ways are not your ways,' shows us that his idea of strength may not be the same as ours either.

In Micah 6:8 we read the profile of a person who is strong in the Lord's strength, characterised by a lifestyle of justice, mercy and humility – the kind of strength that comes from living every moment in tune with God. This person may or may not look strong in themselves; their strength comes from listening, waiting and obeying God, absorbing his compassion, noticing when he signals and gathers them in (verse 8).

I imagine God's love like a giant magnet. As more people allow themselves to be drawn into its scope, so the magnetic field increases its range and intensity; its power gathers in people on the fringes, who respond to the irresistible pull of love.

To be strong in the Lord is to give in to that vital attraction of love that overpowers all our cynical resistance and insecurity. When we become part of his magnetic field, others are drawn by its strength.

† Lord, when we want to do great things, open our hearts instead to your great love that achieves all our hearts' desire.

Monday 22 November
Strong in grief

Read Zechariah 12:6–14

'And I will pour out … a spirit of grace and supplication. They will look on me, the one they have pierced, and they will mourn for him as one mourns for an only child, and grieve bitterly for him as one grieves for a firstborn son.'

(verse 10)

People of different traditions have different ways of expressing mourning. In some Western cultures it's regarded as weak to show grief openly, even in times of bitter loss. Sympathy may be forthcoming in the first few weeks after bereavement but the mourner is soon expected to get back to normal life – almost as if nothing had happened.

Where mention of death is avoided, it leads to avoidance of reality.

In the USA, a country considered among the most sophisticated, modern and progressive in the world, at least half its voters support the death penalty. They argue that murder victims' families have a 'right' to demand the execution of the person who has taken a life, and they promise that this brutal act of revenge will bring 'closure' to the family's grief.

It's a clear example of Western society refusing to grieve or to receive the promised 'spirit of grace and supplication' (verse 10), trying instead to solve or 'close' the inevitable and God-blessed work of mourning. Some victims' families have actually broken this culture by refusing to return violence for violence, instead mourning their loved ones without demanding revenge, and even grieving for the murderer – praying for his or her troubled soul and for their family members, who also have reason to mourn.

Mary and her companions who stood at the foot of the cross, grieving with Jesus through all his sufferings, didn't retaliate or try to rescue him but lent him their strength and compassion. And in doing so, they became stronger in the Lord.

† Jesus, give us courage not to run away from suffering – our own or others' – but to meet it with grace and prayer, in your own spirit.

For further thought
Jesus said, 'Father, forgive them' – not, 'Father, I forgive them.' When I can't forgive, I give our Father permission to do it in my name.

Strong in meltdown

Read Zechariah 13

'This third I will put into the fire; I will refine them like silver and test them like gold. They will call on my name and I will answer them; I will say, "They are my people," and they will say, "The Lord is our God."'

(verse 9)

Sometimes God reduces us to a fraction of our former self – as a huge lump of ore melted down to remove the waste material ends up as a tiny handful of metal, precious and pure.

But only in accepting these meltdown experiences (whether they take the form of loss or failure, sickness or troubling relationships) do God's people become real with him, free to call on the real 'I Am' and to hear him call us clearly.

Paul calls us disciples carrying treasure in clay pots. Under fire, clay may melt and contaminate the precious metal, unless it's separated from it.

When you hear someone say, 'God told me …' in a voice that allows no discussion, it's possible that the message has been interpreted through a filter of their own understanding.

Or when someone says, 'The Bible says … so that's how it is,' they may be lifting a verse out of context, using it to condemn someone or to justify themselves, in a tone of voice that sounds nothing like Jesus Christ's.

God does speak to his people. And his Word – fleshed out and bled out in Jesus Christ – is pure love, pure gold. But we are not – not yet. And we need to make sure we don't stir our own prejudices, ideas and priorities into the gold while we're still engaged in the work of processing it.

Those Christians who constantly re-examine their certainties, in the context of prayer and setbacks and challenges, are a breath of fresh air to the world and a gift of pure gold to the Church.

† Holy Spirit, Refiner's fire, change me and challenge me to become who I am – not the person I'd like to think I am.

For further thought

My actions and choices reveal what I really prioritise and believe. Do they match my 'official' beliefs – or have those become empty theory?

Wednesday 24 November
Strong in power

Read Zechariah 14

The Lord will be king over the whole earth. On that day there will be one Lord, and his name the only name.

(verse 9)

This chapter is terrifying in its descriptions of human violence: the city captured, homes ransacked, women raped, people exiled or abandoned. We know about these shocking obscenities, if not from our own experience then from news reports. We know only too well what can happen when nations or groups seize power for themselves, and when people vote for them.

But there is more violence to come – and it comes from God. The subject of God's anger is an uncomfortable one. It's harder to contemplate the God who can strike all the arrogant with plague, defeat, terror and natural disasters than to think about the gentle baby Jesus in the manger. Maybe the apostles felt the same conflict, seeing their friend comfort the grief-stricken and feed the hungry then turn to anger against rip-off merchants in the temple, or towards religious leaders who bar the entrance to God's kingdom without going in themselves (Matthew 23:13).

But unlike human rage and violence, which explodes like a bomb, throwing pain and wreckage wildly over a random area, God's anger is as precisely targeted as laser surgery. It destroys the destructiveness of the human heart, so that humanity can be revived and recover.

Those who commit inhuman crimes are seriously damaged in their humanity. And the damage is as contagious as a virus: see the faces of people contorted with hatred and rage as they shout for vicious vengeance outside a law court where someone is being convicted of terrible crimes.

But God's rage is saving grace. He overpowers injustice, soothes mortal wounds and turns stony hearts into hearts of flesh.

† Lion of Judah, Lamb of God, you are one. Let us never doubt your love or underestimate your fire: we need both equally.

For further thought

Have you experienced God's anger? Was it against you, as it may have felt – or against something in your life that didn't belong there?

Strong in vulnerability

Beginning at the end: readings from the Minor Prophets – 3 Strong in the Lord

Read Malachi 1

'Oh, that one of you would shut the temple doors, so that you would not light useless fires on my altar!'

(verse 10a)

Imagine inviting someone into your home, welcoming them as part of your closest family, sharing the deepest secrets of your soul – then hearing that they've gone away complaining that the food was rubbish and you are a waste of time, and boasting that the gift they brought you was some unwanted object they had been going to throw away? This reading is an anguished cry from the heart from the generous host – God – whose beloved friends have made a mockery of his house by pretending to worship him while harbouring contempt in their hearts.

We forget that God, in his power and authority, can also be hurt by us. His unconditional love for his people makes him vulnerable, and that is a strength he offers us: he puts us in the strong position, where we are free to reject his hospitality, healing, security and forgiveness, and to walk away sneering and making jokes about him.

Jesus, hanging naked on the cross while people taunted him, spat at him and gambled for his clothes, is an enduring image of the vulnerability and the strength of God. Being invited to follow him is not a soft option.

Some Christians pay for this privilege with their life, or with their reputation, their job, their social acceptance or their family bonds. But, as Paul summarised, when we are weak and open to being hurt, we are strong, because God in his vulnerability is strong in us.

† Lord, give me compassion for all your sufferings. Keep the door of my heart open.

For further thought

What is today's equivalent of bringing second-rate offerings to God's altar? How might I be watering down or contaminating my worship of him?

November

Friday 26 November
Strong in blessing

Read Malachi 3:1–12

'Test me in this,' says the Lord Almighty, 'and see if I will not throw open the floodgates of heaven and pour out so much blessing that there will not be room enough to store it.'

(verse 10)

The beginning of this passage repeats the promise of refining fire for souls who avoid or short-change God, while expecting to receive special favour from him. But God invites his people to experiment with obedience and generosity to him: just try it! Just respond with even the minimum! The results will be oodles of blessing, beyond the wildest dreams!

A couple came to our church Alpha course as a 'last-ditch attempt to see if there's anything in Christianity', to see if God was real and worth following. They listened politely during discussions, asked a few questions, attended some services, but nothing seemed to touch their hearts. One Sunday, people were invited to stand if they wanted to receive more of God. I noticed that they stayed sitting. When prayer ministry was offered, they didn't go forward. When the offering was taken, or donations were invited for free lunches to be provided, they never put anything in. They told me they were still unconvinced that Christian faith had anything to offer them. I suggested they try living for one week as if they were believers.

That week, the man arrived early for a business appointment and, with time to spare, decided to spend it as if he were a Christian. I thought he was going to tell me he talked to a homeless person and bought them a meal, or something similar, but he said he sat in a church and waited to feel something, but didn't. Soon after, the couple gave up on church.

† Lord Jesus, you said it's more blessed to give than to receive. Empower us through that living connection between receiving and giving, so we can both receive and share your blessings.

For further thought

Is there a dividing line between my receiving from God and my giving? Or are both really all about God who gives?

Strength in waiting

Read Malachi 3:13 – 4:6

'But for you who revere my name, the sun of righteousness will rise with healing in its rays. And you will go out and frolic like well-fed calves.'

(verse 4:2)

Away from home as a young student, among friends who didn't believe in God, I felt I was sometimes missing out as others around me experimented with every form of fun. But halfway through the first term, cracks began to show. The fleeting carefree relationships seemed to result in heartbreak or growing cynicism; the chemical highs were followed by dark moods, and the wild parties by hangovers. A few who had called me a sheep for following the rules of some old religion began sheepishly confessing their need for something more permanent and real than the feelgood culture that appeared so enticing.

It's hard sometimes to choose between immediate thrills and long-term (far-off) joy, especially when present-day life feels boring or uncomfortable and any restrictions chafe. Revering God's name does mean rejecting some options in the short term.

But this verse, after all this week's challenging passages where God points out the inevitable negative consequences of rejecting his wisdom, is light at the end of the tunnel: real freedom!

I used to work on a farm where newborn calves were separated from their mothers to be reared in the shelter of the barn. At first they reacted against the dark, confined space, then they adjusted to it. One day, when they were stronger, the barn door would be opened and they would stumble cautiously into the sunlight, stunned by the big wide world ahead of them. Then suddenly they would kick up their heels and leap away into the boundless open space, crazy with joy.

That will be us. And it will be worth waiting for.

† Father God, you don't overprotect us from the power of our free will or from the consequences of our choice – but only in submission to your will for us can we experience the joy of real freedom.

For further thought

If I long for freedom but insist on doing it my way, am I refusing to celebrate my true self and failing to discover the full potential designed for me by God?

Foundations –
1 Chosen for a purpose

Notes by **Liz Clutterbuck**

Liz is a priest in the Church of England and leads a church in North London. She combines parish ministry with research, specialising in exploring how Church impact and Church growth can be better measured. She is also part of Matryoshka Haus, a missional community that eats together every week and intentionally works to build community in London. Liz is passionate about social media, film, baking and travel – and loves it when she manages to combine as many of her passions as possible! Liz has used the NRSVA for these notes.

Sunday 28 November (Advent Sunday)
Founding fathers

Read 2 Samuel 22:29–37

Indeed, you are my lamp, O Lord, the Lord lightens my darkness.

(verse 29)

Today is Advent Sunday, the beginning of a season that anticipates the coming of Christ, the light of the world. In many churches, the first candle on an Advent wreath will be lit, marking the season's start. In the Anglican tradition, this first candle honours the Patriarchs – the founders of Israel. It is a reminder that the Messiah whose birth we are anticipating was long, long awaited. That God's Son followed in the footsteps of those first called by the Father: Abraham, Isaac, Jacob.

Today's words from David's song of thanksgiving in 2 Samuel are a reminder that the God of the Patriarchs was still being true to the promises made to them. That the Lord God of Israel continues to guide like a lamp in the darkness. As David's rule draws to a close, he himself has laid a foundation that the people of Israel built upon, culminating in an heir of David's line being born in Bethlehem and heralding a new era in God's relationship with his people.

As you reflect on the beginning of this new season today, remember the foundations upon which our faith has been built.

† Creator God, we thank you that your light continues to brighten our darkness. May we too be light in the darkness of our world.

Hidden foundations

Read 1 Kings 5

King Solomon conscripted forced labour out of all Israel; the levy numbered thirty thousand men. He sent them to the Lebanon, ten thousand a month in shifts; they would be a month in the Lebanon and two months at home ...

(verses 13–14a)

We are often ignorant of the foundations of great buildings and institutions. Without knowing their history, we are not necessarily aware of their beginnings – who was involved and why. Many global landmarks have a complicated history as far as their origins are concerned. The US Capitol, for example, was in part constructed by enslaved Americans – a fact that is not particularly well known by those who regard it as a symbol of freedom.

In recent years campaigns have launched that raise awareness of the history of institutions or the names attached to them. 'Rhodes Must Fall' emerged at the University of Cape Town in 2015 regarding the commemoration of imperial figurehead Cecil Rhodes. The aim was to highlight institutional racism that stems from the eras of empire and slavery. The movement went on to spread to other South African universities, as well as the universities of Oxford and Harvard.

Prior to today's reading, had you been aware that forced labour was used to build Solomon's temple? The place that contained the Holy of Holies was built by those who had no choice but to fell cedar trees and quarry stones. It is not a fact that will sit comfortably with twenty-first-century readers of scripture. Solomon's actions would have been the norm at the time, but it is something that we now recognise as an abuse of power. It highlights the importance of us recognising that foundations are sometimes hidden from our view.

† Loving God, lead humanity away from its inclination to dominate and oppress. Teach us instead to build our foundations upon equality and justice.

For further thought

Are there campaigns local to you that seek to remove emblems of oppression? Undertake some research and pray over what your response might be.

Tuesday 30 November
Dwelling place

Read 1 Kings 6:7–18

'Concerning this house that you are building, if you will walk in my statutes, obey my ordinances, and keep all my commandments by walking in them, then I will establish my promise with you, which I made to your father David. I will dwell among the children of Israel, and will not forsake my people Israel.'

(verses 12–13)

One of my favourite places of worship is St Paul's Cathedral in London. It's where I was ordained deacon – a day in which many prayers were answered. The history of the building fascinates me; the many buildings that existed before the current cathedral was completed following the Great Fire of London in 1666; and that building's survival of the London Blitz in the Second World War. Whenever I visit I'm aware of the generations of believers who have gone before me in that place. It is very much a 'thin place' for me spiritually, a place where I feel especially close to God.

Israel believed that their Lord God dwelt in the temple, in the Holy of Holies. Access to that part of the temple was strictly restricted, but the presence of the temple was a sign to God's people that he was there. It was a symbol of the covenant God had made with Abraham, and the promise made to King David.

The sight of the dome of St Paul's Cathedral, rising above some buildings and dwarfed by towering skyscrapers in the London skyline, is a sign to me of God's presence in this city. In a place where so many do not know or ignore the good news, the prominence of this place of worship shows God at work still.

But the past devastation of St Paul's, as with the destruction of Solomon's temple, is a reminder that God does not need a building in order to be present among humanity. God does not forsake us.

† Dwell among your people, Lord. Remind us of your eternal and unchanging presence, the promises you continue to keep, and reveal yourself to those who do not know you.

For further thought

Where are there signs of God's presence within your community? Do you have your own 'thin place' locally?

Foundations – 1 Chosen for a purpose

November

Joy and weeping

Read Ezra 3:6–13

*And all the people responded with a great shout when they praised
the Lord, because the foundation of the house of the Lord was laid.
But many of the priests and Levites and heads of families, old people
who had seen the first house on its foundations, wept with a loud voice
when they saw this house …*

(verses 11b–12)

The church of which I am currently vicar worships in a building
that was completed in 1988, but it's not an entirely 'new' building.
For over a century the congregation had worshipped in a large,
Victorian red-brick church that seated over a thousand people. By
the 1970s, the size of the congregation had dwindled. The building
was cold and dark, and the congregation worshipped in the church
hall so it could keep warm. Eventually the painful decision was
taken to demolish the old church, sell off some land and create a
new multi-purpose church building.

Even now, 30 years on, there is still both joy and wailing over
that event in the church's history. The memory of the old lives on
in the older members of the congregation, and in the one part of
the old building that remains. I can well imagine the scenes as the
foundations of the Second Temple were laid – that mix of delight
at what was finally happening, and the grief at what had been lost.

The weeping of the older generation is a reminder to us that it is
very easy to regard restoration as entirely positive, when in fact it
can generate a multitude of emotions. When new is made of old,
there is always some grief for what has gone before and fear of
what may be replacing what was there.

† God of Alpha and Omega, we lift to you our joy and our grief. Rejoice with us,
grieve with us and show us how to navigate the different emotions caught up in
your restoration.

For further thought

Is there a situation you're aware of where joy and grief sit
uncomfortably together? Is there any action you could take to
improve it?

Thursday 2 December
When foundations are shaken

Read Acts 16:16–31

About midnight Paul and Silas were praying and singing hymns to God, and the prisoners were listening to them. Suddenly there was an earthquake, so violent that the foundations of the prison were shaken; and immediately all the doors were opened and everyone's chains were unfastened.

(verses 25–26)

As befits someone who grew up in the Methodist Church, I am a big fan of Charles Wesley's hymns. 'And Can It Be' is a particular favourite, and I love the lines inspired by the earthquake that sets Paul and Silas free. The repeated declaration of 'my chains fell off, my heart was free' is such a glorious lyric, especially when sung with an enthusiastic congregation!

What strikes me about this earthquake is its contrast to what we know about earthquakes – the pictures of destruction displayed on news reports and the many homes and lives lost. But in this instant, the earthquake is not a moment of death, but of life – of many lives.

Not only do Paul and Silas receive their freedom from a prison sentence imposed by those who felt threatened by the good news they brought with them; but their jailer receives freedom from the death sentence he might have received if they had escaped. Spiritual freedom is given too, with the jailer and his whole household receiving the gift of new life in Christ.

The shaking of foundations can be a good thing. It can be a shaking up of a life that needs something new, an opportunity to make a fresh start.

† Shake us up, Lord! Reveal to us again the freedom that is only found in you and help us to share it with those who have not experienced you.

For further thought

What might greater spiritual freedom look like in your life? What needs shaking up?

Foundations – 1 Chosen for a purpose

Nothing left but foundations

Read Jeremiah 51:1–16

Israel and Judah have not been forsaken by their God, the Lord of hosts, though their land is full of guilt before the Holy One of Israel.

(verse 5)

Our world has seen much destruction – even in living memory. Whether it's cities destroyed by war, people groups exterminated through genocide or nations torn apart by difference. One of the most powerful examples of destruction I have encountered is the village of Oradour-sur-Glane in south central France.

Oradour-sur-Glane is known as a martyr village. Its population was massacred by Nazis in June 1944 and the village's buildings set on fire. Although a new village was built nearby after the war, it was decided that the remains of the old village would serve as a memorial to those who had died, and to other similar events that had taken place. It is a stark reminder of what terrible things are possible when humanity goes in the wrong direction.

Chapter 51 of Jeremiah is difficult to read. It is full of violent imagery directed at Babylon, the captors of Jerusalem. It is also a reminder to Christians of the new covenant God formed with us upon Jesus' death, resurrection and ascension. The promise of salvation for all who follow Christ. We know that in Christ, the old laws have fallen away and righteousness is possible for Jew or Gentile. God does not speak in this violent manner under the new covenant.

Oradour-sur-Glane is a reminder of a terrible period in our history, an attempt to teach society how to avoid a descent back into that terrible destruction. Jeremiah's prophecy is similarly an important reminder of what has gone before us. What has laid the foundations for the covenant relationship we now enjoy with our Creator God.

† Loving God, fill us afresh with the power of your Spirit, so that we may do good in our communities. Help us to overcome division and seek the healing of the nations.

For further thought

Take some time to pray through the week's news. Where does violence reign? Where has division overcome unity?

Saturday 4 December
The eternity of the new Jerusalem

Read Zechariah 12:1–5

Then the clans of Judah shall say to themselves, 'The inhabitants of Jerusalem have strength through the Lord of hosts, their God.'

(verse 5)

In today's reading, the prophet Zechariah presents the Lord's vision for the heavenly Jerusalem. A place which would need no earthly foundations, no walls that could be demolished – and there would be no ransacking of the treasures within. The earthly temple, now being rebuilt, was vulnerable to the forces of government and the military, but the heavenly Jerusalem would live forever.

This vision was a stark contrast to what was being experienced at the time Zechariah was writing, and is still a way off from what humanity experiences today. Many in our society have embraced 'throw-away' culture, embracing the latest in technology and thinking little of replacing not-so-old with the newest innovations. Generations have damaged our planet almost beyond repair, causing sea levels to rise, devastating weather events to occur and ice caps to melt. Humanity has come close to destroying the beauty of God's earthly creation.

What is clear from the prophet's vision is that nothing on earth can rock the stability of the new Jerusalem. It is the constant in the midst of the chaos of war and empire building. Whereas earthly foundations might crack from earthquake, fire or demolition, God's heavenly temple is immovable. As the heavenly Jerusalem remains a constant in the chaos humanity has created, so does our God.

† Creator God, we ask for your forgiveness for the damage humanity does to your creation. Help us to focus upon your heavenly kingdom, as we seek to bring about your kingdom on earth.

For further thought

Does your life feel chaotic? Does it need more constancy? Meditate upon the eternity of God's heavenly Jerusalem.

Foundations – 1 Chosen for a purpose

December

Foundations –
2 Building with care

Notes by **Stephen Willey**

For Stephen's biography, see p. 88.
Stephen has used the NRSVA for these notes.

Sunday 5 December
Built together

Read Ephesians 2:11–22

For [Christ] is our peace; in his flesh he has made both groups into one and has broken down the dividing wall, that is, the hostility between us. He has abolished the law with its commandments and ordinances, so that he might create in himself one new humanity.

(verses 14–15a)

A group led by women from Afghanistan hired the church building. 'Toddlers' was not regarded as a church group and therefore the women were not given access to the kitchen cupboards. One day the kitchen flooded and, because all the cupboards were locked, the group couldn't find the mop and bucket. Eventually, with liquid all over the floor, they decided to use a kitchen dishcloth as mop and a washing-up bowl as bucket. Word got around that the toddler group were doing unhygienic things in the kitchen and the church considered cancelling their room booking on health and safety grounds. This would have meant locking the church doors as well as the cupboard doors, separating the church from Toddlers.

A respected, prayerful person offered to speak to the leader of the toddler group. She gently and gracefully listened to the leader's story. As a result of that conversation the church decided to keep the doors to church and mop cupboard unlocked and Toddlers continued to meet. Better still, friendships developed between the church and members of the group. Paul writes to the Ephesians that it is not the law but God's grace that brings unity.

† Christ our peace, you break down the walls of division. By your grace, create in us a new humanity.

Monday 6 December
Built with care

Read 1 Corinthians 3:6–15

For no one can lay any foundation other than the one that has been laid; that foundation is Jesus Christ. Now if anyone builds on the foundation with gold, silver, precious stones, wood, hay, straw – the work of each builder will become visible, for the Day will disclose it.

(verses 11–13a)

Working together it is possible to build something great. On a trip to the manufacturing plant of Jaguar Land Rover (JLR), I was impressed to see people and robots bringing car parts from across the globe together to produce beautiful, shiny cars. However, the JLR car plant has a certain fragility, it has a temporary nature, and each year brings new challenges. Will the business remain profitable? Will JLR stay in the area? God, on the other hand, builds something with much more longevity than a car – even a top-of-the-range car! When churches worked together with voluntary and statutory agencies to build a network of support to prevent human trafficking in the UK Midlands, a web of truth and compassion was created to counter the web of deceit and heartlessness of the traffickers.

Peter (1 Peter 2:5) reminds us that God builds with people, 'living stones'. Here, Paul says, 'you are ... God's building' (verse 9). When people form the building and such a building is founded on a solid and eternal foundation, it is built in eternity through people's lives. With the anti-trafficking web, I hope that through the many and precious gifts of those in the network, vulnerable people will experience love and release from entrapment. Offered with hope, faith, and love, rooted in Christ, the Church's gifts along with the gifts of others can be used by God to bring transformation in the world.

† Jesus our foundation, build in us and our communities a place where eternal gifts like hope, faith and love shine like gold, silver and precious stones.

For further thought

What are our most precious buildings? How does God build within your community?

Careful building

Read Matthew 7:24–29

'Everyone then who hears these words of mine and acts on them will be like a wise man who built his house on rock. The rain fell, the floods came, and the winds blew and beat on that house, but it did not fall, because it had been founded on rock.'

(verses 24–25)

Once, when building a sandcastle with my hands, as a child, I found rock below the sand. When I tried to dig deeper I couldn't, the rock was harder than me! I broke my fingernails and grazed the skin off my young fingers. I decided to build in the sand a little way away and when the sea came up my sandcastle was gone. On the next day, digging in the original place, there was the rock again, just below the surface, as hard as ever.

When he talks about building on the rock, Jesus is talking in the context of our response to the Sermon on the Mount. The words he has spoken to the people are like the rock. Jesus' teachings offer sure foundations. So why would we not want to build on the rock? Well, rock is harder than sand. Jesus' words on the mount are not easy for us. To make peace, to be poor, to weep and mourn, to be persecuted for righteousness' sake … None of this is easily done, but it is the foundation for a lasting reality.

Jesus talks about people like buildings. The two houses – one on the sand and the other on the rock – offer us a way to see our own lives. Few would acknowledge that they were building on sand, but after reading the Sermon on the Mount, and seeing how hard the rock can be, we may wonder again what we are building our lives upon.

† Jesus our hope, show us the truth of our lives. We pray that we may work with the rock of your teachings and not be deterred when it is hard for us.

For further thought

What are the hardest parts of Jesus' teaching for me? Do I know someone who can help me build in those places?

Wednesday 8 December
A rejected stone

Read Luke 20:9–19

'[The owner of the vineyard] will come and destroy those tenants and give the vineyard to others.' When [the people] heard this, they said, 'Heaven forbid!' But [Jesus] looked at them and said, 'What then does this text mean: "The stone that the builders rejected has become the cornerstone"?'

(verses 16–17)

When I was a detached youth worker, the young people I worked with were often in trouble with the authorities for antisocial behaviour. This meant that they were on the streets not just because their parents didn't want them home, but also because many local youth clubs did not want them on their premises. There was one youth project in the area which appeared to be very successful. Having obtained a great deal of grant funding for work with young people from difficult backgrounds, the project had purchased canoes, climbing equipment, tents, resources for fun days, and even a small fleet of minibuses. However, the young people I worked with, who came from some of the most disadvantaged backgrounds, were not permitted to use the equipment. It was said that the leader – the manager of the club and associated schemes – was reluctant to allow *any* young person to use the equipment, as young people tended to 'spoil things and generally cause trouble'. The project which had initially been heralded as a great addition to youth provision had lost its original purpose. Although it had been set up with the best of intentions, it was not providing for those who needed it most; they were now rejected by the project.

The people of Jesus' day said, 'God forbid,' that the stone they were rejecting should become the cornerstone. But when he came among them, they felt that Jesus was disruptive and threatening. Because of their fears, they were no longer willing to share what had been built in their faith. They rejected the cornerstone.

† Disruptive Christ, you who came among us as our cornerstone, help us to keep you at the heart of all our planning and everything we build.

For further thought

Have I ever spent time and energy building up a project and then not wanted to share it with others?

Thursday 9 December
On this rock

Read Matthew 16:13–20

He said to them, 'But who do you say that I am?' Simon Peter answered, 'You are the Messiah, the Son of the living God.' And Jesus answered him, 'Blessed are you ... And I tell you, you are Peter, and on this rock I will build my church.'

(verses 15–18a)

'You are short-sighted,' said the optician when I was 15, 'but we can fix that.' I remember getting my first pair of glasses and, thanks to that optician, I saw, as for the first time, the individual bricks on the house opposite – previously those bricks had just merged into one brown wall. It's easy to see that buildings are made of brick or stone, but sometimes less easy to see the individual stones themselves, especially as the most important stones, like the foundations, are often hidden. Simon Peter, prompted by Jesus, is able to identify who Jesus is in that moment at Caesarea Philippi. Suddenly Simon sees the Messiah, the Holy One of God. A man different from all the other people he'd ever met. Peter's clear-sightedness offers the disciples a new way to see Jesus.

Jesus also has the ability to see who people are, their individuality and potential, and by doing so he opens up new possibilities too. Here, he sees Simon Peter for who he was. He sees his potential. Simon would mature to become the rock on which the Church would be built. Of course, at this point, Simon Peter is hardly a rock and Jesus knows it. Jesus sees that his disciple will deny any knowledge of him before the crucifixion. Jesus, the healer and teacher, sees how things are with this fragile and sometimes wavering man and he gives him the name Peter – the rock. The one Simon identifies as the Son of the living God, nurtures his potential and gives him a new name.

† Lord, call me by my name and nurture me so I might see you in the midst of my everyday life and reach the potential you have placed in me.

For further thought

Are there people in my life I could name and nurture so they could achieve the potential God has given them?

A stumbling stone

Read Isaiah 8:11–18

But the Lord of hosts, him you shall regard as holy; let him be your fear, and let him be your dread. He will become a sanctuary, a stone one strikes against; for both houses of Israel he will become a rock one stumbles over – a trap and a snare …

(verses 13–14a)

I remember, after I had been working in a large successful commercial organisation for several years, going one evening to a small, humble church meeting where we were planning to discuss church business. The week had been a tough one in the company and in the church. Some pretty devastating decisions had been made in the workplace. There were going to be many redundancies with the threat of more redundancies. Company meetings that week had been tense and anxious. I was thinking about this as I drove to the church. They too had had some news. They were losing a minister earlier than they expected.

I arrived just as the meeting started. I sat down without talking with anyone and started to look at the agenda. Then, seemingly out of the blue, the chair of the meeting started singing. It was a simple song, just a biblical phrase about the love and mercy of God, repeated several times. The rest of those present at the meeting joined in, and that was it, I was overcome with emotion. My eyes filled with tears as I saw, for a moment, that meetings in the church and the workplace had felt like rocky places causing me to stumble, but these institutional 'stones' had been transformed as the music of God's holiness broke in on me.

God truly is the rock of our salvation and an encounter with God can stop us in our tracks. On this occasion, as my focus changed, so did my priorities. As my heart was broken open, the Lord became my sanctuary.

† Lord, open our eyes, change our focus so we might see as you see and allow your holiness to break in upon us as the dawn of a new day.

For further thought

What causes my neighbours to be stressed and anxious? Is there a simple song we could sing to enable God's holiness to break through?

Foundations – 2 Building with care

December

347

A foundation for our times

> ### Read Isaiah 33:2–6
> *The Lord is exalted, he dwells on high; he filled Zion with justice and righteousness; he will be the stability of your times, abundance of salvation, wisdom, and knowledge; the fear of the Lord is Zion's treasure.*
>
> *(verses 5–6)*

As I write on my laptop, I am considering Isaiah's times and our times. Things are so different today and yet there are many things we hold in common with the writers of the Hebrew scriptures. Today, unlike Isaiah's time, if we are connected to the internet we can access a huge amount of information, more than any one person could absorb. If we are not connected to the internet, we are excluded from accessing the knowledge which others now take for granted. But all this knowledge, indeed all the knowledge on this earth, can't provide stability for human beings. When I use the internet, every bit of information, knowledge or wisdom seems to carry the same weight. All are accessible by simply clicking on a link on the screen. But how do I know which is which: information or wisdom?

The prophetic writings in the book of Isaiah come from a very different context. Can that poetry speak to me? It does, and Isaiah's words give direction, support and encouragement. Isaiah tells us that God fills Zion with justice and righteousness, and it is God's salvation, wisdom and knowledge which give stability. Here is a foundation which can be built on. If we can acknowledge that God is exalted – high above our thoughts and ways, or indeed our internet-connected world – then we will find treasures in abundance. With God's wisdom and salvation as our foundation, lasting treasures will adorn our lives.

† Creator God, you are high above anything I can understand or imagine, yet you love me. Fill me with your justice and righteousness and by your salvation build in me your wisdom and knowledge.

For further thought
What treasures am I seeking? How can I share the treasure I find with others?

Foundations –
3 The work continues

Notes by **Bola Iduoze**

Bola is a qualified accountant with over 20 years' experience in the marketplace. She has successfully managed Citywall Associates Limited, a business consultancy firm, alongside her husband for over a decade. Bola is also a home business entrepreneur who mentors business owners and an associate pastor at Gateway Chapel, Kent, UK. She is married to Eddie and they are blessed with two children. Bola has used the NIVUK for these notes.

Sunday 12 December
Chosen for a special purpose

Read 1 Peter 2:1–10

But you are a chosen people, a royal priesthood, a holy nation, God's special possession, that you may declare the praises of him who called you out of darkness into his wonderful light.

(verse 9)

As someone who comes from a culture that celebrates the first child as the special one, I can understand the concept of being special and chosen. Despite the culture of my tribe, the Yoruba from West Africa, I had a different experience in my home. I was neither the firstborn nor a boy, but my father made me believe that I was a special kid and could not stop praising me for my intelligence and wisdom. I do not know how he did it – there are six of us, one boy and five girls; yet he made every single one of us feel like we were special, despite the culture we were raised in. We each felt like we were my father's special one.

If my physical father was like that, how much more is God, our heavenly Father?

God has chosen you and me to be his own special people, regardless of our position, intellect or skills. He has chosen us to declare his praise and be great examples to those around us. Let us therefore embrace the calling and enjoy the position, discharging our duties of declaring his praise always.

† Lord, help me to remember that you chose me to declare your praises in all I do. Help me make the most of your calling on my life as a chosen and special person.

Foundations – 3 The work continues

December

Monday 13 December
God will remember your works

Read Hebrews 6:1–12

God is not unjust; he will not forget your work and the love you have shown him as you have helped his people and continue to help them.

(verse 10)

In my teenage years I attended a local Baptist church. The young pastor of this church and his wife were dedicated and hardworking people, and their hard work and interest in the families within their local area brought so many people to church.

When we moved into the area, the church had fewer than 40 people in it. The hard work in their visitation, love and care yielded fruits that saw many more start attending church, just because people felt they needed to reward the love and care of these pastors. The church started growing and within three years the church grew to over 250 people.

When I started at the church, my parents were not dedicated Christians, but the love shown by these pastors won my parents for Church and Christ. My parents both came to Christ in this little church and many great transformation stories can be traced back to this lovely couple.

God rewarded this couple. I saw their local church grow and by the time they were posted elsewhere, their influence and network had grown. Many of us today are still in touch with them and able to trace our lives as Christians as well as our ministry work ethics to them. What a rich life they have had.

God keeps record of our good works and he rewards them as well. As a believer, keep on doing good works, knowing fully well that it is God who will reward you, and not any human being.

† God, enable me to do good works, even when no one is looking, knowing fully well that you are the one who sees. Amen

For further thought

What work can you give your attention to today?

Building up the body

> **Read Ephesians 4:1–16**
>
> *So Christ himself gave the apostles, the prophets, the evangelists, the pastors and teachers, to equip his people for works of service, so that the body of Christ may be built up.*
>
> *(verses 11–12)*

A short while ago, I had the privilege of sitting with a sister whom I have known for over a decade. In this period, her zeal has never flagged. I asked her how she keeps her energy fresh, never showing any sign of discouragement even when no one else is around to assist her. She said, 'I am building this little part of the body and I am very aware of it. If I leave it, that part of the body will suffer and let down the rest of the body.' What a great perspective she has of her service to the whole body.

Many of us may see our service in a church as voluntary and have an 'I will do it when convenient' attitude towards it. Worse still, some have no concerns as to whether the work is done or not. These attitudes will surely not be pleasing to God, the giver of time and talents.

As God has blessed us with different talents, we must understand that they have been given to us, not just for us to enjoy but also for the building of the whole body of Christ. Let us therefore learn from this woman and serve diligently.

The Bible says that Jesus gave each one a gift to equip us for his works of service that will in turn build up the body. A good question to ask ourselves daily is, 'What am I doing to build the body of Christ with the gift God has given me?'

† Lord, as I step out today, help me to be a useful instrument in your hands. Use me and my gifts to build and bless someone today. In Jesus' name. Amen

For further thought
What can you contribute today in your church or community?

Foundations – 3 The work continues

December

Wednesday 15 December
Building up each other

Read 1 Thessalonians 5:1–11

Therefore encourage one another and build each other up, just as in fact you are doing.

(verse 11)

The general principle of life is to take care of number one and do things just for ourselves. But in today's reading, God wants us to think beyond ourselves, choosing to build others up in all things. I want to share with you how I learnt this lesson the hard way.

I am the second of six children, from a culture in which you are expected to be responsible not only for yourself but also for your younger siblings. Whenever my parents were not around and any of my siblings did anything wrong, I was held responsible by my parents. I am generally a cautious person and try not to disobey any rules. But my younger brother seemed to have made it his life mission to break house rules and my sisters did not always fall in line; I was almost always blamed for the misbehaviour of my siblings.

One day, I had to ask my mum why I got punished for other people's misbehaviour. She replied, 'We are family and we must learn to build up each other. Do not just be the good one while everyone else falls out of line. We must learn to build each other up because we are a family.' This was the time my 'me principle' ended. I was disciplined into changing my belief when it came to others. It is no good being the only one enjoying the blessings of the Lord, growing and increasing while there are others around us whom we can help build.

† Lord, thank you for helping me live a life where I can add value to the people around me in the body of Christ. In Jesus' name. Amen

For further thought

Whom around you can you build up today?

A strong faith

Read Colossians 2:6–15

So then, just as you received Christ Jesus as Lord, continue to live your lives in him, rooted and built up in him, strengthened in the faith …

(verses 6–7a)

I dedicated my life to Christ during my very first year in university, and I remember my discipleship teacher emphasising the value of becoming rooted and built up in Christ. He made sure that I and the other disciples understood that the responsibility for growth as well as developing strong spiritual roots and maturity was ours.

I was introduced to the spiritual discipline of valuing the Word of God. I built the daily practice of familiarising myself with the Word of God as written in the Bible. God's Word is a tool that we have all been given to build spiritual muscles and grow, to know who we are and what we have in Christ.

Why is the Word valuable? To be able to live our lives in God, we need to know what God wants us to do and how to do it – all these and more are in the Word of God. As we desire and ingest it, we become more and more as God desires for us to be. Being spiritually built up is possible as a Christian in a busy world like ours, but we cannot attain it without the Word of God.

Get the Word of God into your spirit any way you can – audio Bible, Bible reading, or listening to sermons. There are so many ways of getting the Word into your spirit. The key thing is to decide that you want to take the Word in and make time for it, despite your busy lifestyle and schedule.

† Lord, help me make time for your Word so I can be built up and develop strong faith. In Jesus' name. Amen

For further thought

Thinking back over this year, what has worked in your Bible reading? What needs to change in the coming year?

Foundations – 3 The work continues

December

Friday 17 December
Building on a sure foundation

Read 1 Corinthians 10:1–13

They all ate the same spiritual food and drank the same spiritual drink; for they drank from the spiritual rock that accompanied them, and that rock was Christ. Nevertheless, God was not pleased with most of them ...

(verses 3–5a)

The children of Israel started out on a journey where everyone was under the same provision of God, but Paul says that God was not pleased with most of them. God was not pleased because, rather than enjoy the spiritual food and drink that should have led to their growth, many decided to engage in activities that were against what God desired. Some grumbled and others engaged in idolatry and many other activities that are contrary to God's instructions.

I had always been quite intrigued by this scripture until I came across a real-life situation a little over a decade ago when two gentlemen walked into my church on the same day. They were good friends and a couple of weeks later they both gave their lives to Christ on the same day. They both embarked on the discipleship trainings and were exposed to the same spiritual diet. Over the course of 10 years, one has gone on to build a strong life in his faith and is now a pastor within that same congregation, whereas the other went back to his previous lifestyle. It is surely possible to be under God's provision and still miss out on all the blessings God provides.

It is our responsibility to keep on building on the foundation which we have received so we can enjoy the full benefit of what Christ has got to offer us on our journey of faith.

† Father, help me to take full advantage of the spiritual food and drink you provide to ensure my growth. Help me to live a life you are pleased with, O Lord.

For further thought

Starting out with Christ is great, but we must build on this and develop spiritually acceptable habits that will ensure we keep growing to be more like Christ daily.

Saturday 18 December
A solid foundation

Read 2 Timothy 2:14–19

Nevertheless, God's solid foundation stands firm, sealed with this inscription: 'The Lord knows those who are his,' and, 'Everyone who confesses the name of the Lord must turn away from wickedness.'

(verse 19)

I started out in my Christian walk in a town called Ibadan in Nigeria. During a summer break in the late 1980s, a few friends and I started developing as Christians. After accepting Christ into our lives, we started striving to live by the instructions we studied in discipleship and Bible classes. As the summer break was coming to an end, I started getting quite concerned that I might not continue to grow as a believer if I was not in the company of these friends. My fear led me to go and have a private conversation with my discipleship teacher. The teacher sat me down and then shared the key scripture of today with me, emphasising to me that God's solid foundation stands firm and that I had the seal of God's love and grace upon my life. I need not be afraid.

God's solid foundation indeed stands sure. God's love and grace have been extended to us and as we stretch out our hands and receive without reservation his grace sent to us, we will enjoy the blessings that God has in stock for us. Our faith should not be based on fear but on experiencing and enjoying that which God has generously extended towards us.

Living in the grace and love of God, however, does not mean that we will continue to work in disobedience. But as we have accepted the grace, we need to walk in the path that will be pleasing to God so we can enjoy the fullness of what God has prepared for us.

† Father, help me to recognise your plans for my life, understand your seal upon my life, and enjoy your blessings prepared for me in every area of my life. In Jesus' name. Amen

For further thought

How can you build on the foundation of your faith in the coming Christmas season, and in the coming year?

Foundations – 3 The work continues

December

Christmas with Luke

Notes by **Carla A. Grosch-Miller**

Carla is a practical theologian and poet. Her specialist areas include sexuality and congregational trauma. She is the author of **Lifelines:** Wrestling the Word, Gathering Up Grace *(Canterbury Press, 2020) and* Psalms Redux: Poems and Prayers *(Canterbury Press, 2014), and a co-editor and contributing author of* Tragedy and Christian Congregations: The Practical Theology of Trauma *(Routledge, 2019). She lives in Northumberland with her husband David, where she delights in North Sea swimming and long walks in the countryside. Carla has used the NRSVA for these notes.*

Sunday 19 December
Leaps of faith

Read Luke 1:26–38

But she was much perplexed by his words and pondered what sort of greeting this might be.

(verse 29)

Most of the time we do not know what consequences will flow from our choices. Sometimes we don't want to know (the extra dessert; miles flown over oceans). But occasionally we have a sense that what we are choosing could change everything: the choice to commit to a partner or to bear a child. And not being able to really know the consequences but hearing a voice from beyond call out to us, we take a leap of faith.

Mary stood on a precipice and pondered the possibilities. Before her stood a fullness she could scarcely anticipate. She could have met the stranger with the cynicism due a snake-oil salesman. Something in his being convinced her that this was one whose word was true. It wormed its way into her heart. There it resonated; her heart began to beat with the rhythm of the Great Heart. She sensed the possibility: if she stepped forward, every fibre of her being would be lent to the Love that pulses through the universe.

Not knowing what lay before her, she trusted the beating of her heart and the hint of holiness she sensed in the wind. Not knowing, but trusting, she said yes.

† Tune my heart to the beating of your Great Heart. Fuel my faith, that I may step forward in trust. Receive my yes. Amen

Monday 20 December
Leaps of joy

Read Luke 1:39–45

For as soon as I heard the sound of your greeting, the child in my womb leapt for joy.

(verse 44)

The day I first visited Garrett-Evangelical Theological Seminary near Chicago, Illinois, the wise and wonderful Barbara Troxell welcomed those of us who were beginning our studies there with these words by Frederick Buechner: 'The place God calls you to is the place where your deep gladness and the world's deep need meet' (*Wishful Thinking: A Theological ABC*, Harper & Row, 1973, pp. 118–119). My heart leapt for joy, recognising my own experience in responding to a surprising call to seminary.

That our God-given barometer is joy continues to astonish me. I was raised in a church where the keynote of joy was accompanied by fear, guilt and shame. Faith was about being good, not being happy. Could God really intend my joy? Would joy lead me to the life God had for me? It seemed too good to be true.

But there it is in the Christmas story, the story of Love incarnate. The babe in Elizabeth's womb leaps for joy in recognition of the new thing God is doing in Mary for the world. And I can testify from a few decades of listening for God in my life: joy is a trustworthy companion. There will always be things that just have to be done, but at significant crossroads joy will point the way.

Another wise and wonderful theologian, Howard Thurman, wrote: 'Don't ask what the world needs. Ask what makes you come alive, and go do it. Because what the world needs is people who have come alive' (quoted in *Violence Unveiled*, Herder & Herder, 1996, by Gil Bailie, p. xv).

God knows what the world needs. Leaps of joy mark the way.

† Give me the courage to follow my joy to the place where I can serve you best. Thank you for the gift of joy. Amen

For further thought
Ask what makes you come alive. Go do it.

Tuesday 21 December
Leaps of hope

Read Luke 1:46–56

… for the Mighty One has done great things for me, and holy is [the] name.

(verse 49)

The Magnificat is the crown jewel of the Advent journey, holding in its graced grammar the heart and hope of humankind. The English language does not contain the depths to adequately display its riches. The ancient Greek verbs in the aorist tense are the key. These verbs convey things as already and not yet accomplished at the same time. We read, 'He has brought down the powerful from their thrones, and lifted up the lowly' (verse 52) and think, 'Not really; not yet. When, O Lord, when?' What we are missing is the invitation that the aorist tense accomplishes: God has done this thing and it requires us to complete it.

Just as the conception of Jesus required Mary's yes, so too our own yes is required to fulfil the redemption promised in his birth.

Mary's song is an explosion of joy: that the righting of the world has come and that she would play her part. Favoured and blessed was she indeed! Favoured and blessed are we!

All around the world, Mary's song is sung in Roman Catholic, Anglican and Lutheran places of worship every evening. The radical vision is proclaimed; the invitation issued. With the turning of the Earth, humanity is bursting with joy at nearly every moment for what God has done and will do among us.

Will you add your yes?

† My soul magnifies you, rejoicing in what you have done and will do – in and through me and us. Come, Lord Jesus, reign in the world. Amen

For further thought

Print out the Magnificat; place it where you will see it every day. Let your yes join the great yes ever ringing across the Earth.

Wednesday 22 December
Leaps of trust

Read Luke 2:1–7

… because there was no place for them in the inn.

(verse 7c)

I had my own 'no room at the inn' moment in Bethlehem during my first trip to Palestine and Israel. It was the year 2000. One week into a three-week sabbatical visit, Ariel Sharon stepped on the Mount and the second Intifada started. My walking pilgrimage was cancelled and the Arab travel group in charge of my wandering placed me with a group of Swedes. They had a hotel booked in Bethlehem; I did not. So I found myself standing outside a stone-arched, heavy wooden door watching my guide argue vociferously with the woman of the house in Arabic. She was resolute. Although the priest had a duty to take me in under the ancient rule of hospitality, there was no room at the inn.

As fear began to rise within me, I decided instead to trust that what would be, would be, and that now I would learn to be a guest, here or elsewhere. She finally relented and I was led to a small room with a narrow cot surrounded by laundry. From the window I could see the terrain of Bethlehem. Erase the aerials and it could have been Mary's view 2,000 years earlier.

I imagine her panic as Joseph knocked on door after door, and her relief at the granting of minimal shelter. She had to trust; there was no other option. Soon all fear would disappear in the wonder of the new life she would cradle in her arms.

Every angel says, 'Be not afraid.' Trust erodes fear. There is no other option on the path to love.

† Settle my fears, that I may walk into the unknown and there find the new life you have for me. Amen

For further thought

Courage is not the absence of fear, but stepping ahead in the face of it. When have you faced a fear? What did you learn?

Thursday 23 December
Leaps of insight

Read Luke 2:8–20

I am bringing you good news of great joy for all the people.

(verse 10b)

The angelic chorus lighting up the hillside erupted after a stunning insight. The birth of this child was for all people – not just the rich, the powerful or the famous. All people, period.

American born and bred, I have lived in England for 16 years. When I first emigrated, I was struck by a societal ethos that was more oriented to the common good than my homeland. This has steadily eroded. The UK has more money floating around than ever but it is primarily in the pockets of the rich. Three years ago a slim majority of voters began a process to take us out of the European Union. The problems we face – global warming, terrorism, growing inequality – require a co-ordinated international response. Yet the infection of Me-thinking (my personal profit, my power and my privilege masquerading as freedom) has rendered us less and less able to think in terms of what is good for all people. Around the world, 'strong men' have been elected on nationalist platforms. In my nightmares, the planet will continue to heat up, the flow of climate change refugees will be met by violent hostility, the fear of the Other will continue to breed ugly racism, and our capacity to think and act for the common good will continue to dissipate.

We need a salvation that is good for all living things and the planet. When will a flash of insight transform us from Me-thinking to We-thinking?

† Come, Lord Jesus. We need you now more than ever. Come, give us the transforming insight that we are one interdependent human family whose very existence is at stake. Amen

For further thought

How do you help yourself think beyond your personal self-interest? How may you help others do the same?

Friday 24 December
Anticipation

Read Luke 2:21–40

'… so that the inner thoughts of many will be revealed – and a sword will pierce your own soul too.'

(verse 35)

> *'Another world is not only possible, she is on her way. On a quiet day, I can hear her breathing.'*
>
> Arundhati Roy, War Talk *(South End Press, 2003, p. 75)*

Today is Christmas Eve, a day of great anticipation. The youngest anticipate Santa; the old in our readings anticipated a new world – one where Jerusalem would not be under the boot of Rome and *YHWH* would reign supreme. They had anticipated it their whole lives. Anna's joy erupts from the page. Simeon sighs with relief at the sight of the child and foresees the cost of change.

On 20 September 2019, more than four million people took part in climate change protests around the world. What began with Greta Thunberg's solo protest in front of the Swedish Parliament has become a mass movement among the young and not so young. Many of us want – and all of us need – a new world with sustainable, fair practices. We want our lives to stop costing the Earth.

Simeon's wisdom haunts us. In times like these, the inner thoughts of many are revealed. We have the privilege and pain of witnessing this through social media. Many times my soul has been pierced by the revealed thoughts of people who threaten violence against those who work for change.

Such has it ever been. Simeon's warning to Mary came true. A sword and a cross pierced her to the core as they broke the tender body whose birth we will welcome tomorrow. When God breaks in, a choice is demanded. Will we rise to the challenge, or will we fall prey to base desires?

† When you break in, great God, give me eyes to see and courage to rise to greet you despite the personal cost. Enable me to be the change I long for. Amen

For further thought

Where is God breaking into the world today where you are? How will you participate in God's great work of love in your time?

Saturday 25 December (Christmas Day)
Author of life

Read Isaiah 9:6–7

His authority shall grow continually …

(verse 7a)

I am a child of the 1960s and 70s. From my youth I have treated all who claim authority with suspicion, and as a younger woman I struggled with my own authority. In my lifetime, distrust of institutions that claim authority has continued to grow. We don't trust the Church, the government, the media, the experts. This lack of trust has led of late (2016–2019) to the election of individuals with inordinate trust in themselves alone, with frightening consequences. Just this morning I read an article from the International Policy Digest about the danger of governments led by narcissists.

I want to look at authority from a different perspective, reclaiming the root of the word which is the same as that for 'author'. From the Latin *'auctor'*, the concept is about one who makes or creates. So the question becomes: who or what is the author of your life? How is that working for you and the world God so loves?

Paul writes about the life of a Christian being a letter from Christ (2 Corinthians 3:3). Jesus' authority in our lives is that of an author. His hand guiding the pen with which we write our story, his power is soft but firm. But it requires that we loosen our grip – releasing fear and control – to let him write.

Today the Great Author is born in human flesh, and heaven and earth sing. For the way has been opened for the hand of that author to create a new world from the words that are our lives.

† Loosen my grip on my own life, that your hand may gracefully guide my story. Amen

For further thought
Contemplate what people see when they read the story of your life.

Christmas with Luke

December

Giving and receiving

Notes by **Carla A. Grosch-Miller**

For Carla's biography, go to p. 356.
Carla has used the NRSVA for these notes.

Sunday 26 December
Domination?

Read Genesis 1:26–30

... and let them have dominion over the fish of the sea, and over the birds of the air, and over ...

(verses 26b and 28c)

This ancient text makes me weep. Here the beautiful aspiration that we are made in the image of God is paired with the death-dealing assertion that we have dominion over the Earth. In these verses, we made ourselves to be God.

A friend and I are walking the Cumbria Way this week. We are near the end of our journey. Its beauty has awed us. More than once we have pondered the value of wild places. And we have observed humanity's determination to wrest a living from the land through mining and farming.

The relationship between humanity and the Earth occupies us in the Anthropocene Age. The second creation myth, revealing humanity's purpose to tend and till the land, helps. As does the fact that the Hebrew word used for 'dominion' in Genesis 1:26 is the same word used in 1:8 to describe the dominion of the sun over day – dominion good for the Earth. Whilst we must wrest a living from the land, we are finding it very difficult to know how to do that without ruining everything. Our activity has accelerated a mass extinction of other living beings and may in the end cause our own.

† Soften our footsteps on this precious planet. Teach us right economics. Direct our creativity towards sustainability, justice and peace. Amen

Monday 27 December
I saw Jesus today

Read Luke 19:1–10

He was trying to see who Jesus was …

(verse 3a)

I have a soul sister, Therese, who lives in a remote village in the wilderness with her husband, George. This is her story to tell, which she does in an essay entitled 'Street Walkers' in her book, *Training for a World Doula*.

One tragic day, four young people drowned in the local lake. For days after that, Therese and George walked the streets, being present to the great grief that engulfed the village – listening, holding. When one of her friends who lived far away heard of the community's horrific loss and that they were walking the streets, she said to Therese, 'Oh, they will see Christ in you.' (Therese and George are ordained ministers.) Therese writes, 'That wasn't how it was at all. It was like this. One night on the porch, George looked over at me with tears streaming down his face and said, "I saw Jesus today. I saw him everywhere."'

We tend to think that we will find Jesus in acts of piety – fasting, prayer – or in special holy places – high mountains, cathedrals. We think we need to invite him into our homes and our lives, like we have some control over where he is and what he may do.

Truth is, he is everywhere he is needed. He is in the long hug and the held hand. He is in the broken heart and the whispered 'I am here.' He is in patient listening; he is in streaming tears.

† Thank you, Jesus, for being everywhere you need to be.

For further thought

Where have you seen Jesus recently?

Tuesday 28 December
High-risk strategy – 1

Read Luke 21:1–4

'… but she out of her poverty has put in all she had to live on.'

(verse 4b)

The story of the widow's mite gets under my skin. I read it and think, 'That's a high risk strategy'; what if God does not provide her with the means to live once her pockets are empty?

I am thinking instrumentally, as if our relationship with the Holy is about give and take: I give my all; God provides.

I have seen it work. When I was a minister on the edge of Chicago, a group of French Traditional Catholic nuns and priests from the Fraternité de Notre Dame showed up on the west side of the city – an area rife with poverty, drugs and violence – with nothing but the habits on their backs and the habits of their hearts. In no time they had accumulated the resources to open a centre for hospitality in a disused Methodist church. One nun was seen pulling a refrigerator down the street in a child's wagon! Our liberal Protestant church members responded with an outpouring of cash.

Still, I don't think the story of the widow's mite is the institution of a giving rule. Our relationship with God is not instrumental; it's not about behaving a certain way to get what we need or want. Rather it is about the high-risk strategy of letting love shape our choices. Sometimes that will require us to give our all.

Giving our all is not a rule to live by – we would quickly exhaust ourselves and not necessarily faithfully. It is a discernment. There is a time and a place. God grant that we will recognise them.

† Jesus, who discerned the time and place to give your all, give us the wisdom to know when and how to give ours. Amen

For further thought

What are you being nudged to give? What's holding you back?

Giving and receiving

December

365

Wednesday 29 December
High-risk strategy – 2

Read 2 Corinthians 9:6–15

The point is this: the one who sows sparingly will also reap sparingly, and the one who sows bountifully will also reap bountifully.

(verse 6)

In chapters 8 and 9 of 2 Corinthians, Paul is cajoling the church at Corinth to literally step up to the (offering) plate of the collection for the poor in Jerusalem. The poorer, persecuted churches in Macedonia had begged to be able to contribute despite their straitened circumstances. Paul was embarrassed that the church at Corinth, which started with such enthusiasm, soon fell behind. This collection meant a lot to Paul. It would testify to the unity of Jewish and Gentile Followers of the Way, and allay fears about his mission to the Gentiles. He pulls out all the stops in this passage – promising that they would be enriched in every way for their generosity and that God was able to provide blessings in abundance. It's a bit hard to swallow for the modern reader: if God is able, has God really chosen to withhold the means to live from those who are poor or in desperate circumstances?

Or is it possible that the '*oikos*' (family, household) of God is able to provide blessings in abundance? The testimony of the Bible is that God uses human beings to accomplish God's purposes. We are called and equipped; we are in partnership with the Holy.

God's strategy is high risk. It depends on our faithfulness. As God's power with humans is soft power, cajoling and persuasion may be the only way it can happen. Truly, if we sow sparingly, so shall we – and those we seek to serve – reap sparingly. If we want results, if we want justice to reign for the many, sowing bountifully is required.

† Loosen my grip on my treasure, that I may share it unreservedly, as God has shared Godself with me. Amen

For further thought

What is your relationship with money? Is it a resource, an addiction, a burden? What is it for? Whom is it for?

Giving and receiving

December

366

Thursday 30 December
Searching

Read Matthew 7:1–12

'Ask, and it will be given to you; search, and you will find; knock, and the door will be opened for you.'

(verse 7)

Between 2014 and 2016 my life unravelled. A cascade of shocking bereavements and a confusing work situation left me shattered and unable to pull myself up by my bootstraps. I left the work I had loved and even contemplated leaving church. I could not seek or receive comfort or guidance in my religious faith. I was thrown back on my intuition to feel my way to greater health. I did not pray. I did not draw on religious resources, which seemed empty platitudes to me. I simply concentrated on putting one foot in front of the other, paying attention to what was life-giving, stepping aside from those things that drained or diminished me.

I was searching, but not searching for God. I'd given up on that. I was searching for the Real and the True, for firm ground on which I could stand. I was paying attention to my body – moving (swimming, walking, dancing) and singing – to friendships and to the natural world. These were life-saving and life-giving activities.

As were a peculiar set of unexpected invitations: to study and teach about congregational trauma (which gave me an understanding of what had happened to me), to write, and to gather up a poetry collection. Slowly I began to see how grace was leaching over the lintels of my closed heart door. I may have given up on God, but the Holy showed no signs of letting me go.

We search and we are found. Thanks be to God.

† Holy One, who is always asking, searching and knocking on heart doors, thank you for your perseverance and for the gift of our body selves.

For further thought

How has grace sought you out or surprised you this past year? Give thanks.

Friday 31 December
The Word among us

Read John 1:10–16

And the Word became flesh and lived among us …

(verse 14a)

God has a mission. God's method is conversation. Enfleshed words, clear spoken and lived. Not for God the heavy hand of a bully or the point of a gun. Rather the tease of a story, a parable that engages and disrupts; words that surprise, shimmer and sing.

God is a poet, paying exquisite attention, crafting the words to pull our heartstrings, connecting our pulse to the great pulse of life.

God is a priest, intoning the chants that tie earth to heaven, invoking our prayers, summoning our spirits to reach beyond.

God is a prophet, commanding our attention, provoking our outrage, channelling our best intentions.

God is a song and a celebration. God fixes our consciences, feeds our imaginations, fuels our courage. God breathes life into us and sets our feet to dancing.

We could not know this if we were just given a rule book. We needed a living, breathing presence. We needed his flesh to live among us. We needed to be shaken by his stories. We needed the revelation of death and resurrection to convert us to the reality of God whose love and power can never let us go. We needed, and we received from his fullness, grace upon grace.

† God, ground of our being and of our becoming, make my life a clear word spoken and lived for the sake of this world you so love. Amen

For further thought

Spend five to ten minutes in silence sitting under the loving gaze of God. Be, so that you may become.

Giving and receiving

December

368

IBRA scheme of readings 2022

Join us again next year when we shall be exploring the following themes:

Walking in the light
1. Light in the darkness
2. A light to my path

The Gospel of Luke (1)
1. Healer and teacher
2. Good news for the poor

Weather warnings
1. And it rained!
2. Watering the earth

It started with a kiss

Jonah

The Gospel of Luke (2)
1. Preparing for ministry
2. Down from the mountain

Facing the Darkness
1. Despair
2. Worry & Anxiety
3. Doubt and Fear

The Gospel of Luke (3)
1. The journey to Jerusalem
2. Your king comes to you
3. Your king reigns

All creatures great and small
1. Creatures great
2. And creatures small

Readings from Revelation
1. An open door into heaven
2. A new heaven and a new earth

Body of God: The Bible's divine body imagery
1. Breath of all creation
2. Tears of the divine

Being Church
1. On the way
2. The Church and the churches

Readings in Ezekiel
1. Vision of glory
2. Restored to life

The stranger next door
1. Stranger danger
2. A culture of care

Pain and Hope: The Bible and Para-sport
1. Living with pain
2. Sustained by hope

Setting Sail
1. Make yourself an ark
2. All hands on deck

Ecclesiastes
1. Vanity of vanities
2. Wisdom is better than might

The Rhythm of Life

The Gospel of Luke (4)
1. Faith and opposition
2. Teaching in parables

Brother, Sister, let me serve you
1. What does God require of you?
2. Constant love for one another

Readings from 1 Kings
1. United Kingdom
2. Divided Kingdom

Nation shall speak peace unto nation: The 100th anniversary of the BBC
1. A vision of peace
2. Speaking truth to power

Readings in 1 Corinthians
1. Breaking down divisions
2. Spiritual guidance
3. The higher way of love

A Colourful Bible

The Beauty of Holiness: Tabernacle and Temple
1. The Wilderness Tabernacle
2. The Jerusalem Temple
3. Jesus and the temple
4. The Christian community and the temple

Christmas with Matthew

369

IBRA International Fund

To continue publishing *Fresh From The Word* and providing it overseas for faithful partners to translate, print and distribute we rely on the power of your donations. Would you work with us and help us to enable Christians from different parts of the world to continue to grow in knowledge and love for the Word of God by making a donation of £5, £10 or even £50?

How your donations make a difference:

£5.00 buys four copies of *Fresh From The Word* in Nigeria
£10.00 prints twelve copies in Ghana
£25.00 sends five copies of *Fresh From The Word* (including postage and packaging) to South Africa
£50.00 would fund 1,000 IBRA reading lists to be sent to a country that does not currently receive IBRA materials

Our partners are based in ten countries, but the benefit flows over borders to at least thirty-two countries all over the world. Partners work tirelessly to organise the translation, printing and distribution of IBRA Bible study notes and lists into many different languages, from Ewe, Yoruba and Twi to Portuguese, Samoan and Telugu!

Did you know that we print and sell 6,000 copies of *Fresh From The Word* here in the UK, but our overseas partners produce another 40,000 copies in English and then translate the book you are reading to produce a total of 31,000 copies in seven local languages? With the reading list also being translated into French and Spanish, then distributed, IBRA is still reaching 714,362 Christians around the world.

Faithfully following the same principles developed in 1882, we still guarantee that your donations to the International Fund will support our international brothers and sisters in Christ.

If you would like to make a donation, please use the envelope inserted in this book to send a cheque to International Bible Reading Association, 5–6 Imperial Court, 12 Sovereign Road, Birmingham, B30 3FH or go online to ibraglobal.org and click the 'Donate' button at the top of the page.

Global community

Our overseas distribution and international partners enable IBRA readings to be enjoyed all over the world from Spain to Samoa, New Zealand to Cameroon. Each day when you read your copy of *Fresh From The Word* you are joining a global community of people who are also reading the same passages. Here is how our readings impact people across the globe:

Ghana

Gladys reads *Fresh From The Word* with her devotional group in Ghana every Monday, Wednesday and Friday. She says that the book has been a source of motivation and encouragement for their members, and shared the following about her own experience:

> *Personally, this book has been my source of inspiration during the darkest time of my life. I can emphatically say that it is by the grace of God and the continuous encouragement I get from reading the book that has kept me alive till today.*

India

The Fellowship of Professional Workers in India value the global community of IBRA readers:

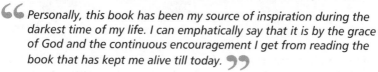

> *The uniqueness of the Bible reading is that the entire readership is focusing on a common theme for each day which is an expression of oneness of the faithful, irrespective of countries and cultures.*

Cameroon

Reverend Doctor Peter Evande of the Redemptive Baptist Church in Cameroon has distributed IBRA daily readings for ten years, and says:

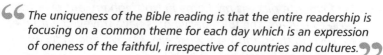

> *The use of writers from different cultural backgrounds makes IBRA notes richer than others. That aspect also attracts people from different backgrounds to love them. The structure and seasons of the Christian year help many people.*

United Kingdom

Sue, from the UK, has read IBRA notes for twenty-two years:

> *I have had many days where it feels as though the notes have been written just for me. I like the short reading for each day as this can easily fit into a daily routine and be kept up with. I also really like reading the views of the writers from overseas for an international view.*

Where people are following IBRA daily readings

We love to hear our readers' favourite places to read and reflect on our daily readings. Get in touch and tell us where YOU'RE reading – perhaps you too have a favourite, or an unusual or exciting place to enjoy your Bible reading. Email ibra@christianeducation.org.uk

66 *My favourite place is my home in Nottingham, but over the past 25+ years, the IBRA daily notes have travelled with me to Nevis in the Caribbean, Australia, Malawi and India as well as many locations in the UK!* 99

66 *Luxembourg – sat with a coffee outside my caravan.* 99

66 *A small hut in Tonga – the very first thing in the morning.* 99

66 *In my sitting room by the side of my wife (so I can share).* 99

66 *2019 has been my first full year with IBRA. Each day starts sitting in bed with tea and the day's reading and prayer.* 99

To find out more visit: **www.ibraglobal.org**

International Bible Reading Association partners and distributors

A worldwide service of Christian Education at work in five continents

HEADQUARTERS
IBRA
5–6 Imperial Court
12 Sovereign Road
Birmingham
B30 3FH
United Kingdom

www.ibraglobal.org

ibra@christianeducation.org.uk

SAMOA
Congregational Christian Church in Samoa
CCCS
PO Box 468
Tamaligi
Apia

asst.gsec@cccs.org.ws / lina@cccs.org.ws

Congregational Christian Church in Tokelau
c/o EFKT
Atafu
Tokelau Island

hepuutu@gmail.com

Congregational Christian Church in American Samoa
P.O. BOX 1537
Pago Pago, AS 96799

gensec@efkasonline.org

GHANA
Asempa Publishers
Christian Council of Ghana
PO Box GP 919
Accra

gm@asempapublishers.com

NIGERIA
IBRA Nigeria
David Hinderer House
Cathedral Church of St David
Kudeti
PMB 5298 Dugbe
Ibadan
Oyo State

SOUTH AFRICA
Faith for Daily Living Foundation
PO Box 3737
Durban 4000

ffdl@saol.com

IBRA South Africa
The Rectory
Christchurch
c/o Constantia Main and Parish Roads
Constantia 7806
Western Cape
South Africa

Terry@cchconst.org.za

DEMOCRATIC REPUBLIC OF THE CONGO
Baptist Community of the Congo River
8 Avenue Kalemie
Kinshasa Gombe
B.P. 205 & 397
Kinshasa 1

ecc_cbfc@yahoo.fr

CAMEROON
Redemptive Baptist Church
PO Box 65
Limbe
Fako Division
South West Region

evande777@yahoo.com

INDIA
All India Sunday School Association
House No. 9-131/1, Street No.5
HMT Nagar, Nacharam
Hyderabad
500076
Telangana

sundayschoolindia@yahoo.co.in

Fellowship of Professional Workers
Samanvay
Deepthi Chambers, Opp. Nin.
Tarnaka, Vijayapuri
Hyderabad 500 017
Telengana State

fellowship2w@gmail.com